RADICAL WORDSWORTH

ALSO BY JONATHAN BATE

Shakespeare and the English Romantic Imagination
Shakespearean Constitutions: Politics, Theatre, Criticism 1730–1830
Romantic Ecology: Wordsworth and the Environmental Tradition
Shakespeare and Ovid
The Genius of Shakespeare
The Song of the Earth
John Clare: A Biography
Soul of the Age: A Biography of the Mind of William Shakespeare
English Literature: A Very Short Introduction
Shakespeare Staging the World (with Dora Thornton)
Shakespeare's Britain (with Dora Thornton)
Ted Hughes: The Unauthorized Life
How the Classics Made Shakespeare

AS EDITOR

Charles Lamb: Elia and The Last Essays of Elia
The Romantics on Shakespeare
The Arden Shakespeare: Titus Andronicus (original and revised editions)
Shakespeare: An Illustrated Stage History (with Russell Jackson)
John Clare: Selected Poems
The RSC Shakespeare: Complete Works (with Eric Rasmussen)
The RSC Shakespeare: Individual Works (with Eric Rasmussen, 34 volumes)
The Public Value of the Humanities
The RSC Shakespeare: Collaborative Plays by Shakespeare and Others
(co-editor)
Worcester: Portrait of an Oxford College (with Jessica Goodman)
Stressed Unstressed: Classic Poems to Ease the Mind (co-editor)

INTRODUCTIONS

Titus: A Film by Julie Taymor
Andrew Marvell: The Complete Poems (Penguin Classics)
The Tempest: A Film by Julie Taymor
The Folio Poets: Lord Byron

CREATIVE WORKS

The Cure for Love (novel)
Being Shakespeare (a one-man play for Simon Callow)
The Shepherd's Hut (poems)

RADICAL WORDSWORTH

THE POET WHO CHANGED THE WORLD

JONATHAN BATE

Yale

UNIVERSITY PRESS

NEW HAVEN AND LONDON

Published with assistance from the Annie Burr Lewis Fund.

First published in 2020 in Great Britain by William Collins and in
the United States by Yale University Press.

Yale University Press books may be purchased in
quantity for educational, business, or promotional use.
For information, please e-mail sales.press@yale.edu (U.S. office)
or sales@yaleup.co.uk (U.K. office).

Typeset in Bembo MT Pro by
Palimpsest Book Production Ltd, Falkirk, Stirlingshire.
Printed in the United States of America.

Library of Congress Control Number: 2020931386
ISBN 978-0-300-16964-5 (hardcover : alk. paper)

This paper meets the requirements of ANSI/NISO Z39.48-1992
(Permanence of Paper).

10 9 8 7 6 5 4 3 2 1

for Mark Lussier

In one of those excursions (may they ne'er
Fade from remembrance!) through the
   Northern tracts
Of Cambria, ranging with a youthful friend,
I left Bethgelert's huts at couching-time,
And westward took my way, to see the sun
Rise from the top of Snowdon . . .

and Christopher Ridgway

   beloved Friend,
When, looking back, thou seest in clearer view
Than any sweetest sight of yesterday
That summer when on Quantock's grassy hills
Far ranging, and among the sylvan coombs
Thou in delicious words with happy heart
Didst speak . . .

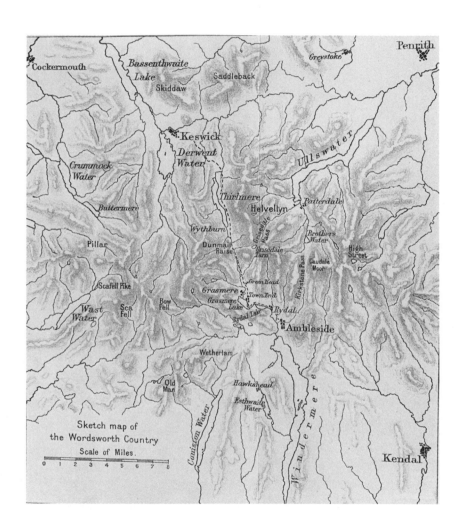

WORDSWORTH'S LAKE DISTRICT

CONTENTS

ILLUSTRATIONS

Wordsworth in Benjamin Robert Haydon's *Christ's Entry into Jerusalem*, beside Newton and Voltaire, with Keats behind (photograph from the author's collection)

Wordsworth on Helvellyn, painted by Benjamin Robert Haydon in 1842 (© National Portrait Gallery, London)

Max Beerbohm, *Wordsworth in the Lake District, at Cross-purposes* (author's collection)

PLACES

Birthplace: the family home in Cockermouth as it is today (author's collection)

Jean Duplessis-Bertaux, *Storming of the Tuileries Palace on 10 August 1792*: Wordsworth witnessed the aftermath (public domain)

Alfoxden as it is today (author's collection)

Dove Cottage as it was when Wordsworth lived there (by permission of the Wordsworth Trust, Grasmere)

Rydal Mount in Wordsworth's time (photograph from the author's collection)

PEOPLE

Annette, presumed miniature portrait (photograph from the author's collection)

Dorothy as a young woman, miniature portrait (photograph © Bonhams)

Dorothy in old age, portrait by Samuel Crosthwaite, photographed in the early twentieth century by Christopher Wordsworth (courtesy of the Wordsworth family, Rydal Mount)

Samuel Taylor Coleridge, portrait after James Northcote (by permission of the Wordsworth Trust, Grasmere)

The New School: detail from James Gillray's caricature *New Morality* (author's collection)

The wedding ring and Dorothy's journal entry for her brother's wedding day (by permission of the Wordsworth Trust, Grasmere)

Charles Lamb by William Hazlitt (© National Portrait Gallery, London)

The lost children: presumed drawing of Thomas and Catharine (by permission of the Wordsworth Trust, Grasmere)

William and Mary in old age (by permission of the Wordsworth Trust, Grasmere)

POEMS AND THEIR INSPIRATION

Title page of *Lyrical Ballads*, 1798 (public domain)

The Quantocks today, with thorn tree, lonesome road and view towards the Bristol Channel, from where it was feared that the French might invade (author's collection)

Symonds Yat today, a few miles above Tintern Abbey, with woods, sylvan river, steep and lofty cliffs (author's collection)

Wordsworth's skates (by permission of the Wordsworth Trust, Grasmere)

'Perfect Contentment, Unity entire': the vale of Grasmere (© Kevin Eames / Dreamstime.com)

Sir George Beaumont's painting of Piel Castle (by permission of the Wordsworth Trust, Grasmere)

Original Goslar manuscript of 'There was a Boy' (by permission of the Wordsworth Trust, Grasmere; photograph by the author)

Title page of first American edition of *The Prelude*, 1850 (author's collection)

PREFACE

Rádical. *adj.* [*radical*, Fr. from *radix*, Latin.]

1. Primitive; original.

2. Implanted by nature.

3. Serving to origination.

> (Samuel Johnson, *A Dictionary*
> *of the English Language*, 1755)

I first went to the Lake District for a family holiday in 1969, when I was eleven. My favourite photograph in the family album is a faded Kodak snapshot in which I am grinning beside my brother and my father (sprightly, happy and youthful-looking, though nearly sixty) on top of Helvellyn, the third-highest mountain in England, with the precipitous Striding Edge snaking below us. The next day we visited Dove Cottage, a few miles down the road in Grasmere. That was my introduction to William Wordsworth. I was amazed that anyone could live and write in rooms so small and dark. A few years later, at school, where I was privileged to have great teachers, we studied the 'Lucy' poems and 'Tintern Abbey'. I worked my way through my father's blue hardback Oxford edition of the complete poems, purchased in 1939, not long before he went from schoolmastering to soldiering. It had tiny print in double columns and a curious arrangement in categories such as 'Poems referring to the Period of Childhood', 'Poems founded on the Affections', 'Poems on the Naming of Places', 'Poems of the Fancy' and 'Poems of the Imagination'.

I discovered that Wordsworth had written a vast number of poems. Every now and then I would find a sequence or a single image that made my heart leap up. But there were great swathes of pomposity and turgidity. I asked myself how a poet who could be so good could also be so bad. Later, I would discover and relish a sonnet by Virginia Woolf's cousin J. K. Stephen, an underrated poet who suffered, like her, from what we now call bipolar disorder. Parodying a grandiloquent sonnet by the man himself which begins 'Two voices are there; one is of the Sea, / One of the Mountains; each a mighty Voice',[1] Stephen identified a distinctly bipolar quality in Wordsworth's imagination:

Two voices are there: one is of the deep;
It learns the storm-cloud's thunderous melody,
Now roars, now murmurs with the changing sea,
Now bird-like pipes, now closes soft in sleep:
And one is of an old half-witted sheep
Which bleats articulate monotony,
And indicates that two and one are three,

That grass is green, lakes damp, and mountains steep:
And, Wordsworth, both are thine.[2]

'Articulate monotony' is a brilliant phrase. Start with the wrong
Wordsworth poems and he will indeed seem ponderous, pedantic,
verbose. You will never want to read him again. Do not on any
account begin with 'To the Spade of a Friend' or the Ecclesiastical
Sonnet on American Episcopacy.

Meanwhile, I puzzled over some of those categories: what was
the difference between the Fancy and the Imagination? My
teacher told me that the answer to that question was to be found
in Samuel Taylor Coleridge's *Biographia Literaria*, and soon the
figures of Wordsworth and Coleridge became inseparable in my
fancy, as they have been in the imagination of generations of
readers. Then at university, when I reread Wordsworth's poems
in chronological order, I began to see that the tangled history
of his relationship with Coleridge might provide a large part of
the answer to my question of how someone who was so good
could be so bad.

During the 1980s, I wrote a doctoral thesis about Wordsworth
and Coleridge, and their successors Keats and Hazlitt, as readers
of Shakespeare. I also had the good fortune to be a tutor on the
Wordsworth Summer Conference, the brainchild of Richard
Wordsworth, an actor best known for his role in the cult 1950s
science fiction horror film *The Quatermass Xperiment*. He was the
poet's great-great-grandson. This was a conference unlike any
other: it lasted for two weeks and, while the mornings and early
evenings were devoted to suitably academic lectures, seminars
and learned papers, the afternoons were spent hiking the fells.
As a tutor, one had to be as adept with a compass and an
Ordnance Survey map as with an edition of Wordsworth and
the latest literary theoretical jargon. Every morning at 7.30 there

was a brisk three-mile walk around Grasmere lake, led by Richard, as fleet of foot in his seventies as my father had been in his sixties and as Wordsworth himself must have been when he ascended Helvellyn at the age of seventy.

I had one frustration as a tutor then, and I still have it today: the desire to give to students – and indeed to anybody who raises an eyebrow when the poet's name is mentioned and the only word that comes to mind is 'daffodils' – a not overlong and not overspecialized book that would make them excited about Wordsworth. He has always lacked the glamour of Coleridge, De Quincey and Byron: he was neither opium addict nor 'mad, bad, and dangerous to know'.[3] He lacked, too, the pathos of Keats, Shelley and John Clare: he failed to make the romantic career move of dying young or going mad. If you try to read a comprehensive account of his entire fourscore years, the chances are that you will lose the will to live somewhere around the halfway mark. Two of the more recent biographies of him, published in 1998 and 2000, are each 1,000 pages long – and one of them covers only the first half of his life.[4] For all their scholarship and their sympathy, they reproduce one of Wordsworth's faults, namely the prolixity that was mocked by Lord Byron:

> And Wordsworth, in a rather long 'Excursion'
>   (I think the quarto holds five hundred pages),
> Has given a sample from the vasty version
>   Of his new system to perplex the sages.[5]

The book I wanted to share was one that was not 1,000 pages long and that explained several things at once, without getting bogged down in too much detail: how the first half of Wordsworth's life was such an extraordinary adventure and the second half so dull; why the poetry of the first half is so memo-

rable, that of the second so forgettable; why William Hazlitt
called his genius 'a pure emanation of the Spirit of the Age';
why he provoked both excoriation and adulation in the next
generation; why the Victorians had no hesitation in regarding
him as the only modern poet to stand in the company of
Shakespeare and Milton. A book, above all, about how Wordsworth
made a difference.

After all these years I have still not found a book that not only
outlines the story of the man and examines the best of his work,
but also places him in the context of his revolutionary age and
traces the vicissitudes of his reputation. So I have attempted it
myself, in the belief that a selective account of the journey from
the visions and experiences that made him a poet to the rays of
influence that made him a force in cultural history will reveal
why his words are still worth reading two and a half centuries
after his birth.

The role of literary as opposed to historical biography should
be to discern and seek to explain the distinctive qualities of the
subject's imaginative power. Why else should one bother to
write, or read, the life of a poet? Wordsworth's best early readers,
most notably Coleridge in his *Biographia Literaria; or, My Literary
Life and Opinions* and William Hazlitt in his essays, recognized
this and accordingly mingled biographical recollection with
literary critical analysis, supported by ample quotation. Some of
Hazlitt's essays and reviews give more space to the words of his
subject than to his own opinions. I have followed the example
of these two in quoting amply from Wordsworth, not only
because they wrote as eyewitnesses but also because they are my
touchstones of literary insight. I therefore have, to adopt a phrase
that Wordsworth used in his Preface to *Lyrical Ballads*, 'one
request I must make of my reader'. Sometimes when we
encounter blocks of indented quotation as we read a biography

or historical work, we skate past them or half-consciously speed
the reading eye. When you come in this book to a passage of
Wordsworth's poetry or his sister Dorothy's prose, or of Coleridge
or Hazlitt, please do the opposite: slow down and savour their
words. Better still, read them aloud. And, as Wordsworth asked,
in 'judging these Poems', decide by your 'own feelings genuinely,
and not by reflection upon what will probably be the judgement
of others'.[6]

★

He was always a mountaineer, so perhaps the conquest of
some vast peak is the best metaphor for his life story. Imagine
it as thirty-six years of arduous but exhilarating ascent to the
summit that was reached with the completion and reading
aloud of the epic work that he called his 'Poem to Coleridge'
and that his family would publish as *The Prelude*. After a
moment of rest, there would be forty-four years of crawling
descent. Any fell-walker will tell you that the joy of the downward journey comes from its speed − as a young man I used
to run down the scree slopes, footpaths and sheep-mown grass
of Wordsworth's native hills. There is nothing more boring
than a gradual decline. So it is that the long life of Wordsworth
tails off into monotony.

This book accordingly offers only a lightning sketch of the
second half of Wordsworth's life. In the spirit of *The Prelude*, it
concentrates on the formative years of youth. For this reason,
my title is *Radical Wordsworth*. The word 'radical' is derived from
Latin *radix*, a root. In Wordsworth's time, it denoted the essential nature of a thing: this book is a quest for the roots, the
fundamentals, of Wordsworth's genius. An organic metaphor is
fitting for the man who was more rooted in the natural world
than any previous poet. Also fittingly, the word 'radical' began

to take on a new meaning in the early nineteenth century: it
became a synonym for 'Jacobinical', used (pejoratively) to denote
an English supporter of the French Revolution.

There are other biographies – I especially recommend those
of Mary Moorman and Stephen Gill[7] – that walk through his
whole story in a straight line from womb to tomb in a steady
tread reminiscent of the way in which, according to William
Hazlitt's account, he composed his verse: 'Coleridge has told
me that he himself liked to compose in walking over uneven
ground, or breaking through the straggling branches of a copse-
wood; whereas Wordsworth always wrote (if he could) walking
up and down a straight gravel-walk, or in some spot where the
continuity of his verse met with no collateral interruption.'[8] The
gravel-walk suited the steady beat of Wordsworth's blank-verse
iambic pentameter, but he did not think that human life
progresses in a straight line. One of his controlling metaphors
in the poem to Coleridge and elsewhere is that of the river or
stream, flowing onwards but sometimes looping back on itself,
sometimes meandering while at other times rushing in a torrent.
A Wordsworthian biography of Wordsworth will be more like
a stream of consciousness than a march from cradle to grave.

It will also acknowledge that his life – any life – is shaped
more by key moments than quotidian routine. As he explained
in *The Prelude*,

> There are in our existence spots of time
> Which with distinct pre-eminence retain
> A fructifying virtue, whence, depressed
> By trivial occupations and the round
> Of ordinary intercourse, our minds
> (Especially the imaginative power)
> Are nourished, and invisibly repaired.[9]

Too often, biographies of Wordsworth have been depressed by trivial occupations and the round of ordinary intercourse. Those are not the things that inspire great poetry. This biography, by contrast, focuses on the spots of time which with distinct pre-eminence fructified, nourished and repaired his imaginative power. It is deliberately fragmentary, momentary, selective. It seeks to open what in book eleven of the poem to Coleridge, which concerns 'Imagination, how impaired and restored', he called 'the hiding-places of my power'.[10]

PRELUDE

A sort of experience like the effect of lightning . . .

(Samuel Taylor Coleridge, *Notebooks*,
late December 1806)

1

THE EPOCH

Christmas 1806. Coleorton, Leicestershire.

He was a long way from the rivers, lakes and mountains of his northern boyhood. A long way, too, from the rolling green hills of the West Country Quantocks where he and his new friend had planned the collection of poems that would come to mark a turning point in literary history. The eastern Midlands of England, all coalfields and low-lying farmland, was not his natural domain. He was there with his family – wife Mary, sister Dorothy, sister-in-law Sara, son Johnny, daughter Dora and new baby Tommy – at a place called Hall Farm. A generous patron, Sir George Beaumont, had given him a sanctuary for the winter of his thirty-seventh year.

Just before Christmas, the friend arrived. Samuel Taylor

Coleridge: overweight, addicted to opium and alcohol, he had recently returned from a long stint in a warmer climate where he had sought to repair his health. He was in the midst of a marital crisis. After weeks of characteristic procrastination, he had left his wife Sara and two young children at the home in the Lake District that they shared with fellow poet Robert Southey and his family (Southey's wife Edith was Sara Coleridge's sister). Coleridge was magnetically drawn to the Wordsworth household not only because of the friendship that had led to the co-written poetry collection *Lyrical Ballads*, but also because he was irredeemably and unrequitedly in love with Sara Hutchinson, William's sister-in-law.

Now he was here at Hall Farm, bringing along his eldest child, ten-year-old Hartley, named after the philosopher David Hartley. There was room enough. The house had three bedrooms on the first floor, and more on the second. The five adults and four children shared a spiced pudding on Christmas Day, Dorothy's birthday.

Wordsworth had a treat for Coleridge and the three women, all of whom loved him in different ways. On the twelve days of Christmas, and for one day beyond, the family gathered around the fireplace in the drawing room to the right of the front door and listened to him reading a blank-verse composition in thirteen books, dedicated to his newly returned friend.[1] It was unlike anything heard before in the history of poetry.

The oldest and most revered form of Western poetry is *epic*. This is where Western culture began: the stories of the demigods in *Gilgamesh*, of the heroes in *The Iliad* and *The Odyssey*. This was the great tradition in which students were drilled through the centuries: the origins of ancient Rome in the *Aeneid* of Virgil, the myths of antiquity in the *Metamorphoses* of Ovid, the Fall of Man in the *Paradise Lost* of John Milton. In what may well have been the boldest act of chutzpah in literary history,

Wordsworth wrote his epic poem not about heroes and gods, not about his nation, not about the spiritual story of humankind from Genesis to Revelation, but about himself. The most ancient of poetic forms was made new and made personal, turned inward to address the growth of the poet's own self.

An epic customarily begins *in medias res*, in the middle of things. Our story accordingly begins at this moment, with the poem ready to be shared. Imagine that we are listening to Wordsworth's voice as he reads his newly minted work to his immediate circle. See them gathered around the fire on a winter evening, deep in the English countryside: the women who have supported him and who are contributing so much to his vision, and the troubled friend who has inspired him to tell in verse the story of his early life.

A new year is about to dawn, but a special trust is about to die.

★

Wordsworth spoke with 'a deep guttural intonation, and a strong tincture of the northern *burr*, like the crust on wine'.[2] He began:

> Oh there is blessing in this gentle breeze
> That blows from the green fields and from the clouds
> And from the sky: it beats against my cheek
> And seems half conscious of the joy it gives.[3]

The breeze was like an instrument carrying the music of nature to his inner self. Soon he was transporting them back from the eastern lowlands to the Lake District in the north-west of England that was their spiritual home.

In the first two books he told of childhood and school time, of stealing eggs from the nests of birds, of rowing an illicitly borrowed boat beneath a towering crag, and of his skates hissing along the polished ice of a lake at night. Then, in the third to fifth books, of university, summer vacation and the influence of books. In the sixth he recalled a walking tour that had taken him across the Alps and in the seventh he tracked his residence in London after going down from Cambridge. Book eight was a philosophical retrospect, entitled 'Love of Nature leading to Love of Mankind'.

And then he plunged into an account of how he had literally walked into the French Revolution and become an 'enthusiast' for the cause. By that winter of 1806–7, however, he had lost faith in the radical politics of his youth. One motivation for writing the poem to Coleridge was to capture before it faded into total oblivion the feeling of hope, of a blissful new dawn for society, that had animated him back in the early 1790s.

On he read, night after night, by firelight and flickering candle, concluding with a vision beheld on the summit of mount Snowdon in North Wales. This climactic memory led into an address to Coleridge asserting that the two of them, these young poets, their art still barely tested in the marketplace, would one day come to be seen as 'Prophets of Nature' with the power to offer humankind 'A lasting inspiration sanctified / By reason and by truth', a philosophy of the love of nature, and a blueprint for 'how the mind of man' may become 'A thousand times more beautiful than the earth / On which he dwells'.[4]

Coleridge replied with a poem of his own. In his manuscript he called it 'To W. Wordsworth. Lines Composed, for the greater part on the Night, on which he finished the recitation of his Poem (in thirteen Books) concerning the growth and history of his own Mind, Jan. 7, 1807, Cole-orton, near Ashby de la Zouch'.[5] It is a poem that makes astonishingly high claims for the work of his friend. Wordsworth is lauded as the first to tell in poetry of 'the foundations and the building up / Of a Human Spirit'. The first to tell of how we are shaped by our childhood environment. Of how we emerge into political consciousness. And, in a magnificent phrase, of how we are eventually summoned homeward 'From the dread watch-tower of man's absolute self' to a place in nature, a vision of the divine, and a sense of community. When 'the long sustainéd Song finally closed' and Wordsworth's 'deep voice' fell silent, Coleridge looked at his friend, and at the three women gathered 'round us both / That happy vision of beloved faces', and then he rose and found himself 'in prayer'. Poetry had taken on the holiness that had traditionally belonged to religious faith.

Wordsworth had three names for his work: 'The Poem to Coleridge', 'The Poem on my own Life' and 'The Poem on the Growth of my own Mind'. But he never gave it a title and never published it. He continued to tinker with it for half a century between its modest beginnings in 1798 and his death at the age of eighty in 1850. For a long time, he conceived it to be a mere overture to a still longer work, which he never completed. That was why when his family saw it into print soon after he died, they gave it the title that has stuck: *The Prelude.* 'The prelude to what?', students will sometimes ask. The old joke among Wordsworthians is that he wrote a *Prelude* to his epic work and an *Excursion* from it, but never wrote the thing itself.

The alternative descriptions recorded on the title page of the first edition when it was finally published are more apt than the lead title: *The Prelude, or Growth of a Poet's Mind; An Autobiographical Poem.* The growth of the subject's mind: that is the most interesting dimension of any biographical endeavour. And an '*auto*biographical' poem: the very word had been coined only a few years before. We might say that Wordsworth's exploration of the growth of his own mind was and remains the original, the exemplary *autobiographia literaria*.

★

Wordsworth and Coleridge both began writing their best poetry when they met each other. They both stopped writing their best poetry when they fell out with one another. When and why did it all begin to go wrong?

Something else happened during that Christmas and New Year visit to Coleorton. Or may have happened. Coleridge scrawled an entry in giant capital letters in his notebook: 'THE EPOCH'. He then gave a date and a place: 'Saturday, 27th December, 1806 – Queen's Head, Stringston, ½ a mile from Coleorton Church, 50 minutes after 10.'[6] It would appear that he had left Hall Farm in horror, crossed the fields and ended up in a pub in the village of Thringstone, where he sat down to drink and to write about what had happened. He was disorientated: I have followed in his footsteps across the fields to Thringstone from the church of St Mary the Virgin, Coleorton (which nestles beside Hall Farm) and it is a walk of three miles, not a mere half.

You can tell from the manuscript that Coleridge's hand was shaking as he wrote. The following three leaves, which would have been densely written in his rapid penmanship, were later ripped from the notebook and destroyed. But their content can be inferred from a notebook entry written some months later, after Coleridge awoke from a dream of tears and an 'anguish of involuntary Jealousy'. He poured out his unrequited love for 'Asra', Sara Hutchinson, describing it as the very ground of his identity: 'Self in me derives its sense of Being from having this one absolute Object.' Then he wrote of his thoughts of suicide. And then this:

O agony! O the vision of that Saturday Morning – of the
Bed / – O cruel! is he not beloved, adored by two – & two
such Beings – / and must I not be beloved *near* him except
as a Satellite? – But o mercy mercy! is he not better, greater,
more *manly*, & altogether more attractive to any the purest
Woman? . . . W. is greater, better, manlier, more dear, by
nature, to Woman, than I – I – miserable I! – but does he
– O No! no! no! he does not – he does not pretend, he does
not wish, to love you as I love you, Sara! – he does not love,
he *would* not love, it is not the voice, not the duty of *his*
nature, to love *any* being as I love you.[7]

Was it not enough for Wordsworth to be adored by his wife
Mary and his sister Dorothy? Was he to be the lodestar of his
sister-in-law Sara, too?

Some months later, Coleridge wrote again of 'that miserable
Saturday morning'. The thunderclouds had been gathering over
his relationship with the Wordsworth household. The dreadful
possibility that Asra might have been in love with William: he
had been staring it in the face, then averting his eyes from it.
Did she not brush off Coleridge when they were physically close
to each other? 'But a minute and a half with *me* and all the time
restless & going.' But with him: 'An hour and more with
Wordsworth – *in bed* – O agony!'[8] Wordsworth's name was written
here in a cipher using Greek characters, Coleridge's way of
shielding himself (and prying eyes) from intimate matters. The
rest of the notebook entry is scored out.

Around the same time, Coleridge wrote a poem in Latin called
'Ad Vilmum Axiologum'. 'Ad Vilmum': to William. 'Axiologum':
a Latinized play on the Greek words for 'words' (*logoi*) and
'worth[y]' (*axios*). Like the generous verses written on hearing
the recitation at Hall Farm, this is a poem 'To William

Wordsworth'. But it is very different in tone. A translation of
the opening lines might read

> Do you force me to endure Asra's forgetting,
> Make me see how she turns her eye from me,
> Make me know that the one I'll always love
> Is false and cruel?

And the end: 'My life is finished. Asra lives on, forgetting me.'[9]
Thanks to Wordsworth, Asra is shown to be an 'empty' woman.
She who was Coleridge's everything has become nothing. In
common with many of Coleridge's poems, this one stitches
together an assortment of literary borrowings, in particular some
virulent and unpleasant lines about sexual infidelity from the
Italian Renaissance poet Ludovico Ariosto.[10] It is hard to read
the poem as anything other than an accusation against Wordsworth
and Sara.

Could it really have been so? Perhaps the image of the pair
of them in bed together was a bad dream or an opium-induced
vision? That was how Coleridge rationalized it many years later:
'Did I *believe* it? Did I not even *Know*, that it *was* not so, *could*
not be so?' Maybe the 'horrid' vision was 'a mere phantasm'.
'And yet what anguish, what gnawings of despair, what throb-
bings and lancinations of positive Jealousy.'[11] Many more years
later, the image was still with him: one night in 1819, he dreamed
of 'Wordsworth and SH' together, her 'most beautiful breasts
exposed'.[12] The frenzied exit to Thringstone and the enduring
force of the memory feel too vivid for the whole thing to have
been a mere imagining. Nor is it plausible that he was under
the delusional influence of opium at the time: Dorothy had made
a point of ensuring that there was no brandy in the house, so
that Coleridge would not have the opportunity to mix a tincture

of laudanum. It was presumably in order to find alcohol in which to dissolve a dose of opium that he headed across the fields to the tavern.

We will never know what Wordsworth and Sara were doing in bed together.[13] The innocent explanation would be that, though the weather that Christmas was unseasonably mild, Hall Farm was a chilly house. Bed was the obvious place to be on a December morning, in order to read together or look through the manuscript of the long autobiographical poem which Wordsworth was preparing to read aloud that evening. Sara had wonderfully clear handwriting and wrote the fairest copies of William's poems. Coleridge did not stop to think that they might have been working together; instead, his memory fixated itself on Sara's beautiful naked breasts.

Wordsworth was a man of strong passions, but there is no external evidence to support Coleridge's perception that he had an affair with his sister-in-law, just as there is no warrant for the idea promoted by some modern critics that the love he bore for Dorothy might have been incestuous. Coleridge's problem was that he could think of love only as something all-consuming. His own insecurity led to his self-perception as a mere 'Satellite' in the sphere of Wordsworth and the three women who supported him in his work. In a letter to his friend Henry Crabb Robinson, a poetry-loving lawyer who got to know nearly all the major authors of the age, Coleridge wrote that 'Wordsworth is by nature incapable of being in Love, tho' no man more tenderly attached – hence he ridicules the existence of any other passion than a compound of Lust with Esteem & Friendship, confined to one Object, first by accidents of Association, and permanently, by the force of Habit & a sense of Duty.'[14] Though the tone of this is negative, Coleridge grants that a compound of lust with esteem and friendship is actually an excellent recipe for an enduring relationship. The Wordsworthian attitude whereby initial sexual desire is subsequently married to respect and companionship will, Coleridge continues, make for 'a good Husband' and a happy life. That is indeed what Wordsworth achieved. Perhaps, though, at the cost of his continued creativity.

There is, says Coleridge, contrasting his own state of mind to Wordsworth's tender attachments, 'such a passion as Love – which is no more a compound than Oxygen'. Coleridge was in close touch with the science of his time: only a few years had passed since Joseph Priestley had demonstrated that oxygen was not a compound and Erasmus Darwin, grandfather of Charles, had popularized its chemical name in his poem *The Botanic Garden*. For Coleridge, love was oxygen, a pure element, uncontaminated by anything so mundane as 'Esteem & Friendship'. One of his poems was called 'Constancy to an Ideal Object', another 'Love and Friendship Opposite'. He wanted Asra, his ideal object, to be constant to him as he vowed he would be to her (having failed to be constant to his wife, the other Sara). And he wanted her to be an all-consuming lover, not a friend. He wanted all or nothing. To use the terms of the novel that Jane Austen published during the very year of this letter to Crabb Robinson, Coleridge was in thrall to 'sensibility', whereas Wordsworth lived and loved with 'sense'. Coleridge was Marianne Dashwood to Wordsworth's Elinor.

Aching with his passion for Asra, Coleridge could not abide the sight of Wordsworth so 'tenderly attached' to his wife, his sister, his sister-in-law and his children. But he was again and again drawn back to the home and family that they offered him. Later in the day, he returned from the Queen's Head. The Wordsworths, for now, were patient. There were probably some stern words, or at least looks, with regard to his drinking and his moodiness. But nothing seems to have been said about the morning encounter, if indeed it ever happened. Over the following evenings, they huddled together around the fireplace in the drawing room and listened to the poet as, with his North Country burr, he read the 8,000 lines of the

POEM
TITLE NOT YET FIXED UPON
BY
WILLIAM WORDSWORTH
ADDRESSED TO
S. T. COLERIDGE

A breach had been opened in the friendship, but for now it was healed by the sharing of poetry as together they inaugurated an epoch in the history of the modern self.

PART ONE

1770–1806:
BLISS WAS IT IN THAT
DAWN TO BE ALIVE

Mr Wordsworth's genius is a pure emanation of the Spirit
of the Age

(William Hazlitt)

2

A VOICE THAT FLOWED
ALONG MY DREAMS

The poem he read to Coleridge on those winter nights in Sir George Beaumont's farmhouse had its origin some eight years earlier. Wordsworth, his sister Dorothy and Coleridge had gone to Germany, ostensibly to learn the language. Coleridge had been urging Wordsworth to write a philosophical epic. Wordsworth was meditating upon his poetic vocation. The question of his destiny led him to think of his origins, and that was where he began:

> Was it for this
> That one, the fairest of all rivers, loved
> To blend his murmurs with my nurse's song,
> And from his alder shades and rocky falls,

And from his fords and shallows, sent a voice
That flowed along my dreams?[1]

Wordsworthian questions may convey a sense of doubt and hesitation, a sense of wonder and surprise, or sometimes both at
once. Was it for this? Negatively: for being stuck in Germany,
far from home, suffering from writer's block on a project that I
don't really believe in, but that I cannot give up on because
Coleridge believes that it is my destiny to be the greatest philosophical poet of the age, the true successor to John Milton.
Positively: perhaps it was for *this*, the act of writing, the very
thing that I am writing now, that I was born. A poetic vision
that would indeed become philosophical, but that begins in
memory, in home, in nature and in childhood.

A vision that begins with the river Derwent flowing beside
the garden wall of the house in Cockermouth where he was
born. With the musical murmur of that river. If you are lucky
enough to be born beside a river – especially in a world without
the hum of traffic and electricity, let alone the white noise of
modern communications – the sound of its water will be a
constant under-presence to your childhood, heard below the
bedtime lullabies, through the drift into sleep and on into your
dreams. The river speaks and asks the nascent poet to respond
in lines that will flow in blank verse across the line endings: 'Was
it for this / That', 'loved / To blend', 'a voice / That flowed'.
The river Derwent was his first muse.

His birthplace, now owned by the National Trust, is elegant
and imposing, Georgian architecture at its best, bathed in light
by way of eight large sashed windows on the lower floor and
nine on the upper. There were spacious, wood-panelled rooms
and ample quarters for family servants. The children's bedroom
was at the back of the house, looking out on the well-stocked

garden that led down to a terraced path by the Derwent. When you open the window, you hear the water. There is a rocky patch on the bed of the river as it flows past the house, causing the water to eddy and to murmur a little louder.

A new build in an old community, this was, and still is, the most handsome dwelling on the main street of Cockermouth, an ancient market town on the north-west fringe of the English Lake District, dominated by a partially ruined Norman castle. The house belonged to a man said to be the richest landowner in England: Sir James Lowther. He was variously known as 'Wicked Jimmy', 'the Bad Earl', the 'Tyrant of the North' and 'Jimmy Grasp-all, Earl of Toadstool'. As well as his rural estates, he owned whole towns, coal mines and the harbour at Whitehaven, the second-busiest port in the land and an engine room of the northern economy. He was master of all he surveyed, exercising control over nine seats in Parliament.

Wordsworth's grandfather Richard had been law-agent for Lowther's properties and dealings in Westmorland until Richard's death in 1760. Wordsworth's father John followed in the family footsteps, training in the law and then entering the service of the Lowthers. In 1764, John Wordsworth was made responsible for their estates in Cumberland (the Lake District is now in 'Cumbria', but it was then two counties, Westmorland on the Pennine side, Cumberland towards the sea). Lowther installed his agent in the impressive house on Cockermouth high street so that everybody would know that his man was someone to be reckoned with.

Eighteenth-century England was a place where property was power. Without it, you couldn't even vote. If you committed a crime against property – poaching, trespass, petty theft – your punishment would be severe. Most of the English land was owned by the all-powerful families of the aristocracy and the gentry, though with some important exceptions, among them the remoter parts of the Lake District. The traditional role for the steward and law-agent of a great landowner was to oversee the estates, collect rents and handle disputes. But John Wordsworth was also tasked with the work of ensuring that eligible voters turned out to support the Lowther interest at election time. To maintain the family's supremacy in the region, it was necessary to keep all those parliamentary boroughs in their pocket. Some votes were openly bought, but most were 'canvassed' by way of the supply of free alcohol. The biggest election expense was the reimbursement of innkeepers, who provided drinks on the house through the several days of polling, in return for the assurance of a vote for their patron. Following the 1774 election, John Wordsworth had to settle a bill just a few shillings short of £200, for 'Victuals and Liquor consumed during the course of the poll'.[2] That is about £30,000 or $40,000 in today's money.

The role of Lowther's agent did not make for popularity. When John Wordsworth's only daughter was a teenager, she complained that 'it is indeed mortifying to my Brothers and me to find that amongst all those who visited at my father's house he had not one real friend'.[3] The only callers were there on business or trying to gain influence with Lowther. One would have expected Mr Wordsworth to be well remunerated for such work. He was not. The house came rent-free, but he had no formal contract or salary. Instead, he was rewarded with interests of his own, such as the tolls on cattle gates and rents on small parcels of land. His financial dependence on his master would become a huge problem for his children.

The year after arriving in Cockermouth, John Wordsworth, now twenty-five, married eighteen-year-old Ann Cookson, daughter of a linendraper from another market town, Penrith, in the east of Cumberland. Within six years, there were five children: firstborn son Richard, the responsible one, destined to become a lawyer like his father; William, born two years later, on 7 April 1770, a temperamental child, the only one his mother ever worried about; Dorothy, the only daughter, born on Christmas Day of 1771; the following December, John, adored by William and Dorothy, 'from his earliest infancy of most lonely and retired habits', and therefore known by his father as 'Ibex', after 'the shyest of all the beasts';[4] then finally, in 1774, Christopher, the scholarly one, who would rise to the supreme position in the academic world, master of Trinity College, Cambridge.

The woman's role was to nurture her children in the Christian faith. At Easter, they would troop to church to say their catechism, dressed in fresh clothes. One of William's few memories of his mother had her pinning to his breast a nosegay of flowers that she had picked and bound for the occasion. With her husband away from home, riding the county on Lowther business, Ann often sent the children to relatives for a change of air. John's elder brother, Richard, was Collector of Customs in the port of Whitehaven. On their first sight of the sea, little Dorothy wept. In old age, William would say that this was the first sign of her remarkable 'sensibility'.[5] On the beach, they picked up shells and took them back to Cockermouth, holding the hollows to their ear and hearing the sound of the sea.

The children also made long visits to Penrith, staying above the linen shop with their mother's parents, whom they found grumpy and critical. This encouraged a rebellious streak in William. He had a temper. Once, he recalled, he was so angry at being told off for some trivial offence that he went up to his grandparents' attic and picked up one of the swords that he knew were kept there, with the intention of killing himself. On another occasion, he and his older brother Richard were whipping their spinning tops on the bare boards of the drawing-room floor. The walls were hung round with family portraits. 'Dare you strike your whip through that old lady's petticoat?' asked William. 'No, I won't,' was goody-goody Richard's inevitable reply. 'Then,' said William, launching his whip, 'here goes.'[6]

William was christened and Dorothy baptized at the same time.[7] They became inseparable. Their favourite place was the terrace by the river at the bottom of the garden, which commanded a fine view of Cockermouth Castle and the hills beyond. Sparrows built their nests in the closely clipped privet and rose hedge that covered the terrace wall. Tearaway William chased butterflies, while sensitive Dorothy feared to brush the dust from their wings.[8]

Standing at the confluence of the river Cocker and the Derwent, the town has always been prone to flooding: in 2009, Wordsworth's birthplace was temporarily inundated by his beloved river. His own earliest memory, he claimed, was of total immersion in the Derwent's crystal water. The first self-image in the first draft of his autobiographical poem is of a naked four-year-old boy making 'one long bathing of a summer's day', basking in the sun, plunging into the stream. And then, when the rain comes pouring down, as sooner or later (usually sooner) it always does in the Lake District, standing alone like 'a naked savage' framed against crag, hill, wood and 'distant Skiddaw's lofty height'.[9]

He would always be pulled back to these mountains, rivers and lakes. But he was also born with the restless spirit of a wanderer. From an early age, his eye would be drawn to a road that led over the hill above the town and on into an unknown distance. Few things, he claims, pleased him more than a 'public road', a sight that

Hath wrought on my imagination since the morn
Of childhood, when a disappearing line,

One daily present to my eyes, that crossed

The naked summit of a far-off hill

Beyond the limits that my feet had trod,

Was like an invitation into space

Boundless.[10]

Wordsworth loved space. He did not want to be bound. At least in retrospect, he imagined himself being called from his home to a vagrant life. He loved nothing more than to walk. Thomas De Quincey, one of his disciples, reckoned that in the course of his life Wordsworth walked some 175,000 miles. The on-the-road conversation with a beggar, a discharged soldier, a dispossessed woman, an impoverished leech gatherer, a shepherd bearing the last of his flock: this would become a hallmark of his poetry.

★

William and Dorothy periodically attended a 'dame school' (kindergarten) in Penrith, where among the fellow pupils was Mary Hutchinson, his future wife, and her sister Sara. At the age of six, William entered the grammar school in Cockermouth. The master spent half a year trying fruitlessly to teach him Latin. But then Wordsworth was educated into strong feeling by harsh experience. Nearly all his greatest poetry is pervaded by a feeling of loss: the loss of childhood, of freedom, of the unmediated relationship with nature symbolized by the four-year-old child plunging naked into the Derwent. For a psychological explanation of this, we need look no further than a day one month before his eighth birthday.

His mother returned from a visit to friends in London. She had been accommodated in the so-called 'best bedroom', that is to say a guest room reserved for special occasions and therefore not regularly aired. The bed was damp. She caught a cold, which turned to a 'decline', probably pneumonia. Soon after her return to her parents' house in Penrith, she died. The seven-year-old William's 'last impression' of his mother was 'a glimpse of her on passing the door of her bedroom during her last illness, when she was reclining in her easy chair'.[11] She was buried at Penrith on 11 March 1778.

He readily admitted that he remembered very little of his mother, yet he firmly believed that it was from her that he learned his love of nature. 'Blest the infant babe', he wrote, as he embarked on his project to use his 'best conjectures' to 'trace / The progress of our being': the baby nursed in its mother's arms or sleeping on its mother's breast is blessed because it is learning the experience of sympathy, the force of love. It is through the bond with our mothers in our infancy that we first claim 'manifest kindred' with a soul other than our own. As the baby at the breast gazes into the mother's eye, it has its first experience of feeling. The reciprocal exchange of 'passion' is like an 'awakening breeze' that in time will extend its force and bind us to our natural surroundings, irradiating and exalting 'All objects through all intercourse of sense':

> Along his infant veins are interfused
> The gravitation and the filial bond
> Of Nature that connect him with the world.[12]

The baby feels safe when 'by intercourse of touch' it holds 'mute dialogues' with the 'mother's heart'. That is the sensation needed to secure the self in the world. This 'infant sensibility' is the 'Great birthright of our being'. So Wordsworth argues, innovatively using poetry to invent a theory of infant psychological development.

But what happens if the mother is lost, the child 'left alone

/ Seeking this visible world, not knowing why'? How will the sense of Self and Other develop if the 'props' of the 'affections' are removed?[13] Wordsworth writes of the baby in his mother's arms, 'No outcast he, bewildered and depressed'. He is reaching back to that unconscious early memory – or perhaps clutching at the beautiful belief of belonging – because his mother's death occurred when he was at a highly sensitive age. The loss made him an outcast, bewildered and depressed.

3

FOSTERED

Dorothy was only six when their mother died. Three months later, she was separated from her brothers. A poignant note in the family account book, now held in the Wordsworth Library at Dove Cottage, reads: 'Dolly Left Penrith for Halifax in a Chaise with Mr Threlkeld and Miss Threlkeld on Saturday 13th June 1778. Mr Cookson gave Miss Threlkred 5 gns towards her conveyance etc.'[1] The Threlkelds, brother and sister, were cousins of Mrs Wordsworth; Mr Cookson, who gave the five guineas for expenses, was William and Dorothy's maternal grandfather. As far as is known, during the next ten years Dorothy never returned from Yorkshire to the Lake District. Nor did her father ever visit her. Many years later, she still held the bitter memory of never being invited to spend 'a single moment under my Father's Roof'.[2] Unlike her brothers, she did not return home annually at Christmas, even though it was also her birthday.

Initially, the brothers remained in Penrith. A year later, the two eldest, Richard and William, were sent to the Free Grammar School at Hawkshead in the vale of Esthwaite. Young John joined them in 1782. The brothers lodged, at a cost of ten guineas each per year, with Hugh (a joiner) and Ann Tyson, whom William would come to regard as a foster mother. William remained in Hawkshead during term time for eight formative years; halfway through his education, he moved with the Tysons from the little town itself to a nearby hamlet called Colthouse. In the summer vacations, as well as at Christmas, the boys returned to Cockermouth or Penrith.

The move to Hawkshead took them from the northern corner of the Lake District to the more mellow landscape of its southern edge. Gently sloping fells led down to the woodland around the lake. Here the seeds were sown for the growth of the poet's mind, as he was fostered daily by beauty and sometimes by fear:

> Fair seed-time had my soul, and I grew up
> Fostered alike by beauty and by fear,
> Much favoured in my birthplace, and no less
> In that beloved vale to which erelong
> I was transplanted.[3]

★

One of the most evocative exhibits in the Wordsworth Museum at Dove Cottage is a pair of ice skates that belonged to the poet. They inspired an exquisite poem by Seamus Heaney.[4] They consist of steel blades hinged onto a wooden bed shaped to fit the foot, with spikes to attach them to the skater's footwear and leather ankle straps to secure them. At the rear, there is a braking mechanism: rock back upon the heels and the wood will come down on the steel, bringing you to a sliding halt. For many readers and students, Wordsworth at first seems a staid figure, as plodding as his later verse. To imagine him on those skates is to set him in motion, to conjure him back to youth, speed and joy.

Such images were among the most forceful of his recollections of his early years. In the memories of 'Childhood and School-time' that begin *The Prelude*, he remembers the 'thundering hoofs' of his horse as he and his friends galloped over Levens Sands, moonlight gleaming in the sea, as they headed home from an excursion to the ruins of Furness Abbey. At such moments, he recalls, he sensed a 'spirit', some form of sublime presence emanating from the rocks and streams.[5]

He felt this spiritual 'transport' again when skating on the lake at twilight in the frosty season. The village clock tolls six as 'All shod with steel / We hissed along the polished ice in games / Confederate'.[6] The sibilance of 'shod', 'steel', 'hissed', 'polished' and 'ice' brings the very sound of the skates to life. And then the boy Wordsworth veers away from the noisy crowd of school-mates, swerving into silent reverie as he cuts 'across the image of a star / That gleamed upon the ice'. In a rare example of a late revision improving *The Prelude*, the final version of the text has 'the reflex of a star' instead of 'the image'. With 'reflex' it is as if an X doubly marks the spot: the star reflected in the ice below the criss-cross of skate trails.[7]

Then he would lean back into a moment of giddy delight:

> and oftentimes
> When we had given our bodies to the wind
> And all the shadowy banks on either side
> Came sweeping through the darkness, spinning still

The rapid line of motion, then at once
Have I, reclining back upon my heels,
Stopped short; yet still the solitary cliffs
Wheeled by me, even as if the earth had rolled
With visible motion her diurnal round.[8]

His body is still but in his head he is moving with the earth, as if he were one with the mysterious force to which, as he moves from narrative to philosophizing, he gives a sequence of names: 'Presence of Nature', 'visions of the hills', 'souls of lonely places'.[9] This will not be the only time that something profound, simultaneously comforting and terrifying, is conjured by Wordsworth's collocation of those words 'earth', 'rolled', 'motion', 'diurnal' and 'round'.

He must have known that the skating scene was one of his best and most characteristic passages because it was one of the few sequences of his verse autobiography that he brought into print. It appeared in 1809 in the – suitably wintery – Christmas issue of Coleridge's magazine *The Friend*. Wordsworth then reprinted it among the 'Poems referring to the Period of Childhood' in his collected poems of 1815, with the title 'Influence of Natural Objects in calling forth and strengthening the Imagination in Boyhood and early Youth'. An explanatory subtitle gestured towards the work that had been in progress for a decade and a half: 'From an unpublished poem'. The descriptive sequence is preceded by a verse paragraph addressed to the 'Wisdom and Spirit of the universe! / Thou Soul, that art the Eternity of thought!' This spirit is said to be the force that gives 'breath' and 'everlasting motion' to forms and images. Working in conjunction with sublime landscapes, it purifies 'The elements of feeling and of thought', bringing us to a recognition of 'A grandeur in the beatings of the heart'.[10] The shift of gear between vivid recollection of childhood and high spiritual-philosophical theory is another Wordsworthian hallmark.

Winters were cold through most of his childhood. There was a particularly prolonged and severe frost in his fifteenth winter, during which not only little Esthwaite Water but even large parts of the vast lake of Windermere were frozen over with thick ice. He often skated in this and other frosty seasons. Several of his peers were very accomplished skaters, though it was always a dangerous sport – one of the best of them, Tom Park, died on Esthwaite when he went through the ice in his twenties.[11]

There is no reason to doubt the autobiographical inspiration of *The Prelude*'s skating scene. At the same time, though, it should be recognized that skating scenes were much favoured in the poetry (as in the painting) of the eighteenth century, so Wordsworth was entering into a literary tradition as well as remembering his own past. The passage was drafted in Germany shortly after he and Coleridge visited the aged poet Friedrich Gottlieb Klopstock. This grand old man of German letters was famous for his odes, one of which, 'Der Eislauf', is an energetic evocation of the art of skating, at which Klopstock excelled. He twists and turns and plays poetically with the sound of skate on polished ice. It was reported that when he met Goethe, Germany's other great poet, they talked about skating more than literature. Both Coleridge and Wordsworth left accounts of their visit to Klopstock, which appears to have been rather disappointing to the young English poets who were so excited to meet the old master. Skating is not mentioned in their recollections, but we cannot rule out the possibility that this encounter was one of the factors that led Wordsworth to turn his own memories of evenings on the ice into poetry.[12]

★

Wordsworth attaches the word 'oftentimes' to the skating scene. This was not a one-time memory. For the most part, we remember our formative years as a blur. In retrospect, each day is very like the next – save for the distinction between schooldays and holidays. We remember long hot summers, freezing cold mornings, the excitement of the first fall of snow. Day upon day, year upon year, of friendship and games, of laughter and tears, will merge together. But if we were fortunate enough to build dens in the woods, skate on frozen ponds and run hallooing in the mountain breeze, then our abiding memory will be of air and light, of the wind upon the face and the arching sky above.

Sometimes, though, we remember in singular flashes. Particular adventures and misadventures become part of family lore. And particular incidents take on symbolic force. These are what Wordsworth called the 'spots of time' that shape our identity. He coined the phrase towards the end of the first part of the autobiographical 'Poem to Coleridge' that he began in late 1798 and early 1799. 'Such moments', he wrote, 'chiefly seem to have their date / In our first childhood'. The very act of recall gives them significance, makes them into the joints and the musculature of the self. Often they come at transitional moments, between light and darkness, marking 'The twilight of rememberable life'.[13] Wordsworth was the first master-poet of memory. That very word 'rememberable' belongs distinctively to him.[14]

At the same time, he was aware of the tricks of memory. His past has 'self-presence', another newly minted turn of phrase, in his heart and yet there is such a gap – a 'vacancy' – between the lived experience of the child and the mind of the poet as he nears the age of thirty and begins to write down his memories that 'sometimes when I think of them I seem / Two consciousnesses – conscious of myself, / And of some other being'.[15] The notion of two 'consciousnesses' was discussed by various eighteenth-century philosophers writing in response to John Locke's theory of human understanding, but the tendency was to argue for the unity of the past and present selves, not a fracture between them. So, for example, Bishop Joseph Butler in his highly influential *The Analogy of Religion* argued that thinking about the relationship between one's past and one's present inevitably raises 'the Idea of personal Identity' and may create the anxiety that we do not have a single stable self, that 'the Consciousness of our own Existence in Youth and Old-age' could constitute 'different successive consciousnesses'. Butler answers the problem by saying that if we are capable of recognizing that we may look at the same thing at different times and have different feelings about it while still knowing that it is the same thing, then we can be confident in the continuity of the self: 'The person of whose existence the consciousness is felt now, and was felt an hour or a year ago, is discerned to be, not two persons, but one and the same.'[16] Wordsworth, by contrast, was interested in exploring his sense of uncertainty about his 'personal Identity', not in the provision of neat logical answers. The question is inevitably raised each time he summons up the remembrance of things past: to which consciousness does the emotional response to the moment belong, that of the original child or that of the adult attempting to piece together the story of the growth of his own mind?

The particular example he gave when defining his idea of 'spots of time' was one of his first horseback rides – he was probably only five – in the company of a servant or groom called James. They became separated on the moors. Afraid, the boy dismounted and with stumbling step led his horse down into a gloomy valley where he saw the mast of an old gibbet upon which a wife-murderer had been hanged years before. The rest of the execution structure was long gone; all that remained was

'a long green ridge of turf' in a shape that resembled a grave.[17]
Hurrying away from the sinister spot, the child went back up
the hill only to see a 'naked pool' and a prominent stone signal-
beacon on the summit. Then he noticed a human figure:

> A girl who bore a pitcher on her head
> And seemed with difficult steps to force her way
> Against the blowing wind. It was in truth
> An ordinary sight but I should need
> Colours and words that are unknown to man
> To paint the visionary dreariness
> Which, while I looked all round for my lost guide,
> Did, at that time, invest the naked pool,
> The beacon on the lonely eminence,
> The woman and her garments vexed and tossed
> By the strong wind.[18]

Wordsworth makes the ordinary seem extraordinary. 'Visionary'
moments and the 'dreariness' of the everyday ought to be oppo-
sites, but the power of memory and imagination 'colours' the
monochrome of the scene.

Why did Wordsworth choose such a bleak 'spot' to illustrate
his proposition that 'There are in our existence spots of time'
that fructify, nourish and repair our minds and 'Especially the
imaginative power'? The presence of the gibbet, the grave-shaped
mound of turf, the Stygian pool and the sepulchral beacon suggest
that the girl with the pitcher on her head, buffeted by the wind,
is struggling through life, walking towards death.

Wordsworth was much possessed by death. In the first version
of the 'Poem to Coleridge', the spot of time immediately before
this one tells of how, just after being taken to live in the Vale of
Esthwaite at the age of nine, he was walking by the lake and

found a pile of clothes on the shore. Despite watching for a full half-hour, he could not see a bather. Shadows fall on the lake, with only the occasional plop of a leaping fish disturbing its 'breathless stillness'. (Poetic convention would advise against the juxtaposition of 'less' and 'ness', but here the image of momentary suspension perfectly captures the mix of calm and foreboding.) The next day, a group of men rowed out to sound the depths of the lake with iron hooks and long poles.

> At length the dead man, 'mid that beauteous scene
> Of trees and hills and water, bolt upright
> Rose with his ghastly face.[19]

It is a moment of horror like something out of a Jacobean tragedy – and indeed in the next line Wordsworth quotes (or rather, slightly misquotes) a phrase that Shakespeare gave to Othello, 'moving accidents by flood and field'. The high drama of the Shakespearean stage is replaced by local 'Distresses and disasters, tragic facts / Of rural history'. We, the people of northern England, Wordsworth is implying, are not the kings, heroes and nobles of traditional tragedy, but we have profound travails of our own and our stories merit the telling. And, as with the girl walking against the wind on the bleak hill, the 'ghastly' – ghostly – face of the dead man, a local schoolmaster who drowned in June 1779 while bathing in Esthwaite Water, impresses itself upon the young Wordsworth's mind and is in later years recalled with very different feelings.

These two spots of time are followed by a third one, in similar vein. This one is a memory of a winter's day when Wordsworth was thirteen. It is the end of school term. He and his brothers are going home for Christmas. Horses are being sent for them. They wait at a crossroads. Once more, it is a threshold moment.

Unsure as to which of the two roads will bring the horses, William leaves his brothers and climbs up a crag onto a ridge in order to look out for them. It is cold and sleety, with mist intermittently obscuring the view. Huddled against a drystone wall, the boy finds himself in the company of a solitary sheep and a bare hawthorn bush that is bristling and whistling in the wind. The moment is implanted in his mind, mixing the 'anxiety of hope' (anticipation of the horses and of Christmas) with a peculiar sense of 'chastisement' arising from the event that followed: ten days later, between Christmas and New Year, his father died. Thirteen, the onset of adolescence, was as bad a time to lose a father as seven, the onset of enduring childhood memory, had been to lose a mother.

Again and again, especially when the rain batters his roof on stormy nights, this spot of time comes back to haunt him, but also, paradoxically, to refresh him:

And afterwards the wind, and sleety rain,
And all the business of the elements,
The single sheep, and the one blasted tree,
And the bleak music of that old stone wall,
The noise of wood and water, and the mist
Which on the line of each of those two roads
Advanced in such indisputable shapes,
All these were spectacles and sounds to which
I often would repair, and thence would drink
As at a fountain.[20]

Sigmund Freud would have called this sequence of *The Prelude* a 'screen memory'. 'There are some people whose earliest recollections of childhood are concerned with everyday and indifferent events which could not produce any emotional effect even in

children, but which are recollected (*too* clearly, one is inclined
to say) in every detail', Freud wrote in his essay 'Screen Memories':
'what is recorded as mnemic image is not the relevant experience
itself [but] another psychical element closely associated with the
objectionable one'.[21] By placing himself in the craggy wintery
landscape of the pre-Christmas journey home, Wordsworth is
evading the actual moment of his father's death. A literary-minded
psychoanalyst would, however, tease out an unconscious memory
of the dead father in the animation of the scene, not only because
of the ghostliness of the figures in the mist, but also because the
phrase 'indisputable shapes' is an inversion of the words that
Hamlet, literature's most famous son, speaks to the ghost of his
dead father: 'Thou com'st in such a questionable shape'.[22]

The primal image of the girl battling against the wind near
the gibbet, the drowned schoolmaster seen soon after the move
to Hawkshead consequent upon his mother's death, and the
'waiting for the horses' scene just before his father followed her
to the grave are defining examples of how Wordsworth's way of
dealing with loss was always to find restorative power in nature,
however bleak the scene. At the same time, like many children
who have lost their parents, he often feels a sense of guilt. Was
it somehow my fault that they died? Did some transgression or
inadequacy of my own precipitate their absence?

It is perhaps for this reason that, though Nature in the early
books of Wordsworth's autobiographical poem is usually his
guardian, nurturing him by her beauty, she is also sometimes a
figure who admonishes, fostering him with fear and trembling.
In the earliest notebook of manuscript drafts for what became
The Prelude, there is a memorable passage composed in the autumn
of 1798, which was duly incorporated into book one of the
full-length poem. It describes an occasion during a summer
holiday ramble when, without permission, he unmoored a shep-

herd's boat and set out across Ullswater by moonlight. In remembering the night, his art of observation does not fail him: there is an exquisite image of how, on either side of the boat, the oars left upon the water

> Small circles glittering idly in the moon
> Until they melted all into one track
> Of sparkling light.[23]

He fixed his gaze on the ridge that formed his horizon, with nothing but the stars above. As he rowed further from the shore, a higher hill, which seemed to the child's eye like 'a huge cliff', reared into sight, blocking out the stars and seeming to pursue him 'like a living thing'. He turned the little boat and stole his way back to the willow tree where it had been moored. For many days thereafter, he writes, 'my brain / Worked with a dim and undetermined sense / Of unknown modes of being'. He was haunted by an inner darkness that turned the familiar shapes of trees and sky and green fields to 'huge and mighty forms that do not live / Like living men'. These spectral shapes 'moved slowly through my mind / By day, and were the trouble of my dreams'.[24] The vividness and intensity of the writing are testimony to the persistence of the memory and the weight with which anxiety pressed upon him, however mysterious – *un*determined, *un*known – its meaning.

After describing the days and nights of fearful visions, Wordsworth tries to identify their origin. Who or what is the spirit that haunts him? In the two-part *Prelude* of 1799, he imagines some combination of the localized nature gods of pagan antiquity and the sprites of native folklore. He begins his invocation: 'Ah! not in vain ye Beings of the hills! / And ye that walk the woods and open heaths / By moon or star-light'.[25] In the more finished

Prelude of 1805, he elevates this force into something grander. The 'Beings of the hills' are replaced by what can only be described as a world-soul:

> Wisdom and Spirit of the Universe!
> Thou Soul that art the Eternity of Thought!
> And giv'st to forms and images a breath
> And everlasting motion! not in vain,
> By day or starlight thus from my first dawn
> Of Childhood didst Thou intertwine for me
> The passions that build up our human Soul,
> Not with the mean and vulgar works of Man,
> But with high objects, with enduring things,
> With life and nature, purifying thus
> The elements of feeling and of thought,
> And sanctifying by such discipline
> Both pain and fear until we recognise
> A grandeur in the beatings of the heart.[26]

It is through his sense of the uncanny that he comes to believe that he has penetrated to the heart of the mystery of being: the human soul is only fully made when, instead of assuming that man is the master of all, we interwine our selves with the 'enduring things' of the natural world.

4

THERE WAS A BOY

In school, he began with Latin. Out of school, with fishing. The usher (deputy to the headmaster) taught him more in a fortnight than he had learned in all his time in Cockermouth. Once fluent in Latin, he took special delight in the *Metamorphoses* of Ovid, with its panoply of mythological tales of humans being transformed into rivers, rocks, flowers, trees and stars. He grew to love and respect the headmaster, Reverend William Taylor, Cambridge-educated, appointed headmaster of Hawkshead at the age of twenty-five, passionate about poetry and described by another poet as a man of 'sound judgment, a modest demeanour and unblemished morals'.[1] Taylor became a substitute father, as Ann Tyson became a second mother.

There was brotherhood too. Not only with Richard and John,

but also with schoolfriends. William and an older boy called Philip Braithwaite carved their names in a window seat in Ann Tyson's cottage. The son of a hatter, Braithwaite had a limp, later exacerbated by an accident when he was apprenticed to a local farmer. This did not stop him from accompanying Wordsworth on long walks. On one occasion they crossed Windermere ferry and explored an unknown valley, where they found an abandoned charcoal-burner's hut. They wondered about spending the night there but thought better of the plan. In the autumn, they would go into Graythwaite woods to gather hazelnuts. As an old man, Braithwaite remembered how William was always asking him questions, eager to learn of the world. When Braithwaite returned from a trip to London, in connection with family legal business, Wordsworth quizzed him about the great city – and was disappointed not to see some visible sign of how his friend might have been transformed by the experience.[2]

Another boy, Thomas Maude, described Wordsworth as 'the uneasiest bedfellow I've ever had'.[3] This chimes with the poet's own memory of nocturnal restlessness. He writes in *The Prelude* of how, when a student at Cambridge, he went home for the summer vacation and lodged again with Ann Tyson, taking comfort in his return to

> That bed whence I had heard the roaring wind
> And clamorous rain, that bed where I so oft
> Had lain awake on breezy nights to watch
> The moon in splendour couched among the leaves
> Of a tall ash, that near our cottage stood,
> Had watched her with fixed eyes, while to and fro,
> In the dark summit of the waving tree,
> She rocked with every impulse of the wind.[4]

Sometimes he would walk out alone at night.

Then there was John Fleming, who also loved poetry. The two teenage boys would get up at sunrise and, before the beginning of school, walk around the lake, reciting lines of rural description from James Thomson's *The Seasons*, the most popular long poem of the eighteenth century. Wordsworth was becoming a voracious reader. During the Christmas and summer vacations, he worked his way through his father's library, especially enjoying 'on the road' novels such as Henry Fielding's *Tom Jones*, Alain-René Lesage's *The Adventures of Gil Blas* in Tobias Smollett's translation, and, father of them all, the *Don Quixote* of Cervantes. In later school years, his teacher lent him all the latest poetry: the meditative *Task* of William Cowper; the Scottish ballads of Robert Burns and the English ones of Thomas Percy's *Reliques*; the pseudo-medieval effusions of the boy wonder Thomas Chatterton; the elegiac sonnets of Thomas Warton and Charlotte Smith; and *The Minstrel* of James Beattie, in which the rise and progress of poetical genius was expounded in florid stanzas filled with Gothic imagery.

These loans came from a new headmaster, because Taylor died, aged just thirty-two, in the summer of 1786. Eight years later, Wordsworth visited his grave near the sea at Cartmel Priory. It was inscribed with lines from Thomas Gray's renowned poem 'Elegy written in a Country Churchyard', chosen by the master himself. Wordsworth, in his habitual guise of a returning wanderer, recalled how, about a week before his death, Taylor had said to him 'My head will soon lie low.' As Wordsworth looked at the turf on the grave, 'those words',

> With sound of voice, and countenance of the man,
> Came back upon me, so that some few tears
> Fell from me in my own despite. And now,

Thus travelling smoothly o'er the level sands,
I thought with pleasure of the verses graven
Upon his tombstone, saying to myself
'He loved the poets, and if now alive
Would have loved me, as one not destitute
Of promise, nor belying the kind hope
Which he had formed when I at his command
Began to spin, at first, my toilsome songs.'

It was indeed Taylor who had set him the exercises that became his first poems: verses on 'The Summer Vacation' (to which the precocious William added a sequel called 'Return to School') and an ode on the power of education, written in commemoration of the bicentenary of the school's foundation.

As Wordsworth approached his father's death obliquely by way of the 'waiting for the horses' passage in *The Prelude*, so he faced the memory of losing Taylor indirectly in a sequence of poems in *Lyrical Ballads* that take the form of dialogues with a teacher called 'Mathew'. The figure was, Wordsworth acknowledged, an amalgam of several schoolmasters and other villagers whom he had known. 'Mathew' is an old man, in contrast to the Taylor who was cut down in his prime. He was partly based on a figure known in Hawkshead as 'Mr John': John Harrison, who for many years kept a small primary (junior) school in the village and who was a keen fisherman. The composite 'Mathew' is a representative of the teacher as father figure.

The finest poem in the group, 'The Two April Mornings', describes how the poet and the schoolmaster go for a walk at sunrise on a beautiful spring morning. 'Mathew' suddenly looks sad. The poet asks him why. He says it is because he has noticed the particular slant of purple light across a cloud over the mountaintop and it has reminded him of another April morning, thirty years ago, when he saw exactly the same fall of light crimsoning a field where the corn was just beginning to show above the ground. On that occasion, he was out with his fishing rod and, passing the churchyard, he stopped to visit the grave of his daughter, who had died at the age of nine. He felt that he had never loved her, or indeed anyone, so much as at that moment:

Six feet in earth my Emma lay,
And yet I lov'd her more,
For so it seem'd, than till that day
I e'er had lov'd before.

He then narrates how, as he turned from the grave, he saw a girl in the full bloom of youth, her flowing hair glistening with the morning dew. She is carrying a basket on her head, tripping along without a care in the world. Mathew sighs with grief as he thinks of his own lost daughter, but then he looks at the girl a second time 'And did not wish her mine'. He accepts his own loss and rejoices instead that life goes on, that the sun comes up another day on another child. Wordsworth ends the poem by reverting to his own memory:

Mathew is in his grave, yet now
Methinks I see him stand,
As at that moment, with his bough
Of wilding in his hand.[5]

The poem peels away layers of memory. Wordsworth wrote it when he was far from home, in Goslar, Germany, in the depths of the freezing winter of 1798–9. The memory of a conversation with an old schoolmaster becomes a memory of his young schoolmaster; when Mathew remembers the earlier April morning, he remembers his dead child and when Wordsworth remembers the conversation, he brings Mathew back to life in his mind's eye, with the fishing rod, cut from the branch of a young tree, that he was carrying not on the morning when he walked with the poet, but when he saw the girl dancing away from the graveyard. And this brings back other memories: not only of the two schoolmasters, but also of that other girl with a pitcher on her head in the screen memory of Wordsworth's mother's death.

Furthermore, the girl who died when 'Nine summers had she scarcely seen' – a similar age to that of Wordsworth at the time of his mother's death – is called Emma. 'Mr John' had a daughter of that name who died as a child, but it was also the name that Wordsworth substitutes for that of his beloved sister Dorothy in several other poems written around the same time. Among these is another spring poem, 'It was an April morning', one of his 'Poems on the Naming of Places' in which he dedicates a secluded dell with lush foliage to 'Emma', making it his 'other home', 'My dwelling, and my out-of-doors abode'.[6] As will be seen, Coleridge thought that the mysterious 'Lucy' poems, also written during the winter in Goslar, were Wordsworth's fearful imaginings of his sister's death. To have been bereaved of her as well as of his mother and father would have been unbearable. By imagining the worst, he was staving off that fear. During the Hawkshead years, his sister was indeed lost to him – she was far away in Yorkshire. Their reunion was one of the most joyful days of his life, and thereafter they would live together for the rest of his days. Symbolically, the joyful girl dancing away from the grave is not only an image of new life, but a figuration of Dorothy brought back from absence into presence.

Wordsworth's acute memory and extraordinary ability to make imaginative connections just below the level of overt consciousness extended from his own experience to his literary inheritance. The carefree girl in the graveyard 'whose hair was wet / With points of morning dew' seemed, he writes, 'as happy as a wave / That dances on the sea'. During his childhood, Wordsworth had seen dancing waves on the coast that edges the Lake District and on more than one occasion prior to the writing of the Mathew poems he had ridden the waves of the English Channel on his way to France. But his choice of simile also came from his reading.

The April morning of the poem is characterized by rebirth: the spring sunshine warms the earth and the fresh corn emerges. For centuries, poets have taken comfort in the cycle of the seasons: human life is linear, leading to the grave, but in the natural world new life comes every spring. At school and then university, Wordsworth read deeply in the classics. A fragmentary manuscript survives in which he translates a passage from Virgil's telling of the story of Orpheus and Eurydice – a tale of a poet's attempt to bring his beloved back from the grave. But the Roman poet whom the young Wordsworth especially loved was Shakespeare's favourite, Ovid. This is hardly surprising: Ovid's *Metamorphoses* is a storehouse of wonder-filled imaginings of the inseparability of the human and the non-human, in which people are transformed into natural objects. It was in Ovid that Wordsworth found the archetypal story of how, as Shelley would put it some years later, 'If Winter comes, can Spring be far behind?'[7] The lovely girl Proserpina, daughter of the goddess of grain and fertility, is abducted by Pluto, god of the underworld, but allowed to return every spring. Her story is an allegory of the seasons.

William Shakespeare was in William Wordsworth's blood-stream, as he was in almost every aspect of the culture of the age.[8] 'Shakespeare', says Henry Crawford in Jane Austen's

Mansfield Park, 'is part of an Englishman's constitution': 'His thoughts and beauties are so spread abroad that one touches them everywhere.' Crawford's rival Edmund Bertram agrees and is more exact: 'we all talk Shakespeare, use his similes, and describe with his descriptions'.[9] Wordsworth was no exception. In *The Winter's Tale*, a play about dead children and second chances, the abandoned and adopted daughter Perdita compares herself to Proserpina. This was Shakespeare's way of indicating that the bleak drama of winter in the first half of the play is turning to joyous spring in the second. In reply to Perdita's invocation of Proserpina, Florizel, in love with her, says 'when you do dance, I wish you / A wave o' the sea, that you might ever do / Nothing but that'.[10] 'As happy as a wave / That dances on the sea': the contextual parallel fleetingly turns the girl in the graveyard in Wordsworth's Mathew poem into Perdita, the lost one who is found.

★

Wordsworth's poetry of memory sought to reanimate the life of childhood, to recover the sensations that fade as we grow to adulthood. In another fragment in his first notebook of jottings towards his long poem of personal memory, he wrote of the early beginnings of his love affair with nature, of the strange affinity he felt between his own existence and 'existing things', of 'The bond of union betwixt life and joy'. 'Yes', he continues, remembering how at the age of ten he

> Held unconscious intercourse
> With the eternal beauty, drinking in
> A pure organic pleasure from the lines
> Of curling mist, or from the smooth expanse
> Of waters coloured by the cloudless moon.[11]

He calls this sensation the 'tranquillizing power' of Nature. It is as if he is her child, drinking nourishment from her smooth breast. Inevitably, though, there is a gulf between the sensations of the ten-year-old child gazing at the lake by moonlight or at the morning mist rising over the hills and the reflective language of the twenty-eight-year-old poet, who was by then both widely read and under the spell of the prodigious intellect of Coleridge. These few lines are very typical of Wordsworth in that they juxtapose precise observation of nature – the curling of the mist, the mirror-like smoothness of water lit by moonlight on a clear night – with abstract, philosophical terms.

'Unconscious intercourse' is a phrase that had never appeared in print before. Eighteenth-century philosophers were very interested in the unconscious workings of the human mind, especially the way in which sense perceptions were organized through a process of mental association. The word 'intercourse' was generally used to refer to social relations, but did sometimes occur in spiritual contexts as a term for communion with the divine. To yoke the two words and attach them to the youthful Wordsworth's communion with a trick of light or a meteorological phenomenon was to imply that children – or at least this child – have an innate sense of natural religion. Similarly, 'eternal beauty' is a phrase that was common in religious works with titles such as *The Practice of Piety: directing a Christian how to walk, that he may please God*.[12] To apply it to a landscape was to venture towards the realm of pantheism, the belief that the divine is to be found immanently in nature, not in some transcendent supernatural realm.

What did Wordsworth mean by his third abstract phrase, 'a pure organic pleasure'? I suspect that he derived the term from one of the most influential books of the Scottish Enlightenment, Lord Kames's *Elements of Criticism*. Published in 1762, this was a

pioneering work of aesthetics, a newly emergent field of intellectual inquiry that asked such questions as 'what is the nature
of beauty?' and 'what constitutes good taste?' The treatise went
through eight editions in twenty years. Kames begins his introduction with a discussion of pleasure, in order to lay the ground
for an argument that the best gardening, architecture, painting,
sculpture, music and poetry give tasteful human beings their most
enduring delights. Pleasure, he argues at the outset, comes from
gratification of the sense organs. The pleasures (and displeasures)
of three of our senses – touch, smell and taste – are intense and
instant because they are felt directly upon the organs that receive
the impressions of external things (skin, nose, tongue). For the
same reason, such pleasures are ephemeral: 'Organic pleasures
have naturally a short duration; when prolonged, they lose their
relish; when indulged to excess, they beget satiety and disgust.'
The pleasures of eye and ear, by contrast, are felt in the mind;
they are of a higher order, occupying a rich holding ground
between the organic and the intellectual. For this reason, they
may be described as therapeutic: 'being sweet and moderately
exhilarating, they are in their tone equally distant from the
turbulence of passion, and the languor of indolence; and by that
tone are perfectly well qualified, not only to revive the spirits
when sunk by sensual gratification, but also to relax them when
overstrained in any violent pursuit'. Our first perceptions, Kames
argues, are of external objects, and our first attachments are to
them. 'Organic pleasures take the lead', but as we mature we
graduate to the higher pleasures of the eye and ear working upon
the mind.[13]

Wordsworth makes this philosophical argument tangible. He
imagines his childhood self *drinking* in pleasure from the lines of
mist, as if feeling the impression of nature upon the tongue. In
emphasizing the *smooth* expanse of waters, he metaphorically

touches the surface of the lake. These childhood pleasures are thus made into physical sensations; they are *purely* organic, without reliance on the conscious mind. Hence the '*unconscious* intercourse', of a kind almost analogous to a sexual union – intriguingly, the *Oxford English Dictionary's* earliest record of the use of 'intercourse' in a sexual sense is Thomas Malthus's *Essay on the Principle of Population*, published in this same year of 1798.

Where Wordsworth departs from Kames is in his mourning for the loss of the child's pure organic pleasure in the landscape. For Kames, the aesthetic sense is a stepping stone that takes the rational man from the baser passions of the body to the higher pleasures of the intellect and ultimately to the realm of reason and morality. For Wordsworth, growing up is a growing away from the child's unmediated unity of self, body and environment. The adult can recapture that primal spirit in moments of memory, but the quest to preserve it in writing requires the intervention of the conscious mind and the working intellect, tainting the purity of the organic pleasure. This in a nutshell is the difference between the Enlightenment philosopher and the Romantic poet.

'But the downward glide / and bias of existing wrings us dry', wrote Robert Lowell, a later poet deeply versed in the Romantic tradition, 'Always inside me is the child who died'.[14] Wordsworth's poetry is essentially elegiac in spirit not only because of the actual deaths that afflicted him in childhood, but also because he knew that he could never recover the child's untrammelled and un-troubled unity with the natural world. In another fragmentary recollection in the notebook in which he began working up scenes for what became *The Prelude*, he places himself beside Windermere or Esthwaite at twilight. The sequence begins in the third person, detaching the remembering adult from the experiencing child: 'There was a Boy . . .' For a moment, the reader wonders who this boy might have been, but as the writing draws the poet fully into the memory, the voice shifts from 'he' to 'I', 'his' to 'my'. The childhood self has come back to life:

> . . . would *he* stand alone
> Beneath the trees or by the glimmering lakes,
> And through *his* fingers woven in one close knot
> Blow mimic hootings to the silent owls,
> And bid them answer *him*. And they would shout
> Across the wat'ry vale, and shout again,
> Responsive to *my* call, with tremulous sobs
> And long halloos, and screams, and echoes loud,
> Redoubled and redoubled — a wild scene
> Of mirth and jocund din. And when it chanced
> That pauses of deep silence mocked *my* skill,
> Then often in that silence, while *I* hung
> Listening, a sudden shock of mild surprize
> Would carry far into *my* heart the voice
> Of mountain torrents; or the visible scene
> Would enter unawares into *my* mind
> With all its solemn imagery, its rocks,
> Its woods, and that uncertain heaven, received
> Into the bosom of the steady lake.[15]

(I have italicized the pronouns to emphasize the shift towards the self.) Coleridge, who knew Wordsworth's poetic voice more intuitively than anyone other than Dorothy, wrote in a letter: 'Had I met these lines running wild in the deserts of Arabia, I should have instantly screamed out "Wordsworth!"'[16] In both style and content, he is sure, this is his friend at his very best, his most characteristic. Let us pause for a moment to test the claim.

Thanks to the influence of Shakespeare, Milton and James Thomson, the supple iambic pentameter blank-verse line — ten syllables, five beats, unstressed, stressed, unstressed, stressed, with rhythmic variation but no neat chime of rhyme – was the favoured medium for meditative poetry in the later eighteenth century. The clipped couplets and urbane wit of Alexander Pope were falling out of favour. Instead, poets such as the manic depressive William Cowper reflected on the solace of rural life in lengthy verse-paragraphs, the fluidity of thought running the sentences across the line endings, setting up a creative tension between the metrical and the syntactical movement. Wordsworth's blank verse moves in the same vein, so why was Coleridge so sure that 'There was a Boy' could have been written only by his friend? What is the difference between Wordsworth and Cowper, whose work was more admired at the time?

In Wordsworth's twenties, when he lived 'Among the fretful dwellings of mankind' in London and Paris, the memory of the river Derwent running beside his earliest home gave him 'A knowledge, a dim earnest, of the calm / Which nature breathes among the fields and groves'.[17] The restorative power of nature was the central theme of his autobiographical epic. This thought was by no means original. The solace of the country as a bulwark against the stress of the city was an ancient poetic theme. 'This is the life which those who fret in guilt, / And guilty cities, never knew', wrote Thomson in *The Seasons*, that paean to rural scenes which was so widely read throughout the eighteenth century.[18] When Wordsworth was fifteen, Cowper published his long blank-verse poem *The Task*, which extolled the virtues of country walks and the sounds of nature that 'exhilarate the spirit' in contrast to the vices of city life. The most famous line in the poem was 'God made the country, and man made the town': for Cowper this distinction explained why 'health and virtue' were to be found in 'fields and groves'.[19]

Wordsworth acknowledged that *The Task* was a significant

precedent for his own project. He described Cowper's work as a 'composite' of 'idyllium' (which he defined as observation of 'the processes and appearances of external nature'), didactic poem (offering 'direct instruction' to the reader) and 'philosophical satire'. His own longer works were just such composites.[20] But there was a key difference. Thomson and Cowper always proceeded from natural description to moral generalization. Wordsworth inherited their art of sermonizing about nature. What he added was a much more individual voice and, above all, a particularity lodged in personal memory. Cowper had his local affections, but the perambulations of *The Task* have a generic quality. The poet could be leading the reader through any English field or grove, whereas when Wordsworth begins his epic task, the starting point is specifically the Derwent of his first home, the alder tree bending into his father's garden, the sound of the river merging into his dreams as he falls asleep as a child and as he dreams that childhood back to life in the act of writing poetry. The power of the unconscious, as manifested in memories and dreams; the child as father of the man: these are not ideas to be found in the 'loco-descriptive' verse of Wordsworth's predecessors.

Cowper's verse moves at a leisurely pace, so in order to make a fair comparison we need to settle into an extended quotation, ideally reading it aloud, imagining ourselves sitting on a sofa by the fire on a winter's night in an English country parsonage:

> Nor rural sights alone, but rural sounds
> Exhilarate the spirit, and restore
> The tone of languid Nature. Mighty winds,
> That sweep the skirt of some far-spreading wood
> Of ancient growth, make music not unlike
> The dash of ocean on his winding shore,

And lull the spirit while they fill the mind,
Unnumbered branches waving in the blast,
And all their leaves fast fluttering, all at once.
Nor less composure waits upon the roar
Of distant floods, or on the softer voice
Of neighbouring fountain, or of rills that slip
Through the cleft rock, and, chiming as they fall
Upon loose pebbles, lose themselves at length
In matted grass, that with a livelier green
Betrays the secret of their silent course.
Nature inanimate employs sweet sounds,
But animated Nature sweeter still
To soothe and satisfy the human ear.
Ten thousand warblers cheer the day, and one
The livelong night: nor these alone whose notes
Nice-fingered art must emulate in vain,
But cawing rooks, and kites that swim sublime
In still repeated circles, screaming loud,
The jay, the pie, and even the boding owl
That hails the rising moon, have charms for me.
Sounds inharmonious in themselves and harsh,
Yet heard in scenes where peace for ever reigns,
And only there, please highly for their sake.[21]

'Languid' is the word. These lines are comforting, but never
startling. Granted, there are many elements that anticipate
Wordsworth in both form and substance: the running on of the
sentences across the line endings ('roar / Of', 'voice / Of', 'slip
/ Through', 'fall / Upon'), the attunement to sounds as well as
sights, the sense of harmony in the natural world ('the *secret* of
their silent course'), the movement between precise description
('loose pebbles', 'matted grass') and a general concept of 'animated

Nature'. But when it comes to the owl whose nightly note 'Nice-fingered art must emulate in vain', there is no personal connection, no specific memory, no sense of the inner being of the child in the landscape. Although the words 'secret' and 'sublime' are used, they have none of the strangeness and fear that animate the Wordsworthian landscape. Cowper finds composure in listening to the wind, the rill and the birdsong, whereas in Wordsworth something much more mysterious occurs.

We may see this by making another comparison. It is possible that some time before writing 'There was a Boy' Wordsworth read a collection of verse dramas by Joanna Baillie, a writer whom he later befriended and for whose work he expressed considerable admiration. In one of her plays, *De Monfort*, he would have found a twilight scene:

> *Enter Rezenvelt, and continues his way slowly across the stage, but just as he is going off the owl screams, he stops and listens, and the owl screams again.*

> REZENVELT: Ha! Does the night-bird greet me on my
>   way?
>   How much his hooting is in harmony
>   With such a scene as this! I like it well.
>   Oft when a boy, at the still twilight hour,
>   I've leant my back against some knotted oak,
>   And loudly mimick'd him, till to my call
>   He answer would return, and thro' the gloom
>   We friendly converse held.[22]

Wordsworth, clearly, was not the first to make poetry out of the memory of a boy mimicking the hoot of an owl in fading evening light. The difference is that in Baillie's play the memory is of

'friendly converse' with the bird, whereas in Wordsworth the
thing that makes the memory a 'spot of time' is the moment
when the owls do *not* reply. It is signalled by one of his most
characteristic line endings: at 'hung / Listening', the pause of
the beat enacts the suspension of sound. And in that moment,
the 'shock of mild surprize' at not getting a conscious answer
from Nature in the form of a response from the owls is transformed into a mystical union in which the voice of water running
from the mountains is carried far into his heart, and the sky
reflected in the lake enters unawares into his mind.

Coleridge was one of the most astute readers of poetry ever
to walk the planet: he was confident that, should he have encountered these lines running wild in the deserts of Arabia, he would
have recognized them as Wordsworth's rather than Cowper's or
Baillie's not only because of the personal voice and the sense of
mystery, but also because no poet before Wordsworth (other than
Shakespeare) had made small words such as 'far' and 'unawares'
do such profound work. When Thomas De Quincey, another
highly astute reader, analysed the poem as an example of
Wordsworthian psychology at its most characteristic, he noted
that 'This very expression, *far*, by which space and its infinities
are attributed to the human heart, and its capacities of re-echoing
the sublimities of nature, has always struck me as with a flash of
sublime revelation'.[23]

Given that these lines were so admired by Coleridge and that
they were among the earliest fragments of what became *The
Prelude*, we might feel a gentle shock of mild surprise on discovering that they do not appear in the opening books of the poem
devoted to 'Childhood and School-time'. Wordsworth published
them independently, as a short poem in the second volume of
Lyrical Ballads. Later, he included them in book five of *The
Prelude*, which is devoted mainly to the influence of books. And

he made a significant revision: the first-person pronouns were removed. The switch to the self has disappeared, leaving the boy a 'he' throughout. Furthermore, a coda was added:

> Fair are the woods, and beauteous is the spot,
> The vale where he was born: the Church-yard hangs
> Upon a slope above the village school,
> And there along that bank when I have pass'd
> At evening, I believe, that near his grave
> A full half-hour together I have stood,
> Mute – for he died when he was ten years old.[24]

In the final 1850 *Prelude*, the age of death is changed to twelve. Wordsworth once told a relative that the grave was of a Hawkshead boy named John Tyson who had been a playmate of his, and whose grave in the churchyard does indeed say that he died at the age of twelve. It is not known whether Tyson excelled at owl-hooting, an art for which Wordsworth's schoolmate William Raincock was renowned.

The coda answers the moment of silence when the boy 'hung / Listening' by way of the image of the churchyard hanging on the slope above the school and the adult Wordsworth standing mute in contemplation of the grave. By transposing what was originally written as his own experience to that of an unnamed boy who died while still a child, Wordsworth transforms the incident into a symbol of how something dies in all of us when we reach our teens and grow into self-consciousness.

This poem was of great importance to Wordsworth. When he gathered his poems for a collected edition in 1815, giving them a distinctive thematic arrangement, he chose to place 'There was a Boy' at the head of 'Poems of the Imagination', the section that included many of his greatest poems, including the 'Lucy' elegies, 'I wandered lonely as a cloud', 'Resolution and Independence', and 'Tintern Abbey'. In his preface he explained that this was because it represented 'one of the earliest processes of Nature' in the development of the faculty of imagination. He describes that process as 'a commutation and transfer of internal feelings, co-operating with external accidents, to plant, for immortality, images of sound and sight, in the celestial soil of the Imagination'. The key, he suggests, is the *surprise* felt at the moment when the 'intenseness' of the boy's mind is 'beginning to remit'. The pattern recurs at several other peculiarly Wordsworthian moments in which intensity is achieved in a moment of relaxation, for example when he realizes that he has crossed the highest point of the Alps without noticing and when he is 'Surprised by joy' while immersed in grief.

On one occasion, he gave his disciple Thomas De Quincey a masterclass in the process: he told of how he would put his ear on the road to listen intently for the sound of an approaching carriage, but then 'at the very instant when the organs of attention were all at once relaxing from their tension, the bright star hanging in the air above those outlines of massy blackness fell suddenly upon my eye, and penetrated my capacity of apprehension with a pathos and a sense of the infinite, that would not have arrested me under other circumstances'.[25] Though a loquacious raconteur, De Quincey was also a good listener. He absorbed the idea and adapted it to his own purposes in his 'Essay on the Knocking at the Gate in *Macbeth*', where he suggests that the moment of most heightened tension in Shakespeare's play comes not with the murder of King Duncan but with the breaking of the silence in its aftermath.

★

One day early in 1783, two of Wordsworth's fellow pupils at the grammar school were scrambling on Yewdale Crags, not far from the village, when they saw a raven's nest high on a ledge. The black raven is a bird with vicious talons and bill, readily capable of pecking out the eyes of a lamb. There was accordingly a bounty on its head, a 'Varmen [vermin] Reward' of fourpence a bird. Wordsworth remembered seeing bunches of unfledged ravens suspended in the churchyard at Hawkshead. For schoolboys, eggs were both a trophy and a contribution to pest control.

The boys went back to the town and found two friends who were accomplished climbers. They took a look: the nest was perched very near the top of the crags, accessible only by a dangerous rope climb. Back they went to town. A lad employed to build drystone walls had a rope and a hook, and was willing to accompany them. A gaggle of other boys went along, including the one they called Bill Wordsworth. They all clawed their way up the crag. Then John Benson, the boy who was supposed to be the best climber, set off along the precipitous ledge, held by a rope and with a satchel on his back to gather the eggs. He got very close to the nest but was then impeded by the overhang of the rock above the ledge. He froze. They tried to talk him down, but he could not make himself move. Some of the boys, among them the two youngest – Bill Raincock and Bill Wordsworth – were sent to get help. It took a long time coming, but eventually a great hulk of a man called Frank Castlehow, together with his equally athletic son Jonathan, scaled the crag, all the way to the top, and Jonathan went down on the ledge to haul up the terrified Benson. Wordsworth's friends the Raincock brothers never went raven's nesting again.[26]

The Prelude has a vivid account of the thrill of such a climb:

> Oh, when I have hung
> Above the raven's nest, by knots of grass,

Or half-inch fissures in the slipp'ry rock,
But ill sustained, and almost, as it seemed,
Suspended by the blast which blew amain,
Shouldering the naked crag, oh at that time,
While on the perilous ridge I hung alone,
With what strange utterance did the loud dry wind
Blow through my ears! the sky seemed not a sky
Of earth, and with what motion moved the clouds![27]

Benson was stuck below the nest, beneath a jutting rock, and with a gang of boys, whereas Wordsworth in this scene is above and alone, clinging to a clump of grass. We can be fairly sure that in Benson's case the lad was merely holding on for dear life, but it is impossible to know whether Wordsworth's sensation of some mystical union with the wind, sky and clouds was felt at the time or imposed in the retrospect of memory. We cannot even be sure that he did ever hang along on a perilous ridge, and that this spot of time is not a fiction embroidered from his recollection of the Benson incident, which became the talk of the town.

Wordsworth himself was eminently aware of the possibility that the act of memory creates rather than recreates a feeling. 'Of these and other kindred notices', he observes at one point in *The Prelude*,

I cannot say what portion is in truth
The naked recollection of that time
And what may rather have been call'd to life
By after-meditation.[28]

Again, writing about 'the impression of the memory', he suggested to himself that things remembered idly 'half seem /

The work of Fancy'.[29] And, in a passage that echoes the emphasis
in 'There was a Boy' on the scene *reflected* in the lake, he compared
memory to the way that if you lean out of a slow-moving boat
on a still clear surface of water and look down to see 'weeds,
fishes, flowers, / Grots, pebbles, roots of trees', you will have
difficulty in separating 'The shadow from the substance', differ-
entiating the things that are really in the depths from the
reflection of the world above. This double vision is, he suggests,
exactly what happens when we scan 'the surface of past time'.[30]
These intuitions do indeed anticipate, with remarkable prescience,
the conclusions of modern psychologists and cognitive scientists
about the nature of memory.[31]

On a series of manuscript pages, replete with half-starts, crossings out, repetitions and variations, Wordsworth argued with
himself about how he had been trying to write 'A history of
love from stage to stage / Advancing hand in hand with power
& Joy', but also to capture the 'reverse' feeling of 'sad perplexity'.[32]
He imagines himself plumbing the depths of the 'mystery of
man' and comes to the conclusion that 'something of the base'
of the human spirit is to be found in 'simple childhood'. In
remembering his own childhood, the 'very fountains' of his
powers 'seem open', but as he approaches them 'they close'. It
is then that he realizes that 'general feelings' are insufficient.
Particular 'incidents' must be 'culled' in order to explain 'the
hiding-places' of his power and the capacity of memory to offer
'restorations'. These ruminations formed the basis of a passage
that he would eventually include between those two key spots
of time – the girl with the pitcher on her head, which I have
linked to his mother's death, and waiting for the horses, which
he explicitly linked to his father's – at the climax of the book
within his verse autobiography that he called 'Imagination, How
Impaired and Restored':

> The days gone by
> Come back upon me from the dawn almost
> Of life: the hiding-places of my power
> Seem open; I approach, and then they close;
> I see by glimpses now; when age comes on
> May scarcely see at all, and I would give,
> While yet we may, as far as words can give,
> A substance and a life to what I feel:
> I would enshrine the spirit of the past
> For future restoration.[33]

Not 'to what I felt' at the time – how can an adult really be sure of what they felt at particular moments when a child? – but 'to what I feel'. The purpose of the writing is to preserve not the letter but the *spirit* of the past, as a way of securing a sense of identity for the present and the future by locking in a personal story before memory vanishes with age.

Sometimes when Wordsworth was a child he had to reach out and touch a tree in order to reassure himself that he actually existed. As an adult he held on to his half-invented memories of being fostered alike by beauty and by fear as a way of giving 'a substance and a life' to his being in the world.

5

WALKING INTO REVOLUTION

14 JULY 1790

Two Cambridge undergraduates were walking through France. They had hatched a summer vacation scheme that their friends thought was 'mad and impracticable': an Alpine walking tour with hardly any money in their pockets and complete uncertainty as to the welcome they would receive. They had crossed from Dover and spent a night in Calais. They were wearing matching coats, purposely made for the journey before they set off from Cambridge. Each of them carried an oak walking stick and bore a bundle of possessions on his head, every bit in the manner of the girl in the mountains carrying the pitcher of water on hers. This, reported one of them to his sister, excited 'a general smile' as they passed through village after village.[1]

As they got into their stride, they would often travel thirteen leagues – about forty miles – a day (a 'league' was originally defined as the distance you could walk in an hour, so roughly three miles). But on this, their first day on French soil, they covered just ten miles, frequently stopping to absorb the festive atmosphere. They had walked straight into a revolution.

It was the first anniversary of the storming of the Bastille. A National Constituent Assembly had been formed and the powers of the monarchy had been curbed. Communities had begun to form democratic *fédérations*. There was genuine hope of a peaceful transition from the tyranny of absolute monarchy to a new regime with a mixed constitution, similar to that in Britain. On both sides of the political spectrum, it was agreed that there should be a *fête* to cement national unity. A day of celebration. The main event was on the Champ de Mars at the edge of Paris, bringing together the king and the royal family, the deputies of the Assembly, delegates from across the nation, and overseas representatives – including John Paul Jones and Thomas Paine from the youngest nation on earth, with its model constitution. They brought along the Stars and Stripes, the first time it was flown outside the United States.

Across the land, each town or village was encouraged to mount its own *fête*. As the two Cambridge students – William Wordsworth and his Welsh friend Robert Jones – walked the ten miles from Calais to Ardres, they encountered people in festive dress, smiling and singing, on their way to celebrate in one town or the other. They spent the night in Ardres and as they journeyed south over the coming days, they would meet many people returning from celebrations elsewhere, including delegates who had been to the great event in Paris. They ate and danced with them, the spirit of hope in the air.

Wordsworth caught the feeling beautifully in the first eight

lines (the 'octave') of a sonnet written when he returned to
northern France twelve years later. The poem is entitled, with
characteristic precision, 'To a Friend, Composed near Calais, on
the Road leading to Ardres, August 7th, 1802':

> Jones! when from Calais southward you and I
> Travell'd on foot together; then this Way,
> Which I am pacing now, was like the May
> With festivals of new-born Liberty:
> A homeless sound of joy was in the Sky;
> The antiquated Earth, as one might say,
> Beat like the heart of Man: songs, garlands,
>   play,
> Banners, and happy faces, far and nigh!

In July 1790, Wordsworth was twenty. He had just completed
three years at university. He was with his best college friend. He
was on foreign soil for the first time in his life, anticipating new
adventures and picturesque sights. And now he was witnessing
a new dawn in human history. In remembering the day, he
projected the joy that beat in his heart onto the earth and the
sky. In 1802, the circumstances, both political and personal, were
very different, as the last six lines (the 'sestet') of the sonnet
reveals:

> And now, sole register that these things were,
> Two solitary greetings have I heard,
> '*Good morrow, Citizen!*' a hollow word,
> As if a dead Man spake it! Yet despair
> I feel not: happy am I as a Bird:
> Fair seasons yet will come, and hopes as fair.[2]

He refused to be cast down, but, as will be seen, his hopes were now more personal than political. By this time, ten years of bloodshed across France and Europe had hollowed out the dream of liberty, equality and fraternity. Even if that had not been the case, he would still have sensed that the youthful joy of July 1790 could never return, which was all the more reason to preserve it in poetry.

★

He had left Hawkshead just over three years earlier, in June 1787, clubbing together with fellow pupils to present some books to the school library. Back in Penrith with his grandparents, the Cooksons, he was at last reunited with his sister Dorothy. They spent much of that summer together, walking and sightseeing, sometimes in the company of her friend Mary Hutchinson. Dorothy wrote to another close friend in Halifax, where she had been living with her late mother's cousin, telling of her joy at seeing her brothers for the first time in nearly ten years: 'They are just the boys I could wish them, they are so affectionate and so kind to me as makes me love them more and more every day.' She thought that William and Christopher were very clever; young John, who was to be a sailor, was less bright, but with 'a most excellent heart'. She went on to describe their misery in the household of their cold-hearted grandparents and the malice of their uncle Christopher Crackanthorpe Cookson. They lived in a perpetual atmosphere of sourness and endured countless petty acts of cruelty and neglect. Dorothy was candid in her letters to her Halifax friend Jane Pollard, who had been like a sister to her. 'Many a time', she wrote, 'have Wm, J, C, and myself shed tears together, tears of the bitterest sorrow, we all of us, each day, feel more sensibly the loss we sustained when we were deprived of our parents.'[3] *Feel more sensibly*: for some writers in the 'age of sensibility' powerful feeling was a performance conjured onto the page, whereas for William and Dorothy Wordsworth it was known in the heart, shaped by the experience of being orphaned and then separated from each other.

More prosaically, their dependence on those cruel relatives was absolute, because of the chaotic state of their father's financial affairs at the time of his death. His executors had spent three years putting together a claim that old John Wordsworth's employer Sir James Lowther (now raised to the peerage as the first Earl of Lonsdale) owed his estate more than £4,500. William's awareness of this lengthy legal battle may have been one reason why he announced to his siblings that he wanted to be a lawyer if his health permitted. He was being troubled by 'violent headaches and a pain in his side'.[4]

The good news was that he had won a place as a 'sizar' – a student in receipt of financial aid – at St John's College, Cambridge, where his uncle was a tutor. Almost everyone who has been to college or university has a vivid memory of their arrival and first few weeks. Wordsworth was the first to capture in autobiographical poetry the combination of excitement and apprehension at such a time. His recollections of undergraduate life are gathered in books three and six of *The Prelude*, with intervening memories of his first 'Summer Vacation' (book four) and of the influence of 'Books' (book five).

He went up in October, accompanied by a cousin who had been admitted to the same college. They travelled via York, where they stayed with the cousin's sister. On the journey south via the Great York Road, he saw a prostitute for the first time, a harbinger of his loss of innocence upon entering into the world. His sensitivity was such that he claimed in *The Prelude* that the sight created within him a sense of a 'barrier' between the spirit of 'humanity' and the human body, 'splitting the race of Man /

In twain, yet leaving the same outward shape'.[5] He would always be a man of strong sexual passions, nearly always repressed or displaced from the 'outward shape' of his poems.

Grey fenny weather. A shiver of delight at the first glimpse of Cambridge's most famous sight, the roof of King's College Chapel. Then, outside the carriage window, a student striding hurriedly along 'in Gown and tassell'd Cap'. Across Magdalene Bridge. Another river along which memories would flow: the Cam. Into the famed university town. The Gothic architecture of the three quadrangles ('courts') of St John's, one of the largest and most prestigious of the colleges.

His first-year room was small, tucked away in an obscure nook of the college, above the noisy kitchens. There were sounds, too, from Cambridge's grandest college, Trinity, which stood next door and which his room overlooked: the clock striking every quarter of an hour, day and night, and the organ bellowing out during divine service or when the scholar was practising. The one good thing about the location was that at night, by moon or starlight, he could gaze down from his bed and see the statue of Sir Isaac Newton in the Trinity antechapel, prism in hand, face rapt in contemplation, 'The marble index of a Mind for ever / Voyaging through strange seas of Thought, alone'.[6] The statue at once invoked the awe-inspiring quality of intellectual inquiry and projected the freshman's loneliness onto an embodiment of genius.

He began to get to know his fellow students. A handful were familiar from school, but as a 'a mountain Youth' – a 'northern Villager' – it felt almost dreamlike to be in Cambridge. 'Questions, directions, warnings, and advice' flowed in from all sides. Preparation for that nervous first tutorial. Settling into a routine of compulsory chapel and morning lectures. Becoming master of your own budget: going to buy an academic gown, which had to be worn whenever out and about, but also a silk dressing gown for posing in one's rooms. 'Invitations, suppers, wine and fruit.' He slicked his hair in the fashionable style, so that it glittered like frost on a tree. Often, though, he would leave the student throng and walk alone across the flat fields, the fenland landscape so different from his own. His communion with the simple, solid things of nature was as much a part of his education as the lectures and tutorials:

> To every natural form, rock, fruit or flower,
> Even the loose stones that cover the high-way,
> I gave a moral life, I saw them feel,
> Or link'd them to some feeling: the great mass
> Lay bedded in a quickening soul, and all
> That I beheld respired with inward meaning.[7]

Where Newton had explained the physical forces of nature, the student Wordsworth tried to discover the agency that binds human feelings to nature. In so doing, his mind turned in on itself, cleaving him to 'Solitude'. He did not seek out some kindred spirit to share his inner quest – that would come later, when he met Coleridge. Instead, he threw himself into casual friendships, lazy reading in 'trivial books' that had nothing to do with the syllabus, riding across the fields or floating down the Cam. He was supposed to be studying classical texts, mathematics and philosophy with a theological slant. He enjoyed geometry and the translation of Latin poetry, but devoted more time to private study of the great English poets who had Cambridge associations – Chaucer, who had set his *Reeve's Tale* down the road in Trumpington village; and Spenser and Milton, who had been students at the university.

When he returned home for the summer vacation at the end

of his freshman year, Wordsworth realized how much he loved his native place. Climbing over a bare ridge, he looked down on Windermere, the lake resembling 'a vast river stretching in the sun':

> With exultation at my feet I saw
> Lake, islands, promontories, gleaming bays,
> A universe of Nature's fairest forms
> Proudly revealed with instantaneous burst,
> Magnificent and beautiful and gay.[8]

He was far more comfortable among the woodmen, shepherds and village 'dames', or listening to the life story of a skeletal and impoverished discharged soldier who had once served in the tropics, than in the academic world of Cambridge.

Back he went for his second year. At this point in *The Prelude*'s narrative of his university years, Wordsworth inserts a dream. In the final version published shortly after his death in 1850, he tells of how, sitting in a rocky cave by the seaside on a still summer day, he had been reading Cervantes' *Don Quixote*, one of the favourite books of his youth. He looked out to sea and began reflecting upon poetry on the one hand and 'geometric truth' on the other. Drifting into sleep, he dreamed that he was in the desert of the Middle East. A figure resembling 'an Arab of the Bedouin Tribes', carrying a lance, rode towards him, perched high on the back of a dromedary. This is clearly a dream version of Don Quixote on his rickety horse Rocinante. The Arab has a stone tucked under the arm that holds his spear. In his other hand, he holds a shell. Glad to have found a guide to lead him through the desert, the dreamer questions the arrivant and is told that the stone is Euclid's *Elements* but the shell, beautifully shaped and brightly coloured, is 'something of more worth'. The dreamer

is told to hold it to his ear, and when he does so he hears, in
an unknown language which he mysteriously understands, 'articulate sounds',

A loud prophetic blast of harmony –
An Ode, in passion uttered, which foretold
Destruction to the Children of the Earth,
By Deluge now at hand.[9]

The Arab then says that he is going to bury his books, presumably so that they would survive the impending deluge. In classic
dream fashion, the dreamer has no difficulty in perceiving the
stone and the shell as books even as they remain stone and
shell. By the same account, the figure remains the Arab but
now explicitly becomes Don Quixote as well. He rides on,
with the dreamer initially keeping pace. Then the Arab looks
back over his shoulder, sees a glimmer of light and says that it
is the waters of the deep gathering upon them, causing him to
speed his camel into the distance across the desert sands, 'With
the fleet waters of the drowning world / In chace of him'. At
which point Wordsworth awakes in terror, and sees the real sea
in front of him, his copy of *Don Quixote* beside him. He then
interprets his own dream: it will be his destiny to follow the
example of the Arab and ensure that the great books of the
past will survive beyond the catastrophe that he sensed was
about to engulf the present. He would hold in his hand a book
by Shakespeare or Milton ('Labourers divine') and imagine it
as an 'earthly casket of immortal Verse'. Rather than burying
it beneath the desert sand, it would be his task to absorb the
spirit of the mighty dead into his own poetry and so to keep
their legacy alive.[10]

Wordsworth's placing of the dream at this point in his autobiographical narrative, together with the image of the prophetic ode being of more worth than Euclid's mathematical textbook, might be read as a moment of awakening akin to that in the oft-recounted dream of a later Cambridge student who would eventually follow in Wordsworth's footsteps as Poet Laureate: Ted Hughes. In his dream, Hughes is slaving over a literature essay late at night in his room at Pembroke College when a tall figure, half-man, half-fox, comes through his door, puts a burning paw-mark on the essay and tells the writer that by engaging in critical analysis he is killing the thought-creatures of his imagination. Hughes interpreted this as a call to switch his degree from English to Archaeology and Anthropology. In the spirit of Wordsworth's line 'We murder to dissect', Hughes determined to abandon literary criticism and turn instead to a rich body of mythological and ritualistic lore that would provide him with raw material for poetic creation. By analogy, the Arab is telling Wordsworth to become a visionary poet instead of following in his uncle's footsteps and remaining in academe (which is what his brother Christopher did, with such success that he eventually rose to the pinnacle of becoming master of Newton's college). In his second and third years at Cambridge, Wordsworth did indeed begin to believe that it was his vocation to become a poet. He grew in confidence that the past masters could be as friends rather than inhibiting shadows:

> Those were the days
> Which also first encouraged me to trust
> With firmness, hitherto but lightly touch'd
> With such a daring thought, that I might leave
> Some monument behind me which pure hearts
> Should reverence. The instinctive humbleness,
> Upheld even by the very name and thought

Of printed books and authorship, began
To melt away; and further, the dread awe
Of mighty names was soften'd down, and seem'd
Approachable, admitting fellowship
Of modest sympathy.[11]

The fellowship of the literary tradition instead of the College
Fellowship that was the ambition of many of his contemporaries
and the expectation of his relatives: a symbolic licensing of this
vocation seems to have been Wordsworth's intention in claiming
the Arab dream for himself in the final version of *The Prelude*.

But this was a trick: in the original version of the poem, it
is a 'studious friend' who has the dream and narrates it to
Wordsworth. The friend is not identified. It is not Coleridge,
to whom *The Prelude* is addressed — as when, directly after the
narration of the Arab dream, Wordsworth writes 'O Friend! O
Poet! Brother of my soul, / Think not that I could ever pass
along / Untouch'd by these remembrances'.[12] The strong likeli-
hood is that it was the third Lake Poet, the exceptionally 'studious'
Robert Southey, who became close to Wordsworth in the early
1800s, when *The Prelude* was being drafted, and who at exactly
this time was having terrifying dreams of the world being engulfed
by a deluge. Indeed, Southey contemplated writing an epic poem
on the subject.[13] Poems, like dreams, absorb and conflate different
sources and memories, so other influences were also at work,
including that of a very unusual man whom Wordsworth would
meet in France.

★

He didn't do badly at Cambridge. In the college exams at the
end of the first term of his second year, he was among 'those
who did not go thro' the whole of the examination and yet had

considerable merit' — that is to say, he ran out of time, but did well on the questions that he succeeded in answering. When it came to the end-of-year exams, he was unclassed but got a distinction in the Classics paper. A year later, in June 1790, he was again unclassed but showed 'considerable merit' in the subjects that he undertook.[14] He was content to get by. He knew by this time that he would not be seeking to stay on and gain a Fellowship. For all his love of books and his breadth of reading through his teenage years and at Cambridge, he always knew that his greatest inspiration was what John Keats would call 'the poetry of earth'.

Immediately after the passage in *The Prelude* where he recalls the sense of vocation that grew during his time at Cambridge, he tells of how he found happiness in 'loveliness of imagery and thought'. At dusk, he would walk in the groves along the Backs of the colleges until he heard the porter's bell summoning him to the nightly curfew. He remembers looking intensely upon a single ash tree lit by moonlight on a sharp frosty evening:

> Up from the ground and almost to the top
> The trunk and master branches every where
> Were green with ivy; and the lightsome twigs
> And outer spray profusely tipp'd with seeds
> That hung in yellow tassels and festoons,
> Moving or still.[15]

There is a natural historian's precision in the art of observation here, combined with a poet's gift for the choice of animating words. He was beginning, as he would put it in 'Tintern Abbey', to 'see into the life of things'.

His love of nature meant that his summer vacations were his most joyful months. Doubly so, because he was with Dorothy, and sometimes Mary Hutchinson as well. They wandered through their native ground, into Dovedale and across into the Yorkshire Dales. By the end of his third year, though, he was ready to broaden his horizons. It was time to witness Nature in her grander aspect. He came up with the idea of walking to the Alps. He had made a good friend in a fellow grammar-school boy from the north, Robert Jones, son of a Welsh lawyer. Though of very different temperaments, they were drawn together by a love of mountain terrain and a passion for walking. Wordsworth – tall, with a long face and a serious expression – was 'apt to be irritable in travelling', and in Jones – tubby, round-faced and red-cheeked – he was lucky enough to find a companion who was 'the best-tempered Creature imaginable'.[16] The Welshman was game. They had crossed the Channel before Wordsworth wrote to tell his family where he was.

★

Casting off the burdens of academe, they strode through France. In just over a week, they were at Troyes in the Loire Valley, in another at Chalon on the river Saône, where they embarked on a boat to Lyons, along with a group of delegates returning from the festivities in Paris.

Three years later, Wordsworth published an account of their journey under the title *Descriptive Sketches. In Verse. Taken during a Pedestrian Tour in the Italian, Grison, Swiss, and Savoyard Alps.* In the poem's dedication to Jones, Wordsworth wrote of how two travellers plodding along the road side by side 'each with his little knapsack of necessaries upon his shoulders' will inevitably have a closer bond – 'more of heart' between them – than 'two companions lolling in a post-chaise'. Walking also grounds the pedestrian more firmly in the landscape. Moving at human pace and without the sound of hoof or wheel, walkers see and hear their surroundings more fully, more immediately, than travellers borne at speed to their destination.

Wordsworth and Jones were following in the tracks of a pair of student adventurers sixty years before, the Etonian poet Thomas Gray and his intimate friend the novelist Horace Walpole – though they had gone by carriage and sometimes horse, not on foot. Following Gray's death in 1771, his letters home describing their journey through France, over the Alps and into Italy had been published with his poems in 1775. His account of the approach to the monastery of the Grande Chartreuse high in the mountains of Savoy inspired generations of artists and students to head for the wild landscapes of the south:

> It is six miles to the top; the road runs winding up it, commonly not six feet broad; on one hand is the rock, with woods of pine trees hanging over head; on the other, a monstrous precipice, almost perpendicular, at the bottom of which rolls a torrent, that sometimes tumbling among the fragments of stone that have fallen from on high, and some-times precipitating itself down vast descents with a noise like thunder, which is still made greater by the echo from the mountains on each side, concurs to form one of the most solemn, the most romantic, and the most astonishing scenes I ever beheld.[17]

This is a highly influential early usage of the word 'romantic' to describe mountain scenery. It is also a classic instance of what Edmund Burke classified as a 'sublime' as opposed to a 'beautiful' scene, the distinction being that the sublime creates a reaction of awe with an element of fear, in this case created by the raging torrent, the noise resembling thunder, the echo from the mountain walls. For Wordsworth and Jones, as for Gray and Walpole before them, the approach to the Grande Chartreuse was one of the most 'astonishing' scenes that they ever beheld. Astonishment – being struck dumb with awe – was the hallmark of the sublime.

They spent two days hosted by the monks, contemplating the 'wonderful scenery' with ever-increasing pleasure.[18] As they reached the mountainous terrain of the south, Wordsworth began to think about how to capture his sensual immersion in the landscape. There was a conventional language available to him in the form of the 'picturesque': literally, composing the scene as if it were a picture. He originally thought of calling his poem of the tour *Picturesque Sketches,* but came to the conclusion that 'the Alps are insulted in applying to them that term'. 'The cold rules of painting' were an obstacle to the work of giving the reader an idea of the emotions which the Alps had 'the irresistible power of communicating to the most impassive imaginations'. In describing a fiery sunset over the Swiss mountains after a storm, he refused to follow the picturesque convention of always mingling light with shade. Instead, he explained in a footnote to the poem, 'I consulted nature and my feelings': 'The ideas excited by the stormy sunset . . . owed their sublimity to that deluge of light, or rather of fire, in which nature had wrapped the immense forms around me; any intrusion of shade, by destroying the unity of the impression, had necessarily diminished its grandeur.'[19] The key words here are 'sublimity' and 'grandeur'.

Their next destination was Geneva, then the glaciers of the Alps, the Vale of Chamonix and the sight of snow-capped Mont Blanc. Wordsworth's attempt to describe it in the poem of his tour was among his first efforts at rendering the sublime:

Alone ascends that mountain nam'd of white,
That dallies with the Sun the summer night.

Six thousand years amid his lonely bounds
The voice of Ruin, day and night, resounds.
Where Horror-led his sea of ice assails,
Havoc and Chaos blast a thousand vales.[20]

Constrained by his chosen form of rhyming couplets and reaching
for hand-me-down abstractions out of the realm of Gothic (Ruin,
Horror, Havoc, Chaos), the apprentice poet has not yet found
a voice of his own.

Both his style and his emphasis were very different in *The
Prelude* a decade later, when he once again reconstructed his
walking tour in verse. This time his memory was of how his
heart leapt up when he looked down into the Vale of Chamonix.
The valley presented him with an image of what he calls a 'green
recess' inhabited by an 'aboriginal' community of pastoral dwellers
in simple huts resembling 'Indian cabins'. He is conjuring up an
image of humankind living harmoniously in what Jean-Jacques
Rousseau, citizen of Geneva, called the 'state of nature'. 'The
summit of Mont Blanc', by contrast, offered 'a soulless image
on the eye' that 'usurped upon a living thought / That never
more could be'. The limitation of the sublime, he implies, is
that its power to astonish may erase the little things and ordinary
working people that deserve the affections of the human heart.
Looking down on Chamonix, he trained his eye on 'small birds'
warbling in 'leafy trees', a reaper binding 'the yellow sheaf' and
a young woman spreading a haystack in the sun.[21]

The literal high point of an Alpine tour was the moment
when one reached the summit of the Simplon Pass. Wordsworth
and Jones made their way up the 'steep and rugged road' in the
company of a group of traders carrying their wares on mules.
They all stopped for lunch. Their mountain guide wanted to get
going, but the Englishman and the Welshman lingered a while.

When they set off, they followed a path downwards until it came to a dead end by a stream. The only path now visible was on the other side of the stream, winding back up the mountainside. So they waded across and climbed quickly, trying to catch up with the group. Failing to find them, they began to panic. Fortunately, they met a mountain-dwelling peasant. He told them that they needed to go back down to the stream and to follow its course further downwards. They were puzzled and kept questioning him: shouldn't they be going up, not down? The peasant was insistent. Comprehension then dawned. The language barrier was 'translated by [their] feelings': they realized '*that we had crossed the Alps*'.

It was a profound moment of anticlimax. But in *The Prelude* the mature Wordsworth would recuperate it by way of a reflection on the power of the human imagination.[22] In recollecting moments of sorrow or disappointment and turning them to poetry, we can remake them as visions of a better world. Human greatness, he proposes, resides in this capacity to transport us from what we see to what we desire. Paradoxically, it is as if a flash of mental lightning illuminates us in the very instant that physical light is darkened by a cloud: 'When the light of sense / Goes out in flashes that have shewn to us / The invisible world'.[23] Our mental triumphs, Wordsworth argues, are in the anticipation and not the realization, the hope and not the achievement:

> Our destiny, our nature, and our home,
> Is with infinitude – and only there;
> With hope it is, hope that can never die,
> Effort, and expectation, and desire,
> And something evermore about to be.[24]

In Wordsworth's Christian society, most people hoped for – or were told to hope for – salvation and an eternity in heaven with Jesus. Wordsworth is saying, albeit less explicitly, something akin to William Blake's provocative aphorism in *The Marriage of Heaven and Hell*: 'all deities reside in the human breast'. The human imagination is the only place where heaven is to be found on this earth.

Wordsworth was steeped in the poetry of John Milton. He was thrilled that one of his Cambridge friends was lucky enough to be bunked in rooms at Christ's College that were once Milton's. Some of the most glorious poetry in *Paradise Lost* occurs when Adam and Eve give voice to a morning hymn in which they exhort all living things to join them in praise of the goodness and power of God: 'On Earth join, all ye creatures, to extol / Him first, him last, him midst, and without end.'[25] Wordsworth remembered and adapted these lines as he sought to prove his argument about the transformative power of imagination by turning the anticlimax of having missed the moment of crossing the Alps into a climactic vision of the divine power of the sublime landscape of the Ravine of Gondo, through which they subsequently passed:

>   The immeasurable height
> Of woods decaying, never to be decayed,
> The stationary blasts of waterfalls,
> And everywhere along the hollow rent
> Winds thwarting winds, bewildered and forlorn,
> The torrents shooting from the clear blue sky,
> The rocks that muttered close upon our ears –
> Black drizzling crags that spake by the way-side
> As if a voice were in them – the sick sight
> And giddy prospect of the raving stream,

The unfettered clouds and region of the heavens,

Tumult and peace, the darkness and the light,

Were all like workings of one mind, the features

Of the same face, blossoms upon one tree,

Characters of the great apocalypse,

The types and symbols of eternity,

Of first, and last, and midst, and without end.[26]

Where Milton's Adam and Eve praised an invisible transcendent God, Wordsworth finds the voice, mind, and face of the divine in the awe-inspiring environment of the ravine.

All this is part of the retrospective ordering of his narrative of the growth of a poet's mind. At the time, crossing the Alps with Jones, he noticed the 'Black drizzling crags, that beaten by the din' of the waterfalls 'Vibrate, as if a voice complain'd within'.[27] He did not, however, transpose the scene into an allegory of eternity or a vision of apocalypse now. Writing to Dorothy at the time, he took the more orthodox view that the wonders of nature were to be read as a sign of the power of God the Creator: 'Among the more awful scenes of the Alps, I had not a thought of man, or a single created being; my whole soul was turned to him who produced the terrible majesty before me.'[28] Jones, no doubt, had similar sentiments: he went on to become a clergyman.

Throughout *The Prelude*, Wordsworth was writing in the aftermath of his disillusionment with the turn to violence taken by the French Revolution. In the summer of 1790, like many young political radicals, he dared to hope that the New Jerusalem was about to dawn, that heaven could be brought to earth through social justice. Looking back, more than a decade later, he could not prevent his memories from being contaminated by subsequent events. The night after the crossing of the Alps, Wordsworth lodged in an 'alpine house' called the Spittal of Gondo. He could not sleep. In *The Prelude* he described the lodging as

> A dreary mansion, large beyond all need,
> With high and spacious rooms, deafened and stunned
> By noise of waters, making innocent sleep
> Lie melancholy among weary bones.[29]

Something very strange happened thirty years later, when Wordsworth and Dorothy went on a continental tour. They visited the Spittal of Gondo, but Dorothy could not persuade her brother to go inside. They moved on, forced to lodge elsewhere.[30] Wordsworth's phobic reaction has never been explained, but there may be a hint in that phrase 'innocent sleep'. The description of the mansion, with its high-ceilinged bedrooms, bears an uncanny resemblance to another hotel where Wordsworth spent a sleepless night in Paris two years later. And that, as will be seen, was the moment when his dream of the dawn of the New Jerusalem was shattered.

★

'I am a perfect Enthusiast in my admiration of Nature in all her various forms', Wordsworth wrote to Dorothy from a village beside Lake Constance.[31] The rest of the tour was more watery than mountainous: Lake Maggiore, the Lake of Lugano, Como (where Wordsworth was mildly smitten by the sight of dark-eyed peasant girls dancing on the shore), the Lake of Zurich, the Lake of Lucerne, the Falls of the Rhine at Schaffhausen, the valley of Unterwalden, the mountains rising above Grindelwald, a boat bought in Basel and sailed along the Rhine to Cologne. There was the occasional adventure, for example a night in the woods when the two travellers were separated in a storm, but the landscapes of this second half of the tour conformed to the Burkean 'beautiful' as opposed to the 'sublime'. Having sold the boat in Cologne, they continued on foot once again, past Aix-la-Chapelle and thence to the coast. They encountered some Belgian troops on the move, a military presence that cast the merest shadow of a cloud on the political horizon. They hurried their step, needing to get back to Cambridge to complete their degrees.

Wordsworth spent the week before his final exams reading Samuel Richardson's novel *Clarissa* instead of revising. He sat the exams in the Cambridge Senate House in January 1791, duly scraping through his BA without distinction – he was classed among the hoi polloi.[32] He had no idea what to do next. Like many a graduand before and after, he drifted aimlessly to London. Book seven of *The Prelude* records his memories of being thrown into the vortex of the city: the crowds, the noise, 'Stalls, barrows, porters, midway in the street / The scavenger that begs with hat in hand', peep shows, street performers, hawkers shouting their wares, migrants from across the globe, the freak shows of Bartholomew Fair, a blind beggar propped motionless against a wall with a 'written paper' on his chest telling his story, 'His fixed face and sightless eyes' admonishing Wordsworth as if 'from another world'.[33]

It was a lonely time. In May, however, he was reunited with Jones at his home Plas-yn-Llan, in the village of Llangynhafal in Denbighshire. A handsome redbrick house, long and with high windows, it rather resembled Wordsworth's childhood home in Cockermouth. A letter of Dorothy's suggests that her brother's spirits were lifted by both the place and the company: 'Who would not be happy enjoying the company of three young ladies in the Vale of Clwyd and without a rival?' she joked, explaining that 'His friend Jones is a charming young man, and has *five*

sisters, three of whom are at home at present, then there are
mountains, rivers, woods and rocks, whose charms without any
other inducement would be sufficient to tempt William to
continue amongst them as long as possible.'[34] Wordsworth would
not have been the first young man to enjoy a little flirtation with
his best friend's sisters. Sadly, one of them, Margaret, died soon
after, aged just sixteen. Years later, Jones, writing with regret that
they had been out of touch for so long, mentioned another of
the girls, who was two years older than Margaret: 'Mary you
may perhaps remember something of.'[35]

The two young men spent the whole summer together. They
went off on another walking tour, covering much of North
Wales. They climbed the precipitous mountain of Cader Idris,
which had been made famous in a painting by the landscape
artist Richard Wilson; they wandered by the winding river Dee.
In Powys, a little further south, they visited the shrine of a female
saint called Melangell and Wordsworth got into an altercation
regarding the powers of the Welsh language that led to him being
threatened with a carving knife by a local priest who had drunk
too much strong ale.

The most memorable of these summer excursions was a
midnight ascent of Snowdon, the highest mountain in Wales
(higher, too, than any in England).[36] After taking supper in a
rugged thatched cottage in a hamlet called Beddgelert, they
proceeded to the foot of the mountain, where they roused a
shepherd who supplemented his income by acting as a guide. It
was a close warm night with a 'dripping mist' threatening a
storm. They climbed through the fog, trusting their guide, whose
sheepdog ran ahead of them, unearthing a hedgehog among the
crags. As they got higher, 'the ground appeared to brighten'. A
flash of light illuminated the turf and, all of a sudden, the moon
was out. Wordsworth looked down. They were above the mist,

which now resembled a sea with the peaks of the surrounding mountains emerging like the backs of whales. In the distance, they saw the mist dipping and swirling into the real sea. And somewhere between the mountains and the sea, they spotted 'a blue chasm, a fracture in the vapour',

> A deep and gloomy breathing-place thro' which
>   Mounted the roar of waters, torrents, streams
> Innumerable, roaring with one voice.

'In that breach', Wordsworth writes in *The Prelude*, 'Through which the homeless voice of waters rose', Nature had lodged 'The soul, the imagination of the whole'.[37] This idea of the imagination filling a gap, emerging from an abyss of emptiness, and indeed of homelessness, is at the core of Wordsworth's vocation. His poetry, the work of his imagination, filled the void of the losses – of parents, of home, of political ideals, and later of friends, siblings and children – that afflicted him.

Wordsworth then makes his habitual move from description to philosophizing:

> A meditation rose in me that night
> Upon the lonely Mountain when the scene
> Had pass'd away, and it appear'd to me
> The perfect image of a mighty Mind,
> Of one that feeds upon infinity,
> That is exalted by an underpresence,
> The sense of God, or whatsoe'er is dim
> Or vast in its own being.[38]

Here there is a measured uncertainty as to whether the 'underpresence' – the gleam or intimation that in book two of *The*

Prelude he called 'an obscure sense / Of possible sublimity'[39] — is an epiphany of the divine or a recognition of the profundity of human potential. Is the 'mighty Mind' God's or our own?

As with the crossing of the Alps in the middle of *The Prelude*, the cognitive conclusion drawn from the ascent of Snowdon at the poem's climax may belong to the act of memory, not the moment itself. We cannot be sure that the meditation really did arise in him that night rather than in the act of remembering and writing about the night. Equally, although there is no reason to doubt that he and Jones had the experience of standing above the sea of mist, the language in which the scene is described bears an uncanny resemblance to that of the standard guidebook which they had almost certainly consulted in planning their picturesque tour. During their perambulations, they actually visited the book's author, Thomas Pennant. It was his *A Tour in Wales* that had given them the idea of an ascent of Snowdon timed so as to see the sun rise from the summit. There Wordsworth would have read of how

A vast mist enveloped the whole circuit of the mountain. The prospect down was horrible. It gave an idea of numbers of abysses, concealed by a thick smoke, furiously circulating around us. Very often a gust of wind formed an opening in the clouds, which gave a fine and distinct visto [*sic*] of lake and valley. Sometimes they opened only in one place; at others, in many at once, exhibiting a most strange and perplexing sight of water, fields, rocks, or chasms, in fifty different places.[40]

★

Though Wordsworth frequently wrote in Rousseauistic terms about nature providing a better education than books, he was always hungry for books and gladly acknowledged that the development of his writing was dependent on his reading. His first extended poem, 'The Vale of Esthwaite', written during the summer holidays when he was just seventeen, borrows its language from James Beattie's highly popular *The Minstrel*, while his first published poem, *An Evening Walk*, on which he worked during his long vacations from Cambridge, has the conventional vocabulary and perky rhyming couplets of a dozen other 'loco-descriptive' poems of the eighteenth century, not to mention classical sources and indeed guidebooks. Wordsworth acknowledged as much by adding footnotes along the lines of 'from Thomson' (that is to say, borrowed from Thomson's *The Seasons*), 'See Burns' Cotter's Saturday Night', 'See a description of an appearance of this kind in Clark's *Survey of the Lakes*', and 'Much of this paragraph alludes to Horace's beautiful ode to Bandusia of which the author has attempted a translation.'[41]

The now forgotten Beattie was one of the most important of these early influences. He anticipated Wordsworth in arguing for the power of places in summoning up memories:

> The sight of a place in which we have been happy or unhappy renews the thoughts and feelings we formerly experienced there. With what rapture, after long absence, do we revisit the haunts of our childhood and early youth! A thousand ideas, which had been many years forgotten, now crowd upon the imagination, and revive within us the gay passions of that romantick period. And from these, and other associations of a like nature, arises in part the love of our country, our friends and fellow citizens, a fondness for the very fields and mountains, the vales, rocks and rivers which formed the scenery of our first amusements and adventures.[42]

Wordsworth's early poems, notably his *Evening Walk* tracking his youthful perambulations around Derwent, Rydal, Grasmere, Esthwaite and Winander (Windermere), conform exactly to this model. And he did come to believe that love of country, friends and fellow citizens grew in part from love of nature.

But his most powerful memories – the windswept girl, the gibbet, the admonishing cliff rising over the stolen boat, the grip of the crag-fast boy, the thunderous sound of falling water in the Ravine of Gondo, the abyss below Snowdon – have a much darker and more mysterious tone than that suggested in Beattie's evocation of the 'gay passions' of the 'romantick period' of childhood and early youth. Perhaps the first moment when Wordsworth found his own voice as a poet came in a passage of the 'The Vale of Esthwaite', which he never published, when he dispensed with the flummery of Gothic fantasia stitched from his reading – the style that dominates the poem – and summoned up that memory of the December day when, aged thirteen, he was waiting for the horses to take him home for the Christmas holiday during which his father followed his mother to the grave:

> One Evening when the wintry blast
> Through the sharp Hawthorn whistling pass'd
> And the poor flocks all pinch'd with cold
> Sad drooping sought the mountain fold
> Long Long upon yon steepy rock
> Alone I bore the bitter shock
> Long Long my swimming eyes did roam
> For little Horse to bear me home
> To bear me what avails my tear
> To sorrow o'er a Father's bier.[43]

John Wordsworth, working on Lowther business, had ridden out to a far corner of Cumberland and lost his way home on a pitch-dark December evening. He spent the freezing night on Cold Fell and never recovered from the exposure. William followed his father's 'bier' to the grave in Cockermouth churchyard on a day of snow and wind. The death of his parents, and his consequent separation from his sister, shaped his whole life. He remained a poet of twilight and mourning, long after the fading of the glad morning of hope that he experienced with Jones on the road to Ardres in July 1790.

6

TWO REVOLUTIONARY WOMEN

The extended Wordsworth family was well embedded in the establishment of the Anglican Church. In September 1791, a cousin wrote to offer William a curacy in the south-east of England. Saying goodbye to Jones and his sisters, he travelled to London to explain that he was not of a legal age to enter Anglican holy orders. He was glad of the excuse. But he was still drifting. At the beginning of term, he went back to Cambridge. There was talk of him studying oriental languages, but he did not enrol. Instead, he returned to France. He intended to spend the winter in Orleans, perfecting his French. It was not quite clear how this would prepare him for the learning of biblical Hebrew that would be the next step in the event that the ecclesiastical plan should eventually come to fruition.

Nevertheless, the family was willing to give him £40 to set him on his way.

By late November he was in Brighton, waiting four days for the wind to change so that he could embark for France. He took the opportunity to write to another college friend, William Mathews, complaining of his own lack of resolution with regard to a career: 'I am doomed to be an idler throughout my whole life.'[1]

His host in the seaside town, sticking with him until the moment he left, was a fellow poet, Charlotte Smith, author of a volume of *Elegiac Sonnets* that he particularly admired. His connection came from the fact that her family lawyer, John Robinson, was a distant cousin of Wordsworth's, who had worked as a clerk for Wordsworth's grandfather and gained the patronage of Sir James Lowther. He had gone into politics while maintaining his legal career. He was not averse to the art of political advancement through the backhander – once, in the House of Commons, the supremely witty Whig politician and playwright Richard Brinsley Sheridan spoke out against bribery and there were cries to name the chief instigator, to which Sheridan replied 'I could name him as soon as I could say Jack Robinson.'[2]

Charlotte Smith, born in 1749, was a generation older than Wordsworth. The eldest child of a Sussex landowner, she was, as she put it, 'sold into marriage' at the age of fifteen to a man named Benjamin Smith. Violent and dissolute, Smith came from a family that derived their wealth from West Indian slave plantations. Charlotte bore him twelve children while he wasted the family fortune. In 1783, she spent several months with him in debtors' prison. This was when she set to work on her *Elegiac Sonnets* in the hope of making some money. A few years later, she separated from her husband and began supporting her children through her pen. This led her to turn to the novel, which had a bigger market than poetry. In the summer of 1789, she published *Ethelinde; or the Recluse of the Lake*, a novel set in a Gothic house called Grasmere Abbey and containing many rhapsodic descriptions of Lake District scenery. The heroine Ethelinde wanders at dusk beside Grasmere lake, clutching her copy of the published letters of the poet Thomas Gray, 'in which he with the clearest simplicity describes this small lake': 'she pursued her way, now over "eminences covered with turf, now among broken rock" till she reached the village which stands on a low promontory projecting far into the lake'.³ This was the village that Wordsworth would one day call home, just as *The Recluse* was a title that he would one day seek (without success) to make his own. Late in life, he sometimes complained that tourists only wanted to see the site of Smith's fictional 'Grasmere Abbey' – locals would tease them by directing them to a broken sheepfold on the hillside, perhaps the very one that inspired Wordsworth's poem 'Michael'.

The two poets would have talked not only of the Lakes in the north, but also of events across the English Channel. Everyone was talking politics, a national debate having been stirred by Edmund Burke's admonitory *Reflections on the Revolution in France* and Thomas Paine's pro-revolutionary reply *The Rights of Man*. Smith had spent the year 1791 researching a new novel, *Desmond*, which marked her entry into the arena of political controversy. She explained in a preface when it was published the following year that 'the political passages dispersed throughout the work' were 'drawn from conversations to which I have been a witness, in England, and France, during the last twelve months . . . I have given to my imaginary characters the arguments I have heard on both sides.'⁴ The novel accordingly includes many quotations from, and debates about, Burke's attack on the revolution and Paine's defence of it. Smith nailed her colours firmly to the radical mast. Indeed, the following year when news came of the slaughter of the personal bodyguards of King Louis XVI, Charlotte scandalized a gentleman who was visiting her in Brighton. 'I liked her well enough', he wrote, save for 'a demo-cratic twist (which I think detestable in a woman)' – until 'she disgusted me completely on the account arriving of the Massacre of the Swiss Guards at the Tuileries by saying that they richly deserved it'.[5] From this time forward, she was a marked woman.

In the course of her research for *Desmond*, she had even visited Paris, where she met with one of the leading figures among the revolutionaries: Jacques-Pierre Brissot. He had cut his political teeth writing anti-monarchical pamphlets and forming an anti-slavery group known as the Society of the Friends of the Blacks. When Smith met him in Paris in 1791, he was making speeches in the Jacobin Club, editing the *Patriote français* and writing for a newspaper called *Le Républicain* that he had established, along with Thomas Paine and the Marquis de Condorcet. At the time of the storming of the Tuileries, he headed the Legislative Assembly. From this point on, cracks were beginning to appear within the revolutionary leadership. They all wanted a republic to be proclaimed, but they could not agree over the fate of King Louis, Queen Marie Antoinette and the rest of the royal family. Should they be kept alive, under house arrest, or would that run the risk of a revival of the monarchy in the event of foreign invasion or counter-revolutionary reaction? The Jacobins argued for a final solution, whereas Brissot emerged as the leader of a more moderate faction, who became known as the Girondins because many of them came from the region of the Gironde – though they were often called the Brissotins.

Charlotte Smith gave Wordsworth a letter of introduction to Brissot. She also gave him one addressed to a fellow poet who was residing in Paris: Helen Maria Williams. This was a woman whose work Wordsworth admired even more.

Born in 1761, Helen Maria, together with her sister and half-sister, was raised by her mother in Berwick-upon-Tweed on the Scottish border after her father died while she was an infant. She wrote poems from an early age. Brought to London in 1781, she was taken up by a Presbyterian minister called Dr Andrew Kippis. He wrote a preface praising her first published poem, *Edwin and Eltruda*, published when she was just twenty-one years old. Set in the time of the English civil war, it tells the story of lovers whose families fight on opposite sides, ending with their tragic deaths.

Doomed or thwarted lovers of this kind were a favourite theme in the literature of the late eighteenth century. *Romeo and Juliet* was one of the most frequently staged of Shakespeare's plays, while the bestselling secular book of the age was Jean-Jacques Rousseau's novel *La nouvelle Héloïse*, which went through over seventy editions in print by 1800, besides being imitated in numerous other novels. It was so popular that publishers could not print enough copies to keep up with the demand, so they rented it out by the day or even the hour. Rousseau was overwhelmed with fan mail, telling him of the tears, swoons and ecstasies provoked in his readers. A modern reworking of the medieval story of Héloïse and Abelard, the novel tells the story of a passionate love affair that crosses the boundaries of class, religious piety and decorum. The full title was *Julie, ou la nouvelle Héloïse*, though when first published in Amsterdam in 1761 it was called *Lettres de deux amans* – 'letters of two lovers, living in a small town at the foot of the Alps'. The lover is Julie's tutor, Saint-Preux. Under the *ancien régime* a posh girl cannot marry her tutor, especially if he is a holy man. But living in the sublime landscape of the Alps and rowing on a beautiful lake, they cannot resist their passions. Their affair must, however, come to an end when upper-class Julie dutifully marries a baron chosen for her by her father. Saint-Preux goes off on a world tour. Six years later he returns and is employed once more, this time as tutor to Julie's children. They live happily and virtuously together, enjoying a simple country life, all passion duly restrained. But Julie has an epiphany when her child almost drowns: she has never stopped loving Saint-Preux, and soon she expires as if from pure emotional excess, an extreme of what was known as 'sensibility' (the temperament anatomized by Jane Austen in the character of Marianne Dashwood in *Sense and Sensibility*). For readers, the book demonstrated the power of passion over the demands of duty and the social order. The Catholic Church duly placed it on the index of prohibited books. But, however often priests and moralists inveighed from pulpit and pamphlet against the dangers of novel-reading, especially for women, the authorities could not prevent the spread of the cult of 'sensibility' – and there was no literary form more suited to the expression of extreme emotion than poetry.

Helen Maria Williams' particular gift was the transposition of a Rousseauistic narrative of passion into verse and into an English setting. The character of Eltruda in her poem is a young woman of extreme sensibility, whose sympathetic imagination extends to every living thing:

> For the bruis'd insect on the waste,
> A sigh would heave her breast;
> And oft her careful hand replac'd
> The linnet's falling nest.

The naming of a specific species of finch and the tender care for a bird's nest: such details prefigure the delicate poetic brushwork of the most sensitive of all poets of nature, John Clare. One may also see the young Helen Maria Williams anticipating

Wordsworth at his best. Eltruda is compared to a 'lonely flower' that 'smiles in the desert vale'.[6] That is a conventional enough image, an echo of Thomas Gray's famous lines in his 'Elegy written in a Country Churchyard': 'Full many a flower is born to blush unseen / And waste its sweetness on the desert air'. But in their rhythm of alternating tetrameters and trimeters (four- and three-stress lines), the following lines from *Edwin and Eltruda* feel very like a dry run for Wordsworth's mysterious and mesmerizing 'Lucy' poems. Thus Williams:

> So liv'd in solitude, unseen,
>> This lovely, peerless maid;
> So grac'd the wild, sequester'd scene,
>> And blossom'd in the shade.[7]

And Wordsworth:

> She dwelt among th' untrodden ways
>> Beside the springs of Dove,
> A Maid whom there were none to praise
>> And very few to love.

Women were cautious about exposing their identity in print. Like all the novels which Jane Austen would publish in her lifetime, Williams' first book of poetry was anonymous. But in 1784 she boldly put her name on the title page of an epic poem called *Peru*. Two years later, she gathered her early works together with many new ones in a two-volume collection simply entitled *Poems*. It was published by the method of subscription, whereby purchasers paid up front to cover the cost of production. Over 1,500 people signed up, a remarkable number for a volume of poetry by a young woman.

In the spring of 1787, a London-based but cosmopolitan-inspired monthly journal called the *European Magazine* included in its poetry pages the first published work of a young man on the brink of his seventeenth birthday. It was entitled 'Sonnet on seeing Miss Helen Maria Williams Weep at a Tale of Distress'. The octave reads as follows:

> She wept. – Life's purple tide began to flow
> In languid streams through every thrilling vein;
> Dim were my swimming eyes – my pulse beat slow,
> And my full heart was swell'd to dear delicious pain.
> Life left my loaded heart, and closing eye;
> A sigh recall'd the wanderer to my breast;
> Dear was the pause of life, and dear the sigh
> That call'd the wanderer home, and home to rest.

These few lines epitomize the Rousseauist sensibility. 'She wept', as did so many readers of *Julie, ou la nouvelle Héloïse*, especially female ones. In connecting with a book – a tale of distress that might equally be a novel, a narrative poem or a true story – the reader also connects with the full tide of Life with a capital L. The heart reaches out in the spirit of fellow feeling with suffering humanity.

Extreme 'sensibility' of this kind was generally regarded as unmanly. Many readers of this sonnet in the *European Magazine* would have expected it to have been written by a woman. It was not. The poem was signed 'Axiologus', that classically inspired codename for Words-worth that Coleridge would use in his bitter poem about Sara Hutchinson. This was the teenage William's first appearance in print. The sonnet is indeed a poem about the worth of words, the power of poetry. Wordsworth would go on, in company with Coleridge, to make unprecedented

claims for that worth, for poetry as a form of salvation, a revolution of the self.

The sonnet's key metaphor is that of a stream — a stream of
consciousness, perhaps, that will eventually flow into the sea of
the unconscious. The fluvial imagery is then internalized: the
poet's eyes swim with tears in sympathy with those of Miss Helen
Maria Williams, as she in turn weeps in sympathy with the
distress about which she is reading. Life flows along the blood-
stream, 'thrilling' the veins. And then the pulse slows and the
heart is swelled to 'dear delicious pain'. Sympathy, or what we
would now call empathy, brings, as a later and much greater
Wordsworth poem would put it, 'sensations sweet, / Felt in the
blood, and felt along the heart'. *Sensations*, the swelling heart,
the excited flow of blood in the veins, the beating of the pulse,
the idea that pain might have something delicious about it, above
all that verb *felt*: these are going to be key words in poetry for
the next forty years. One might almost say that the entire sensibility of another precocious poet, John Keats, is bound within
the nutshell of this cluster of images. One thinks of the 'Ode to
a Nightingale' and its cry 'Now more than ever seems it rich to
die'. At the core of 'Sonnet on seeing Miss Helen Maria Williams
Weep at a Tale of Distress' is the idea that a poem can offer a
momentary 'pause of life'. In momentarily suspending what a
later sonnet would call the 'getting and spending' of daily routine
in which we 'lay waste our powers', poetry can call the wanderer
home, bring us 'home to rest'. What we come home to is a
bond, a sympathy for the still sad music of humanity.

He had not literally *seen* Miss Helen Maria Williams weeping
at a tale of distress. He had *read* her poems and projected an
image of her as the sympathetic poet. His sonnet was almost
certainly inspired by a passage in *Peru*. Williams' epic concerns
the Spanish massacre of the Incas. It is a manifestation of her

anti-imperial, pacifist sensibility. In a footnote, she expressed the
hope, in anticipation of the coming revolutions such as that led
by Toussaint L'Ouverture in the Caribbean, that 'these injured
nations may recover the liberty of which they have been so
cruelly deprived'. 'Liberty' is another of the poetic watchwords
of the age. At the climax of *Peru*, Williams introduced a person-
ification of Sensibility, weeping for the Incas. A visionary figure
descends from the clouds: 'It lights on earth – mild vision! gentle
form – / 'Tis Sensibility!' Then, 'Wet with the dew of tears',
the 'ray of pity' beaming from her eyes, she addresses

> Ye to whose yielding hearts my power endears
> The transport blended with delicious tears,
> The bliss that swells to agony the breast,
> The sympathy that robs the soul of rest.[8]

One can see the source of the language of Wordsworth's sonnet.
His clever device was to elide this figure with its creator: he
makes Helen Maria Williams into the very embodiment of
Sensibility. His reading is fully justified by the presence in her
collection of a poem called 'To Sensibility', which argued – against
the (nearly always male) critics who attacked what we might call
the School of Sensibility – that strong emotion, weeping especially, is an essential part of what it is to be human because it
answers to the moral imperative to feel for others and show
benevolence towards them, or, as Wordsworth puts it in the
closing line of his sonnet written in response to his reading of
her, 'To cheer the wand'ring wretch with hospitable light'.

In 1788, Williams published an anti-slavery poem, then early
in 1790 her first novel appeared. Its very title, *Julia*, revealed the
influence of Rousseau. In a digression in its second volume,
Williams introduced a new poem of her own, under the pretence

that it was written by a friend of the loser in the novel's love triangle – written while he was in a terrible prison but dreaming prophetically of the destruction of that place. It was called 'The Bastille, A Vision'.

Soon after her novel was published, Helen Maria Williams set off for France. She arrived in Paris on the very day that Wordsworth and Jones arrived in Calais on their student walking tour: the eve of the first anniversary of the fall of the Bastille. She had gone straight into the eye of the revolutionary storm. Later that year she published her *Letters written in France, in the Summer 1790, to a friend in England; containing, various anecdotes relative to the French Revolution.* 'I arrived in Paris', she began her first letter, 'the day before the federation' (the 'Fête de la Fédération' witnessed by those travellers whom Wordsworth and Jones met in the following weeks). She gave thanks for the good fortune of a speedy journey: 'Had the packet which conveyed me from Brighton to Dieppe sailed a few hours later; had the wind been contrary; in short, had I not reached Paris at the moment I did reach it, I should have missed the most sublime spectacle which, perhaps, was ever represented on the theatre of this earth.'[9] Week by week, she reported from the front line, praising every aspect of the early days of the revolution:

It was the triumph of human kind; it was man asserting the noblest privileges of his nature; and it required but the common feelings of humanity to become in that moment a citizen of the world. For myself, I acknowledge that my heart caught with enthusiasm the general sympathy; my eyes filled with tears; and I shall never forget the sensations of that day.[10]

In the act of becoming one of her country's few field correspondents at the scene of the epoch-making events, she moves

her vocabulary of sensibility – heart, sympathy, tears, sensations
– into the political arena.

Wordsworth, then, was on a mission, poetically, politically and
in terms of his literal destination: his desire was to follow in the
footsteps of Helen Maria Williams. He arrived in Paris by night,
at the end of November, only to discover that she had moved
to Orleans.

BUT TO BE YOUNG
WAS VERY HEAVEN

Having missed Helen Maria Williams, Wordsworth acti-
vated the second letter of introduction provided by
Charlotte Smith: to her friend Jacques-Pierre Brissot.
This took him into the heart of the French Revolution. Brissot
arranged for him to visit the National Assembly, where the
deputies were remaking the government of the realm. He also
attended a clamorous debate at the Jacobin Club, where he saw
'the revolutionary power / Toss like a ship at anchor, rocked
by storms'.[1] In the manner of a pilgrim, he visited the sites
associated with the revolutionary events of the previous two
and a half years: the Champ de Mars, where the Feast of the
Federation had been held on his memorable first day in France
back in 1790; the Faubourg Saint-Antoine, the quarter near

the Bastille that harboured many of the most radical of the
sans-culottes; the Panthéon, where Rousseau and Voltaire had
been reburied in honour of their literary work as harbingers
of the revolution. He sat among the dust in the Place de la
Bastille,

> And from the rubbish gathered up a stone,
> And pocketed the relick in the guise
> Of an enthusiast.[2]

'Enthusiast', like the term 'patriot', which he also applied to
himself, was code for a passionate supporter of the revolution.

After a few days, he headed south to Orleans. Once he got
there, he discovered that he had again missed Helen Maria
Williams. He found lodging with a hosier, at eighty francs a
month. His host was virulent in anti-revolutionary feeling, as
were his fellow lodgers, who were cavalry officers. He met an
Englishman, Mr Foxlow, who owned a cotton factory in the
city. Just before Christmas, he fell in with a family called Dufour,
together with a friend of theirs, a notary's clerk called Paul Vallon.
He was moving among respectable burghers, nearly all of them
royalists.

Vallon's sister Marie-Anne – known as Annette and four
years older than Wordsworth – was visiting from the city of
Blois, some forty miles further along the river Loire. Since
Wordsworth was short of cash, he decided not to enrol with
a professional tutor, but to improve his French by means of
conversation with the Dufours and the Vallons. And since
Annette was the one who did not have a job to go to, she
became his de facto tutor: in an age when everyone knew
Rousseau's *Nouvelle Héloïse*, the intimacy of the tutorial was
all too likely to light the fuse of romance. Early in 1792,

Annette returned to Blois. And Wordsworth went with her.
They had fallen in love.

*

In *The Prelude* there is an especially vivid memory of a member
of the garrison in either Orleans or Blois fuming over the daily
news from Paris that was read out in public. His voice was
'disarmed' and his 'yellow cheek' fanned 'Into a thousand colours'.
He denounced the deputies of the Assembly, even the moderate
Girondins such as Carra and Gorsas, as 'locusts' devouring the
land. Wordsworth listened to these military 'defenders of the
crown' with respect, but he resisted their attempts to win him
over to their cause. Coming from 'a poor district', one of the
places in England with the fewest number of aristocrats exercising
power through 'wealth or blood', and having then been educated
in the intellectual 'republic' of Cambridge, where every student
stood 'upon equal ground' as 'brothers / In honour, as of one
community', his natural sympathies leaned towards 'the government of equal rights / And individual worth'.[3] Many officers
were deserting and going to join the émigré army that was
mustering on the French border, with support from Austria and
Prussia. As he walked the public roads, exploring the Loire Valley,
he encountered 'patriot' soldiers marching off to defend the
revolution against the impending invasion. Tears came to his eyes
as he saw the local women saying goodbye to their loved ones.

In contrast to Orleans, there were very few foreigners in Blois.
There is accordingly a strong possibility that Wordsworth was
one of the two Englishmen who, a surviving record informs us,
were granted permission to sit in on the meetings of the city's
pro-revolutionary group, the Friends of the Constitution. What
is certain is that he also made the acquaintance of a man whose
politics were very different from those of the conservative burghers

of Orleans, the well-to-do Vallons and the great majority of the officer class.

Captain Michel-Armand Beaupuy was from an ancient aristocratic family in the Bordeaux region; his mother was descended from the great sixteenth-century essayist Michel de Montaigne. Brought up in the spirit of the Enlightenment *philosophes*, he was an ardent democrat, deeply concerned about the plight of the poor. Wordsworth put his conversations with this remarkable man at the heart of his account in books nine and ten of *The Prelude* of 'Residence in France and French Revolution'. Beaupuy gave him his political education:

> oft in solitude
> With him did I discourse about the end
> Of civil government, and its wisest forms,
> Of ancient prejudice, and charter'd rights,
> Allegiance, faith, and laws by time matured,
> Custom and habit, novelty and change.[4]

Wordsworth turned one of their roadside encounters into the most politically charged of his spots of time, in which Beaupuy gives him a lesson on the need to eradicate poverty and inequality:

> And when we chanced
> One day to meet a hunger-bitten girl
> Who crept along, fitting her languid self
> Unto a heifer's motion − by a cord
> Tied to her arm, and picking thus from the lane
> Its sustenance, while the girl with her two hands
> Was busy knitting in a heartless mood
> Of solitude − and at the sight my friend
> In agitation said, ''Tis against that

Which we are fighting,' I with him believed
Devoutly that a spirit was abroad
Which could not be withstood, that poverty,
At least like this, would in a little time
Be found no more, that we should see the earth
Unthwarted in her wish to recompense
The industrious, and the lowly child of toil,
All institutes for ever blotted out
That legalized exclusion, empty pomp
Abolished, sensual state and cruel power,
Whether by edict of the one or few –
And finally, as sum and crown of all,
Should see the people having a strong hand
In making their own laws, whence better days
To all mankind.[5]

As she slowly walks, barefoot, knitting a garment to protect against the weather, the ill-fed girl seems the very embodiment of the inequality of society.

The word 'agitation', which Wordsworth chooses to evoke Beaupuy's response, meant far more than it does today: it suggests a sensitivity in the nervous system, a strength of 'sensibility', an activation of the spirit of philosophic sympathy. Dr Samuel Johnson's definition of 'agitation' was 'violent motion of the mind; perturbation; disturbance of the thoughts', but Wordsworth was more influenced by the philosopher David Hartley, the man honoured in Coleridge's naming of his first son, who proposed that sensation or feeling was the result of 'vibration' or 'agitation' in the particles of the nervous system. In this, Hartley was a pioneer of the idea that there is an integral relationship between psychic and physiological states, a key Wordsworthian tenet. Joseph Priestley, Hartley's most influential expositor, argued that the degree of nervous 'agitation' determines the strength of a feeling and the force of a memory in the mind. The theory of nervous 'agitation' was accepted even by those who argued more generally against Hartley's philosophy of 'the association of ideas'. Thus Joseph Berington: 'That many of our affections follow mechanically the nervous agitation, is not at all to be doubted. Such are, in the first place, all *sensations*.'[6] Wordsworth's was indeed an age of *sensation* in every sense of the word.

At the same time, 'agitation' was suggestive of social unrest, revolutionary sentiment. Wordsworth's language of sensation allied him to radical new ideas in both philosophy and politics. The act of feeling on behalf of the hunger-bitten girl was the first step towards an acknowledgment of her human rights and thence to a revolution in the social relations that constrained both France and Britain. In mingling the language of democratic politics with that of strong feeling, Wordsworth was channelling the spirit of Jean-Jacques Rousseau via Michel Beaupuy, yoking the cult of sensibility embodied in *La nouvelle Héloïse* to the revolutionary clarion call of Rousseau's *Social Contract*, with its idea that government should be based not on the inherited authority of the few but on the 'general will' of the people.

In the version of *The Prelude* completed in 1805, Wordsworth moved directly from the memory of the girl with the heifer to a story in the spirit of *La nouvelle Héloïse* that, he claimed, he had heard from Beaupuy 'And others who had borne a part therein'.[7] It was a Romeo and Juliet tale of lovers called Vaudracour and Julia, facing parental resistance to their affair because the young man's father was an aristocrat, the girl from the middle class. In the context of this social and familial gulf, the girl's name would appear to be a nod to both Rousseau's heroine and Shakespeare's. But the distinctive thing about this story is that she bears Vaudracour an illegitimate child.

Wordsworth subsequently removed the story from *The Prelude* and published it as an independent poem. In the notes on the origins of his poems that he dictated to his friend Isabella Fenwick in his final decade, he said that it was 'Faithfully narrated, though with the omission of many pathetic circumstances, from the mouth of a French Lady, who had been an eye and ear-witness of all that was done and said.' He added that 'Many long years after, I was told that Dupligne [the origin of Vaudracour] was then a monk in the Convent of La Trappe.'[8] All this was an attempt to remove any suspicion that the story might have had an autobiographical resonance. But it did. His relationship with Annette Vallon was so important to his life that he felt compelled to write about it in his poetic autobiography. He could not, however, openly admit to it in print. During the Victorian era, to have done so would have been ruinous to his reputation for probity and moral seriousness. More than half a century passed after his death before anyone outside the circle of his immediate family and friends would come to know that, during the year in the Loire when he was talking politics with Beaupuy, his relationship with Annette Vallon grew into a fully-fledged affair.

On 15 December 1792, a child, born that same day, was baptised in the cathedral church of Sainte-Croix in Orleans. Paul Vallon stood as godfather and Madame Dufour as godmother. The father was absent. Before leaving the city, he had given legal power to Monsieur Dufour to stand as his proxy. The clerk filled in the register: 'Anne Caroline Wordswodsth [*sic*], daughter of Williams Wordswodsth, Anglois, and of Marie Anne Vallon.'[9] Just two weeks before the ninth anniversary of his father's death, Wordsworth, now twenty-two, had become a father.

No love poem from William to Annette survives, but a passage that he inserted into 'Vaudracour and Julia' when developing it as an independent poem reflects the youthful bliss of their affair, heightened by a sense of illicit excitement but tinged with the sorrowful knowledge that Wordsworth's poverty and his status as an itinerant foreigner meant that they could never marry:

> The vacant city slept; the busy winds,
> That keep no certain intervals of rest,
> Moved not; meanwhile the galaxy displayed
> Her fires, that like mysterious pulses beat
> Aloft; – momentous but uneasy bliss!
> To their full hearts the universe seemed hung
> On that brief meeting's slender filament.[10]

Wordsworth's device of ending a line with the suspense of the word 'hung' creates a pause, as if the lover's heart is missing a beat, while the notion of the entire universe resting on the single thread of a stolen nocturnal encounter brilliantly captures the sense one has when young and in love for the first time that nothing else in the world matters but this moment.

Wordsworth had left the Loire Valley at the end of October. Annette was heavily pregnant and there was no prospect of him getting work locally. Over the summer, word had come from Paris that the revolution was becoming more extreme. The three-year experiment of a constitutional monarchy came to an end with the deposition of the king in August. The Parisian sans-culottes stormed the Palace of the Tuileries and killed about 800 of the royal Swiss guards and domestic staff. Then in early September, after Verdun fell to the counter-revolutionary Prussian invaders, royalists and common prisoners were massacred after peremptory show trials. On 20 September, the revolutionary army effected a reverse, defeating the Prussians at Valmy. The next day a National Convention was opened in Paris and the day after that France was formally declared a republic. The prospect of war with Britain was becoming more likely by the day, with unknown consequences for a young Englishman far from home. The only sensible option was for him to return to England, commence a career and send such funds as he could for the support of his child.

Wordsworth had grown used to goodbyes by this time, what with his parents' deaths, his long separation from Dorothy and the death of his beloved schoolmaster. Yet this would not have diminished the pain of parting from his lover and their unborn child. The impropriety of the liaison was such that he could not write about it directly, but he projected his feelings into the narrative of the separation of Vaudracour from Julia:

> Once again
> The persevering wedge of tyranny
> Achieved their separation: and once more
> Were they united, – to be yet again
> Disparted, pitiable lot! But here
> A portion of the tale may well be left
> In silence, though my memory could add
> Much how the Youth, in scanty space of time,
> Was traversed from without; much, too, of thoughts
> That occupied his days in solitude
> Under privation and restraint; and what,
> Through dark and shapeless fear of things to come,
> And what, through strong compunction for the past,
> He suffered – breaking down in heart and mind![11]

In the story, it is parental 'tyranny' that parts the lovers; in Wordsworth's experience it was the prospect of national and international political tyranny. Poetically, the word 'disparted' is a fine example of his mastery of the negative prefix; biographically,

it is a hint that the passage is informed by his own disappointment, indeed despair, over his parting from Annette and the
knowledge that he might never see his first child. There is a
revealing reticence as part of the story is left 'in silence', then a
tell-tale introduction of the first-person voice ('*my* memory could
add / Much'). The 'fear of things to come', 'strong compunction
for the past', the suffering and the breakdown of 'heart and mind'
are his own.

He also found a way of processing his sorrow at not witnessing
his daughter's early years by having Vaudracour bear his infant
child away and nurse it as a single father:

> His eyes he scarcely took,
> Throughout that journey, from the vehicle
> (Slow-moving ark of all his hopes!) that veiled
> The tender infant: and, at every inn,
> And under every hospitable tree
> At which the bearers halted or reposed,
> Laid him with timid care upon his knees,
> And looked, as mothers ne'er were known to look,
> Upon the nursling which his arms embraced.[12]

This is a fantasy that imagines the impossible circumstance of
him taking the baby with him when he left France. But then
the poem ends in bereavement: 'the precious child . . . by some
mistake / Or indiscretion of the Father, died'. In penance,
Vaudracour becomes a hermit and an elective mute. Not even
'the voice of Freedom' resounding through France can rouse him
back into society. The most psychologically revealing line of the
poem occurs just after the child dies: 'Theirs be the blame who
caused the woe, not mine!'[13] Given that he is allegedly narrating
the story at second hand, there was no need for Wordsworth to

introduce any mention of blame being attached to himself. Clearly, he did blame himself for the reality that from the point of view of his daughter, as she grew into consciousness of family and circumstance, her father might as well have been dead.

Between parting from the pregnant Annette and writing these lines, Wordsworth witnessed Coleridge's paternal care of his son Hartley. And he read his friend's 'Frost at Midnight', one of the most beautiful poems ever written about a father's love for his baby: 'at my side / My cradled infant slumbers peacefully . . . My babe so beautiful! It thrills my heart / With tender gladness thus to look at thee'.[14] Deprived of such moments, Wordsworth compensated by nurturing his imaginary children: his poems.

★

On a beautiful autumn day, he left the vineyards, orchards and meadows of the Loire for the 'fierce metropolis' of Paris.[15] Once again, he ranged through the city, judging the mood of the people, weighing the hope brought by the proclamation of the republic against the fear that followed from the slaughter of the palace guards and the September Massacres. He spoke to fellow English radicals who had witnessed these events. One of them, James Watt, wrote home to his father, the inventor of the steam engine:

> I am filled with involuntary horror at the scenes which pass before me and wish they could have been avoided, but at the same time I allow the absolute necessity of them. In some instances the vengeance of the people has been savage and inhuman. They have dragged the dead naked body of the Princess de Lamballe through the streets and treated it with all sorts of indignities. Her head stuck upon a Pike was carried through Paris and shown to the King and Queen, who are in hourly expectation of the same fate.[16]

In *The Prelude*, Wordsworth elides the two bloody events of August and September as he remembers walking across the vast Place du Carrousel in front of the Tuileries Palace, where the bodies of the Swiss Guard and other victims had been piled up and burned:

> I crossed – a blank and empty area then –
> The Square of the Carousel, few weeks back
> Heaped up with dead and dying, upon these
> And other sights looking as doth a man
> Upon a volume whose contents he knows
> Are memorable but from him locked up,
> Being written in a tongue he cannot read,
> So that he questions the mute leaves with pain,
> And half upbraids their silence.[17]

He was beginning to question his own complicity with the revolution, to upbraid himself. His own loyalties were by now divided: he had shared in Beaupuy's revolutionary fervour, but at the same time he was in love with Annette, whose family were staunch royalists. What would happen to them if Robespierre and the other hardliners tightened their grip not just on Paris, but on the provinces? Was it a harbinger of things to come that, before he had left Orleans, more than fifty political prisoners had been transferred from that city to Versailles, where they were slaughtered in the street by the very same sans-culottes who were responsible for the massacres? That night, he lay awake in his lodgings, feeling 'most deeply' in what a world he now found himself:

> My room was high and lonely, near the roof
> Of a large mansion or hotel, a spot
> That would have pleased me in more quiet times –

Nor was it wholly without pleasure then.
With unextinguished taper I kept watch,
Reading at intervals. The fear gone by
Pressed on me almost like a fear to come.
I thought of those September Massacres,
Divided from me by a little month,
And felt and touched them, a substantial dread.[18]

'A fear to come', so close to the 'dark and shapeless fear of things
to come' in the 'Vaudracour and Julia' sequence, is a sign that
his fears are not only for himself but also for Annette and his
child.

Unable to sleep, he is haunted by a voice of remembrance
and admonishment, conjured out of some combination of recent
experience and 'tragic fictions'. The language has a distinctly
Shakespearean feel, signalled by an allusion to the voice that cries
'sleep no more' to Macbeth, murderer of an anointed king:

'The horse is taught his manage and the wind
'Of heaven wheels round and treads in his own steps,
'Year follows year, the tide returns again,
'Day follows day, all things have second birth;
'The earthquake is not satisfied at once.'
And in such way I wrought upon myself
Until I seem'd to hear a voice that cried
To the whole City, 'Sleep no more.'[19]

Wordsworth can only be comparing himself to Macbeth because
he feels in some sense responsible for the blood that has just
stained the Place du Carrousel, even for the execution of the
French royal family that was soon to follow. Had he not welcomed
the revolution? Having heralded the dawn, he was implicated in

the consequences that were unfolding in the cold light of day. Blood will have blood, as Macbeth says. Wordsworth generalizes the thought into the old sense of the word revolution: 'Course of any thing which returns to the point at which it began to move . . . Rotation; circular motion'.[20] Actions have consequences; once violence begins, a cycle of retribution will follow. Does that mean, Wordsworth wonders, that the pure ideals of liberty, equality and fraternity will never be realized throughout society and that the task of the writer may be to think about individual choice and liberty instead?

He was, of course, writing this passage a decade after the event, circling back in retrospect. And he would revise his account on several occasions in later years, moderating the language of books nine and ten of *The Prelude* in order to distance himself more and more from his youthful self, as the politics of his middle age and later years revolved to conservatism. We will never know whether he really heard an inner voice of admonition during that restless night. In the act of writing, it is his mature self in flight from the young idealist he once was.

During the month that he spent back in Paris, he furthered his acquaintance with the Girondin faction. It is possible that the very house in which he spent that sleepless night belonged to the man to whom Charlotte Smith had introduced him. An edition of Wordsworth's poems published in Paris in 1828 includes an anonymously written introduction, which claimed that he 'was acquainted with many of the leaders of the revolutionary party, and lodged in the same house with Brissot'.[21] Brissot lived in a tall four-storey town house in the Rue Grétry, a few blocks from the Palais Royal, to which Wordsworth remembered walking on the morning after his dark night of the soul, so both the structure and the location of the house make the identification plausible. The older Wordsworth denied that he actually lodged

with Brissot: in his seventieth year he annotated a manuscript
memoir by a writer called Barron Field, in which the claim from
the 1828 Paris edition was repeated: 'There is much mistake here
which I should like to correct in person.' He also crossed out
the phrase about Brissot and wrote 'a mistake' above it in the
manuscript.[22] This may, however, be an obfuscation on the part
of the old Tory, eager to underplay the extent of his involvement
with the revolution.

Whether or not the house was Brissot's, there is no doubt that
at this time Wordsworth supported the Girondins against the
extremist Jacobins. The Palais Royal, just to the north of the
Louvre, was the home of the king's cousin, the Duke of Orleans,
who had come out in favour of the revolution and even changed
his name to the Duc d'Egalité. He had opened the palace grounds
to the public and now it was a place where people thronged to
hear the latest news. When Wordsworth walked round the corner
from his lodgings into the 'Palace Walk of Orleans' on the morning
after his sleepless night, he heard hawkers crying 'Denunciation of
the crimes / Of Maximilian Robespierre'. They were selling copies
of a pamphlet in which the moderate Jean-Baptiste Louvet, a
close associate of Brissot, accused Robespierre of seeking dictator-
ial power. The Prelude gives an account of the circumstances:
Brissot had attacked Robespierre in the Convention and
Robespierre had responded by challenging anyone accusing him
of tyrannical ambition to confront him face to face. 'Whereat',
writes Wordsworth, evoking a moment of vivid theatricality:

> When a dead pause ensued and no one stirred,
> In silence of all present, from his seat
> Louvet walked singly through the avenue
> And took his station in the Tribune, saying
> 'I, Robespierre, accuse thee!'[23]

A pause, a silence, and then a moment of strong emotion: this is the Wordsworthian moment of suspension, as in 'There was a Boy', transposed to the seat of high politics.

Just how close Wordsworth was to the Girondin cause is apparent from the official memoir published by his nephew Christopher Wordsworth shortly after his death. The family of the recently deceased Victorian Laureate was eager to dismiss the young poet's radical phase as a juvenile aberration, but the memoir nevertheless acknowledged that 'If he had remained longer in the French capital, he would, in all probability, have fallen victim among the Brissotins, with whom he was intimately connected, and who were cut off by their rivals, the Jacobins, at the close of the following May.'[24]

In that same district of Paris, on the north bank of the Seine, close to the Palais Royal, there was a narrow street called the Passage des Petits-Pères. This is another possible location for Wordsworth's lodging. It housed both the Hôtel des Etats-Unis and the Hôtel d'Angleterre, also known as White's Hotel. These two lodgings provided the hub for the pro-revolutionary Americans and British who had descended upon Paris. On 18 November 1792, halfway through Wordsworth's sojourn, about a hundred men and women met for a banquet at White's, during which they formed themselves into 'The Society of the Friends of the Rights of Man', celebrating the creation of the republic and the values of liberty, equality and fraternity. Thomas Paine himself, author of *The Rights of Man* and one of the chief architects of both the American and French revolutions, was there. So were Helen Maria Williams; renegade Irish lord, Edward Fitzgerald; radical Welsh philosopher, David Williams; publisher of revolutionary pamphlets, John Hurford Stone; and freethinker John Oswald, who believed that rights should be extended not merely to all men, women and slaves, but even to animals and to nature itself. Fifty of them signed a petition addressed to the National Convention that advocated 'a close union between the French republic and the English, Scotch, and Irish nations, a union which cannot fail to ensure entire Europe the enjoyment of the rights of man and establish on the firmest bases universal peace'.[25] Wordsworth may well have been among those who were present but did not sign.

Another acquaintance he made in Paris at this time was John Stewart, an eccentric figure known as 'Walking Stewart'. His nickname came from the fact that he had walked halfway round the world, from Madras, through Persia, Arabia, Abyssinia, much of North Africa, and every country in Europe as far as Russia. He refused to take carriages because they were both elitist and cruel to horses. He came to believe that there was an impending 'universal empire of revolutionary police terror' that would 'bestialize the human species and desolate the earth'. The police state would ban his books, so he urged readers to translate them into Latin (a precaution against the supposed decay of the English language) and bury them seven feet underground. Their locations would be passed down orally until the dawn of the age of the Stewartian man made their disinterment possible. Despite these bizarre beliefs, Thomas De Quincey, who wrote a wonderful essay about him, said that his political views 'seemed to Mr Wordsworth and myself every way worthy of a philosopher'.[26]

Stewart's philosophy, expounded in books with titles such as *The Apocalypse of Nature* and *The Revelation of Nature*, was a theory of materialism, influenced by Spinoza and Holbach, combined with a distinctive belief in a single universal consciousness, an idea partly inspired by his travels in the East. Spinoza's pantheism, the belief that there is no transcendent or personal deity, that God is to be found in nature, in *things*, was abhorrent to the church. It would fascinate Coleridge. As for Baron d'Holbach, his pseudonymously published anti-religious polemic *The System of Nature*, with its argument that there is 'no necessity to have recourse to supernatural powers to account for the formation of things', underpinned the state-decreed atheism of the French Revolution.[27] The universe, Holbach argued, was nothing more than matter in motion.

Wordsworth learned of Spinoza from Coleridge, but probably never read him; he did not own a copy of Holbach's *System of Nature* until 1805. His acquaintance with Walking Stewart in Paris meant that he didn't need a first-hand knowledge of these influential radical thinkers. In *The Apocalypse of Nature*, Stewart praised Holbach for completing 'the destruction of error' and purging the human mind of prejudice. He made a series of claims that were profoundly formative of Wordsworth's mind. Stewart began with matter and motion. 'MOTION is the force or soul of matter, and cause of all action': hence Wordsworth's conception, expressed in 'Tintern Abbey', of a *motion* that impels all thinking things and all objects of all thought. 'MAN. This machine is formed of particles of matter, organized so as to resemble a corded instrument of music of five strings which correspond with the five senses': this idea chimed with Coleridge's notion, which would soon also influence Wordsworth, of the human mind as an aeolian harp – a stringed instrument played by the wind – trembling into thought. For Stewart, as for Wordsworth, the self and nature are inextricably linked: 'Self, as a part of all Nature, is immortal and universal . . . self pervades all Nature in its revolutions and operations, and self is as much concerned in the present or future health and happiness of all Nature, as the hand is concerned in that of the body.'[28] The further one reads into *The Apocalypse of Nature*, the more deeply one understands that the animated nature of Wordsworth's poems, the insight into 'the life of things' that a few years later he would

be articulating in 'Tintern Abbey', is deeply bound to the philos-
ophies of pantheism and materialism that were at the ideological
heart of the French Revolution.

Wordsworth asserted in *The Prelude* that in the early 1790s his
love of nature gave way to a love of humankind. This was inspired
by Beaupuy and the other radicals whom he met in France, and
whose courage he saluted: 'For great were the auxiliars which
then stood / Upon our side, we who were strong in love', he
wrote in book ten. At the same time, he never renounced his
primary love of nature. At the core of his system of belief there
remained what Walking Stewart at the climax of his *Apocalypse
of Nature* called 'The RELIGION of NATURE', its first tenet
being 'Nature is the great integer of being, or matter and motion,
without beginning as without end.'[29] Nature would always offer
Wordsworth a sense of wholeness and what he called in the same
passage of *The Prelude* a 'pleasant exercise of hope and joy'.
Through that spring and summer in the Loire, inspired by river
and valley, radicalized by Beaupuy, and in love with Annette, he
breathed a vision of hope and joy for both nature and society.
He believed for the while that 'Not favored spots alone, but the
whole earth, / The beauty wore of promise'. He was able to say

> Bliss was it in that dawn to be alive,
> But to be young was very heaven.[30]

STEPPING WESTWARD

He was back in London by Christmas 1792. He told a friend about the 'story he had heard' of the love affair between Vaudracour and Julia. He said that he was thinking of turning it into a novel. Wordsworth the romantic novelist is an intriguing road not taken.

The year 1793 is possibly the most obscure in his life. For much of the time, he lodged with his older brother, the lawyer who certainly did not share his political views. Wordsworth seems to have disappeared into the life of the city. Thanks to *The Prelude* and a number of other poems – if his memory can be trusted – his beliefs are easier to trace than his movements. He arrived amidst a growing movement for the abolition of the slave trade and swiftly came to the conclusion that if the revolution pros-

pered in France, then the spirit of humanitarianism would spread
and bring an end to the vile trade in human flesh. At the same
time, he watched anxiously as the forces of reaction took hold
and his native land moved inexorably towards armed confronta-
tion with the new republic across the Channel.

His first priority was to find a way of supporting his lover
and his child. The prospect of ordination was now ruled out:
he could hardly marry a Roman Catholic Frenchwoman while
being a Church of England minister. Dorothy, who was still in
the north, wrote with the hope that he might find a job as a
tutor, while living with her in a cottage in the English countryside. The plan was shared with Annette. She and William
were keeping in touch with each other by post, though only
two of her letters survive – one to William and one to Dorothy,
whom she had never met but whom she nevertheless repeatedly
calls 'my dear sister', saying that she embraced her with '*tout
mon coeur*' ('all my heart').[1] This was in response to a series of
touching letters, now lost, that Dorothy had sent her. Annette
wrote of how the image of William was never out of her mind,
how she would read his letters alone in her bedroom, almost
believing that he was there with her. Halfway through this long
letter, she digressed into an address to William in which she
dreamed of a reunion and echoed the idea of unity of feeling
that was so central to his vision of happiness:

> When you are surrounded by your sister, your wife, your
> daughter, who will breathe only for you, we will have but
> one feeling, one heart, one soul, and everything will hang
> upon my dear Williams. Our days will flow in tranquillity. I
> will at last enjoy the calm that I cannot feel save when I am
> with you, in telling *out loud* that I love you.[2]

To William himself, she poured out her heart in in a beautiful love letter, linking him to his daughter:

> Come, my love, my husband, receive the tender kisses of your wife, of your daughter. She is so pretty, this poor little one, so pretty that the tenderness I feel for her makes me lose my head whenever she is not in my arms. She resembles you more and more by the day. I believe I'm holding you in my arms. Her little heart often beats against mine; I believe in order to feel that of her father.[3]

★

During his time in France, wandering along the banks of the river Loire and its tributary Loiret, he had been writing *Descriptive Sketches*, the poetic narrative of his Alpine tour with Jones. Having also polished his undergraduate poem *An Evening Walk*, he submitted them both to a publisher called Joseph Johnson.

A literary revolution cannot be made without the work of the book trade, and no publisher did more to foster the new poetry and ideas of the age than Johnson. He was a Unitarian in religion – a brand of Nonconformity that emphasized the gospel of love above the authority of dogma and the hierarchies of the established church. He gathered a circle of radical writers, who met for dinner parties at his house at three o'clock in the afternoon. Among them were the scientist and philosopher Joseph Priestley (whose house in Birmingham was attacked by an angry mob as a result of his revolutionary sympathies), the writer and educationalist Anna Barbauld, the radical couple William Godwin and Mary Wollstonecraft (her writing of the *Vindication of the Rights of Woman* was Johnson's idea), the painter Henry Fuseli and the visionary William Blake. Johnson had a long track record of publishing defences of the American Revolution, Nonconformist polemics, and textbooks for use in the Dissenting Academies that were giving opportunities for education and social mobility to people excluded from the ancient universities of Oxford and Cambridge on the grounds of their refusal to express formal loyalty to the established Church of England. He also had an eye for innovative poetry, having seen into print such influential works as Cowper's *The Task* and a long two-part poem in heroic couplets by Charles Darwin's grandfather Erasmus Darwin. Entitled *The Botanic Garden*, it combined an ingenious versification of the principles of Linnaean botany with praise of scientific innovation and a theory of sexual reproduction as the key to evolution, along with footnotes that mingled natural history and radical politics.

Johnson agreed to publish both Wordsworth's poems. They sold poorly and received only a handful of lukewarm reviews, but they gave Wordsworth the satisfaction of seeing his name on a title page. *An Evening Walk* was furnished with an explanatory subtitle that quietly acknowledged his love for Dorothy: *An Epistle, in Verse. Addressed to a Young Lady, from the Lakes in the North of England. By W. Wordsworth, BA of St John's College Cambridge.* Interviewed late in life about his poetic development, Wordsworth explained that *An Evening Walk* was begun at school, then developed in his Cambridge summer vacations; that the 'young lady' to whom it was dedicated was indeed Dorothy; and that every image in it was based on personal observation as opposed to poetic convention or literary inheritance. He said that even in his seventy-third year he could still vividly remember the time and place where each image was inspired. A shepherd waving his hat to direct his dog to retrieve stray sheep from a cliff: that was on Dunmail Raise, the pass above Grasmere, on the way to Keswick. An oak tree in evening light, the 'darkening boughs' entwined with the 'leaves' in 'stronger lines':

This is feebly and imperfectly exprest; but I recollect distinctly
the very spot where this first struck me. It was in the way
between Hawkshead and Ambleside, and gave me extreme
pleasure. The moment was important in my poetical history;
for I date from it my consciousness of the infinite variety of
natural appearances which had been unnoticed by the poets of
any age or country, so far as I was acquainted with them: and
I made a resolution to supply in some degree the deficiency.
I could not have been at that time above 14 years of age.[4]

It does not matter whether or not the old man's memory was
entirely accurate: the point of the remark is to stress that a
particular *moment* and a minute observation of nature constituted
the wellspring of his poetic art.

Although the language of *An Evening Walk* is confined by the
conventions of eighteenth-century descriptive verse, Wordsworth
was already seeking an unprecedented precision and emotional
engagement in his relationship with his environment. Immediately
after the description of the oak tree, the poem recounts his pleasure
in walking by Esthwaite as a schoolboy and observing the movement of a swan through water: the swelling of the chest, the
backward bend of the neck towards the 'towering wings', the
reflection in the wake making the water resemble 'the varying
arch and moveless form of snow'.[5] With his preternatural power
of memory, he again recalled the source of his inspiration in detail
when interviewed about his poems half a century later:

The description of the swans, that follows, was taken from
the daily opportunities I had of observing their habits, not
as confined to the gentleman's park, but in a state of nature.
There were two pairs of them that divided the lake of
Esthwaite and its in-and-out flowing streams between them,

never trespassing a single yard upon each other's separate domain. They were of the old magnificent species, bearing in beauty and majesty about the same relation to the Thames swan which that does to the goose.[6]

By the time he wrote this, he was an elderly and very proper gentleman himself. His memory of the swans of his boyhood takes him, momentarily, back to 'a state of nature'.

★

A few days after the publication of his poems, England declared war on France. Now he was torn: throughout his youth he had 'with the breeze' played as 'a green leaf on the blessed tree / Of my beloved country', yet now he had to reconcile his pride and joy in the English land with his commitment to Annette, baby Caroline and the values espoused by Beaupuy.[7] He was, however, determined to stay true to his political principles. That January, a pamphlet had appeared with the title *The Wisdom and Goodness of God in having made both Rich and Poor*. Written by a fellow Cumbrian, the Bishop of Llandaff, it consisted of an old sermon along the lines of 'we need the poor so that we can exercise charity', together with a new appendix attacking the French revolutionaries and praising the unwritten English constitution, the legal system and the poor laws. For Wordsworth, it was especially galling that the bishop, Richard Watson, had hitherto been on the liberal wing of the church and had even given a cautious welcome to the revolution in its early years. His politics had now turned as a result of the execution of King Louis XVI. Wordsworth responded with a draft pamphlet of his own, en- titled *A Letter to the Bishop of Llandaff on the Extraordinary Avowal of his Political Principles*. Provocatively, it carried the attribution *By a Republican*.

He argued for universal suffrage and praised the democracy of the Swiss cantons. He attacked hereditary monarchy and nobility as forms of decadence that lead to idleness, gambling and prostitution; he called out poverty as an impediment to stable marriage; he denounced war as an exploitation of the labouring classes who found themselves conscripted and their women left deserted or widowed. He was especially virulent in his assault on the English legal system: 'I congratulate your lordship upon your enthusiastic fondness for the judicial proceedings of this country. I am happy to find that you have passed through life without having your fleece torn from your back in the thorny labyrinth of litigation.' The image of the fleece torn from the back was a particularly appropriate metaphor to include in a verbal assault on a pastor from sheep-farming country. Writing from the bitter experience of the endlessly protracted litigation over the Lowther debt, Wordsworth continued in proto-Dickensian vein, suggesting that, as a member of the House of Lords which served as the ultimate court of appeal, 'your lordship cannot, I presume, be ignorant of the consuming expense of our never-ending process, the verbosity of unintelligible statutes, and the perpetual contrariety in our judicial decisions'.[8] The pamphlet was offered to Johnson but, for all his radical sympathies, he thought that it was too dangerous to publish. Some years later, Johnson took the risk on another polemic – a response to a further outburst from the Bishop of Llandaff – and was imprisoned for his pains. By that time, the government was cracking down ever harder on seditious publication.

A Letter to the Bishop of Llandaff offers the written voice of a Wordsworth who might have had a future as a political journalist. The following year, he did indeed lay out plans for the publication of a monthly magazine to be called *The Philanthropist* – a word associated with radical politics (from the Greek *philein*, to love, *anthropos*, all humankind). He imagined that he might employ correspondents to report on the progress of the revolution, commission biographies of 'eminent men distinguished for their exertion in the cause of liberty', review books that encouraged 'benevolence' (another key word in the radical lexicon), and include features on 'Poetry, Painting and Gardening' that he would contribute himself.[9] The project failed for lack of funds, which was probably good for Wordsworth's safety: his brother Richard, the lawyer, wrote to him with the warning 'I hope you will be cautious in writing or expressing your political Opinions . . . by the suspension of the Habeas Corpus acts the Ministers have great power.'[10]

Though the Llandaff letter reveals Wordsworth as a radical critic of his own government and legal system, his enthusiasm for events in France was brought to an abrupt halt. News was emerging from Paris of the purging of his friends the Girondins, of the nascent Terror under Robespierre and of the sinister Committee of Public Safety. In *The Prelude*, Wordsworth refers explicitly to the imprisonment and execution of Madame Roland, a leading Girondin whose last words on the guillotine were said to have been 'O Liberty, what crimes are committed in thy name.' He voiced his sorrow that the town of Arras, through which he and Jones had passed in the happy early days of Liberty, was now irrevocably associated with Robespierre, who was born there and who now, like Satan in Milton's *Paradise Lost*, 'Wielded the sceptre of the Atheist crew'.[11] At this point in *The Prelude*, Wordsworth jumps forward a year and recalls the moment in the summer of 1794 when, crossing Levens Sands at low tide, he heard the news of Robespierre's fall. Rejoicing, he spurred on his horse, recapturing the spirit of that earlier ride across the treacherous estuary when with his schoolfellows 'Along the margin of the moonlight sea, / We beat with thundering hoofs the level sand'.[12] Though he was glad that 'Authority put on a milder face' after the execution of Robespierre and his crew, he would never again feel the same about France. By the time he came to write up his experiences in *The Prelude*, Napoleon had taken power, with imperial ambition overtaking democratic idealism. In December 1804, ancient privilege and ritual was reasserted as Napoleon called Pius VII from Rome to Paris, and so

> finally to close
> And rivet up the gains of France, a Pope
> Is summoned in to crown an Emperor –
> This last opprobrium, when we see the dog
> Returning to his vomit.[13]

★

Failing to progress in his quest for a career, Wordsworth had no reason to refuse an invitation from a well-to-do schoolfriend, William Calvert, to go on a summer walking tour in the West Country. They spent several weeks on the Isle of Wight, which was becoming popular for its mild climate and sea air. From there, they witnessed the English fleet at Spithead, getting ready to go to war, creating more conflicted feelings in Wordsworth. On leaving the island, their gig (a speedy little two-person one-horse carriage known as a 'whiskey') was broken by the horse that was pulling it. Calvert rode off to get help and Wordsworth was left to wander alone on Salisbury Plain, a place rich in English historical lore. During this peregrination, he took a siesta at Stonehenge. It was a time of mental disturbance and strange visions, which he would turn to poetry. Stonehenge was associated at the time with (unfounded) beliefs about the ancient Druids and the practice of human sacrifice. In his state of disorientation, Wordsworth dreamed of victims being burned alive in a Wicker Man, perhaps a displacement of the image of his friends the Girondins being sent to the guillotine.

Seeking the anchor of friendship, he headed north in order to see Jones in North Wales again. This involved a long walk up the beautiful river Wye, its meandering course and wooded banks reminding him of the Loire, and inevitably of Annette. He passed through the ruins of Tintern Abbey and he began to talk to people who would give him seed corn for later poems: a little girl in a churchyard at Goodrich Castle who challenged his sense of the border between life and death, a 'wild rover' who walked with him to Hay-on-Wye and gave him an image for the 'countenance, gait and figure' of the hawker he would call Peter Bell.[14]

There is some uncertainty as to what happened next. In late 1793 and for the whole of 1794, he lived an itinerant life in the north-west of England, moving between family and friends in Whitehaven on the coast, Halifax in Yorkshire, where Dorothy had been brought up, and Windy Brow, a house with a spectacular setting in the Vale of Keswick, where he was inspired to develop his nature poetry. But there are some tantalizing fragments of evidence that he didn't go there straight from Jones's comfortable home Plas-yn-Llan.

Late in Wordsworth's life, he received a visit from the writer Thomas Carlyle, who recorded that 'He had been in France in the earlier or secondary stage of the revolution; had witnessed the struggles of *Girondins* and *Mountain*'. The latter were the Girondins' extremist opponents, led by Danton and Robespierre, with the Parisian sans-culottes as their foot soldiers. They were sometimes known as Jacobins and sometimes as La Montagne (or the Montagnards) because they sat on the highest benches in the National Convention. This reminiscence would at first sight seem to be a reference to Wordsworth's sojourn in Paris in

November 1792. But it was only with the trial of King Louis XVI the following month and his execution in January 1793 that the Mountain really formed into a coherent group and dedicated themselves to the downfall of the Girondins.

The next detail that Carlyle recalled from his conversation is startling. He reported that Wordsworth witnessed 'in particular the execution of Gorsas, "the first *Deputy* sent to the Scaffold"'. Carlyle added that Wordsworth 'testified strongly to the ominous feeling which that event produced in everybody, and of which he himself still seemed to retain something: "Where will it *end*, when you have set an example in *this* kind?"'[15] Jean-Antoine Gorsas was a leading anti-monarchical journalist. When elected to the National Assembly he initially sat with the Mountain, but he was a close associate of Brissot and Madame Roland. In the debate about what to do with the king, he voted for detention and eventual banishment, not execution. Thereafter, he became a firm Girondin. In March 1793, his printing shop was ransacked after he published a denunciation of the leading Jacobin, Jean-Paul Marat. That summer, as the Girondins were removed from power, Gorsas escaped to the provinces, but he returned to Paris in the autumn. He was arrested, and guillotined on 7 October 1793.

Carlyle had undertaken extensive research for his voluminous history of the French Revolution. He was absolutely correct that Gorsas was the first deputy to be sent to the scaffold. More than twenty of the leading Girondin deputies were placed under house arrest in the summer of 1793 – the assassination of Marat by Charlotte Corday on 13 July gave the Jacobins a further excuse to tighten their control of the city – but it was not until late October that they were brought before the Revolutionary Tribunal and summarily guillotined. Carlyle failed to find any other reference to a public outcry in Paris, let alone England, following the execution of Gorsas, so he could only assume that Wordsworth had indeed been present as a witness.

There can be no doubt about Wordsworth's acquaintance with Gorsas. In his copy of volume seven of the collected works of Edmund Burke, he noticed a reference to Gorsas. He put a cross beside the name and wrote in the margin 'I knew this man. W. W.'[16] Unless there was indeed some confusion of memory, one can only infer that – perhaps after opening his heart to Jones – Wordsworth made a rash decision to return to France, presumably in the hope of seeing Annette and baby Caroline. He would have arrived in Paris at the worst possible time, as the Girondins were about to undergo their show trials. The previous year, Wordsworth had seriously considered offering his services as a journalist on their behalf. Now one of their leading journalists, a man he knew, was on the guillotine. To have witnessed the sharp edge of the guillotine coming down on the neck of a friend and political mentor, in front of a baying crowd in the great open square that is now Place de la Concorde, at the height of the Terror instigated by the Committee of Public Safety under Robespierre: this is hardly an event to invent or misremember.

The thought that it could have been Wordsworth himself on the scaffold is suggested by a passage in *The Prelude* in which he imagines 'ghastly visions' of despair

> And tyranny and implements of death,
> And long orations which in dreams I pleaded
> Before unjust Tribunals.[17]

There is circumstantial evidence that an 'old republican' Irishman called Thomas Bailie told him that he needed to leave the country immediately, causing him to 'decamp with great precipitation'.[18] Any hope of a return visit to the Loire would have been aborted.

A week after the execution of Gorsas, the authorities started rounding up Englishmen resident in Paris and imprisoning them. By the end of the month, Queen Marie Antoinette had gone to the guillotine, as had Brissot, Madame Roland and dozens of other Girondins. Whether Wordsworth witnessed the guillotine in action at first hand, as Carlyle believed he did, or whether he heard of the Terror through report, these events were at the core of the spiritual and political crisis that he went through in his mid-twenties.

★

In the first half of 1795, we find him in London, mixing with a group of leading political radicals, most notably the philosopher and novelist William Godwin, who would soon enter into a partnership of love and philosophy with the feminist Mary Wollstonecraft.

Edmund Burke had sparked the great debate on how Britain should react to the French Revolution in the autumn of 1790. His *Reflections on the Revolution in France* was published two weeks after Helen Maria Williams' *Letters written in France*, when Wordsworth was back in Cambridge after his Alpine walking tour. Burke described the uprising of the French people as 'the most astonishing that has hitherto happened in the world'.[19] As well as arguing eloquently for the importance of tradition and evolution in society, as opposed to innovation and revolution, he plucked at the strings of sensibility by painting an unforgettable picture of Marie Antoinette:

> It is now sixteen or seventeen years since I saw the queen of France, then the dauphiness, at Versailles; and surely never lighted on this orb, which she hardly seemed to touch, a more delightful vision. I saw her just above the horizon,

decorating and cheering the elevated sphere she just began to move in, – glittering like the morning-star, full of life, and splendour, and joy. Oh! what a revolution! and what a heart must I have to contemplate without emotion that elevation and that fall! . . . little did I dream that I should have lived to see such disasters fallen upon her in a nation of gallant men, in a nation of men of honour, and of cavaliers. I thought ten thousand swords must have leaped from their scabbards to avenge even a look that threatened her with insult. But the age of chivalry is gone. That of sophisters, economists, and calculators, has succeeded; and the glory of Europe is extinguished for ever. Never, never more shall we behold that generous loyalty to rank and sex, that proud submission, that dignified obedience, that subordination of the heart, which kept alive, even in servitude itself, the spirit of an exalted freedom.[20]

This provoked Thomas Paine's magnificent riposte in *The Rights of Man*, in which he castigated Burke for his betrayal of the liberal principles that had made him a supporter of the American Revolution back in the 1770s:

He pities the plumage, but forgets the dying bird. Accustomed to kiss the aristocratical hand that hath purloined him from himself, he degenerates into a composition of art, and the genuine soul of nature forsakes him. His hero or his heroine must be a tragedy-victim expiring in show, and not the real prisoner of misery, sliding into death in the silence of a dungeon.[21]

Whether one was a Burkean opponent of the revolution or, like Paine and a dozen other pamphleteers, a defender of it, everyone agreed that Europe was at a watershed moment in history. The Whig politician Charles James Fox described the fall of the Bastille as the greatest event that had ever happened in the world and much the best.

For the more intellectual among the English supporters of the revolution, a book as important as Paine's *Rights of Man* was William Godwin's *Enquiry concerning Political Justice*, published in the spring of 1793, shortly after the guillotining of the French king and England's declaration of war with France. It provided a philosophical basis for pro-revolutionary sentiment by, in Wordsworth's paraphrasing of the book's central ideas, 'abstract[ing] the hopes of man / Out of his feelings'. Godwin argued that human beings tend to base their actions on their feelings rather than on reason. Rational thinking can, however, enable us to weigh up the consequences of different feelings and thus to regulate our actions for the good of society. All through history, the strong have dominated over the weak. Laws do not derive from God or nature or the wisdom of our ancestors; rather, they are the product of the passions, fears and ambitions of the powerful. Nevertheless, humankind has an innate goodness, as witnessed by our sensibilities, our capacity for empathy. A rational society would accordingly shake off 'The accidents of nature, time, and place, / That make up the weak being of the past' — that is to say, the hierarchies of monarchy and rank, the constraints of government, law and property, the conformities of education and marriage — and achieve 'social freedom' on the sole basis of 'The freedom of the individual mind'.[22] *Political Justice* was, in essence, a sophisticated manifesto for philosophical anarchy, the freedom of the individual to make their own laws instead of submitting to inherited authority, providing always that they do not harm others.

For a time, Wordsworth was seduced by this attempt to 'Build social upon personal Liberty', but he soon came to see that the theory could all too easily become a justification for selfishness and even manipulative power play.[23] Between autumn 1796 and spring 1797, reflecting on both Godwinian theory and the progress of the revolution in France, he wrote his only play, *The Borderers*. He knew that a successful verse drama staged at Drury Lane or Covent Garden would net far more money than a volume of poetry ever could. Shakespeare was all the rage, and many writers tried their hand at neo-Shakespearean blank-verse tragedies or history plays, usually with scant success but just occasionally creating a huge hit. Wordsworth decided to set his drama in the age of King Henry III. The barons had achieved a degree of *liberté* and *fraternité* with the signing of Magna Carta in the previous reign, that of Henry's father King John. But now the country was descending into lawlessness, especially along the Scottish border. Wordsworth saw the analogy with contemporary France – first the limitation of monarchical abso-lutism, but then a chaos of faction and violence. He created a compelling villain called Rivers who is partly an Iago figure, tempting the noble outlaw Mortimer into crime, but also in his rhetorical powers of persuasion and lack of remorse for his ruthlessness a figure analogous to Wordsworth's conception of Robespierre, that man of 'great bad actions'.[24] The Robespierre-like Rivers frames his arguments precisely in the manner of Godwin's *Political Justice*, rejecting the old morality of church and state, which he calls 'tyranny', in favour of what Wordsworth in the Godwinian section of *The Prelude* calls

> The freedom of the individual mind,
> Which, to the blind restraint of general laws
> Superior, magisterially adopts
> One guide – the light of circumstances, flashed
> Upon an independent intellect.[25]

The language in the play is almost identical:

> You have taught mankind to seek the measure of justice
> By diving for it into their own bosoms.
> To day you have thrown off a tyranny
> That lives but by the torpid acquiescence
> Of our emasculated souls, the tyranny
> Of moralists and saints and lawgivers.
> You have obeyed the only law that wisdom
> Can ever recognize – the immediate law
> Flashed from the light of circumstances
> Upon an independent intellect.[26]

Wordsworth wrote a prefatory essay explaining that his intention in creating the character of Rivers was to represent 'a young Man of great intellectual powers, yet without any solid principles of *benevolence*' (my italics – the term was Godwin's criterion for moral worth). 'He has deeply imbibed a spirit of enterprize in a tumultuous age. He goes into the world and is betrayed into a great crime.'[27] Rivers is, in short, a Romantic idealist breaking bad. By the time Wordsworth wrote the play, he and Coleridge had become close collaborators. Their shared interest in characters 'betrayed into a great crime' would be one of the wellsprings of 'The Ancient Mariner'.

Richard Brinsley Sheridan, the manager of Drury Lane theatre, expressed some interest in looking at a play by Wordsworth, but *The Borderers* was never staged. In later years, Wordsworth said, a touch disingenuously, that it had always been intended as a 'closet drama', to be read and not seen. Late in life, he revised it for publication, changing the names of the characters. Rivers becomes Oswald, which happens to have been the name of one of the English Jacobins active at White's Hotel in Paris. The link was probably not conscious, but it is a sign that the play was written out of Wordsworth's disillusionment with the turn of the revolution from idealism to violence. He was explicit about this in a note appended to the published text of 1842:

> The study of human nature suggests this awful truth, that, as in the trials to which life subjects us, sin and crime are apt to start from their very opposite qualities, so are there no limits to the hardening of the heart, and the perversion of the understanding to which they may carry their slaves. During my long residence in France, while the Revolution was rapidly advancing to its extreme of wickedness, I had frequent opportunities of being an eyewitness of this process, and it was while that knowledge was fresh upon my memory, that the Tragedy of 'The Borderers' was composed.[28]

As well as reflecting Wordsworth's evolving political beliefs, *The Borderers* played an important role in the development of his poetic art. *An Evening Walk* and *Descriptive Sketches* had been written in the conventional rhyming couplets of eighteenth-century descriptive poetry, but in *The Borderers* he created a supple, at times genuinely Shakespearean, blank-verse style that at its best gave the impression of catching a thought on the wing:

> Action is transitory, a step, a blow –
> The motion of a muscle – this way or that –
> 'Tis done – and in the after vacancy
> We wonder at ourselves like men betray'd.
> Suffering is permanent, obscure and dark,
> And has the nature of infinity.[29]

★

Wordsworth's itinerant life was changed by two strokes of fortune. At Windy Brow near Keswick during 1794, he spent many months nursing the dying Raisley Calvert, brother of the school-friend who had invited him to the West Country and from whom he had become separated on Salisbury Plain. Though it was a sorrowful task, his kindness brought him a reward in the form of a legacy, paid at £70 a year, that would eventually amount to the substantial sum of £900 (the equivalent of about £120,000 today).

He then returned to London. This time, instead of lodging with his brother, he stayed with another lawyer, Basil Montagu, who was living in chambers while studying for the bar. Montagu was a Cambridge contemporary, a clever young man with a difficult background: he was the son of the fourth Earl of Sandwich (the man who allegedly invented the sandwich, in the form of a piece of salt beef between two slices of toasted bread) and his mistress, Martha Ray, a famous singer who was shot dead on the steps of Covent Garden Theatre by her stalker, a vicar called James Hackman. While still a student, Basil had married against his father's will. His young wife had died and he was left as a single father, bringing up their little boy. Also called Basil, the child was four when Wordsworth befriended Basil senior. A plan was hatched for the benefit of all parties: Wordsworth would take his sister Dorothy away from the round of relatives between whom she had been passed for so many years and they would bring up little Basil in the countryside, leaving his father with his melancholy and his legal studies. The boy was actually called Basil Caroline Montagu (in honour of his late mother's name), and at some level he would serve for Wordsworth as a substitute for his own daughter Caroline while she was trapped in France – as Dorothy would serve as a substitute for Annette.

Montagu had some pupils in the law called John and Azariah

Pinney, brothers whose father was a Bristol merchant who had made a fortune from his sugar plantation on the island of Nevis. If one may judge from a letter Pinney senior once wrote to his new manager in the West Indies, he was one of the slightly less harsh slave-owners: 'I hope it is unnecessary to recommend to you a mild (not cruel) treatment of my Negroes and more especially so at the time of their Sickness, a merciful Man is so, even to his Beast.'[30] Nevertheless, he had no compunction about the money he made from the trade in human flesh. He lived in a grand house in the slave port of Bristol, but also owned a country place in Dorset, which he rarely used. His sons proposed this as a home for Wordsworth, Dorothy and little Basil. They did not tell their father that they were offering it rent-free. The offer of a home was another piece of good luck for Wordsworth.

While waiting for Dorothy to come south, he stayed with old Mr Pinney in Bristol. It was at this time that he met Samuel Taylor Coleridge. They had overlapped at Cambridge, but not known each other. Coleridge was in Bristol trying to raise funds to buy a ship to take him and fellow poet Robert Southey to America, where they proposed to establish a utopian commune on the banks of the Susquehanna river, taking with them a pair of sisters, the Fricker girls. Southey had married Edith and Coleridge was about to marry Sara. Their name for the scheme, 'Pantisocracy', meant 'government by all'. They also vowed to practise 'Aspheterism': property held in common. But now Southey was getting cold feet. Coleridge, meanwhile, was also delivering a series of political lectures, including one advocating the abolition of the slave trade. Abolition would not have been good news for Mr Pinney, but it did not stop Wordsworth from getting into occasional conversation with his fellow aspiring writer. He also met Southey, along with Joseph Cottle, who published both authors.

Dorothy arrived in late September 1795 and for the next two years she and William lived with little Basil Montagu at Racedown Lodge, Pinney's spacious country retreat on the road from Crewkerne in Somerset to Lyme Regis in Dorset. About fifty miles from Bristol, the house sat on high ground facing westward, just below Pilsdon Pen, the highest hill in Dorset. For the first time since the death of their mother seventeen years before, brother and sister had the opportunity to live a settled existence. For Dorothy, this was the fulfilment of a long-held dream of a rural life with her brother. Over the previous years, she had poured out her heart to her friend Jane Pollard. On a warm July evening she strolled into a neighbouring meadow and listened to the birdsong. The only imperfection in her pleasure was the absence of her friend and her 'dear William'. She compensated by conjuring the two of them into imaginary presence:

> I hear *you* point out a spot where, if we could erect a little cottage and call it *our own* we should be the happiest of human beings. I see my Brother fired with the idea of leading his sister to such a retreat . . . our parlour is in a moment furnished; our garden is adorned by magic; the roses and honeysuckles spring at our command; the wood behind the house lifts at once its head, and furnishes us with a winter's shelter, and a summer's noonday shade.[31]

The same letter conveys the depth of her affection for her brother:

> You must forgive me for talking so much of him . . . I am willing to allow that half the virtues with which I fancy him endowed are the creation of my Love, but surely I may be excused! He was never tired of comforting his sister, he never

left her in anger, he always met her with joy, he preferred her society to every other pleasure, or rather when we were so happy as to be within each other's reach he had no pleasure when we were compelled to be divided.[32]

This was *fraternité* on the profoundest personal level. Dorothy was a woman, to use the jargon of the time, of exceptional 'sensibility', with extraordinary facility in what she called 'the language of the heart'.[33] She longed for intense companionship after the many years when she was isolated from her siblings because of her exile to Yorkshire after their mother's death. Her long epistles to Jane Pollard read like love letters in which there is equal feeling for her brother and her friend:

> I entreat you my love to think of me perpetually, to think of what will be our felicity when we are again united if we meet with health and strength equal to our vivacity and youthful ardour of mind, think of our moonlight walks attended by my own dear William, think of our morning rambles when we shall − after having passed the night together and talked over the pleasures of the preceding evening, steal from our lodging-room, perhaps before William rises, and walk alone enjoying all the sweets of female friendship. Think of our mornings, we will work, William shall read to us . . . I have nothing to recommend me to your regard but a warm honest and affectionate heart, a heart that will be for ever united to yours by the tenderest friendship, that will sympathize in all your feelings and palpitate with rapture when I once more throw myself into your arms.[34]

She is longing for the kind of vivacious and youthful (physical, but not actively sexual) *ménage à trois* that she and William would eventually inhabit, though it would be with Coleridge rather than Jane Pollard as the third party.

Soon after her arrival at Racedown, Dorothy, writing with her acute eye for detail, described their idyllic existence to another friend:

> I have been making Basil coloured frocks, shirts, slips, etc. . . . We walk about two hours every morning – we have many very pleasant walks about us and what is a great advantage, the roads are of a sandy kind and are almost always dry. We can see the sea 150 or 200 yards from the door . . . We have hills which seen from a distance almost take the character of mountains, some cultivated nearly to their summits, others in their wild state covered with furze and broom. These delight me the most as they remind me of our native wilds. Our common parlour is the prettiest little room that can be; with very good furniture, a large book[case?] on each side the fire, a marble chimney piece, bath stove, and an oil cloth for the floor.[35]

For her brother, a home in the country, the presence of his sister, the novelty of a foster child and the prospect of a legacy provided the security he needed for his writing to flourish.

During his 'lonesome journey' north to Jones in the summer of 1793, he had conceived and begun a poem set on Salisbury Plain. Dorothy had copied it into a notebook during their residence at Windy Brow the following year. In the peaceful setting of Racedown he expanded and polished it until it was ready to send to Joseph Cottle in Bath, who had offered to look at Wordsworth's work. 'Salisbury Plain' was a long poem in rhymed stanzas of nine lines each, with an extra poetic foot in each concluding line, a form that had been invented in Shakespeare's time by Edmund Spenser for his epic *The Faerie Queene*. The Spenserian stanza was a popular medium for narrative verse in the eighteenth century; James Beattie had used the form for *The Minstrel*, that poem which so impressed the schoolboy in Hawkshead.

This was Wordsworth's first foray into extended narrative. As originally drafted, the poem begins with a traveller wandering – as he had done himself – in the bleak landscape of Salisbury Plain. He rests for the night in a derelict house, where he encounters a female vagrant, also taking shelter there, who tells her story of being widowed after losing her husband and children in war overseas. Her descent into beggary leads Wordsworth to expostulate against oppression and tyranny. In revising the poem at Racedown, he built up the character of the male traveller: now it is a pressganged sailor who, returning from the war, robs and kills a man on the road. The two vagrants stick together, but then encounter a distraught woman whose child has been beaten by his father. The Sailor turns over the child, who is lying on the ground. Looking at the injury, he sees a 'Strange repetition of the deadly wound / He had himself inflicted' on the man on the road. This moves him to tears and tenderness, which duly reconcile the violent father to his wife and child. The Sailor and the Female Vagrant walk on and then encounter a dying woman in a cart. She tells her story: of how her husband was away in the navy, leaving her with her young children, and how she had grown scared because a murder was committed near their house, and there had been a rumour that it had been committed by her husband on his return to the neighbourhood, but that could not possibly have been the case because 'My husband's loving kindness stood between / Me and all worldly harms and wrongs however keen'.[36] The Sailor realizes that it is his own wife and asks her forgiveness as she expires. Penitent, he turns himself in and is hanged in chains. The conclusion to be derived from the story is that poverty and war turn men from benevolence to violence.

Wordsworth took the bold step of sending the poem, via the Pinney brothers, to his new acquaintance Coleridge, in order to get his opinion of it. He hoped that this might lead to Coleridge putting in a good word on his behalf with publisher Cottle. John Pinney told Wordsworth that Coleridge had read it carefully, interleaving the manuscript with blank sheets of paper on which he would write down editorial comments and advice. When they next met, Wordsworth read the poem aloud. Coleridge would long remember the 'sudden effect' it produced on his mind, the sense that here was a 'union of deep feeling with profound thought' that marked a new beginning in English poetry.[37]

Cottle, however, declined to publish 'Salisbury Plain', though he acknowledged its promise and offered to look at some other poems. Wordsworth would extract the story of 'The Female Vagrant' and include it in *Lyrical Ballads*, while the rest of the poem languished in manuscript until 1842, when the whole thing was published, with further revisions, under the title 'Guilt and Sorrow'. Though the language is uneven and there are still many traces of the overwrought 'Gothic' Wordsworth, the writing and rewriting of 'Salisbury Plain' made him see that he was well suited to the poetry of roadside encounters and narratives told from the point of view of the rural poor. Still at Racedown, he returned to this vein in 'The Old Cumberland Beggar', a protest against the practice of confining vagrants to the poorhouse. The poet's argument is that the aged mendicant has so little that he should at least be granted the dignity of spending his last days in the freedom of the open air: 'As in the eye of Nature he has liv'd, / So in the eye of Nature let him die'.[38]

In the spring of 1797, on completing *The Borderers*, Wordsworth began a new poem exploring the effect of poverty on women. The following year, he would expand it and give it the working title 'The Ruined Cottage'. It would not be published until 1814, when it provided the opening narrative of his epic philosophical poem *The Excursion*. Coleridge always wished that it had been published independently, because it would have formed 'one of the most beautiful poems in the language'.[39] This was the work in which Wordsworth truly found his narrative voice: he took the blank-verse style of *The Borderers* and combined it with a story in a similar vein to that of 'Salisbury Plain'. The protagonist, Margaret, is a woman whose husband enlists in the war against France in order to receive a militiaman's bounty of ten guineas to support his family in a time of bad harvests and rising bread prices. She ekes out a living, waits on her doorstep for news of her husband, and as she decays so does her cottage. At the end she dies, 'Last human tenant of these ruined walls'.[40] Wordsworth was developing his art of what the Victorian sage John Ruskin would call the 'pathetic fallacy': matching the mood of an environment to the emotions of its observer or inhabitant.[41] For Wordsworth, this was not a fault but the essence of the poet's art of sympathy with both the poor and the natural world. Poetry 'proceeds', he wrote, 'from the soul of Man, communicating its creative energies to the images of the external world'; objects 'derive their influence not from properties inherent in them, not from what they are actually in themselves, but from such as are bestowed upon them by the minds of those who are conversant with or affected by those objects'.[42]

Wordsworth worked and reworked his lines, seeking a matter-of-fact style in which there is little drama but profound emotion created out of apparently inconsequential details: a swallow's nest that has dropped to the ground with the crumbling of the smoke-stained chimney stack of the cottage, the dull clanking of a horseshoe mingling with 'the heavy sound / Of falling rain', the dampness of Margaret's clothes even as she sits by her fireside.[43] With Dorothy to encourage him, Wordsworth was forging a new poetry of the human heart. Infused with the rural calm, walking and standing by secluded rivers or on the gentle rolling hills of Dorset, he began thinking back to his childhood environment in the north and sketching out poetic fragments in a new and highly personal voice:

> and yet once again,
> Standing beneath these elms, I hear thy voice,
> Beloved Derwent, that peculiar voice
> Heard in the stillness of the evening air,
> Half-heard and half-created.[44]

His native river and his beloved sister are as one, inspiring him to what in 'Tintern Abbey' he would call 'tranquil restoration'. Listening, half remembering and half creating, he is on the road to 'the poem on my own life'.

A NEW SPIRIT IN POETRY

On an early June afternoon in 1797, Samuel Taylor Coleridge came down the road to Racedown Lodge from Crewkerne, crossing the county line from Somerset into Dorset. He cut a corner by leaping over a gate and bounding across a field. The gateway is still there, though the gate is now of metal. The field slopes down into the wooded valley. Looking to the right as you make for the handsome, tall square-fronted house of red brick, you see the hill on the far side of the valley and imagine the prospect of walks in the lush pastures and fresh air.

Wordsworth would never forget this moment. The collaboration was about to begin. He immediately read 'The Ruined Cottage' to his new friend. After tea, Coleridge read out two

and a half acts of a play he was working on, called *Osorio*.
Wordsworth responded the next morning with a reading of *The
Borderers*. Coleridge would stay until the end of the month. Half
a century later, his children Sara and Derwent would call this
year of shared creativity the *annus mirabilis*.[1]

Dorothy was delighted with their house guest. She described
him in a letter to her future sister-in-law Mary Hutchinson:

> You had a great loss in not seeing Coleridge. He is a wonderful
> man. His conversation teems with soul, mind, and spirit. Then
> he is so benevolent, so good-tempered and cheerful, and like
> William interests himself so much about every little trifle. At
> first I thought him very plain, that is for about three minutes.
> He is pale and thin, has a wide mouth, thick lips, and not
> very good teeth, longish loose-growing half-curling rough
> black hair. But if you hear him speak for five minutes, you
> think no more of them. His eye is large and full, not dark
> but grey . . . it speaks every emotion of his animated mind.
> It has more of 'the poet's eye in a fine frenzy rolling' than I
> ever witnessed. He has fine dark eyebrows, and an overhanging
> forehead.[2]

They decided that they had to live closer together. In order to
make arrangements, Coleridge returned to the little cottage in
the Somerset village of Nether Stowey that he rented from Tom
Poole, a wealthy tanner by trade, a political radical by inclination,
and a lover of poetry. A few days later, Coleridge was back at
Racedown, ready to bring William and Dorothy to his home.
They travelled over in Tom Poole's one-horse chaise.

Coleridge loved company. 'I shall have six companions', he
had written upon making the move to Nether Stowey at the
beginning of the year. He identified the six as Sara, his wife;

Hartley, his baby; his 'own shaping and disquisitive mind'; his books; his 'beloved friend Thomas Poole'; and 'lastly, Nature looking at me with a thousand looks of beauty, and speaking to me in a thousand melodies of Love'.³ A further companion had arrived in February. Charles Lloyd was the son of a Quaker financier whose family name remains one of the most famous in the history of banking. But he didn't want to go into the business: he wanted to be a poet and philosopher like Coleridge, who had become his mentor. Joseph Cottle of Bristol was about to publish a collection of poems by Coleridge and Charles Lamb, who had been a close friend of Coleridge's since their schooldays at Christ's Hospital. Generously, Coleridge persuaded Cottle to include some of Lloyd's work as well, suggesting that the young man's commercial connections would shift some extra copies. The volume duly appeared in June: *Poems by S. T. Coleridge, Second Edition. To which are now added Poems by Charles Lamb, and Charles Lloyd.* By this time, however, Lloyd had left Nether Stowey, suffering from what Lamb described as an exquisiteness of feeling that bordered on derangement. Coleridge spoke of his protégé's nightmares, somnambulism and '*agoniz'd Delirium*'.⁴ Lloyd would later suffer from severe mental illness and violent hallucinations. He would be confined in a private asylum and, upon arriving on the doorstep of Dove Cottage when it was inhabited by Thomas De Quincey, claim to be the Devil. From Coleridge's point of view, William and Dorothy brought the prospect of far less high-maintenance house guests.

They loved the area: 'There is everything here,' wrote Dorothy to Mary Hutchinson, 'sea, woods wild as fancy ever painted, brooks clear and pebbly as in Cumberland, villages so romantic.' Brother and sister wandered out and found 'a sequestered water-fall in a dell formed by steep hills covered with full-grown timber trees'. The whole place had 'the character of the less grand parts of the neighbourhood of the Lakes'.[5] Walking in the rolling Quantock hills above the village, they spotted a fine house called Alfoxden in the nearby village of Holford. They discovered that it was available to let. Within a week, Wordsworth had signed a one-year lease, and a week after that they moved.

Coleridge's cottage was proving far too small to house them all, especially as Charles Lamb had now come to stay. He was wonderful company: tiny in stature, bow-legged, stammering, warm, witty and able to laugh even at his own history of mental illness. The year before, he had written to Coleridge:

> I know not what suffering scenes you have gone through at Bristol, – my life has been somewhat diversified of late. The six weeks that finished last year and began this your very humble servant spent very agreeably in a mad house at Hoxton – . I am got somewhat rational now, and don't bite any one. But mad I was – and many a vagary my imagination played with me, enough to make a volume if all told.[6]

His visit to Nether Stowey was respite from the trauma of the previous autumn, when, in a fit of madness, his sister Mary had stabbed their mother to death with a kitchen knife during a row about the treatment of a serving girl. Mary was being held in a lunatic asylum, from which she would subsequently be released on condition that Charles watched over her. They became the closest of companions, writing stories together, including their *Tales from Shakespeare*, novelistic retellings of the comedies and tragedies that introduced generations of children to the plays.

It was perhaps due to the sheer number of bodies in the tiny cottage, which can still be visited today, that Sara Coleridge accidentally spilt a skillet of boiling milk on her husband's foot. This confined him to the cottage and its garden, depriving him of walks across the hills in the company of William, Dorothy and Charles. Instead, sitting in a lime-tree bower, he followed them in imagination, flexing his poetic muscles in the easeful conversational style of blank verse that he and Wordsworth would perfect over the ensuing months:

> Well, they are gone, and here must I remain,
> This lime-tree bower my prison! I have lost
> Such beauties and such feelings, as had been
> Most sweet to have remember'd, even when age
> Had dimm'd my eyes to blindness! They, meanwhile,
> My friends, whom I may never meet again,
> On springy heath along the hill-top edge
> Wander in gladness, and wind down, perchance,
> To that still roaring dell, of which I told . . .
>   . . . Now my friends emerge
> Beneath the wide wide Heaven, and view again
> The many-steepled track magnificent
> Of hilly fields and meadows, and the sea
> With some fair bark perhaps which lightly touches
> The slip of smooth clear blue betwixt two isles
> Of purple shadow! Yes! They wander on
> In gladness all.[7]

'Friends' is the key word here. It connoted not only a close bond of love but also the idea of a group of people who took the same side in political debates during times of war and contention. The young Coleridge was in constant search of a community of friends. That had been one of the impulses behind the ill-fated 'Pantisocracy' scheme with Southey. The Lloyd family, meanwhile, were highly prominent members of the 'Society of Friends', otherwise known as the Quakers. 'Friends' at this time inevitably suggested the spirit of Quakerism, which originated during the civil war when the English killed their king. The movement was associated with the American Revolution and the campaign to abolish slavery, and with values of democracy and equal rights. At the same time, it embraced a tradition of 'quietism', suggesting pacifism and retreat from political engagement. In the spiritual realm, Quakers believed that everyone could find an 'inner light' and that God was to be found there, not in the rituals and priestly hierarchies of the established church. Both politically and spiritually, the Friends shared many beliefs and values with that other Nonconformist sect, the Unitarians, who counted Coleridge and Lamb among their number. Wordsworth shared these beliefs and values, too, but held back from joining any kind of dissenting 'church'. While Coleridge preached from Unitarian pulpits, Wordsworth found his faith as he walked in the hills.

The gentle Quantock landscape was evoked by Dorothy in vivid prose in another of her letters to Mary Hutchinson, in which she also described Alfoxden House. It was a large mansion with enough furniture for a dozen families. The parlour that would soon become their favourite room faced a garden that was well stocked with vegetables and fruit. There was a courtyard in front, with a grass plot, gravel walks, shrubs and moss roses in full bloom. The house looked out on a hill covered with trees and ferns, deer and sheep moving among them. They could glimpse the sea – the Bristol Channel – across the countryside of woodland and meadow. They strolled in the nearby woods, listening to the waterfall in the glen, and then they would take off, walking for miles across the smooth-topped hills.[8]

★

Within days of Charles Lamb's departure, another visitor arrived in Nether Stowey. This was John Thelwall, regarded by some in government as the most dangerous man in Britain. He had been a leading figure in the London Corresponding Society, which had welcomed the French Revolution and called for political reform at home. 'Citizen' Thelwall became the public voice of the cause of universal suffrage and the anti-war movement. In 1794, he and two colleagues were charged with the capital offence of high treason. He was imprisoned in the Tower until his trial at the Old Bailey. The event was a public sensation, widely reported and ending in his acquittal – a triumph for both the radical cause and the independence of the judiciary. But he inevitably remained a marked man. His public lectures were targeted by right-wing protesters, causing him to retreat from active politics. He entered into a correspondence with Coleridge after the latter had delivered his political lectures in Bristol. Now he was on a walking tour of the West Country and took the opportunity to call on Coleridge.

When they woke up on the morning after the first night of his stay, they walked over to Alfoxden before breakfast. Coleridge had prepared him for a meeting with 'A very dear friend of mine, who is in my opinion the best poet of the age'. He was convinced that they would get on well because 'this man is a Republican and at least a *Semi*-atheist'.[9] They spent the day with Wordsworth, rambling in the hills, talking poetry, philosophy and politics. Looking out over the beautiful scenery, Coleridge remarked, only half-jokingly, 'Citizen John, this is a fine place to talk treason in.' Thelwall replied. 'Nay, Citizen Samuel, it is rather a place to make a man forget that there is any necessity for treason!'[10] That, at least, is how Coleridge remembered the exchange. Wordsworth recorded it in less inflammatory language. Coleridge: 'This is a place to reconcile one to all the jarrings and conflicts of the wide world.' Thelwall: 'Nay, to make one forget them altogether.'[11] That evening, Thelwall wrote to his wife, waxing lyrical about his day:

> Everything else but my Stella & my Babes are now banished from my mind by the Enchanting retreat (the Academus of Stowey) from which I write this, & by the delightful Society of Coleridge & Wordsworth – the present occupier of Allfox Den. We have been having a delightful ramble today among the plantations & along a wild romantic dell in these grounds thro which a foaming, murmuring, rushing torrent of water winds its long and artless course – There have we sometime sitting on a tree – sometimes wading boot-top deep thro the stream & again stretched on some mossy stone or root of a tree, a literary & political triumvirate passed sentence on the productions and characters of the age – burst forth in poetical flights of enthusiasm – & philosophized our minds into a state of tranquillity which the leaders of nations might envy.[12]

A new 'literary and political triumvirate' was in the making. In the mind's eye of Coleridge, having moved on from the early partnership of 'Coleridge and Southey' to that of 'Coleridge, Lamb and Lloyd', now there was the prospect of 'Coleridge, Wordsworth and Thelwall'.

Gossip spreads quickly in small rural communities – especially in time of war. As Jane Austen wrote in the novel on which she was working this very year, in the villages of England 'every man is surrounded by a neighbourhood of voluntary spies'.[13] A few days after Thelwall's arrival, Tom Poole's cousin recorded in her diary that people in the neighbourhood were shocked to hear that he was in the vicinity. 'Alfoxden house is taken by one of the fraternity', she added, using a term loaded with French revolutionary connotations, 'To what are we coming?'[14] That same Sunday, Wordsworth read his politically charged play *The Borderers* to Thelwall under the trees in the grounds of Alfoxden.

In the evening, he hosted a dinner party for fourteen, including the Coleridges, Thelwall, Tom Poole and various other locals. Helping at table was a man called Thomas Jones who lived in a farm building on the estate. He was taken aback by the turn of the conversation, especially when 'a little Stout Man with dark cropt Hair', distinctively dressed in 'a White Hat and Glasses', stood up after dinner and started loudly declaiming with political passion. Jones became convinced that he was either among French spies or treasonous domestic conspirators. He got in touch with a friend named Charles Mogg, a former employee on the Alfoxden estate.

Mogg had left the area, but returned to investigate. Jones told him that the Wordsworths were French emigrants. They had no respect for the Sabbath, what with the suspicious dinner party and their habit of spending the Lord's day of rest washing and mending clothes instead of going to church. Worse still, Wordsworth didn't have a wife: 'only a woman who passes for his Sister'. An alarmingly bohemian set-up. Sniffing around some more, Mogg was told by a retired huntsman called Christopher Trickie, who lived in the former dog pound at the end of the driveway to Alfoxden, that these new French tenants were wandering around the countryside with notebooks, taking plans of all the houses in the area. They had allegedly asked Trickie whether the brook that ran past the dog pound was navigable down to the Bristol Channel. He had even seen them going out onto the hills at night with 'Camp Stools' and a 'Portfolio in which they enter their observations, which they have been heard to say were almost finished'.[15] The obvious conclusion was that they were making maps and plans, which could be transmitted to France so as to assist an invading army in making their way inland from a beachhead on the Bristol Channel.

This fear of invasion was not entirely fanciful. England had been at war with France for four years. Earlier that year, a French force of about 1,400 men had landed at Fishguard on the Welsh coast, with the intention of marching on Bristol. They surrendered to a small and gallant company of the Pembroke Yeomanry, following a brief encounter that constituted the last battle with a foreign power on British soil. There was at the time no knowing whether the French might make a second attempt.

Mogg decided to take action. He went to Bath and spoke to another former Alfoxden employee, a cook who was now working for a doctor. He told her what he had heard from Jones and Trickie; she told the doctor; the doctor wrote to the Home Secretary. 'These people', he said of the Wordsworths, 'may possibly be under Agents to some principal at Bristol.' The case was passed to a Home Office spy called James Walsh, who had earlier infiltrated Thelwall's public lectures. He relished the prospect of being the agent who might bring Thelwall back into custody, along with his new cronies. But Walsh's investigation did not start well. He began by interviewing the primary informer, but had to report that 'Mr Mogg is by no means the most intelligent Man in the World.'

Walsh was then furnished with cash and instructed to proceed to Alfoxden, 'taking care on your arrival so to conduct yourself as to give no cause of suspicion to the Inhabitants of the Mansion house'. He was told to 'narrowly watch their proceedings, and observe how they coincide with Mogg's account'. He was to gather intelligence such as their names and appearance, and to trail them if they suddenly moved out of the area. Walsh was soon filing reports from the Globe Inn at Stowey. Thelwall had left. The man who had taken the big house was called

Wordsworth, a name known to the security services. The locals had taken to referring to him and his family and friends as 'Rascalls'. These wild tenants of Alfoxden hall were 'not French, but they are people that will do as much harm as all the French can do'. They were 'a mischiefuous gang of disaffected Englishmen . . . a Sett of violent Democrats'. However, in the absence of any firm evidence of treason, Walsh was recalled and no action was taken. The Home Office took the view that without the prize of Thelwall, it wasn't worth leaving an agent in the field.

Walsh's belief that the name of Wordsworth was known in the espionage community might lead one to believe that his activities in revolutionary France back in the early 1790s had been clocked by an informer. That would, however, be to follow a false trail: it seems that the name was known because a cousin of the poet's called Robinson Wordsworth was an exciseman at Harwich on the Essex coast. With the war making Channel crossings impossible, this North Sea port was a key line of communication for the transmission of goods and intelligence to and from the continent, so the local Customs officer was a valuable source of information. A couple of years later, Home Secretary and spymaster the Duke of Portland would authorize a payment to Robinson Wordsworth for assistance in arresting and taking to London two men accused of treason.

Coleridge later made a joke of the appearance of Walsh in the Quantocks: 'A SPY was actually sent down from the government *pour surveillance* of myself and my friend.' He told of the agent's 'three weeks of truly Indian perseverance in tracking us':

He had repeatedly hid himself, he said, for hours together behind a bank at the sea–side (our favorite seat) and overheard our conversation. At first he fancied, that we were aware of our danger; for he often heard me talk of one *Spy Nozy*, which he was inclined to interpret of himself, and of a remarkable feature belonging to him; but he was speedily convinced that it was the name of a man who had made a book and lived long ago. Our talk ran mostly upon books, and we were perpetually desiring each other to look at *this*, and to listen to *that*; but he could not catch a word about politics.[16]

Turning Walsh into a version of Shakespeare's bumbling constable Dogberry, Coleridge imagines him misinterpreting a conversation about the philosophy of Baruch Spinoza as whispers of espionage.

The irony of this is that the Dutch philosopher, though indeed 'a man who had made a book and lived long ago', was arguably a more dangerous figure than Citizen Thelwall. Throughout the eighteenth century, all across Europe, Spinoza was considered to be the chief proponent of a materialist philosophy that denied the received truths of revealed religion, the Bible as divine word and the notion that kings and governments derived their authority from God.[17] In this respect, his ideas were regarded as atheistic and subversive underpinnings of revolutionary thought. Spinoza's phrase *Deus sive Natura* ('God or Nature') was interpreted as meaning that the only God *was* Nature. The terms 'Spinozism' and 'pantheism' were used interchangeably. Coleridge was utterly compelled by Spinoza's sophisticated philosophical vision of the unity of all things and the identity of spirit and nature, even as he wrestled with that vision's incompatibility with his Christian faith. Among his *Poems on Various Subjects*, published as he was forging his friendship with Wordsworth, was a blank-verse meditation called 'Effusion XXXV. Composed August 20th, 1795, at Clevedon, Somerset' (later renamed more economically as 'The Eolian Harp'), in which he asked in pure Spinozistic fashion,

And what if all of animated nature

Be but organic Harps diversely framed,

That tremble into thought, as o'er them sweeps

Plastic and vast, one intellectual Breeze,

At once the Soul of each, and God of all?[18]

The poem then upbraids the thought by imagining Coleridge's beloved (as she was then, though not for much longer) wife Sara reproving him for this 'unhallowed' thought and bidding him 'walk humbly with my God'.

Wordsworth was never as intellectual as Coleridge, never so deeply read in philosophy. But as Coleridge talked to him of Spinoza while they walked and contemplated nature in the Quantocks, he saw the analogy between Spinoza's ideas and his own image of the corresponding breeze that linked the human spirit to nature. As Poet Laureate John Dryden once said of Shakespeare, Wordsworth needed not the spectacles of books to read nature. He found his pantheism in the very landscapes around him. That did not, however, stop politically conservative critics from perceiving his poetry of nature as emanating from the same spirit of Spinozism which was thought to have contributed to the execution of the king and the suppression of the church in France.

From the vantage point of the *Biographia Literaria*, written two decades later when both Coleridge and Wordsworth had settled into political conservatism themselves, Spinoza and the Spy Nozy affair could be brushed off lightly. At the time, Coleridge took it far more seriously. Thelwall had so enjoyed both the Quantock environment and the company of his new friends that he expressed the wish to move there permanently and find a cottage of his own, in which he could retreat from politics into poetry. Coleridge was quick to scotch the plan:

Very great odium T. Poole incurred by bringing *me* here –
my peaceable manners & known attachment to Christianity
had almost worn it away – when Wordsworth came & he
likewise by T. Poole's agency settled here – You cannot
conceive the tumult, calumnies, & apparatus of threatened
persecutions which this event has occasioned round about us.
If *you* too should come, I am afraid, that even riots & dangerous
riots might be the consequence – *either* of us separately would
perhaps be tolerated – but *all three* together – what can it be
less than a plot & damned conspiracy – a school for the
propagation of demagogy & atheism?[19]

A few weeks later, Coleridge helped Tom Poole to draft a letter
to the owner of Alfoxden, who was becoming nervous about
the rumours concerning her new tenant. It said (falsely) that
Thelwall's arrival in the area was a chance call, not a planned
visit; that Wordsworth had merely shown common hospitality;
that he did not know Thelwall and disapproved of his politics;
that he would never wish to cause any trouble in the neighbourhood; and indeed that he had never concerned himself with
politics – a claim that would hardly have stood up if the incendiary *Letter to the Bishop of Llandaff* had ever seen the light of
day.

In *The Prelude*, Wordsworth alluded only obliquely to the
incident. In writing of what he called his 'juvenile errors' during
the time of the French Revolution, he deflected the reader's
attention away from 'Reality too close and too intense', but did
make a brief reference to the gagging acts and treason trials of
Pitt the Younger and his government. He speaks of the 'shepherds' of the state thirsting to turn 'the guardian Crook of Law'
into 'A tool of Murder'. Despite the 'awful proof before their
eyes / That he who would sow death reaps death' – a reference

to Robespierre's Terror, echoing the language of the passage concerning the voice that he imagined hearing in the Parisian night at the time of the September Massacres – the authorities in Britain imitated the perfidious methods of Robespierre and the Committee of Public Safety. 'In their weapons and their warfare base', Wordsworth then writes of the crackdown on domestic dissent,

As vermin working out of reach, they leagued
Their strength perfidiously, to undermine
Justice, and make an end of Liberty.[20]

This is the only time in his entire oeuvre that he uses the word 'vermin'. The image of an invisible rat, combined with those of perfidy and an assault on Justice and Liberty, condemns Pitt's regime of oppressive surveillance. The older, politically conservative Wordsworth removed these lines from his later revision of *The Prelude*. And even in the 1805 text, he created the illusion that he was not personally a victim of the vermin: the following lines read 'But from these bitter truths I must return / To my own History'.

Wordsworth never mentioned Thelwall by name in his poems, but he paid indirect homage to him in a lovely little poem written at Alfoxden some months after his departure from the Quantocks. By that time, having been brushed off by Coleridge, Thelwall and his wife had found a cottage in which to make their rural retreat – in Wordsworth phrase, to 'take refuge from politics'. It was in the village of Llyswen in the Wye Valley on the Welsh border. In Wordsworth's poem, which is called 'Anecdote for Fathers', he has been enjoying a seaside walk with Basil Montagu, aged five. He asks the child if he would rather be at Kilve, a pretty nearby village with a sea view, or far away at Llyswen. To

Wordsworth's surprise, the boy opts for Llyswen. The reason? Basil says that it is because there are no weathercocks in Kilve. The origin of the poem was this very remark from little Basil, though what he pointed to was the large weathercock on Alfoxden House, shining in the sun. The purpose of the poem was to suggest that there is a special kind of wisdom in the innocence, the instinctiveness and the delightful irrationality of a young child's conversation – a theme further developed in Wordsworth's longest poem in *Lyrical Ballads*, 'The Idiot Boy'. The weathercock is displaced from Alfoxden so as to heighten this sense: after all, Basil probably pointed to it because it sat on top of the place that had become his home and made him feel secure. That was not the point of the poem, so the weathercock had to be transported across the Bristol Channel. The choice of Llyswen as the alternative point of reference is an indication that Thelwall's journey from radical politics to rural retreat remained very much on Wordsworth's mind.

Indeed, the case of Thelwall was giving him the idea for the main theme of the long poem that Coleridge was encouraging him to write. In 1793, at the height of his radical activism, Thelwall published a curious book, mostly in prose but with bursts of verse, entitled *The Peripatetic; or, Sketches of the Heart, of Nature and Society; in a Series of Politico-Sentimental Journals, in Verse and Prose of the Eccentric Excursions of Sylvanus Theophrastus*. The 'peripatetics' were the philosophical students of Aristotle, whose school met in a Lyceum with covered walkways. Aristotle was said to walk up and down as he lectured. For Thelwall, as for Wordsworth, walking was conducive to creative thought. The pen name alludes to Theophrastus, a student of Aristotle's who was known as the father of botany: he believed that wisdom could be derived from observation of the natural world. Sylvanus, meanwhile, was the tutelary deity of woods and fields. Reading

Thelwall, and talking to him about his work, Wordsworth would have discovered a kindred spirit. *The Peripatetic* consists of a series of meditations inspired by natural phenomena (a skylark, a night-scape) and encounters on the road with characters such as a pair of beggars, an old sailor, a melancholy wanderer, and a solitary who has gone into retreat from the world of politics. There are dialogues with a 'friend' and pantheistic apostrophes to nature. Like Wordsworth, Thelwall believed that there was an intimate connection between the rights of man and the rights of nature. When Edmund Burke launched his second assault on the French Revolution, *Letters on a Regicide Peace*, Thelwall responded with a pamphlet called *The Rights of Nature against the Usurpations of Establishments. A series of letters to the people of Britain, on the state of public affairs, and the recent effusions of the Right Honourable Edmund Burke.*

As a result of Coleridge's exclusion of Thelwall from the West Country 'triumvirate', Wordsworth absorbed the influence of 'Citizen John' rather than collaborating with him directly. It was probably Thelwall's notion of peripatetic, his figure of the melancholy wanderer and his paean to the beauties of nature that gave Wordsworth the idea of returning to his narrative of Margaret and her ruined cottage, but introducing a backstory for the wanderer whom the first-person narrator meets outside the tumbledown dwelling. He becomes a Pedlar who takes inspiration from, on the one hand, a tradition of working-class lyric song, embodied most notably in the poetry of Robert Burns, and, on the other, the mountainous landscapes of northern Britain among which he has wandered throughout his adult life:

> His eye
> Flashing poetic fire, he would repeat
> The songs of Burns, and as we trudged along

Together did we make the hollow grove
Ring with our transports. Though he was untaught,
In the dead lore of schools undisciplined,
Why should he grieve? He was a chosen son:
To him was given an ear which deeply felt
The voice of Nature in the obscure wind
The sounding mountain and the running stream.
To every natural form, rock, fruit, and flower,
Even the loose stones that cover the highway,
He gave a moral life; he saw them feel
Or linked them to some feeling. In all shapes
He found a secret and mysterious soul,
A fragrance and a spirit of strange meaning.[21]

Eighteenth-century poets, not to mention the exiled duke in Shakespeare's *As You Like It*, had moralized upon the forms of nature; Thelwall had linked them to strong feelings; Coleridge, under the influence of Spinoza, had ascribed a kind of divinity to natural things; but no poet before Wordsworth had descended to such minute particulars or thought to give a *feeling* and a fragrance to 'the loose stones that cover the highway'.[22] These lines are the first draft of a thought that Wordsworth attributed to himself instead of the Pedlar in the Cambridge book of *The Prelude* (quoted in chapter 5, above).

He began to see that the Pedlar and Margaret might become characters in a much larger project. Picking up on Thelwall's subtitle *Sketches of the Heart, of Nature and Society*, he announced in a letter of early March 1798 that 'I have written 1,300 lines of a poem in which I try to convey most of the knowledge of which I am possessed. My object is to give pictures of Nature, Man, and Society. Indeed I know not any thing which will not come within the scope of my plan.'[23] This would be like *The*

Peripatetic, but unified – and all in verse, not mostly prose. The proposed poem was furnished with a name in another letter a few days later, in which Wordsworth also announced a new plan to go to Germany with Dorothy and Coleridge. It would be called *The Recluse or Views of Nature, Man, and Society*. To judge from notebooks of the time, the bulk of these 1,300 lines consisted of the expanded 'Ruined Cottage' including the story of the Pedlar, together with a moving description of an encounter with a discharged soldier met by the roadside, in which the poet listens to the voice of an impoverished war veteran neglected by his country.

It was Coleridge's influence as well as Thelwall's example that gave Wordsworth the idea of combining a peripatetic narrative focused on sympathy for the poor with more philosophical reflections. Coleridge was planning a similar project himself. It was for this reason, not some treasonable plot, that he and his friends were tracing the course of the brook that ran past Alfoxden, making sketches and notes.

He tells the story in the *Biographia Literaria*: 'I sought for a subject, that should give equal room and freedom for description, incident, and impassioned reflections on men, nature, and society, yet supply in itself a natural connection to the parts, and unity to the whole. Such a subject I conceived myself to have found in a stream.' The poem would begin 'from its source in the hills', follow the stream 'to the first break or fall, where its drops became audible, and it begins to form a channel', thence to 'the peat and turf barn, itself built of the same dark squares as it sheltered; to the sheep-fold; to the first cultivated plot of ground; to the lonely cottage and its bleak garden won from the heath; to the hamlet, the villages, the market-town, the manufactories, and the seaport'. The daily walks on the top of the Quantocks, and 'among its sloping coombs', with 'pencil and memorandum book' in hand, were for the purpose of 'making studies, as the artists call them', and 'moulding my thoughts into verse, with the objects and imagery immediately before my senses'. The poem 'was to have been entitled THE BROOK'. Coleridge then rounds off his account with a laugh at spy Walsh's expense:

> Had I finished the work, it was my purpose in the heat of the moment to have dedicated it to our then committee of public safety as containing the charts and maps, with which I was to have supplied the French Government in aid of their plans of invasion. And these too for a tract of coast that from Clevedon to Minehead scarcely permits the approach of a fishing boat![24]

Coleridge only ever succeeded in composing fragments of 'The Brook', but his conception of using a stream – a stream of consciousness, one might say – to structure a long poem that mixed 'description, incident, and impassioned reflections on men, nature, and society' gave Wordsworth the inspiration for several key elements of *The Prelude*: its opening with the Derwent, its meandering structure, its recurring images of the flow of water. Furthermore, the closest either poet came to completing a project on the principles of 'The Brook' was Wordsworth's sonnet sequence of 1820 *The River Duddon*, probably his last work with moments of enduring poetic quality.

Bristol publisher Joseph Cottle intuited that neither 'The Brook' nor *The Recluse* would be ready for him any time soon. But he wanted to go on publishing Coleridge and, although he had shied away from 'Salisbury Plain', he was keen to take on Wordsworth. Could they not put together a collaborative collection of shorter poems for the interim? Their walks around the village and on the Quantock hills were providing inspiration.

And in the absence of Thelwall, a new triumvirate was coming into being.

The third member was Dorothy, who had started keeping a journal.[25] Its earliest surviving entry reveals her astonishing eye for natural detail:

ALFOXDEN, January 20th, 1798. The green paths down the hill-sides are channels for streams. The young wheat is streaked by silver lines of water running between the ridges, the sheep are gathered together on the slopes. After the wet dark days, the country seems more populous. It peoples itself in the sunbeams . . . The purple-starred hepatica spreads itself in the sun, and the clustering snow-drops put forth their white heads, at first upright, ribbed with green, and like a rosebud when completely opened, hanging their heads downwards, but slowly lengthening their slender stems. The slanting woods of an unvarying brown, showing the light through the thin net-work of their upper boughs. Upon the highest ridge of that round hill covered with planted oaks, the shafts of the trees show in the light like the columns of a ruin.[26]

This is prose poetry of the highest order, conjured from an acute gift for observation, a fluent and wide vocabulary, and a precise botanical expertise. William sometimes described how he would compose his poems as he walked with Dorothy, speaking them aloud, measuring the iambic rhythm to their tread. Dorothy's prose often shares the same beat: 'the púrple-stárred hepáticá' is a perfect iambic tetrameter.

Dorothy had a remarkable sense of colour. 21 January: 'Walked on the hill-tops – a warm day. Sate under the firs in the park. The tips of the beeches of a brown-red, or crimson. Those oaks, fanned by the sea breeze, thick with feathery sea-green moss, as a grove not stripped of its leaves. Moss cups more proper than acorns for fairy goblets.' She also had a constantly inquiring mind. 22 January: 'The day cold – a warm shelter in the hollies, capriciously bearing berries. Query: Are the male and female flowers on separate trees?'[27]

Each day's entry is a thing of wonder, a window onto a life of unity between the little group of companions and their natural environment:

> February 3rd. A mild morning, the windows open at breakfast, the redbreasts singing in the garden. Walked with Coleridge over the hills. The sea at first obscured by vapour; that vapour afterwards slid in one mighty mass along the seashore; the islands and one point of land clear beyond it. The distant country (which was purple in the clear dull air), overhung by straggling clouds that sailed over it, appeared like the darker clouds, which are often seen at a great distance apparently, motionless, while the nearer ones pass quickly over them, driven by the lower winds. I never saw such a union of earth, sky, and sea. The clouds beneath our feet spread themselves to the water, and the clouds of the sky almost joined them. Gathered sticks in the wood; a perfect stillness.[28]

Dorothy *sees* the union of earth, sky and sea, noting in prose. Wordsworth reflects upon it, philosophizing in verse. Walking over to Tom Poole's house after tea one day, they noticed, in Dorothy's words,

> The sky spread over with one continuous cloud, whitened by the light of the moon, which, though her dim shape was seen, did not throw forth so strong a light as to chequer the earth with shadows. At once the clouds seemed to cleave

asunder, and left her in the centre of a black-blue vault. She
sailed along, followed by multitudes of stars, small, and bright,
and sharp.[29]

William turned this observation into verse, first copying and
expanding the language:

> The sky is overcast
> With a continuous cloud of texture close,
> Heavy and wan, all whitened by the Moon,
> Which through that veil is indistinctly seen,
> A dull, contracted circle, yielding light
> So feebly spread, that not a shadow falls,
> Chequering the ground . . .

He then introduces a human figure: a lonesome traveller who
sees above his head 'The clear Moon, and the glory of the
heavens'. With this, he reverts to Dorothy's words:

> There, in a black-blue vault she sails along,
> Followed by multitudes of stars . . . small
> And sharp, and bright.[30]

The little poem then ends with the idea of how, after the vision
closes, the mind, 'Not undisturbed by the delight it feels', settles
into calmness. Wordsworth, as always, is interested in the effect
of nature upon the mind; and as so often, he expresses his thought
with deliberate tentativeness. Rather than 'disturbed' or 'moved',
he writes 'not undisturbed'.

Coleridge perceived that Dorothy's eye and William's mind
worked in perfect harmony. He was deeply impressed by her
ardent and impressive manners, 'Her information various. Her

eye watchful in minutest observation of nature; and her taste a perfect electrometer. It bends, protrudes, and draws in, at subtlest beauties and most recondite faults.'[31] Some time later, writing of himself and her and William, he said 'Though we were three persons, it was but one God.'[32] Coming from Coleridge the religious Unitarian, this trinitarian image could be read two ways: did he mean that they were a creative Trinity, three-in-one and one-in-three, or, more negatively, that their creativity was triune but the credit was taken entirely by the God-like William?

It is impossible – and perhaps undesirable – to disentangle the shared creativity. From a modern feminist point of view, Dorothy looks like the silenced partner. Yet she shied away from the possibility of becoming a published author and she never complained about William using her journals as raw materials for his poems. It is possible indeed that some of the images she wrote down after their daily walks were originally William's, spoken as they looked and listened and shared their impressions. Intriguingly, those exquisite four first sentences in the diary entry for 20 January 1798 appear not only in the posthumously published text of Dorothy's now lost journal, but also in William's hand in his Alfoxden notebook, where they are scribbled fluently in a way that suggests a first draft rather than a painstaking secondary copy.[33]

In The Prelude, Wordsworth acknowledges the twin inspiration of Coleridge and Dorothy. Indeed, in recalling the passage of his life when disillusionment with the French Revolution set in and the idea of a poetic revolution took its place, he gave many more lines of credit to his sister than to his friend. Coleridge lends a hand in regulating his soul, but Dorothy does far more:

> Ah! then it was
> That Thou, most precious Friend! about this time
> First known to me, didst lend a living help

To regulate my soul, and then it was,
That the beloved Woman, in whose sight
Those days were pass'd, now speaking in a voice
Of sudden admonition like a brook
That does but cross a lonely road, and now
Seen, heard, and felt, and caught at every turn,
Companion never lost through many a league,
Maintain'd for me a saving intercourse
With my true self: for, though impair'd and changed,
Much, as it seem'd, I was no further changed
Than as a clouded, not a waning moon.
She in the midst of all preserv'd me still
A Poet, made me seek beneath that name
My office upon earth, and nowhere else,
And lastly, Nature's self, by human love
Assisted, through the weary labyrinth
Conducted me again to open day,
Revived the feelings of my earlier life,
Gave me that strength, and knowledge full of peace,
Enlarged, and never more to be disturb'd,
Which through the steps of our degeneracy,
All degradation of this age, hath still
Upheld me, and upholds me at this day.[34]

As they walked the deserted tracks along the top of the Quantocks, Coleridge may have been the one to come up with the idea of writing a long poem that twisted and flowed like a brook, but it was Dorothy who offered 'sudden admonition like a brook / That does but cross a lonely road' and in so doing returned her brother to his 'true self', guiding him on his path to his true vocation as a poet responsive to 'Nature's self'. It was his sister who spurred him to revive 'the feelings' of his 'earlier life'.

From Coleridge's point of view, Thelwall was too dangerous a collaborator, Lamb was too preoccupied with looking after his mentally ill sister back in London, and Lloyd had blotted his copybook by publishing a novel called *Edmund Oliver*, which included a sequence that lightly fictionalized the embarrassing episode when, as an undergraduate of Jesus College, Coleridge absconded from Cambridge and enlisted in the regiment of the Horse Dragoons (even though he was no rider) under the name Silas Tomkyn Cumberbatch. Wordsworth, he was now convinced, was the chosen one: 'Wordsworth is a very great man, the only man to whom *at all times* and in *all modes of excellence* I feel myself inferior . . . The Giant Wordsworth – God love him!'[35]

Wordsworth himself was growing in confidence. In April 1798, he had his portrait taken, a token of faith in future fame. It was commissioned by Cottle, as was a drawing in profile (with a very large nose) by another artist, Robert Hancock, who had previously drawn Coleridge and Southey. The oil portrait was by William Shuter, a Bristol-based artist who was better known as a flower painter. It captures a boyish look, bright blue eyes, rosy cheeks and what another portraitist, William Hazlitt, described as 'a convulsive inclination to laughter about the mouth' – a very different image from the sober, contemplative figure captured in later, better-known images of Wordsworth.

*

Hazlitt was the next visitor to Nether Stowey and Alfoxden. The son of a dissenting minister, a passionate believer in the cause of revolution, an aspiring philosopher and writer as well as a painter, he first met Coleridge when he tramped for miles over the fields from his native Wem in Shropshire, solely in order to hear him preach. He boldly befriended the master and got himself an invitation to Nether Stowey.

Hazlitt stayed for three weeks. On his first afternoon, Coleridge took him over to Alfoxden. William was not there, but Dorothy gave them tea and 'free access to her brother's poems, the *Lyrical Ballads*, which were still in manuscript'. He stayed over, in an atmospheric bedroom, where the walls were adorned with blue hangings and old portraits of ancestors of the gentry family who owned the house. Then the next morning:

> as soon as breakfast was over, we strolled out into the park, and seating ourselves on the trunk of an old ash tree that stretched along the ground, Coleridge read aloud, with a sonorous and musical voice the ballad of *Betty Foy*. I was not critically or sceptically inclined. I saw touches of truth and nature, and took the rest for granted. But in the *Thorn*, the *Mad Mother*, and the *Complaint of a Poor Indian Woman*, I felt that deeper power and pathos which have been since acknowledged . . . as the characteristics of this author; and the sense of a new style and a new spirit in poetry came over me. It had to me something of the effect that arises from the turning up of the fresh soil, or of the first welcome breath of Spring.[36]

That night, he and Coleridge walked back to Stowey, talking philosophy and theology. Coleridge launched into an analysis of Wordsworth as poet: he didn't believe sufficiently 'in the traditional superstitions of the place', meaning that there was 'something corporeal, a–matter-of-fact-ness, a clinging to the palpable, or often to the petty, in his poetry'; his genius 'was not a spirit that descended to him through the air; it sprung out of the ground like a flower, or unfolded itself from a green spray, on which the goldfinch sang'. This objection, though, was confined 'to his descriptive pieces'; his 'philosophic poetry', by contrast, 'had a grand and comprehensive spirit, in it, so that his soul seemed to inhabit the universe like a palace, and to discover truth by intuition, rather than by deduction'.

The next day Wordsworth arrived from Bristol at Coleridge's cottage. Twenty-five years later, Hazlitt still remembered his first sight of him. A tall, 'Don Quixote-like' figure, 'quaintly dressed' in a brown fustian jacket and striped pantaloons:

> There was something of a roll, a lounge in his gait, not unlike his own Peter Bell. There was a severe, worn pressure of thought about his temples, a fire in his eye (as if he saw something in objects more than the outward appearance), an intense, high, narrow forehead, a Roman nose, cheeks furrowed by strong purpose and feeling, and a convulsive inclination to laughter about the mouth, a good deal at variance with the solemn, stately expression of the rest of his face. He sat down and talked very naturally and freely, with a mixture of clear, gushing accents in his voice, a deep guttural intonation, and a strong tincture of the northern burr, like the crust on wine. He instantly began to make havoc of the half of a Cheshire cheese on the table.

Looking out of the low, latticed window, Wordsworth said, 'How beautifully the sun sets on that yellow bank!' Hazlitt thought to himself, 'With what eyes these poets see nature!' For ever after, he would think of Wordsworth whenever he observed evening light bouncing off an angled object or a slanting landscape.

The next day they were back at Alfoxden, where Wordsworth read his long ballad *Peter Bell* in a chant-like voice. It was a poem that would not be published for many years. Later, Hazlitt 'got into a metaphysical argument with Wordsworth, while Coleridge was explaining the different notes of the nightingale to his sister'. On another occasion, Hazlitt walked with Coleridge through a place called the Valley of Rocks, near the sea. Coleridge told him of the writing plans that he and Wordsworth had hatched while they were there. On this same walk, he explained that 'the *Lyrical Ballads* were an experiment about to be tried by him and Wordsworth, to see how far the public taste would endure poetry written in a more natural and simple style than had hitherto been attempted; totally discarding the artifices of poetical diction'.

Hazlitt was the first person outside Wordsworth's immediate circle of family and friends to read and hear the *Lyrical Ballads*. His intuition that he was witnessing 'a new style and a new spirit in poetry' would play a pivotal role in creating the perception that the 'Lake Poets', as they would come to be called, were seeking to create a cultural revolution in its way as radical as the political revolution on the other side of the English Channel.

10

THE BANKS OF THE WYE

During May 1798, Joseph Cottle visited Wordsworth and Coleridge, in order to make plans for publication of their joint volume of poetry. In his memoirs, he gave a colourful account of how soon after this Wordsworth was forced to leave Alfoxden because of the suspicions of the locals. One said that 'he had seen him wander about by night, and look rather strangely at the moon!' Another said that he had heard him mutter, as he walked, in some outlandish brogue that nobody could understand. Another accused him of being a smuggler. Yet another, of brewing illegal alcohol in the cellar of the big house. And there was still the rumour that he was 'surely a desperd [desperate] French jacobin; for he is so silent and dark that nobody ever heard him say one word about politics'.[1] In old age,

Wordsworth said that this was all an exaggeration, that he never intended to stay beyond the one year of his lease on Alfoxden House and that he did not know about the Spy Nozy business until after he had left the area.

Whatever the precise circumstances, William and Dorothy were ready to move on. Plans were being laid for Germany. Little Basil Montagu would have to be left behind. Dorothy thought that it would now be good for him to receive some education among other children, instead of living alone with them. They departed for Bristol, where they stayed with Cottle. From there, they went on to the home of James Losh, a fellow Cumbrian political radical who had also been in Paris in 1792 and whom Wordsworth had met when he was moving in the circle of William Godwin in London. Then on 10 July, William and Dorothy set off on a short walking tour of the Wye Valley. It would inspire one of his very greatest poems.

They crossed the Severn Ferry and walked about ten miles further to the ruined Cistercian abbey at Tintern. The next morning they walked along the river, through Monmouth and then on to another ruin, that of Goodrich Castle. Having travelled nearly twenty miles that day, they slept well. On the third day, they retraced their steps to Tintern and went some miles further south to Chepstow. Wanting to spend another night at Tintern, they took a boat upstream to the village that nestled by the abbey ruins. Then on the fourth and final day, 13 July, they returned all the way to Bristol, completing their journey in a small sailing vessel. In all, they had walked about fifty miles, through one of the most scenic valleys in Britain, which had by this time become an especially popular destination for tourists seeking the 'picturesque'.

When describing the origin of his poems to Isabella Fenwick forty-five years later, Wordsworth said

No poem of mine was composed under circumstances more
pleasant for me to remember than this: I began it upon leaving
Tintern, after crossing the Wye, and concluded it just as I
was entering Bristol in the evening, after a ramble of 4 or 5
days, with my sister. Not a line of it was altered, and not any
part of it written down till I reached Bristol.[2]

Quite apart from being recalled so long after the event, this
memory is not especially helpful, since William and Dorothy left
Tintern three times on the tour: going north on the second day,
south on the third, and again on the fourth after their return
upstream. The Fenwick note seems to imply that the poem was
created in a burst of creativity on the journey back to Bristol,
after crossing the river and leaving Tintern for the last time. That
would mean it was composed downstream from the abbey, and
yet the very precise title is 'Lines written a few miles above
Tintern Abbey, On revisiting the banks of the Wye during a
tour, July 13, 1798'. Besides, on another occasion, Wordsworth
said that it took him four days to compose the poem.[3]

This would suggest that he began thinking the poem,
composing it in his head, perhaps – as was his wont – speaking
some of its lines to Dorothy, on day two of the tour, having
walked several miles north of the abbey ruin. The date 13 July
would then refer to the writing down of the poem, not its
original composition. Perhaps that is why in later editions of his
poetry Wordsworth changed the title from 'Lines written a few
miles above Tintern Abbey' to 'Lines *composed* a few miles above
Tintern Abbey'.[4]

Wordsworth provides a hint as to the location of the poem's
inspiration in a footnote to its fourth line. He begins with a
remembrance of the solitary journey up the Wye Valley that he
had made back in 1793:

Five years have passed; five summers, with the length
Of five long winters! and again I hear
These waters, rolling from their mountain-springs
With a sweet inland murmur.[5]

The river has an *inland* murmur, the footnote informs the reader, because it is not affected by tides a few miles above Tintern. The Wye was a busy river, with commodities being shipped downstream towards the major port of Bristol. At Llandogo, six miles north of Tintern, it was still tidal, allowing large flat-bottomed boats to be used. Further north, it was not.

Twenty-first century peripatetics can follow the 'Wordsworth Walk' to Cleddon Shoots waterfall above Llandogo, then sit on the 'Bread and Cheese Stones', looking down on the valley. A pamphlet published by the tourism office of the local council informs them that this is the location traditionally thought to have inspired the poem: 'He may even have sat on these stones!'[6] The problem with this claim is that the scene does not really match the topography of the next few lines:

– Once again
Do I behold these steep and lofty cliffs,
Which on a wild secluded scene impress
Thoughts of more deep seclusion; and connect
The landscape with the quiet of the sky.
The day is come when I again repose
Here, under this dark sycamore, and view
These plots of cottage-ground, these orchard-tufts,
Which, at this season, with their unripe fruits,
Among the woods and copses lose themselves,
Nor, with their green and simple hue, disturb
The wild green landscape. Once again I see

> These hedge-rows, hardly hedge-rows, little lines
> Of sportive wood run wild; these pastoral farms
> Green to the very door; and wreathes of smoke
> Sent up, in silence, from among the trees.

There are no 'steep and lofty cliffs' hanging over the Wye at Tintern or at Llandogo. For a walker as vigorous as Wordsworth, 'a few miles above Tintern' might well have been as many as fifteen miles. That would have taken him and Dorothy to Symonds Yat, north of Monmouth, a tall rocky outcrop which afforded some of the finest views of the Wye. From there, one can indeed see 'steep and lofty cliffs', hear the non-tidal murmur of the water, look out on cottages and orchards, woods and copses, laid hedgerows and 'pastoral farms / Green to the very door'.[7] This is a much more 'wild secluded scene' than that at Tintern.

Later in the poem, Wordsworth contrasts his response to the landscape on this return visit with his reaction five years earlier when he was at the same spot:

> The sounding cataract
> Haunted me like a passion: the tall rock,
> The mountain, and the deep and gloomy wood,
> Their colours and their forms, were then to me
> An appetite: a feeling and a love,
> That had no need of a remoter charm,
> By thought supplied, or any interest
> Unborrowed from the eye.

These are lines that have puzzled critics and biographers who have sought to place the poem closer to Tintern, since there are no sounding cataracts and tall rocks to be found there. But this is what William Gilpin wrote of Symonds Yat – known then as New-Weir – in his guide for tourists seeking the picturesque (a book which Wordsworth knew well and may have carried with him on the tour):

> But what peculiarly marks this view, is a circumstance on the water. The whole river, at this place, makes a precipitate fall; of no great height indeed; but enough to merit the title of a cascade: tho' to the eye above the stream, it is an object of no consequence. In all the scenes we had yet passed, the water moving with a slow, and solemn pace, the objects around kept time, as it were, with it; and every steep, and every rock, which hung over the river, was solemn, tranquil, and majestic. But here, the violence of the stream, and the roaring of the waters, impressed a new character on the scene: all was agitation, and uproar; and every steep, and every rock stared with wildness, and terror.[8]

At Symonds Yat, the Wye was indeed a 'sounding cataract' with a 'tall rock' hanging over it.

Gilpin was, to use the distinction inaugurated by Edmund Burke, saying that further downstream the Wye is 'beautiful', but here it is 'sublime'. That sublimity is what Wordsworth responded to on his first visit, when his youthful revolutionary passion was still upon him. It created for him a peculiar connection with landscapes such as this. The gift he has received from this part of the Wye Valley has been something 'Of aspect more sublime':

>   that blessed mood,
> In which the burthen of the mystery,
> In which the heavy and the weary weight

Of all this unintelligible world
Is lighten'd: − that serene and blessed mood,
In which the affections gently lead us on,
Until, the breath of this corporeal frame,
And even the motion of our human blood
Almost suspended, we are laid asleep
In body, and become a living soul:
While with an eye made quiet by the power
Of harmony, and the deep power of joy,
We see into the life of things.

His eye for landscape and his capacity for strong feeling fostered this reaction, but it required the philosophical mind of Coleridge to give him the ability to articulate this special state of mind as explicitly as he does here. Some months earlier, Coleridge had written to Thelwall,

I can *at times* feel strongly the beauties, you describe, in themselves & for themselves − but more frequently *all things* appear little − all the knowledge, that can be acquired, child's play − the universe itself − what but an immense heap of *little* things? − I can contemplate nothing but parts, & parts are all *little* − ! − My mind feels as if it ached to behold & know something *great* − something *one & indivisible* − and it is only in the faith of this that rocks or waterfalls, mountains or caverns give me the sense of sublimity or majesty! − But in this faith *all things* counterfeit infinity![9]

Wordsworth achieved what Coleridge was struggling towards in this letter: the thought that *all* things − little things such as hedgerows as well as sublime things such as rocks and waterfalls − are part of some quasi-divine harmony:

> I have felt
> A presence that disturbs me with the joy
> Of elevated thoughts; a sense sublime
> Of something far more deeply interfused,
> Whose dwelling is the light of setting suns,
> And the round ocean, and the living air,
> And the blue sky, and in the mind of man,
> A motion and a spirit, that impels
> All thinking things, all objects of all thought,
> And rolls through all things.

Coleridge would have called that motion and spirit 'God' or 'the Infinite Mind'. Wordsworth locates it firmly in the landscape in which he is walking, and that is why 'Tintern Abbey' was regarded by some as the work of a pantheist:

> Therefore am I still
> A lover of the meadows and the woods,
> And mountains; and of all that we behold
> From this green earth; of all the mighty world
> Of eye and ear, both what they half-create,
> And what perceive; well pleased to recognize
> In nature and the language of the sense,
> The anchor of my purest thoughts, the nurse,
> The guide, the guardian of my heart, and soul
> Of all my moral being.

Towards the end of the poem, Wordsworth explicitly calls himself 'A worshipper of Nature'. To a conservative Christian sensibility, this was not merely blasphemous but dangerously close to the materialism of those revolutionary thinkers who influenced the unorthodox ideas of radicals such as Walking Stewart.

Wordsworth acknowledges in 'Tintern Abbey' that he has changed since the time when nature to him was 'all in all'. The memory of the Wye has brought him mental restoration in times of stress, especially during his lonely nights in the city. But the French experience – both his radicalization and the disillusionment that followed from witnessing such terrible violence – has made him see that pastoral visions, though they might inspire 'little, nameless, unremembered acts / Of kindness and of love', are not enough: the poet's duty is also to hear 'the still, sad music of humanity'. Yet he finds moral guidance not in the teachings of the church, but in 'nature and the language of the sense'.

This is why it is so important that the poem is *not* about Tintern Abbey. The fact that William and Dorothy doubled back on their tracks in order to spend another night staying near the abbey shows that they were impressed by the ruins. A decade later, in a fragment intended for *The Recluse*, Wordsworth did choose to write about the assault on the Catholic Church during the French Revolution and to make a comparison with the dissolution of the monasteries during the Reformation centuries earlier in Britain. On that occasion, he conjured up a fresh memory of his Wye tour:

Fallen, in a thousand vales, the stately Towers
And branching windows gorgeously array'd,
And aisles and roofs magnificent that thrill'd
With halleluiahs, and the strong-ribb'd vaults
Are crush'd, and buried under weeds and earth
The cloistral avenues . . .
          . . . the Piles that rose
On British lawns by Severn, Thames, or Tweed
And saw their pomp reflected in the stream,
As Tintern saw; and, to this day, beholds
Her faded image in the depths of Wye.[10]

In the poem written during the tour, by contrast, he pointedly omits any reference to the abbey or its surroundings. Previous tourist poets, who were often clergymen, had placed Tintern at the heart of their 'loco-descriptive' verses on the Wye. Wordsworth slyly gestures towards convention by naming it in his title, but then he deliberately heads several miles upstream and worships instead at the altar of the landscape.

Furthermore, writing at a time when women were habitually represented as keepers of the simple flame of religious piety, he ends the poem by enlisting Dorothy in his cause. In her 'wild eyes' and her voice of enthusiasm for the beauties of the landscape, he catches an echo of his own idealistic youthful self. He incorporates her into a prayer addressed not to God but to Nature. Ecclesiastical language – 'chearful faith' and 'blessings', 'zeal' and 'holier love' contrasted with 'evil tongues' and 'the sneers of selfish men' – is taken away from the abbey and into a world of solitary walks, 'misty mountain winds' and 'the banks of this delightful stream'. The sense of the infinite is internalized as the human mind becomes 'a mansion for all lovely forms', and Dorothy's memory, instead of God's church or indeed His heaven, becomes the 'dwelling-place / For all sweet sounds and harmonies'. The poem ends, as it began, with the 'steep woods and lofty cliffs' of a 'green pastoral landscape' untouched by the ruin of a failed faith.

★

Their return to Bristol was timely. The volume of poetry was about to go to press, and Cottle just had time to insert the new poem – which ran to 160 lines – at the end. He would have appreciated the inclusion of a landscape poem because he had written one himself. Back in February, he had lent Wordsworth a copy of his *Malvern Hills: A Poem*, which also describes a

'blessed spot' to which the poet retreats in 'holy quietness' from
the stresses and strains of the world. Where Cottle might have
been disappointed was in the way that Wordsworth's 'Lines' –
despite their talk of the 'still, sad music of humanity' – paid little
attention to the poverty that was visible in the Wye Valley.
Though there is a passing reference to 'vagrant dwellers in the
houseless woods', the consequence of the poem being composed
miles upstream, in the more secluded reaches of the valley, is
that Wordsworth does not write, as other visitors to Tintern did,
of how beggars loitered in the ruins of the abbey and charcoal
burners eked out a living along the banks of the river. Cottle's
poem, by contrast, included a section concerning 'the effects of
extreme poverty' on society. Its preface argued that every poor man
should receive 'a stipend from the state', 'rising in proportion to
the number of his children'.[11] This was an opinion diametrically
opposed to that of Thomas Malthus, who argued in his *Essay
concerning Population*, also published in 1798, that the way to deal
with hunger was to force limits on the population growth of the
poor.

   With his habit of recording specific dates for his poems,
Wordsworth was inevitably mindful of the fact that 13 July was
the date on which he had first landed in France, and walked
with Jones into the celebrations of the first anniversary of the
storming of the Bastille and the hope for a new society of liberty,
equality and fraternity in which poverty would be no more.
Consciously or not, by focusing in his poem on the bond between
the individual spirit and the landscape, he was signalling his retreat
from radical politics even as he was articulating a radical alternative religion of nature.

11

THE EXPERIMENT

The materials for poetry, Wordsworth claimed in the opening sentence of the 'Advertisement' that prefaced *Lyrical Ballads*, 'are to be found in every subject which can interest the human mind'. The statement sounds bland, but was in fact profoundly political. Eighteenth-century conventions of decorum suggested that only *certain* subjects provided fit material for the elevated form of utterance that is Poetry. By the same account, the language of poetry was supposed to be exclusive. Vulgar words were frowned upon.

Wordsworth and Coleridge were in rebellion against these norms. They wanted poetry to be inclusive, in both subject matter and language. 'The majority of the following poems', Wordsworth continued in the 'Advertisement', 'are to be considered as experiments'. The purpose of the experiment was to democratize poetry: 'They were written chiefly with a view to ascertain how far the language of conversation in the middle and lower classes of society is adapted to the purposes of poetic pleasure.'[1] The elevated poetic form of 'lyric' would be yoked to the vernacular form of the ballad, which was associated with popular culture, oral tradition and such labouring-class poets as Robert Burns.

By 1798, it was clear that a revolution in government was not coming to Britain and that the enfranchisement of the middle and lower classes of society in France had led not to a new dawn of universal rights, but to repression and war. In Paris, a year later, on 18 Brumaire according to the new revolutionary calendar, there would be a *coup d'état* led by Napoleon; France was on the road to a dictatorship and the eventual proclamation of Napoleon as emperor. Wordsworth and Coleridge, abandoning the field of parliamentary reform, were proposing that liberty, equality and fraternity should be introduced into the realm of high culture instead.

Coleridge was aware that the experiment might prove dangerous, and not merely because of the recent attentions of the Home Office spy. A backstory is required in order to explain the wider context.

In the bestselling *Rights of Man* of 1791 Thomas Paine had refuted Edmund Burke's anti-revolutionary arguments. The following year, Paine had published a second part, arguing for more representative government at home and a system of progressive taxation to assist the poor. This led not only to a heated pamphlet war, but to Paine's indictment for seditious libel, which carried the death penalty. He fled to France, where he was offered honorary citizenship, along with some of the American Founding Fathers, such as George Washington, Benjamin Franklin and

Alexander Hamilton, all of whom had been inspired by Paine's earlier book *Common Sense*. In revolutionary Paris, Paine aligned himself with the Girondins. This led to his arrest at the time of the purges, but his release was secured, largely due to the work of James Monroe, the American minister, who argued that Paine was now an American citizen and thus not a citizen of a country at war with France.

During this period, Paine had also been writing about the relationship between religion and the state, attacking the corruption and politicization of the priesthood. In 1794 and 1795 he published two parts of a new book called *The Age of Reason*. This was a work in the eighteenth-century tradition of deism: the belief that religious revelation was an illusion, but that the order and beauty of the natural world were sufficient to prove the existence of a Supreme Being. Deism had a long and respectable intellectual pedigree among the educated, but Paine's book was considered seditious because it was aimed at the masses. The church, after all, was as important as the law in maintaining the moral order, and thus the social and political system, of the nation. In 1797, Paine's English publisher was sentenced to a year's hard labour for distributing the book.

In Paris, Paine had put his theories into practice by establishing a new natural religion called Theophilanthropy. The Theophilanthropists, 'Friends of God and Man', were originally a small sect, mixing one part Rousseau with one part Robespierre. The idea was to cater for the religious instincts of the people while jettisoning the priestcraft of the Catholic Church and the hierarchical notion of God the transcendent patriarch. The cause was subsequently taken up by Louis Marie de La Révellière-Lépeaux, a prominent figure in the Directory, the small committee that took over the government of France following the fall of Robespierre and the disbanding of the Committee of Public

Safety. Theophilanthropic ideas were beginning to circulate in England, especially after the publication in 1797 of a translation of the *Manual of the Theophilanthropes, or Adorers of God, and Friends of Men.*[2]

It was also in 1797 that, a new weekly magazine called the *Anti-Jacobin* was launched by the deputy Foreign Secretary in the Tory government, George Canning, a close ally of Prime Minister Pitt and a strong supporter of his measures to control the press. Canning was a talented satirical writer, who contributed much of the material himself. The issue of 9 July 1798, the day before William and Dorothy set off on their Wye tour, included a long poem by Canning called 'New Morality'. It took aim at Theophilanthropy, representing a motley crew of pamphleteers as disciples of Paine and worshippers at the Theophilanthropic shrine of Lépeaux. Among them, he named a group of poets:

> And ye five other wandering Bards that move
> In sweet accord of harmony and love,
> C-----DGE and S--TH-Y, L---D and L--B and Co.
> Tune all your mystic harps to praise LEPAUX!

The poet as wanderer, the language of harmony and love, and especially the clear reference to 'The Eolian Harp', Coleridge's poem on the 'one life' of the mind and nature: Canning had all the values shared within the Coleridge circle in his gunsight. He was aware of Coleridge's collaborations both with Lamb and Lloyd and with Southey – whose 'democratic' poetry was the object of some superb parodies in other issues of the *Anti-Jacobin*. The fifth wandering bard, 'Co', is Cottle: 'and Co', suggesting a company, is a play on his double identity as both poet and publisher. He was one half of 'Biggs and Cottle', printers and booksellers; indeed, some of their products, including the *Annual Anthology* which published many of Coleridge's and Southey's poems, bore the imprint 'Printed by Biggs and Co'.[3]

The *Anti-Jacobin* had become the most talked-about anti-revolutionary publication of the time partly because Canning had hired James Gillray, the outstanding caricaturist of the age (perhaps of any age), to produce plates based on material in the magazine. Caricatures were displayed in print-shop windows, where crowds pressed against the glass to see them. The medium was as powerful as television in the twentieth century or social media in the twenty-first as a way of disseminating political debate, controversy and scandal to a wide urban public. On 1 August 1798, as Cottle was preparing *Lyrical Ballads* for print, Gillray issued a blazing caricature based on Canning's poem. Entitled 'New Morality; – or – The Promis'd Installment of the High-Priest of the Theophilanthropes', it shows the figures named in the poem bowing down in homage before the shrine of three bedraggled-looking goddesses labelled Justice, Philanthropy and Sensibility. Justice wears the inflammatory French word *Egalité* around her waist; Sensibility holds a copy of Rousseau; Philanthropy is treading on 'Ties of Nature' (meaning family and marriage) and '*Amor Patria*' (love of the fatherland), implying that these traditional values are threatened by the philanthropes' notion of a universal love shared equally among all humankind.

The caption to the caricature consisted of an extract from the poem, including the lines naming the 'wandering Bards'. Coleridge, one of whose poems had been written in sympathy for a donkey beaten by its master, appears in the caricature, wearing an ass's head, as does Southey. Lamb and Lloyd are represented as a frog and a toad, holding a volume labelled 'BLANK-VERSE' – the title of their latest joint publication, which had included poems by Lloyd that attacked the war and praised the communist 'pantisocratic' scheme of Coleridge and Southey.[4]

The Gillray caricature demonstrates that the political temperature was so hot at this time that the idea of 'sensibility' – fellow feeling for another sentient being – could be regarded as dangerous radicalism. Even the very act of writing blank verse, as opposed to ordered rhyming couplets, might be considered transgressive. The 'New Morality' was considered so insidious of the established church that deism, pantheism and atheism were lumped together and considered to be subversive practices. By this account, 'Tintern Abbey' could have been perceived as a revolutionary poem, even though it lacked the explicit politicizing of Cottle's *Malvern Hills*. As for the term 'Philanthropy', that came to the very heart of Wordsworth's and Coleridge's poetry of friendship and fellow feeling. *The Philanthropist* was, after all, the name that Wordsworth had chosen for his abortive project of launching a magazine. Coleridge was also conscious of the reputation he had gained as a friend of Justice, Sensibility and Philanthropy, following his public lectures in Bristol attacking the state, the established church and the barbarity of the slave trade.

Wordsworth's name was as yet beneath the radar of Canning and his crew. *An Evening Walk* and *Descriptive Sketches* had sold few copies and received only a handful of reviews, in which they were praised for their descriptions of Lake District and Swiss scenery, but they were perceived as conventional poems of place, with no particular political resonance. 'Salisbury Plain' and the *Letter to the Bishop of Llandaff* were unpublished. His obscurity might have been a political shield, but his name would have done nothing to promote sales. Coleridge's name, meanwhile, would run the risk of provoking another attack in the *Anti-Jacobin* and elsewhere. In the light of all this, Coleridge suggested to Cottle that anonymity might be the best strategy for the new publication: 'Wordsworth's name is nothing', he wrote, and 'to a large number of persons mine stinks'.[5] *Lyrical Ballads, with a few other Poems* was duly published in the autumn of 1798 without any author's name on the title page.[6]

Coleridge's anxiety to maintain the anonymity of the authors was such that he removed one of his contributions to the collection while it was in the press: a poem called 'Lewti, or the Circassian Love-Chant', a ballad of unrequited love that he had developed from an unfinished schoolboy ode by Wordsworth, had already been published (albeit pseudonymously) in the *Morning Post* newspaper. In theory, it could have been traced back to him. It was therefore replaced by 'The Nightingale, a Conversational Poem'. Some copies of the first edition accordingly include 'Lewti', while most have 'The Nightingale'. Since the substitute poem was longer than the original one, the pagination in the later-printed copies runs 69, blank, 69, 70. Aesthetically, though, it was a happy turn of events: 'The Nightingale' is a much finer poem, written in fluid blank verse, beautifully recalling a night when Coleridge carried his crying baby Hartley out into the garden and calmed him with the sight of the moon.

Wordsworth's 'Advertisement' explaining the purpose of the poems was also an insertion late in the publication process. The trouble with well-to-do, highly educated poets, he implies, is that they don't speak the language of ordinary people. They all too frequently resort to the 'gaudiness and inane phraseology' of many modern writers. This book, by contrast, would seek only to offer 'a natural delineation of human passions, human characters, and human incidents'. Though 'natural', 'human' and 'passions' are seemingly innocuous terms, in the febrile wartime climate of the late 1790s they carried resonances of Theophilanthropy, Sensibility and *Egalité*.

★

The inclusion of 'Tintern Abbey' meant that the volume was bookended by two wholly contrasting long poems, for it begins with Coleridge's 'The Rime of the Ancyent Marinere, in Seven Parts' (in the 1798 edition, the poem used archaic spellings). Between them, these two celebrated poems occupy more than sixty out of 210 pages. Another lengthy ballad, 'The Idiot Boy', occupies a further thirty pages. There are twenty shorter poems, seventeen of them by Wordsworth.

The idea for 'The Rime of the Ancyent Marinere' was hatched on one of their West Country excursions. In early November 1797, William, Dorothy and Coleridge took a walking tour to Lynton on the Devon coast, a distance of some thirty-six miles each way, in which they passed through the picturesque Valley of Rocks. Periglacial and notable for its fossils, the place had a primitive quality that got them talking about a sprawling, rhapsodic and surprisingly widely read German prose-poem on the subject of *The Death of Abel*.[7] Coleridge came up with the idea of a jointly written sequel to be called *The Wanderings of Cain*. The plan was that Wordsworth would write the first canto, Coleridge the second, and whoever finished first would take on the third. Coleridge dispatched his part of the task 'at full finger-speed' and hurried to Wordsworth with his manuscript, only to witness a 'look of humorous despondency fixed on his almost blank sheet of paper' and then a 'silent mock-piteous admission of failure struggling with the sense of the exceeding ridiculousness of the whole scheme – which broke up in a laugh: and the Ancient Mariner was written instead'.[8]

Wordsworth did, however, make a contribution. He explained

that much the greatest part of the story was 'Mr Coleridge's invention', but that he had suggested certain parts: 'For example, some crime was to be committed which should bring upon the Old Navigator, as Coleridge afterwards delighted to call him, the spectral persecution, as a consequence of that crime and his own wanderings.' Over the previous few days, Wordsworth had been reading an early eighteenth-century travel book, George Shelvocke's *Voyage round the World by way of the Great South Sea*, in which he had come across a passage about how, as they were rounding Cape Horn, the crew took comfort in the companionable sight of albatrosses, 'some extending their wings 12 or 13 feet'. But the second mate shot one of them. 'Suppose', Wordsworth suggested to Coleridge, 'you represent him as having killed one of these birds on entering the South Sea, and that the tutelary Spirits of these regions take upon them to avenge the crime.' It was also Wordsworth who 'suggested the navigation of the ship by the dead men'.[9] He also recalled that 'We began the composition together on that to me memorable evening: I furnished two or three lines at the beginning of the poem, in particular "And listened like a three years' child; / The Mariner had his will".' The simile of the listening child is typically Wordsworthian. Then, however, 'As we endeavoured to proceed conjointly (I speak of the same evening) our respective manners proved so widely different that it would have been quite presumptuous in me to do anything but separate from an undertaking upon which I could only have been a clog.'[10] The rest of the poem was left to Coleridge.

Wordsworth's 'Advertisement' acknowledged that 'The Rime of the Ancyent Marinere', with its archaic spellings, was stylistically different from the rest of the volume. He argued, however, that it shared with the collection as a whole a commitment to 'the spirit of the elder poets' – by which he meant the popular culture of medieval ballads and the plays of Shakespeare, with their mingling of kings and clowns, the elite and the people. The message of Coleridge's poem, that all living things are sacred and to be blessed, is in accordance with the spirit of nature worship and strong fellow feeling ('sensibility') that unifies the collection. The poem asks the reader to feel for the albatross, just as Wordsworth felt for the subjects that he gleaned from his perambulations in the Lakes, the Wye Valley and the Quantocks. The inspiration for the encounter with the little girl in 'We are Seven' came on his first walk through the Wye Valley in 1793; several of the poems hark back to his years in Hawkshead; the shepherd bearing the last of his flock was met in the village of Holford on a walk from Alfoxden, while the old huntsman trying to dig out the root of a tree is given the name Simon Lee, but was actually based on Christopher Trickie of the old dog pound at the end of the drive to the big rented house – the man who, unknown to Wordsworth, had been one of the informants against him at the time of the Home Office investigation.

Wordsworth's recollection of Coleridge's vision for the collection was that it should consist of 'Poems chiefly on supernatural subjects taken from common life but looked at, as much as might be, through an imaginative medium'.[11] But in Wordsworth's contribution there is more naturalism than supernaturalism. The poem of his that was closest to 'The Ancyent Marinere' – in many ways a direct response to it – was *Peter Bell*, but it was agreed with Cottle that, largely for reasons of length, this ballad should be excluded. Of the poems that were included, the one closest in spirit to 'The Ancyent Marinere' was 'The Thorn'. It tells the story of a woman in an isolated setting, haunted by the memory of a terrible crime that she has committed (curiously, Wordsworth gave her the name of Martha Ray, the celebrated mistress of little Basil Montagu's grandfather). The ballad had its origin in a walk on the hills above Alfoxden:

> Arose out of my observing, on the ridge of Quantock Hill, on a stormy day a thorn which I had often past in calm and bright weather without noticing it. I said to myself, 'Cannot I by some invention do as much to make this thorn permanently an impressive object as the storm has made it to my eyes at this moment.'[12]

Dorothy recorded the occasion in her journal: 'March 19th. Wm and Basil and I walked to the hill-tops, a very cold bleak day. We were met on our return by a severe hailstorm. William wrote some lines describing a stunted thorn.'[13] Coleridge had given a dramatic quality to his 'Mariner' poem by introducing a narrator who interrogates the protagonist; Wordsworth imagined something similar for 'The Thorn'. He explained in the 'Advertisement' that, 'as the reader will soon discover', the poem was 'not supposed to be spoken in the author's own person: the character of the loquacious narrator will sufficiently shew itself in the course of the story.' But the reader discovers no such thing: the ballad reveals nothing of its supposed narrator, with the result that those elements of its loquacity that bordered upon pedantry could be ascribed by hostile critics to Wordsworth himself. The description of the pond near the stunted thorn became notorious:

> Not five yards from the mountain-path,
> This thorn you on your left espy;
> And to the left, three yards beyond,
> You see a little muddy pond
> Of water, never dry;

I've measured it from side to side:
'Tis three feet long, and two feet wide.

In defence of this degree of particularity, it is important for the sake of the story to know that a pond of these dimensions is just large enough in which to drown an unwanted baby, but the labour of the writing would lead to much mockery.

One might imagine 'The Thorn' as a supernatural tale told in order to elicit a shiver of fearful delight in five-year-old Basil Caroline Montagu, who was on the walk that day when they were caught in the hailstorm. The pervasive presence of children and a child's way of seeing in Wordsworth's contributions to *Lyrical Ballads* is partly a consequence of Basil's presence in the Alfoxden household. One of Wordsworth's favourite techniques was to begin a poem as if it were a simple rhyme for children, but then to introduce adult matter. 'Goody Blake, and Harry Gill, A True Story' is an example. It begins

Oh! what's the matter? what's the matter?
What is't that ails young Harry Gill?
That evermore his teeth they chatter,
Chatter, chatter, chatter still.
Of waistcoats Harry has no lack,
Good duffle grey, and flannel fine;
He has a blanket on his back,
And coats enough to smother nine.

Yet before long this becomes a poem about poverty, property and the need for firewood in a hard winter.

Young Basil's presence is also important because one of Wordsworth's themes in the collection was the question of education. In the autumn of 1797, Tom Wedgwood, of the wealthy pottery family who would prove to be Coleridge's most important patrons, visited Nether Stowey and Alfoxden with the purpose of interesting Wordsworth and Coleridge in a scheme he had dreamed up whereby they would supervise the education of a hypothetical child genius by removing all distractions and providing a forced immersion in improving books. Explaining his project to William Godwin, whose ideas on human perfectibility had greatly influenced him, Wedgwood said that the key would be for the child never to go out of doors or leave his own apartment. Above all, there should be no opportunity for 'idleness'. This was the very opposite of the Rousseauistic idea of letting a child wander free in nature. Unsurprisingly, Wordsworth wanted nothing to do with the Wedgwood scheme. The poem 'Lines written at a small distance from my house, and sent by my little boy to the person to whom they are addressed', which comes immediately after 'Goody Blake, and Harry Gill', turns Wedgwood's proposal on its head. It is 'the first mild day of March', so Wordsworth sends Basil with a message to Dorothy, telling her to stop doing housework. Instead, the three of them should spend the day out in the sunshine, doing nothing. The repeated chorus is 'And bring no book; for this one day / We'll give to idleness'. Politicians, preachers and landowners were forever railing against the idleness of the poor, so to write in praise of it was a subversive gesture. Furthermore, the poem is imbued with its own natural religion, a linking of pantheism and sensibility:

Love, now an universal birth,
From heart to heart is stealing,
From earth to man, from man to earth,
– It is the hour of feeling.

The word 'universal' carried special weight for Wordsworth, in that it suggested the unity of all things, the idea of universal rights for humankind, and the unbreakable bond between spirit and environment, as expressed in the ice-skating passage of *The Prelude*, which includes a powerful image of 'The surface of the universal earth' being filled 'With meanings of delight, of hope and fear'.[14]

The idea of education through nature instead of books is also the key to a pair of poems called 'Expostulation and Reply' and 'The Tables Turned', provoked by that metaphysical argument with Hazlitt which took place while Coleridge was explaining the different notes of the nightingale to Dorothy. As Wordsworth put it in the 'Advertisement', these pieces 'arose out of conversation with a friend who was somewhat unreasonably attached to modern books of moral philosophy':

Books! 'tis a dull and endless strife,
Come, hear the woodland linnet,
How sweet his music; on my life
There's more of wisdom in it.

And hark! how blithe the throstle sings!
And he is no mean preacher;
Come forth into the light of things,
Let Nature be your teacher.

She has a world of ready wealth,
Our minds and hearts to bless —
Spontaneous wisdom breathed by health,
Truth breathed by chearfulness.

One impulse from a vernal wood
May teach you more of man;
Of moral evil and of good,
Than all the sages can.

Sweet is the lore which nature brings;
Our meddling intellect
Mishapes the beauteous forms of things;
– We murder to dissect.

Enough of science and of art;
Close up these barren leaves;
Come forth, and bring with you a heart
That watches and receives.[15]

This poem is an epitome of the Wordsworthian vision of nature
as teacher. The music of birdsong replaces the preaching of
theologians. The language of moral philosophy is taken out from
the library and into the woods. 'We murder to dissect' brilliantly
transposes an image associated with the anatomical training of a
surgeon from the physical realm to the intellectual. Wordsworth
offers instead the wise passiveness of the receptive heart. As in
'Tintern Abbey', he is responsive to the *things* of the natural
world: in that poem their inner 'life', in this one their 'beauteous
forms'.

★

William Hazlitt's argument with Wordsworth about metaphysics
during that summer of 1798 made him into the negative exemplar in 'The Tables Turned'. In later years, Hazlitt made
Wordsworth into a negative political exemplar: the young radical
turned middle-aged conservative. Yet although Hazlitt became

disillusioned with Wordsworth the man, he never lost faith in his conviction that a new age of poetry dawned in the Quantocks in 1798.

The first poem by Wordsworth that the reader encounters in *Lyrical Ballads* is about a baby abandoned at birth.[16] The two longest are about, respectively, a Down's syndrome boy and a female vagrant. Others are about impoverished old people, a shepherd fallen on hard times, a convict, an old man travelling to a hospital to visit his war-wounded son, and a dungeon that might as well be the Bastille. Not to mention a 'Mad Mother' and 'a forsaken Indian Woman'. To Hazlitt, this subject matter was turning poetry on its head: gone was the polished wit of Alexander Pope writing satiric rhyming couplets about a lady at her dressing table, or pronouncing urbanely from a coffee house that 'Whatever is, is right'.[17] Hazlitt saw *Lyrical Ballads* as nothing less than the English literary equivalent of the French political revolution. He argued that towards the end of the eighteenth century England's 'poetical literature' had 'degenerated into the most trite, insipid, and mechanical of all things, in the hands of the followers of Pope and the old French school of poetry':

> It wanted something to stir it up, and it found that something
> in the principles and events of the French revolution . . .
> The change in the belles-lettres was as complete, and to many
> persons as startling, as the change in politics, with which it
> went hand in hand. There was a mighty ferment in the heads
> of statesmen and poets, kings and people. According to the
> prevailing notions, all was to be natural and new. Nothing
> that was established was to be tolerated. All the common-
> place figures of poetry, tropes, allegories, personifications,
> with the whole heathen mythology, were instantly discarded;
> a classical allusion was considered as a piece of antiquated

foppery; capital letters were no more allowed in print, than letters-patent of nobility were permitted in real life; kings and queens were dethroned from their rank and station in legitimate tragedy or epic poetry, as they were decapitated elsewhere; rhyme was looked upon as a relic of the feudal system, and regular metre was abolished along with regular government.[18]

Hazlitt was teasing and praising at one and the same time. 'It was a time of promise, a renewal of the world and of letters; and the Deucalions, who were to perform this feat of regeneration were the present poet-laureat [Southey] and the two authors of the Lyrical Ballads.' This was written during the Regency years, by which time all three of the Lake Poets had, in Hazlitt's view, sold out to the establishment. Because of this apostasy, his account has fun at Wordsworth's expense, but there is no doubting the underlying seriousness of the argument that the 'new school' of poetry was founded on principles of 'sheer humanity' and 'pure nature void of art'. Wordsworth and Coleridge, Hazlitt says, brought the Muses into company with 'a mixed rabble of idle apprentices and Botany Bay convicts, female vagrants, gipsies, meek daughters in the family of Christ [a quotation from Coleridge's poem 'The Eolian Harp', published prior to Lyrical Ballads], of ideot boys and mad mothers' – not to mention 'owls and night-ravens'. 'They took the same method', Hazlitt concludes, 'which Rousseau did in his prose paradoxes – of exciting attention by reversing the standards of opinion and estimation in the world. They were for bringing poetry back to its primitive simplicity and state of nature, as he was for bringing society back to the savage state.'[19]

Wordsworth was by no means the first to make poetry out of poverty and to reach out in sympathy to beggars and transients,

the marginalized and the outcasts. The ephemeral magazine verse
of the 1790s was full of ballads and descriptive poems with titles
such as 'The Idiot', 'Ellen, or the Fair Insane', 'The Female
Convict', 'The Unfortunate Cottager', 'The Poor Debtor's
Lamentation', and 'The Complaint of a Transport in Botany
Bay'.[20] Some of these used the four-line stanza of the traditional
ballad, others mixed ballad elements with the longer and more
intricately rhymed stanzas of the lyric form, anticipating the
practice of *Lyrical Ballads* (though the nomenclature on Wordsworth
and Coleridge's title page was original). However, the tendency
of the magazine verse, and indeed of many other poetry collections in the 1790s, was either to represent the poor as picturesque
details in a landscape or to use them as the occasion for the
expression of sentimental sympathy together with explicit or
implicit moral pronouncements on the importance of charity.
This was the stance that William Blake attacked in a bitterly
ironic couplet in one of his *Songs of Experience*: 'Pity would be
no more / If we did not make somebody Poor'.[21] The new and
radical thing about Wordsworth's treatment of this subject matter
was the sense of personal encounter on the 'public road'.

Consider, by way of contrast, a passage from the allegedly
dangerous revolutionary John Thelwall. In his magazine *The
Tribune*, he told of his custom of rambling 'in the true democratic
way, on foot, from village to village'. To walk, rather than to
ride or to take a carriage, was an act of solidarity with the poor,
a sign that one was a 'democrat' – a word associated far more
closely with revolutionary politics than it is today. Thelwall then
writes that he would go into the pubs and chat to 'the rough
clowns, whose tattered garments were soiled with their rustic
labours; for I have not forgot that all mankind are equally my
brethren . . . I love the labourer then, in his ragged coat, as well
as I love the Peer in his ermine; perhaps better'.[22] Thelwall's

heart was wholly in the right place; with the phrase 'equally my brethren', he echoes the French revolutionary values of *égalité* and *fraternité*. But in his tone, he could not escape paternalistic condescension. In the words of the historian E. P. Thompson, 'the advanced reformers of the time found it more easy to advocate the political programme of equality – manhood suffrage – than they did to shed the cultural attitudes of superiority'.[23]

Wordsworth's reflective voice, heard for example in the lines in *The Prelude* that follow his conjuring of the early childhood memory of the road leading away from Cockermouth, is quite different. Of his encounters with 'vagrants' on the public highways, he writes:

> when I began to inquire,
> To watch and question those I met, and held
> Familiar talk with them, the lonely roads
> Were schools to me in which I daily read
> With most delight the passions of mankind,
> There saw into the depth of human souls,
> Souls that appear to have no depth at all
> To vulgar eyes. And now convinced at heart
> How little that to which alone we give
> The name of education hath to do
> With real feeling and just sense.[24]

The word 'vulgar' was traditionally applied to the lower classes. Wordsworth turns it around: the 'vulgar eyes' are those of the privileged and respectable, who fail to see that 'the passions of mankind' and the authenticity of the human spirit are to be found among the poor, out on the road. It is precisely because they have not undergone 'education' into polite society that these vagrants can speak with 'real feeling and just sense'. Wordsworth's poetry uses them to offer a re-education of the feelings for those who have had their humanity knocked out of them by what passes for education in schools and colleges. Once again, this is an idea shaped by Rousseau, whose *Emile; or, on Education* was an attempt to create a system of natural as opposed to denaturing education.

Wordsworth's complaint in the 'Advertisement' to *Lyrical Ballads* was that the 'gaudiness and inane phraseology' – the self-consciously literary language – of contemporary verse set up a barrier between the poet and the people. He detected fakery as opposed to 'real feeling and just sense' in the language of well-to-do poets. He channelled instead his own experience as a homeless wanderer in the years after he left university – an experience so different from that of the typical gentleman-poet writing from the comfort of a vicarage or with the support of an annual income. Instead of verbally portraying the poor in the manner of a Dutch genre painting, he listened to their stories.

So too with his poems of place. Titles such as 'Lines written in early spring' or the more elaborate 'Lines left upon a Seat in a Yew-tree which stands near the Lake of Esthwaite' would have been familiar to readers from magazine verse and volumes of poetry, where there were numerous pieces along the lines of 'Description of a Morning in May' or 'Inscription for a Coppice near Elsfield'.[25] Equally, 'Tintern Abbey' was in a long tradition of meditative verse inspired by particular landscapes. The most accomplished practitioner of this kind of poetry was William Cowper. Dozens of lesser poets shared his sense of the beauties of nature as a sign of God's order and goodness, the idea that civilization and city life cut humankind off from primal connection with the environment, and that the poetry of nature offered both spiritual balm and moral improvement. Wordsworth follows in Cowper's footsteps, but with a difference: in 'Tintern Abbey' there is no God but nature itself, while the work of the poem is a process of self-realization through the mind's connection with nature, not an exhortation to orthodox piety and good deeds within a settled moral and social order. It was for this, as well as for his stripping away of poeticisms and his attunement to little things and suffering voices, that Hazlitt would champion Wordsworth as 'the most original poet now living' and call his poetry 'a pure emanation of the spirit of the age'.[26]

12

LUCY IN THE HARZ
WITH DOROTHY

On 14 September 1798, Wordsworth, Dorothy and Coleridge left London for the East Anglian port of Yarmouth. They were accompanied by John Chester, a shy Nether Stowey man who had become obsessed with Coleridge.[1] Two days later, they set sail across the turbulent North Sea; the Channel ports were closed because of the war, so there was no quick route to the continent. Dorothy was violently seasick and spent the entire forty-eight-hour voyage in her cabin. Wordsworth was also sick, Coleridge not. Once they reached the still waters of the river Elbe, Dorothy emerged and drank tea. After a delay due to fog, they sailed up the Elbe to Hamburg. They ate a bad dinner at a dirty and expensive inn called the Wild Man, where they would lodge for a fortnight. During that time, Wordsworth paid several visits to the grand old man of German letters, Friedrich Gottlieb Klopstock.

A survivor from the early eighteenth century, Klopstock had been one of the first to steer German literature away from French models. Germany was not yet a nation but rather a collection of principalities, of which Prussia was the most powerful. The language of the aristocracy and the courts, of politics, diplomacy and public life, was French. And the culture was accordingly dominated by French models, French neoclassical values. Klopstock, by contrast, wrote odes and dramas in German, seeking to dignify his native tongue. A translation of Milton's *Paradise Lost* inspired him to write a biblical epic himself, over which he laboured for decades. Entitled *The Messiah*, it proved controversial because it was written in blank verse as opposed to the rhyming 'Alexandrine' couplets of such French models as Voltaire and Boileau. Klopstock told Wordsworth that at the age of seventeen he had begun a three-year process of planning the poem. He did not complete it until he was nearly fifty. This perhaps gave Wordsworth the reassurance that there was no hurry to complete his own epic *Recluse*. After their first meeting, Dorothy wrote in her journal that she could not help looking upon 'the father of German poetry' without 'the most sensible emotion' – because he was now an old man with swollen legs, clearly close to death. She did not take to his second wife: 'much younger than he, a fine fresh-looking woman, but with an unpleasant expression of countenance, vain, and not pleasing in her manner'.[2]

Dorothy also described Klopstock as 'the benefactor of his country'. William relished his conversations with him because he found himself in the company of a poet who had made a difference. Klopstock's influence on the poetry and drama of late eighteenth-century Germany was immense. His first disciple was the self-educated philosopher, essayist, theologian, poet and critic Johann Gottfried Herder. As the young Hazlitt would be to Wordsworth, so Herder had been to Klopstock: on discovering Klopstock's poetry, Herder said that it was like 'a festive morn rising up over icy mountains'.[3] He regarded Klopstock as the equal of Shakespeare in his knowledge of the human heart and his ability to express the passions, especially in his love poetry. 'They are creators and exhibitors of the human soul,' Herder wrote, 'they present the operation of all motives, the play of all impulses. Thus they bestir the blood, overwhelm the mind, and arouse the sympathy of their readers.' Like Shakespeare, Klopstock was 'poet, philosopher, and psychologist, all in one'.[4] Wordsworth's highest aspiration was to be the same.

Herder was a key figure in the early phase of German Romanticism that became known as the *Sturm und Drang* – 'storm and stress'. He committed himself to the overthrow of classical restraint and to the espousal of a native German culture in opposition to all things French. He despised Prussian autocracy and its code of military nationalism, arguing instead that the true spirit of Germany was to be found in the traditions of the *Volk* – in ballads and songs, the traditions of the peasantry and the land. The models to follow were not the polished elite French ones such as the writings of Voltaire and the tragedies of Racine, but rather the raw, energetic, native plays and poems of Britain – Shakespeare's history plays, in which he gave the people the history of their own nation, and, on the Celtic fringe, the poems of the legendary bard Ossian. Herder's battle cry was taken up by Goethe and Friedrich Schiller, the founders of a distinctively national German drama. They wrote in the German language, about German stories, in the style of Shakespeare. Between October 1798 and April 1799, the exact period of Wordsworth's residence in Germany, the rebuilt Hoftheater in Weimar staged

Schiller's *Wallenstein*, under the direction of Goethe. This trilogy of historical dramas was at the centre of the cultural efflorescence that became known as Weimar classicism, in which Goethe and Schiller sought to yoke the impassioned sensibilities of the *Sturm und Drang* to an elevated Enlightenment sense of human freedom and dignity. Coleridge, who planned to go to Weimar to meet the authors but was discouraged by the cost of travel, would translate two of the three plays into English on his return from Germany. He went instead to Ratzeburg and then studied at the University of Göttingen, becoming fluent in the language and immersing himself in German literature.

Coleridge also had unfulfilled plans to visit another university, where two brothers, Friedrich and August Wilhelm Schlegel, were developing a theory of what – pioneeringly – they called 'Romantic' art. They were in a circle of profoundly well-read writers based in the university town of Jena. They welcomed the new political, philosophical and literary innovations of the age. Friedrich proclaimed that the spirit of the age was best captured by the French Revolution, the philosophical theories of Johann Gottlieb Fichte (who divided his vision of the world into the 'I' and the 'Not-I'), and Goethe's novel *Wilhelm Meister's Apprenticeship*, the archetypal *Bildungsroman*, or 'coming of age' tale, in which the protagonist grows into his mature self by joining a company of actors and inhabiting the part of Hamlet.

For Friedrich Schlegel, *Wilhelm Meister* was a perfect example of the 'organic' artwork – as indeed, according to Goethe's novel, was *Hamlet*. Whereas neoclassical works were perceived as 'mechanical', their form determined by a prescribed set of rules (as laid down in learned French literary treatises influenced by the *Poetics* of Aristotle), the Romantic artwork was 'organic', its laws governed only from within, its growth more like that of a tree than a building. Schlegel developed this idea in an essay in

Athenaeum, a journal that he and his brother launched in 1798. His brother would develop the theme in his lectures and from there Coleridge would develop the idea further – partly by means of liberal plagiarism from the Schlegels – in his literary-critical and philosophical autobiography, *Biographia Literaria*.

The first issue of *Athenaeum* also included nearly 150 pages of aphoristic fragments, ranging from gnomic remarks about the nature of irony as the 'alternation of self-creation and self-annihilation' to a lengthy riff on 'Romantic poetry' as 'a progressive, universal poetry'. The Romantic mixes 'poetry and prose, inspiration and criticism, the poetry of art and the poetry of nature', embracing everything from a universal system of creative belief to 'the sigh, the kiss that the poetizing child breathes forth in artless song'. Romantic poetry, Schlegel rhapsodizes, is 'a mirror of the whole circumambient world, an image of the age', but at the same time it is never finished and can never be fully analysed. It is in a state of perpetual evolution, soaring beyond the boundaries of genre and form that had constrained poets in previous generations:

> That, in fact, is its real essence: that it should forever be becoming and never be perfected. It can be exhausted by no theory . . . It alone is infinite, just as it alone is free; and it recognizes as its first commandment that the will of the poet can tolerate no law above itself. The romantic kind of poetry is the only one that is more than a kind, that is, as it were, poetry itself: for in a certain sense all poetry is or should be romantic.[5]

Never before had such high – and inherently unrealizable, paradoxical – claims been made for the art and passion of poetry. Elder brother August Wilhelm offered a more concise definition of the new cultural spirit of the age in his course of lectures on literature that deeply influenced Coleridge. There he described Goethe's other early novel, *The Sorrows of Young Werther*, the zenith of *Sturm und Drang*, as 'a declaration of the rights of feeling in opposition to the constraint of social relations'.[6]

Reading the contemporary Germans, Coleridge came to see that the literary revolution was more psychological than political. Poetry was being reinvented as the expression of the self. A cult of personality was emerging, along with a special valuation of the idea of sincerity – and there is no poet more sincere than Wordsworth. The late eighteenth century witnessed the birth of the belief that nothing matters more to us as human beings than our sensations, our *feelings*, and accordingly the notion that individualism and an individual's ideals – whatever they may be – define our freedom and our modernity. It was under the influence of the Jena school that Coleridge came to believe that 'the first step to knowledge' was to dare to 'commune with our very and permanent self'.[7] And it was this belief that led to his high estimation of *The Prelude* as the poem that penetrated 'the dread watch-tower of man's absolute self'.

It is impossible to imagine anybody before this era writing a letter of self-analysis like one that Coleridge penned to William Godwin in 1802. Here Coleridge argued that inaction and reverie were the necessary preconditions for creativity even as they were a form of mental sickness: 'Partly from ill-health, & partly from an unhealthy & reverie-like vividness of Thoughts, & (pardon the pedantry of the phrase) a diminished Impressibility from Things, my ideas, wishes, & feelings are to a diseased degree disconnected from motion & action. In plain & natural English, I am a dreaming & therefore an indolent man.'[8] One can see why Hamlet was the favourite Shakespearean character of nearly all those writers who have come to be called the Romantics.

Self-definition through literary models was one of their most effective devices. 'I am a Starling self-incaged, & always in the Moult, & my whole Note is, Tomorrow, & tomorrow, & tomorrow', Coleridge's letter continues, yoking the caged bird of Laurence Sterne's novel of sensibility *A Sentimental Journey* to the ennui of Macbeth contemplating the meaninglessness of life.

Coleridge went on to lament his own lack of 'the self-impelling self-directing Principle', his loss of 'Self-estimation' ('I evade the sentence of my own Conscience by no quibbles of self-adulation'), his failures of 'steadiness & self-command'.[9] Where once a man would have confessed his failings to a priest, here relentless self-examination takes a new form to which Coleridge gave a new name: 'psycho-analytical understanding'.[10] The Romantics were their own psychoanalysts and poetry was their therapy.

Coleridge's preoccupation in Germany was reading up on the new idealist philosophy in which Immanuel Kant and his disciple Fichte wrestled with the question of the relationship between the things of the world as they are in themselves and our idea of things as represented in the mind. His voracious appetite for books and his restlessly self-questioning mind, together with his increasing ill health and reliance on opium, paralysed him from completing any of his major writing projects. Wordsworth, by contrast, found his true voice of personal feeling during his months in Germany. He made the connection between the 'I' and the 'Not-I' poetically as opposed to philosophically.

Having split up from Coleridge and Chester, William and Dorothy went south to Goslar, a picturesque town in Lower Saxony, nestling 1,000 feet above sea level on the slopes of the wooded Harz mountains. Wordsworth vividly remembered that winter when he explained the origin of a poem called 'Lines written in Germany on one of the coldest days of the century'. It was composed, sitting beside his sister, in their lodgings 'at a draper's house in the romantic imperial town of Goslar on the edge of the Hartz Forest', a place retaining 'vestiges of ancient splendour' from the days of the German emperors of the Franconian line.

> So severe was the cold of this winter, that when we past out of the parlour warmed by the stove, our cheeks were struck by the air as by cold iron. I slept in a room over a passage that was not ceiled [sealed]. The people of the house used to say, rather unfeelingly, that they expected I should be frozen to death some night. With the protection of a pelisse lined with fur, and a dog's-skin bonnet such as was worn by the peasants, I walked daily on the ramparts, or in a sort of public ground or garden in which was a pond. Here I had no companion but a Kings fisher, a beautiful creature that used to glance by me. I consequently became much attached to it.[11]

Confined to their lodgings by the weather, Wordsworth veered between bursts of extreme creativity and physical symptoms that sound as if they were manifestations of mild depression. In the absence of books, he explained to Coleridge in a letter, he was obliged 'to write in self-defence':

> I should have written five times as much as I have done but that I am prevented by an uneasiness at my stomach and side, with a dull pain about my heart. I have used the word pain, but uneasiness and heat are words which more accurately express my feelings. At all events it renders writing unpleasant. Reading is now become a kind of luxury to me. When I do not read I am absolutely consumed by thinking and feeling and bodily exertions of voice or of limbs, the consequence of those feelings.[12]

The writing out of his memories was working as a form of catharsis, in an analogous process to the psychotherapeutic talking cure. In order to avoid being 'consumed' by his feelings, he had to express them – to push them out – in writing. But his darker thoughts also expressed themselves in physical pain, preventing him from writing. When that happened, his self-defence was absorption in the imaginary worlds of such books as he could lay his hands on.

Several notebooks from this period survive.[13] They are crammed with fragments, rough drafts, new poems sometimes written out partly in William's hand and partly in Dorothy's, together with material by Dorothy such as notes on German grammar and an account of their journey from Hamburg to Goslar. It was here that William wrote more ballads and the 'Mathew' poems, 'Nutting' and 'There was a Boy'. And it was here that he began *The Prelude*, composing such memory flashes as the skating scene and the stolen-boat incident. Dorothy reported that her brother was working very hard – more at his poetry than his German language. 'His mind is always active,' she wrote, 'indeed, too much so; he overwearies himself, and suffers from pain and weakness in the side.'[14]

Being far from his birthplace but in a not dissimilar landscape, Wordsworth's childhood memories were unlocked. By the time they left Goslar in the early spring, he had completed most of a version of what eventually became 'Book first: Childhood and School-time'.[15] This early version, which scholars call the two-part *Prelude* of 1799 (the second part was written later that year), included the 'spots of time' passage, exemplified by the girl with the pitcher on her head and the waiting-for-the-horses incident, those sequences linked to the deaths of his parents. In Goslar, thoughts of the grave seem to have weighed especially heavily on Wordsworth's mind.

They moved on in the early spring of 1799, wandering through Germany. There was a brief reunion with Coleridge in Göttingen, but those memories of childhood were calling them home. They talked of how they would continue to live close to Coleridge once back in England. 'I am sure I need not say', he told Wordsworth, 'how you are incorporated into the better part of my being.'[16] He was jealous of the bond between brother and sister, to which the companionship of the worshipping John Chester bore no comparison: 'William, my head and my heart! dear William and dear Dorothea! You have all in each other; but I am lonely, and want you!'[17] The trouble was, he was keen to return to Nether Stowey, whereas their hearts were set on the Lake District.

The Wordsworth family was now scattered, and brother and sister could not afford a place of their own, so on their arrival back in England they had to rely on the kindness of old friends. They headed far north to Sockburn in County Durham, where they spent several months staying in the comfortable farmhouse of the Hutchinson family. 'It is a grazing estate,' Dorothy explained in a letter to a friend written during an earlier visit, 'and most delightfully pleasant, washed round by the Tees (a noble river) and stocked with sheep and lambs which look very pretty.'[18] For William, it was a chance to become reacquainted with Mary Hutchinson, whom he had not seen since those precious summer excursions in the Lakes and the Yorkshire Dales during the long vacations in his Cambridge days.

★

In April 1799, Coleridge wrote to Tom Poole from Göttingen, replying to a letter containing tragic news: Coleridge's second son, Berkeley, had died of consumption at the age of eight months. 'Death – the death of an Infant – of one's own Infant!

– I read your letter in calmness, and walked out into the open fields, oppressed, not by my feelings, but by the riddles.'[19] The riddle, that was, of a benevolent God allowing an infant to die. Death made him ask questions about the nature of life and of consciousness. The philosopher George Berkeley, for whom he had named his child, had wrestled with the question of how we know that the world is real when all we can know for sure is the idea of the world that we hold in our minds. 'I refute him thus', said the commonsensical Dr Samuel Johnson, kicking a stone. The pain from the impact was real, so the stone must be real. But consciousness of pain comes from the mind, so that wasn't really a refutation. Berkeley's answer to the radical scepticism known as Pyrrhonism was that, while the human mind could know only ideas of things as opposed to things in themselves, everything had a true reality in the mind of God. All this was on Coleridge's mind because he was immersing himself in the 'idealism' of Kant, which took off from that of Berkeley (his habit of naming his children after philosophers was teased in *Nightmare Abbey*, Thomas Love Peacock's hilarious satirical novel about the Romantics, in which Flosky, the character based on Coleridge, names his son Immanuel Kant Flosky).

Now, though, little Berkeley's death and the question of whether there was some kind of afterlife for his spirit had Coleridge thinking about that stone which Dr Johnson had kicked in protest against the potential nihilism of Berkeley's philosophy of 'immaterialism': 'What if the vital force which I sent from my arm into the stone, as I flung it in the air and skimm'd it upon the water – what if even that did not perish! – It was *life*! it was a particle of *Being* – ! it was *Power* – ! and *how could* it perish? *Life, Power, Being!*'[20] These thoughts were shaped not only by philosophy, but also by a poem. Coleridge continued the letter to Poole:

Some months ago Wordsworth transmitted to me a most sublime Epitaph / whether it had any reality, I cannot say. – Most probably, in some gloomier moment he had fancied the moment in which his sister might die.

> Epitaph
> A Slumber did my spirit seal,
> I had no human fears:
> She seem'd a Thing that could not feel
> The touch of earthly years.
>
> No motion has she now, no force;
> She neither hears nor sees;
> Roll'd round in Earth's diurnal course
> With rocks, & stones, and trees![21]

Wordsworth's poem gave Coleridge an epitaph for Berkeley and at the same time a possible answer to the problem of Berkeleyan philosophy: the first stanza offers an idea in the mind – a moment of complete happiness in which the beloved is imagined to be untouchable by time – while the second suggests that in death the human subject is united with the material world of rocks and stones and trees.

Wordsworth always associated children and love and Dorothy with motion, with intense hearing and seeing and delicate touch. The quadruple negatives of the second quatrain take all this away from the beloved 'she' of the first. She becomes passive instead of active. The lines initially seem to be the negation of the joyful spiritual presence that animates 'Tintern Abbey', the 'motion and a spirit, that impels / All thinking things, all objects of all thought, / And rolls through all things'. And yet even in the first stanza 'she' seems 'a thing'. A reader as immersed in

Wordsworth as Coleridge was will remember that his poetry finds life in all things, even 'rocks and stones and trees', so in some sense the person in the grave is still alive, now connected to the diurnal course of the earth in a way that she was not in the first stanza's possessive, even egotistical, dream of immortality. As a student, Wordsworth had translated a famous ancient Greek poem called the 'Lament for Bion'. It contrasted the annual renewal of nature (even 'the lowliest children of the spring', violets and snowdrops, will 'breathe another year') with human mortality:

> But we the great the mighty and the wise
> Soon as we perish in the hollow earth
> Unwakeable unheard of, undisturbed
> Slumber a vast interminable sleep.

The 'sublime Epitaph' reverses this age-old thought: the poet's spirit slumbers while the beloved is alive, whereas when she is dead she follows the same diurnal course as the things of nature.

Few poets in the English language other than Wordsworth – Shakespeare is one, of course, perhaps Emily Dickinson another – could have packed such profundity and complexity into lines so seemingly simple. Coleridge saw that this was his friend writing at his best, that the poem is a universal epitaph, applicable to the feelings of anyone who has loved and lost. It answers to the measure of true poetry, namely its ability to, in the words of John Keats, 'strike the Reader as a wording of his own highest thoughts, and appear almost a Remembrance'.[22] Understandably, though, Coleridge could not resist speculating about its origin: after all, as he could judge from other poems that Wordsworth was sending from Goslar to Göttingen, passages that would form the bedrock of The Prelude, the sublime epitaph was written at the very time when Wordsworth was becoming the English language's first fully autobiographical poet.

Wordsworth was nearly always happy to answer questions about the sources of his inspiration, most fully in the notes that he dictated to Isabella Fenwick near the end of his life as he turned over the pages of a six-volume edition of his *Poetical Works*. But when it came to 'A slumber did my spirit seal', all that he said to Isabella Fenwick was '1799. Germany.'[23]

The letter in which Wordsworth sent the poem to Coleridge is lost, but another one survives in which Dorothy copied out 'two or three little Rhyme poems which I hope will amuse you'.[24] They are similarly possessed by death. One of them, later published in a pared-down version with the first line 'She dwelt among th'untrodden ways', begins in a style reminiscent not only, as I suggested earlier, of Helen Maria Williams, but also of the ballad tradition which underwent a revival after the publication in 1765 of Thomas Percy's *Reliques of Ancient English Poetry*. Wordsworth's poem ends, however, with a highly innovative intrusion of the poet's self. Many a ballad created a jolly roll of rhymes by ending alternating lines with the choral exclamation 'O'. Wordsworth transforms the convention into an aching expression of personal loss, by means of a singular 'Oh' followed by one of his trademark pauses at the line ending:

Long time before her head laid low
   Dead to the world was she:
But now she's in her Grave, and Oh!
   The difference to me.[25]

The other 'little rhyme poem', as Wordsworth's self-deprecatingly called these lyrics, describes a moonlit ride to a lover's cottage and the sudden fear, provoked by the dropping of the moon behind its roof, that she might be dead. In this one, the woman is given a name: 'Lucy'. And when Wordsworth published the one about the girl who, like 'A violet by a mossy stone / Half-hidden from the eye', dwelt in a secluded vale near the source of the river Dove, he changed the beginning of the final stanza to 'She *liv'd* unknown, and few could know / When Lucy ceased to be'. These poems were gathered in a cluster in the second edition of *Lyrical Ballads*, creating the impression that the subject was the same person. So was 'Lucy' a code name for Dorothy? Or was there a 'real' Lucy, perhaps some lost first love residing in Dovedale, or around Hawkshead, or in some secluded Lake District valley, a figure akin to Mary Joyce, the childhood sweetheart who haunted the poetry of John Clare?[26] Thomas De Quincey, who lived in Grasmere for more than a decade, reported that Wordsworth 'always preserved a mysterious silence on the subject of that "Lucy", repeatedly alluded to or apostrophized in his poems, and I have heard, from gossiping people about Hawkshead, some snatches of tragical story, which, after all, might be an idle semi-fable, improved out of slight materials.'[27]

The problem with the 'Lucy as Dorothy' argument is that Wordsworth did include the figure of Dorothy in other poems, but on those occasions he encoded her as 'Emma'. Coleridge's speculation about fear of Dorothy's death as the origin of 'A slumber did my spirit seal' may well have been correct; after all, Wordsworth would have been utterly bereft without her, given that he had been orphaned long ago, he was not close to his lawyer and academic siblings, his beloved brother John was away at sea, and Annette and Caroline were unreachable in France. But that would still not make Dorothy into 'Lucy', since Wordsworth never explicitly branded the sublime epitaph as a 'Lucy' poem. The efforts of biographers to find a real Lucy, or identify her as the dead sister of either Mary Hutchinson or

Robert Jones, have been fruitless. It is more probable that she was indeed, to use Coleridge's term, a 'fancy'. The name is first used when the light of the moon disappears behind the cottage. Lucy means light, so Wordsworth gives the name to the beloved of the horseback rider as he imagines that the light of his life has gone out. Then, in revising for publication the ballad about the girl in Dovedale, he gave her the same name.

He used it again in another exquisite Goslar poem, this time an imagining of a child who has died at the age of three. She is so lovely that Nature decides to take her for herself. Instead of lying in the grave, as in 'A slumber', she is transformed into a dancing nature spirit, an 'overseeing power' in the landscape, an embodiment of the 'vital feelings of delight' evoked by beautiful places:

> She shall be sportive as the fawn
> That wild with glee across the lawn
> Or up the mountain springs,
> And hers shall be the breathing balm
> And hers the silence and the calm
> Of mute insensate things.
>
> The floating clouds their state shall lend
> To her, for her the willow bend,
> Nor shall she fail to see
> Even in the motions of the storm
> A beauty that shall mould her form
> By silent sympathy.
>
> The stars of midnight shall be dear
> To her, and she shall lean her ear
> In many a secret place

Where rivulets dance their wayward round,
And beauty born of murmuring sound
Shall pass into her face.[28]

What Lucy represents here is the unmediated relationship between child and nature. The idea of her death, like that of the 'Boy' of Winander/Windermere, is a cipher for Wordsworth's own sense of the loss of his childhood. What has been left to him, he writes in the poem's closing lines, is 'The memory of what has been, / And never more will be'.

So many of Wordsworth's poems are tied to the memory of specific places, but the only place mentioned in the Lucy poems (other than a generic rural England in 'I travelled among unknown men', a sequel to 'She dwelt among' written a year and a half later) is the upper reach of the river Dove. There are several rivers of that name. The likeliest candidate for a location of a 'real' Lucy is the one that flows through the beautiful valley of Dovedale in the Peak District of Derbyshire, where Wordsworth wandered in the summer vacations during his Cambridge years. If we are to insist on finding specific biographical origins for the feelings behind these poems, we should perhaps go no further than proposing that they might be read as elegies not only for childhood and youth in general, but also for those remembered summers when he was in his late teens, released from his studies, reunited with Dorothy and beginning, though not fully realizing as much, to fall in love with their fellow rambler Mary Hutchinson. 'Lucy' *might* be regarded as simultaneously a composite of these two beloved women, a search for lost time, and an anxiety dream about the chasm that would be created if there were another death in the family.

★

Back in England in 1799, Wordsworth began to take in the reception given to *Lyrical Ballads*. Sara Coleridge, who was not feeling well disposed towards her husband in the light of his absence abroad at the time of their baby's death a few weeks before, reported to Tom Poole that 'The Lyrical Ballads are laughed at and disliked by all with very few exceptions.'[29] This was not entirely true. Francis Jeffrey, who would soon become Wordsworth's most vocal critic, enthused to a friend that 'I have been enchanted with a little volume of poems, lately published, called "Lyrical Ballads", and without any author's name.'[30]

The public reception was mixed. The first substantial review was by Coleridge's former collaborator Robert Southey. Like many writers, Wordsworth could hear only the criticism, not the praise. 'The bulk of the poems he has described as destitute of merit', he wrote to his publisher from Sockburn on reading the review.[31] The note in the 'Advertisement' about the narrator of 'The Thorn' had backfired: 'The author should have recollected that he who personates tiresome loquacity, becomes tiresome himself.' As for 'The Ancyent Marinere', 'Genius has here been employed in producing a poem of little merit.' On the one hand, Southey quoted from 'Tintern Abbey' and said 'In the whole range of English poetry, we scarcely recollect any thing superior to a part of the following passage'; on the other hand, he complained that 'On reading this production, it is impossible not to lament that he should ever have condescended to write such pieces as the Last of the Flock, the Convict, and most of the ballads.'[32] It is Southey who is condescending here: the whole point of these latter poems had been to write about the poor and the oppressed without condescension.

Dr Charles Burney, friend of Dr Johnson, influential figure in London literary society, and father of the novelist Frances Burney who was so admired by Jane Austen, was equally impressed by

'Tintern Abbey': 'The reflections of no common mind; poetical, beautiful, and philosophical.' He did not, however, approve of its 'gloomy, narrow, and unsociable ideas of seclusion from the commerce of the world'. Was it not sociability and commerce, the 'busy hum of men' in the city, that set us apart from 'the savage'? Surely a taste for 'beautiful scenery, and sublime objects of nature enjoyed in tranquillity' was the product of 'education and the culture of the mind' – the very things that the author seemed to be attacking elsewhere in the volume? Again, for Burney, while 'distress from poverty and want' was 'admirably described' in many of the poems, commiseration was misplaced when offered to 'The Convict', 'one condemned by the laws of his country, which he had confessedly violated'. Granted, 'The Female Vagrant' was 'an agonizing tale of individual wretchedness; highly coloured, though, alas! but too probable'. For Burney, the problem with the story was that

> As it seems to stamp a general stigma on all military transactions, which were never more important in free countries than at the present period, it will perhaps be asked whether the hardships described never happen during revolution, or in a nation subdued? The sufferings of individuals during war are dreadful: but is it not better to try to prevent them from becoming general, or to render them transient by heroic and patriotic efforts, than to fly to them for ever?[33]

Burney's criticisms were manifestly political, his implication being that it was not appropriate to publish such poems when the nation was at war and in peril of invasion.

The *New London Review* was unimpressed with the volume's 'experiment': 'The language of *conversation*, and that too of the *lower classes*, can never be considered as the language of *poetry*.'[34]

This was the kind of response that frustrated Wordsworth. Not only did such reviews reek of snobbery; they suggested that the whole purpose of the experiment had not been understood.

Much of the negative response had been directed at 'The Ancyent Marinere'. Its prominence, occupying the first fifty pages of the book, was clearly a problem. It was, Wordsworth told publisher Cottle, 'an injury to the volume, I mean that the old words and the strangeness of it have deterred readers from going on'. If there were to be a second edition, perhaps it could be replaced with 'some little things which would be more likely to suit the common taste'.[35] He was thinking of the lyric poems and shorter ballads he had been writing in Goslar. But what would his co-author make of such a displacement?

Cottle and Coleridge visited the Wordsworths at Sockburn in the autumn of 1799, following a letter from William reporting that he was in poor health. Little was said of *Lyrical Ballads*. Sales had been poor, despite the onward sale of the sheets to a more prominent publisher in London. The three men went off on a walking tour, heading towards the Lake District. It was Coleridge's first time in the north. They parted from Cottle at Greta Bridge. Wordsworth led Coleridge on, eager to show him the places that had shaped him in his childhood and that he had been recalling in the autobiographical verses he had shared in Germany.

One vale in particular enchanted Coleridge: that of Grasmere and Rydal. He drank in the world of his friend: the mountain of Helvellyn, the walk to Grisedale Tarn, the upper waterfall at Rydal. They talked about settling in the area, Wordsworth fantasizing about building a house by Grasmere lake. For now, though, they would have to rent. William wrote to Dorothy, who was still with the Hutchinsons on Teeside: 'There is a small house at Grasmere empty which perhaps we may take, and purchase furniture but of this we will speak.'[36]

Coleridge would not be able to join them there. He had received an offer to write for the *Morning Post* newspaper. He needed the money, but it would necessitate living in London. He returned to Sockburn to bid farewell to Dorothy. There was an evening of 'Conundrums and Puns and Stories and Laughter' with the Hutchinson family. 'Stood round the Fire', Coleridge scribbled in his notebook, '*et Sarae manum a tergo longum in tempus prensabam . . .*' Or, in English: 'and I held Sara's hand behind her back for a long time, and in that time, then first, love pierced me with its arrow – poisoned, and alas! incurable'.[37]

He left for London just before William returned to say his goodbye and thanks to the Hutchinsons, and to take Dorothy to their new abode. They began on horseback, with Dorothy clinging onto George, one of the Hutchinson siblings, and William riding Sara's mare called Lily. Once in Yorkshire, George returned with the horses, leaving William and Dorothy to walk the rest of the way, which took three freezing December days. As they came closer to the Lakes, they were spurred on by a brisk tailwind. Wordsworth's heart rose with the joyful anticipation of a homecoming:

When hitherward we journeyed, and on foot,
Through bursts of sunshine and through flying snows,
Paced the long vales – how long they were, and yet
How fast that length of way was left behind,
Wensley's long Vale and Sedbergh's naked heights.
The frosty wind, as if to make amends
For its keen breath, was aiding to our course
And drove us onward like two Ships at sea.
Stern was the face of nature; we rejoiced
In that stern countenance, for our souls had there
A feeling of their strength. The naked trees,

The icy brooks, as on we passed, appeared
To question us. 'Whence come ye? To what end?'
They seemed to say. 'What would ye?' said the shower,
'Wild Wanderers, whither through my dark domain?'
The Sunbeam said, 'Be happy.'[38]

13

BY W. WORDSWORTH

t had once been a small inn called the Dove and Olive Branch. In Wordsworth's time it had no name; only later would it be christened Dove Cottage.

'We have both caught troublesome colds in our new and almost empty house, but we hope to make it a comfortable dwelling', Wordsworth told Coleridge in a long letter written over Christmas 1799.[1] The upstairs chimney smoked like a furnace, but the fire drew well in the little living room downstairs, which was, in the words of its later occupant Thomas De Quincey, 'an oblong square, not above eight and a half feet high, sixteen feet long, and twelve broad; very prettily wainscoted from the floor to the ceiling with dark polished oak, slightly embellished with carving'. There was just one window at the front, 'with little diamond panes, embowered, at almost every season of the year, with roses; and, in the summer and autumn, with a profusion of jessamine and other fragrant shrubs'.[2]

Dorothy was plagued by toothache and other ailments, but she found refreshment in the orchard outside. From the top of the garden, which ascended a steep bank, you could see over the roof of the cottage to the lake, the church in the centre of the village (they were half a mile away in a cluster of dwellings known as Town End), the little mountain of Helm Crag behind and most of the vale of Grasmere beyond. It was bitterly cold – 'Rydale is covered with ice, clear as polished steel, I have procured a pair of skates and tomorrow mean to give my body to the wind'[3] – but brother and sister were together in what at last felt truly like a home.

They would soon be joined by William's brother John, whom they had barely seen since he had gone away to sea at the age of fourteen. He was the shy one in the family. He twice approached the door of the cottage, put his hand on the latch, then stopped and turned away 'without the courage to enter'.[4] He went to the local inn and sent word of his arrival. He stayed for eight months, on leave as he waited for the return of the ship he had been appointed to command, the *Earl of Abergavenny*. One of the largest 'East Indiamen', built to carry cargo for the company that dominated world trade, it was on its way back from China, captained by his uncle, another John Wordsworth.

Through those months, the two brothers and Dorothy walked in the woods and hills, laying emotional claim to their environment. William wrote his 'Poems on the Naming of Places': a pool in a clearing in the beech wood of Rydal Park dedicated to Mary Hutchinson; a rock chiselled with the name of her sister Joanna; a place by the lake where, on one of their walks, they initially mistook a man too sick to work for an idler, giving rise to the name 'Point Rash-Judgment'; a secluded dell named for Dorothy (coded as 'Emma'); and for William himself, a claiming of Stone Arthur, the rocky outcrop on the eastern side of the vale of Grasmere. When Mary Hutchinson came to visit, John struck up a close friendship with her; Dorothy noticed that they were always out walking together. Later, he seems to have developed an affection for her sister Sara.

John left Grasmere in September 1800. William and Dorothy walked with him as far as Grisedale Tarn, a mountain pond between Fairfield and Dollywagon Pike, where over the course of the previous months their visiting brother had often gone alone, to fish and to indulge 'his love of solitude and of the mountains'. From there, they could see down into Patterdale and as far as the head of Ullswater. They stood until they could see him no longer, 'as he *hurried* down the stony mountain'.[5]

★

Their closest friends in the locality were Thomas and Catherine Clarkson.

Coleridge's lectures advocating the abolition of the slave trade had brought him into the orbit of the man who did more than anyone else in England to secure that end. Thomas Clarkson was ten years older than Wordsworth. The son of a clergyman, he had gone to Cambridge, where he won an essay prize on the set topic of whether slavery was ever justified. By his own account, he then had a religious epiphany on the road, in which God revealed to him that it was his destiny to fight for abolition. He published his essay, which propelled him into a circle of like-minded men, mainly Quakers and Nonconformists, with whom in 1787 he formed the Society for Effecting the Abolition of the Slave Trade. Over the following decade he tirelessly gathered evidence by interviewing sailors and traders; he published more pamphlets and gave public lectures illustrated with the barbaric implements of the slaving vessels. He travelled thousands of miles on horseback, criss-crossing the country, taking the cause to the people, agitating for a sugar boycott that had the potential to bankrupt the plantation owners. Everywhere he went, he distributed medallions with the insignia of the Society for Abolition: designed by Coleridge's patron Josiah Wedgwood, it showed a manacled African slave, his chains extending to the ground, kneeling with hands clasped in supplication, surrounded by the words 'Am I not a man and a brother?'

Exhausted by his work, Clarkson retreated to the Lake District, where he commissioned the building of a handsome house called Eusemere at Pooley Bridge on Ullswater, a nine-mile-long glacial lake, second only in size to Windermere, overlooked by Helvellyn on one side and the plateau-like fell called High Street on the other. It was here that Clarkson married a woman called Catherine Buck. Coleridge took Wordsworth to call on them when they were walking in the Lake District in late 1799. 'I must tell you', Catherine wrote to a friend, 'that we [had] a Visit from Coleridge and W. Wordsworth who spent a whole day with us.' She offered a lovely vignette of the character of the two men and the relationship between them:

C was in high Spirits and talk'd a great deal. W. was more reserved but there was neither hauteur nor moroseness in his Reserve. He has a fine commanding figure is rather handsome and looks as if he was born to be a great Prince or a great General. He seems very fond of C. laughing at all his Jokes and taking all opportunities of shewing him off and to crown all he has the manners of a Gentleman.[6]

Pursuing the acquaintance, the Clarksons visited William and Dorothy at Town End. Catherine, who was convinced of William's genius, would become Dorothy's most intimate correspondent. Thomas Clarkson would later advert to Wordsworth's poetry of nature as an illustration of the spirit of Quakerism: 'the man, who is attentive to these divine notices, sees the animal, the vegetable, and the planetary world with spiritual eyes. He cannot stir abroad, but is taught in his own feelings, without any motion of his will, some lesson for his spiritual advantage.'[7]

When the slave trade was finally abolished by Act of Parliament, Wordsworth immortalized his friend's achievement in a sonnet entitled 'To Thomas Clarkson, On the final passing of the Bill for the Abolition of the Slave Trade, March, 1807':

Clarkson! it was an obstinate Hill to climb;
How toilsome, nay how dire it was, by Thee
Is known, – by none, perhaps, so feelingly;
But Thou, who, starting in thy fervent prime,
Didst first lead forth this pilgrimage sublime,
Hast heard the constant Voice its charge repeat,
Which, out of thy young heart's oracular seat,
First roused thee. – O true yoke-fellow of Time
With unabating effort, see, the palm
Is won, and by all Nations shall be worn!
The bloody Writing is for ever torn,
And Thou henceforth shalt have a good Man's calm,
A great Man's happiness; thy zeal shall find
Repose at length, firm Friend of human kind![8]

Here the vocabulary that Wordsworth more often applies to nature – 'feelingly', 'sublime', 'the constant Voice' – is applied to the work of abolition. 'Friend' is always a key word in

Wordsworth's lexicon, and it often carries political as well as personal heft, suggesting the 'friends of Liberty', those who agitated for the extension of freedom to all 'human kind' ('kind' itself suggesting 'kindred', a unifying bond). He was proud that this friend of humankind was his personal friend. Whereas his faith in the universal *fraternité* heralded by the dawn of the French Revolution had crumbled in the bloodstained dust of the Place du Carrousel after the storming of the Tuileries, he could now celebrate Clarkson's work to gain recognition that the slaves on the Caribbean plantations were men and women, brothers and sisters.

Modern historians point out that the Wedgwood medallion, which was reproduced on a huge variety of merchandise, became a fashion statement – rather as the politically correct of the late twentieth century would sport a Campaign for Nuclear Disarmament logo. It was a symptom of the first age of mass consumerism as well as a symbol of the cause. To own a medallion was to express allegiance to the Christian – and gentlemanly – virtues of pity and charity.[9] By the same account, Wordsworth's sonnet might be criticized for its focus on his friend the abolitionist, as opposed to the suffering of the slaves themselves. In response, one might point out that Wordsworth's own commitment to the end of slavery and the rights of all human beings is equally apparent in another sonnet, written in memory of Toussaint L'Ouverture, the slave who led the Haitian Revolution in 1801.[10] Its sestet gloriously imagines the spirit of the dead freedom fighter living on in both the elements of nature and the best aspirations of humankind:

> Live, and take comfort. Thou hast left behind
>   Powers that will work for thee; air, earth, and skies;
> There's not a breathing of the common wind

> That will forget thee; thou hast great allies;
>
> Thy friends are exultations, agonies,
>
> And love, and Man's unconquerable mind.[11]

'Am I not a man and a brother?' the Wedgwood medallion had asked. For Wordsworth, Toussaint was both the embodiment of 'Man's unconquerable mind' and a brother of the forces of nature.

★

In April, four months after William and Dorothy's arrival in Grasmere, Coleridge came to visit. When he left a month later, he took with him a number of Wordsworth's new poems. At the end of June, he was back, accompanied by his wife Sara and son Hartley. They were on their way to take up residence at Greta Hall in Keswick, in the heart of the Lakes, some thirteen miles north of Grasmere. Over the course of the summer, the two friends prepared materials for a second volume of *Lyrical Ballads*; they also wrote to Cottle proposing corrections and rearrangements of the first collection.

Cottle's publishing business had been struggling financially, causing him to sell his copyrights in late 1799 to the well-established London firm of Longman. They evaluated the rights to the 1798 *Lyrical Ballads* as worthless, so Cottle gave the copyright back to Wordsworth instead – which hardly pleased him, since he thought that the copyright was his all along and that Cottle had merely been given permission to produce the first edition and license it to another publisher in London.[12] Rather surprisingly, when it came to talk of a second edition in the summer of 1800, Longman offered £80 (the equivalent of about £6,500 today) for the rights, inclusive of the second volume of new poems.

Wordsworth had two people to thank for this: Coleridge

and a very remarkable woman.[13] Coleridge's new position as a political columnist for the *Morning Post*, working closely with the editor Daniel Stuart, connected him to the London literary world, where he indefatigably promoted his friend as the most gifted poet since John Milton. He also befriended the poetry editor of the paper, Mary Robinson. Born in 1757, she had been married off in her teens, confined with her husband to debtors' prison, then discovered as an actress by Richard Brinsley Sheridan and David Garrick, the age's leading playwright-producer and actor. A young woman of radiant good looks and irrepressible vivacity, she caught the eye of the Prince of Wales when playing the role of Perdita in Garrick's adaptation of Shakespeare's *The Winter's Tale*. Prince George sent her love letters signed with the name of Perdita's disguised royal lover Florizel. Their affair became the talk of the town and ended with rumours of blackmail and purloined letters. Abandoning the stage, Mary reinvented herself as a fashion icon and became the constant subject of the celebrity gossip that filled the London newspapers and magazines. Painted by all the lead-ing society portraitists – Sir Joshua Reynolds, Thomas Gainsborough, George Romney and John Hoppner – she was reputedly the most beautiful woman in England. In Reynolds' studio, she met Colonel Banastre Tarleton, a dashing Liverpudlian soldier who had gained an equal reputation for courage and cruelty in the war in the American colonies. They embarked on a long and turbulent affair, but in 1783 she was crippled by rheumatic fever. After a period seeking convalescence in various European spas, accompanied by her only daughter, she returned to London and remade herself again, this time as a writer.

Using the pseudonym Laura Maria, she began publishing verse in the florid style of the group of poets known as the 'Della

Cruscans', who had a taste for words such as 'tinsel' and 'pearly'. She then turned to the more financially rewarding medium of fiction; she was always short of money. In the early 1790s she produced several successful novels in a style of intense 'sensibility'. Sales were boosted by coded references to her colourful love life, and perhaps by pity for her disability (her public appearances by this time were in a wheelchair), but she was also a serious-minded political campaigner on the liberal side and an advocate for women's rights, moving in the circle of William Godwin and Mary Wollstonecraft. One of her books was a treatise in the Wollstonecraft vein, in which she argued, long before it became a reality, that women should be allowed to go to university. In the last years of the decade, despite a further decline in her health, she became the most prolific contributor of poetry, written under various pen names, to the *Morning Post*, which under Stuart's dynamic editorship had become the highest-circulating newspaper in the land.

At the end of 1799 Mary Robinson was appointed as the paper's poetry editor. She made it her general rule to print only new poetry, but in April 1800 she made an exception for Wordsworth, reproducing 'The Mad Mother' from the 1798 collection and introducing it with an enthusiastic headnote: 'We have been so much captivated with a beautiful piece, which appears in a small volume LYRICAL BALLADS, that we are tempted to transgress the rule we have laid down for ourselves. Indeed, the whole collection, with the exception of the first piece, which appears manifestly to be written by a different hand, is a tribute to genuine nature.'[14] Robinson had, of course, inside knowledge of the authorship of *Lyrical Ballads* from her fellow contributor to the *Morning Post*, the author of that first piece, 'The Ancyent Marinere'. Coleridge was at this time growing in admiration for Robinson and her poetry: 'She is a woman of undoubted Genius', he wrote to Southey, 'I never knew a human Being with so *full* a mind.'[15]

At the same time, Robinson so admired Wordsworth's poetry that she determined to publish a new collection of her own poems – a similar mix of narrative ballads and lyrical verses – with the imitative title *Lyrical Tales*. No doubt prompted by Coleridge, who was becoming more diffident by the day about his own poetic talent, she became the first person to refer to the 1798 collection as if it belonged exclusively to Wordsworth, writing to various publishers with her book proposal, saying that it would 'consist of Tales, serious and gay, on a variety of subjects in the manner of Wordsworth's Lyrical Ballads'.[16] She even asked Biggs and Cottle if they could produce her book in the same typeface as Wordsworth's. In the light of her celebrity, her sales and her connections in the newspaper world, Wordsworth in turn considered changing the title of his second edition, so that it would not be overshadowed by her forthcoming collection.

Wordsworth owed a debt to Robinson in her twin capacity as promoter and imitator of his poetry, but her close relationship with Coleridge carried risks. Her reputation remained mixed because of past sexual scandals and there may have been an element of mischief in the gossip Coleridge passed on to her. When her *Lyrical Tales* was published just a few weeks before the second edition of *Lyrical Ballads* – both collections being printed by Biggs and Cottle in Bristol for Longman in London – it included a ballad called 'The Granny Grey', which tells of the forbidden love between two characters called William and Annetta. The choice of the name Annetta is either a remarkable coincidence or a hint that Coleridge told Mary Robinson – who, like Annette Vallon, spent much of her life as a single parent to a daughter – more about Wordsworth than the fact that he was the principal author of *Lyrical Ballads*.

Robinson's point about 'The Ancyent Marinere' being so different in style from the other poems in the 1798 collection confirmed Wordsworth's sense that readers and reviewers regarded it as an impediment. However, rather than omit it altogether, he persuaded Coleridge and Cottle that in the new edition it should come near the end of volume one, instead of at the beginning. In addition, much of the archaic vocabulary was removed. Coleridge was demoting himself to the role of amanuensis, editor and advisor. It was he who urged Wordsworth to write a preface containing the two men's 'joint opinions on Poetry', but he took no credit for this in print.[17]

*

The fruit of many conversations with Coleridge, the 1800 Preface to *Lyrical Ballads* was Wordsworth's manifesto for the new poetry of feeling. His starting point was to expand upon the core idea of the 1798 'Advertisement'. The purpose of the collection was to explore 'the manner in which we associate ideas in a state of excitement'. Why, though, were ordinary people living in humble circumstances chosen for the experiment? Wordsworth's answer was now environmental, linked to the sense he had developed in the course of the 1790s, as he thought about his own feelings in Grasmere in contrast to London, that the human spirit is alienated in the city but somehow authentic, and connected to place, when 'amidst the beautiful and permanent forms of nature':

Low and rustic life was generally chosen, because in that situation the essential passions of the heart find a better soil in which they can attain their maturity, are less under restraint, and speak a plainer and more emphatic language; because in that situation our elementary feelings exist in a state of greater simplicity and consequently may be more accurately contemplated and more forcibly communicated; because the manners of rural life germinate from those elementary feelings; and from the necessary character of rural occupations are more easily comprehended; and are more durable; and lastly, because in that situation the passions of men are incorporated with the beautiful and permanent forms of nature.[18]

The logic of this position was that the ills of society were better addressed by a nature cure stimulated through poetry than by political measures to eradicate poverty and create equality. The Wordsworth of 1800 had become a very different person from the firebrand republican who penned the *Letter to the Bishop of Llandaff*.

He was keen to make careful discriminations and to avoid guilt by association. In particular, he wanted to distinguish his attempt to use 'a selection of the real language of men in a state of vivid sensation' from what he considered the lurid, unhealthy mental arousal offered by the popular fiction and drama of the time that we now call 'Gothic'. Such works, he thought, were signs of a dangerous urban decadence: he attributes the 'craving for extraordinary incident' which created the taste for 'frantic novels, sickly and stupid German Tragedies, and deluges of idle and extravagant stories in verse', to 'the increasing accumulation of men in cities'. His little volumes were a modest attempt to counteract the 'degrading thirst after outrageous stimulation' that had led to the taste for German melodramas and novels of sensation (one thinks here of Jane Austen's *Northanger Abbey*, written a year or two before Wordsworth's Preface, with its delicious parody of the naïve heroine's immersion in Mrs Radcliffe's *The Mysteries of Udolpho*).

The Marquis de Sade had a slightly different explanation for the *fin de siècle* delight in gloomy castles, medievalism and villainous religious hypocrites. He thought that Matthew Lewis's Gothic shocker *The Monk* (which features a sex-maniac rapist monk, incest, demonic influence, the Wandering Jew, a castle of sadistic nuns, a rampaging mob, and the Spanish Inquisition) was the greatest novel of the age. Sade suggested that the bloody Terror of the French Revolution had rendered everyday reality so horrific that only the demonic and the supernatural were sufficient to create a greater horror in the realm of literature. Sade himself regarded libertinism as of a piece with the spirit of revolution. He wrote his most notorious work, *120 Days of Sodom*, while incarcerated in the Bastille and for a time he represented the Jacobin cause at its most radical – before he was dispatched to prison by Napoleon (and then transferred to a lunatic asylum), for having written *Justine or The Misfortunes of Virtue* and its sequel *Juliet or the Prosperities of Vice*, in which disquisitions on theology, morality, aesthetics and politics jostle with extreme pornographic scenes from the happy and successful life of an amoral nymphomaniac murderess.

Sade is a far cry from Wordsworth, though it is notable that the latter attributed the taste for sensationalism not only to the accumulation of the population in cities but also to 'the great national events which are daily taking place', by which he meant war, revolution and counter-revolution. In England the 'anti-Jacobin' press did not hesitate to attack *The Monk* as a manifestation of the same subversive and atheistic tendencies as those of the poets and philosophers who represented the 'New Morality'. James Gillray's caricature *Tales of Wonder* shows a group of women poring over the book in pursuit of what the viewer is clearly intended to consider to be 'outrageous stimulation'. In idealizing the older way of life of rural communities, where news and new tastes penetrated far more slowly than in the cities, if at all, Wordsworth was subtly detaching himself from some of the radical associations of his own past.

The Preface was also an opportunity to explain what he meant by his reference in the 1798 'Advertisement' to the 'gaudiness and inane phraseology' of the recent poetic tradition. As an example, he singled out a sonnet by Thomas Gray on the death of his friend Richard West. Gray, he says, was 'curiously elaborate in the structure of his own poetic diction'. Wordsworth reproduced the sonnet, italicizing the lines that he thought were good, such as '*I fruitless mourn to him that cannot hear, / And weep the more because I weep in vain*', in order to contrast them with those that he thought were bad, such as

And reddening Phœbus lifts his golden fire:
The birds in vain their amorous descant join,
Or cheerful fields resume their green attire.[19]

He admires those lines in which Gray expresses strong feeling – anguish, the melting heart, joy rising and fading in the heart, mourning, above all weeping – but he condemns the poetic elaboration of 'reddening Phoebus' for the sun, birds amorously descanting and fields in 'green attire'. His own aim was to combine strong feeling with a more grounded language. What did 'Phoebus' have to do with the poet's task of expressing how human beings behave at times of extreme emotional stress such as when they are bereaved?

In particular, he explains, he had sought to tap into some of the 'great and universal passions' that the urbane and polished poetry of the previous century had all too often neglected. The 'maternal passion', for instance: the subject of 'The Idiot Boy' and 'The Mad Mother'. Then there were 'The struggles of a human being at the approach of death', as in 'The Complaint of a forsaken Indian Woman'. And 'the perplexity and obscurity which in childhood attend our notion of death, or rather our utter inability to admit that notion'. This last idea is wonderfully conveyed by the ballad 'We are Seven', in which an adult confronts a little girl, one of a family of seven children, two of whom have died. 'A simple child', it begins,

> That lightly draws its breath,
> And feels its life in every limb
> What should it know of death?[20]

Breath, feeling and life are Wordsworth's touchstones, but to the calculating adult voice that speaks the poem, 'If two are in the churchyard laid, / Then ye are only five'. For the child who sits and sings to her siblings in the grave, there is no acknowledgment of death: 'Nay, we are seven!'

Again, among the most peculiarly haunting of the 1798 *Lyrical Ballads* is 'The Idiot Boy'. This must be the first poem in any language on the subject of a Down's syndrome child. It is at once touching, funny and just a little holy. It says something about the special grace both of children with special needs and those who care for them.

Motherhood, children, death. Wordsworth saw that to bring the three subjects together would be to open the floodgates of feeling. And to do that would return poetry to its primal source, for, in the Preface's most famous phrase, 'all good poetry is the spontaneous overflow of powerful feelings'. Wordsworth believed that 'the deeper passions' and poetry have a natural connection. Metrical arrangement, however rudimentary, is the means of both expressing and ordering all those strong but inchoate emotions that are stirred by love and loss:

The music of harmonious metrical language, the sense of difficulty overcome, and the blind association of pleasure which has been previously received from works of rhyme or metre of the same or similar construction, all these imperceptibly make up a complex feeling of delight, which is of the most important use in tempering the painful feeling which will always be found intermingled with powerful descriptions of the deeper passions.[21]

This is literary criticism of the highest order, recognizing that poetry can be a balm, tempering the darker emotions, because it is complex, because its rhythms are as important as its words, and because a fine new poem can bring back the pleasurable memory of a fine older one. The authentic poet must, however, escape received 'poetic diction' and root out all 'falsehood of description'. True poetry, the Preface argues, comes from simplicity and sincerity. The language of good poetry is no different from that of good prose. The gaudy phraseology and figures of speech traditionally associated with verse-writing choke the true voice of feeling.

Wordsworth would not have sought to deny that a great deal of very bad verse comes from the spontaneous overflow of powerful feelings – the poetry of teenagers in love might come to our minds. Mindful that raw emotion is not enough, he went on to say that the feelings need to be modified by deep thoughtfulness ('habits of meditation'), and indeed that the best poetry often comes not in the moment of strong feeling but when an emotion is 'recollected in tranquillity'. The recollection triggers a process whereby the feeling is reanimated. For Wordsworth, this is the essence of the creative process: 'the emotion is contemplated till, by a species of reaction, the tranquillity gradually disappears, and an emotion, kindred to that which was before the subject of contemplation, is gradually produced, and does itself actually exist in the mind. In this mood successful composition generally begins, and in a mood similar to this it is carried on'.[22] A psychoanalyst might compare this to the mechanism that occurs during the 'talking cure'.

The act of fixing recollection in words has the potential to bring back what Wordsworth would later call 'the hour / Of splendour in the grass, of glory in the flower'. In this respect, poetry is a way of defying time. The poet thus has a unique, almost sacred calling. 'What is a Poet?', Wordsworth asks. 'And what language is to be expected' from a poet? A poet should speak to all people. In defining the characteristics of the true poet, Wordsworth uses the male pronoun, as was customary. This does not mean that he neglected the female poets: so, for example, in a later preface he especially extolled Anne Finch, Countess of Winchilsea, as one of the few writers of the eighteenth century gifted with authentic as opposed to artificial poetic diction.[23]

The poet, he continues, is 'endowed with more lively sensibility, more enthusiasm and tenderness . . . a greater knowledge of human nature, and a more comprehensive soul, than are supposed to be common among mankind'. Poets rejoice in their 'own passions and volitions', call up 'the spirit of life' that is within us all, waiting to be awakened; they delight in contemplating 'similar volitions and passions as manifested in the goings-on of the Universe'. 'To these qualities', Wordsworth concludes, the poet 'has added a disposition to be affected more than other men by absent things as if they were present; an ability of conjuring up in himself passions . . . especially those thoughts and feelings, which, by his own choice, or from the structure of his own mind, arise in him without immediate external excitement.'[24]

John Dryden, a poet whom Wordsworth greatly admired (he told Klopstock that he believed Dryden to be more accomplished than Pope), described Shakespeare as 'the man who of all modern and perhaps ancient poets had the largest and most comprehensive soul' and who had 'all the images of nature . . . present to him'.[25] Wordsworth – who, with Dorothy, read deeply in Shakespeare during the Grasmere years – takes Dryden's praise and layers onto it the terms associated with his own era of strong feeling: 'sensibility', 'enthusiasm', 'tenderness'. He adds the quality of being 'affected by absent things as if they were present' and the ability to conjure up passions without direct external stimulation: these are gifts that Coleridge would define in his *Biographia Literaria* as the essence of the poet's *imagination*.

★

In the manuscript of the Preface Wordsworth wrote that he would not 'have ventured to present a second volume to the public' without including a new long poem by Coleridge, the Gothic ballad 'Christabel', in which 'a lovely lady' is seduced in the woods by a 'lady strange' called Geraldine who, when she undresses and they go to bed together, reveals upon her breast some undescribed sight of horror with allegedly magical powers.[26] The completed first part of this poem was sent enthusiastically to Cottle, who began printing it. Then on Saturday 4 October, while William and Dorothy were having dinner, Coleridge arrived, very wet from his walk from Keswick in the pouring rain (he was visiting Grasmere frequently, sometimes taking a detour to traverse the summit of Helvellyn on the way). He read the second part of the poem to them. Although it ended abruptly, they were, according to Dorothy, 'exceedingly delighted'. He read it again on Sunday and they had 'increasing pleasure'. On Monday, however, Dorothy wrote in her journal 'After tea read The Pedlar.

Determined not to print Christabel with the LB.'[27] The extent
to which the determination was a collective decision of the three
of them is unclear.

A few days later, Coleridge explained the reasoning behind
the decision in a letter to his friend the scientist Humphry
Davy. The poem was long and 'was so much admired by
Wordsworth, that he thought it indelicate to print two Volumes
with *his name* in which so much of another's man was included';
more importantly, it was 'in direct opposition' to the intention
of the collection, which was to experiment with the passions
arising from 'the incidents of common Life'. And again, to
Josiah Wedgwood, who together with his brother had supplied
him with an annuity: 'my poem grew so long and in
Wordsworth's opinion so impressive, that he rejected it from
his volume as disproportionate both in size and merit, and as
discordant in its character'.[28] The idea seems to have been that,
because it was lengthy and because it was good, 'Christabel'
merited publication in a separate volume, along with 'The
Pedlar', Wordsworth's expanded version of 'The Ruined
Cottage' that they all thought was equally substantial and impressive. This did not happen.

Coleridge does not seem to have objected to the removal of
'Christabel'. He was aware that he couldn't find a satisfactory
way of finishing it, so publication would have been premature.[29]
Wordsworth wanted to get on and publish the collection, but
now the second volume was too short. He proposed that the
gap could be filled by Coleridge writing some 'Poems on the
Naming of Places' to go alongside his own, but Coleridge was
unable to write to order. Instead, Wordsworth laboured for several
weeks over a new poem with the working title 'The Sheepfold'.
Coleridge assisted by copying out part of it for Cottle. It eventually occupied the last twenty or so of the 154 pages of the

volume that was published in January 1801 with a title page (dated 1800) that read *Lyrical Ballads, with other Poems. In two volumes. By W. Wordsworth.*

That was an honest description of the second volume, which could be purchased independently, and indeed sold better than the first. Coleridge did not object to the false impression it gave that the poems in the first volume were also all 'By W. Wordsworth'. In his darker moments, he was thinking of giving up on verse and becoming a mere literary critic: 'I abandon Poetry altogether – I leave the higher and deeper kinds to Wordsworth, the delightful, popular and simply dignified to Southey; and reserve for myself the honorable attempt to make others feel and understand their writings, as they deserve to be felt and understood.'[30]

★

The reordered first volume of *Lyrical Ballads* began with 'Expostulation and Reply' and 'The Tables Turned', in effect making 'Let Nature be your teacher' into the theme for the entire collection. Volume two bore a superficial structural resemblance to volume one, in that it began with a rhyming ballad and ended with a long poem in blank verse, but there are major differences. The ballad was called 'Hart-Leap Well', the name of a spring near Richmond in Yorkshire that William and Dorothy passed on their winter journey from Teeside to Grasmere. A local peasant had told them the story of how the place was cursed because it was where a hart, exhausted by the chase, had breathed its last.

'To freeze the blood I have no ready arts', wrote Wordsworth, as if to indicate that the story was much more mundane than that of the Mariner and the albatross. There is, however, a similar conclusion: as 'The Ancient Mariner' (its title no longer archaized)

ended with the sentiment 'He prayeth best, who loveth best /
All things both great and small', so 'Hart-Leap Well' ends by
urging sympathy for 'the meanest thing that feels':

> The Being, that is in the clouds and air,
>
> That is in the green leaves among the groves,
>
> Maintains a deep and reverential care
>
> For them the quiet creatures whom he loves.

The sentiment is in the same vein as such works as *The Cry of
Nature or An Appeal to Mercy and Justice on Behalf of the Persecuted
Animals* by John Oswald, one of those English radicals who
moved in the same circles as Wordsworth in Paris in 1791. This
was the period of the emergence of both vegetarianism and
animal-rights activism: in 1824, a Society for the Prevention of
Cruelty to Animals was established, building on the example of
the campaign to abolish the slave trade. Basil Montagu Sr was
among the founding members, several of whom used a
Wordsworthian language of sympathy in their arguments for the
rights of animals.[31]

From the well in Yorkshire, the collection moves to specific
Lake District settings. The second poem is 'There was a Boy'
and the third is 'The Brothers', which is furnished with an
explanatory footnote apologizing for the abruptness of its
opening on the grounds that 'This Poem was intended to be
the concluding poem of a series of pastorals, the scene of
which was laid among the mountains of Cumberland and
Westmoreland'.[32] It is a long poem about 'brother Shepherds
on their native hills' who are 'the last of all their race' – the
latter became one of Wordsworth's most quoted phrases
throughout the nineteenth century. For Coleridge, the poem
was the model of English pastoral. It transposes an ancient

genre from the sunny Mediterranean vales of Arcadia, where imagined shepherds seemed to spend more time singing of heartbreak than working with their flocks, to the harsh reality of the northern hill farms. In contrast to the ease (Latin '*otium*') of traditional pastoral, Wordsworth creates a world in which shepherds are 'buffeted with bond, / Interest and mortgages'.

At Ennerdale, during Coleridge's and Wordsworth's reconnaissance of the Lakes in 1799, they had been told a story about how a shepherd had dozed off at the summit of a rock called the Pillar, then sleepwalked over the edge, leaving his staff caught midway in the cliff, where 'for many years / It hung – and moulder'd there'. The story becomes the occasion for a lengthy blank-verse dialogue between a local priest and the unrecognized returning brother of the dead shepherd, exploring the hardships of the rural economy and the enduring bond among the hill farmers ('Your dalesmen, then, do in each other's thoughts / Possess a kind of second life') and between them and their environment:

> I warrant, every corner
> Among these rocks and every hollow place
> Where foot could come, to one or both of them
> Was known as well as to the flowers that grow there.

This firm yoking to location is the most innovative feature of the second volume of *Lyrical Ballads*. So, for example, 'The Idle Shepherd-Boys' sounds like a traditional title for 'A Pastoral', but the poem is given the subtitle 'or Dungeon-Gill Force', which is duly amplified by a footnote: 'Gill in the dialect of Cumberland and Westmoreland is a short and for the most part a steep narrow valley, with a stream running through it. Force is the word universally employed in these dialects for Waterfall.'

At the same time, Wordsworth stamps his personal mark on the lakes and hills by means of the 'Poems on the Naming of Places' and the inclusion of 'There was a Boy' and 'Nutting', written in Goslar as part of the autobiographical project. The latter, in which the gathering of hazelnuts is represented as a violation of virgin nature, ends with a (hardly necessary) exhortation to Dorothy to move gently 'for there is a Spirit in the woods', but of all the poems in the collection it is the one in which the word 'I' is used most sustainedly – and it even has a footnote referring to 'The house at which I was boarded during the time I was at School'. This release of the personal voice inevitably led readers to speculate that the 'I' throughout the collection was Wordsworth himself and that there might therefore be some autobiographical origin for the figure of 'Lucy'.

The concluding poem begun as 'The Sheepfold' – Wordsworth's slow work on it was duly noted by Dorothy in her journal – was eventually called 'Michael, a Pastoral Poem'. It became one of Wordsworth's best-loved works. Here he succeeds fully in integrating his feeling for the hills around Grasmere with his sympathy for the dalesman. 'Having felt the power / Of Nature', he writes, 'by the gentle agency / Of natural objects' he has been 'led on to feel / For passions that were not my own'. He is convinced that the shepherds themselves feel the same way that he does:

And grossly that man errs, who should suppose
That the green Valleys, and the Streams and Rocks
Were things indifferent to the Shepherd's thoughts.
Fields where with chearful spirits he had breath'd
The common air; the hills, which he so oft
Had climb'd with vigorous steps; which had impress'd

So many incidents upon his mind
Of hardship, skill or courage, joy or fear;
Which like a book preserv'd the memory
Of the dumb animals, whom he had sav'd,
Had fed or shelter'd, linking to such acts,
So grateful in themselves, the certainty
Of honorable gains; these fields, these hills
Which were his living Being even more
Than his own Blood – what could they less? had lay'd
Strong hold on his Affections, were to him
A pleasurable feeling of blind love,
The pleasure which there is in life itself.

As in 'The Brothers', the narrative turns on a shepherd leaving his native vale – this time it is a son rather than a brother – just as Wordsworth himself had left the Lakes. The sense of absence makes these pastorals into poems of yearning and of loss. At the end of the poem the old shepherd Michael, in his eighties, waits for news of his son who has gone to the city and then overseas, falling into a dissolute life. Each day Michael returns to the sheepfold that they had begun to build together, but, the locals believe, he 'never lifted up a single stone'. The poem ends, as it begins, 'Beside the boisterous brook of Green-head Gill', just above the village of Grasmere where generations of Wordsworth lovers have gone in search of 'the remains / Of the unfinished Sheep-fold'.

Michael's grief for his lost son is conveyed with an intensity matching that with which Shakespeare represented the anguish of King Lear on losing his daughter, albeit in a quieter voice. In composing a tragic poem about a dalesman, Wordsworth was seeking to show that 'men who do not wear fine cloaths can feel deeply'. That is what he wrote in a letter sent to Charles

James Fox, the leading Whig politician of the age, upon publication of the new *Lyrical Ballads* in January 1801. Wordsworth
explained that he was sending the book solely for the purpose
of asking Fox to read 'The Brothers' and 'Michael'. Fox, he said,
had a reputation for 'a constant predominance of sensibility of
heart' in his public character, unmatched by any other politician.
Wordsworth believed that Fox would accordingly value the way
in which the poems drew attention to the 'rapid decay' of the
traditional way of life of 'the lower orders of society' in rural
England. The spread of manufacturing industry, workhouses,
soup shops, even 'the heavy taxes on postage' were eroding the
spirit of community, family and 'independent domestic life'.[33] In
particular, families were being separated by the decline of the
rural economy and the concomitant need for young people to
go to the city in pursuit of work. When Fox eventually got
around to replying, he said that his favourite poems in the collection were 'Harry Gill', 'We are Seven', 'The Mad Mother' and
'The Idiot'. Of 'Michael' and 'The Brothers', he said that he
was 'no great friend to blank verse for subjects which are to be
treated with simplicity'.[34]

It would be some time before a wider readership would come
to appreciate – as Coleridge did from the start – Wordsworth's
innovative democratization of the medium of blank verse that
Shakespeare had used in high tragedy and Milton in religious
epic. Sales were modest, though sufficient for a reprint of an
additional 500 copies to appear in 1802. For publisher Thomas
Longman, this was as nothing to compare with the success he
achieved with another volume of rural verse, *The Farmer's Boy*
by the Suffolk cobbler-poet Robert Bloomfield. Also published
in 1800, it went through five editions and 20,000 copies in two
years, with another 30,000 over the following two decades.[35]

The new volume of *Lyrical Ballads* did, however, firmly establish 'W. Wordsworth' as the poet of very specific, little-known northern places. The first words in the collection to meet the reader were 'Hart-Leap Well'. The last were 'Green-head Gill'. He was now emphatically a poet of the north.

14

HOME AT GRASMERE

Willliam and Dorothy's most intimate friendship was now with each other. Dorothy's Grasmere journal provides a day-by-day account of their walks, their reading, the ups and downs of William's health (his sleepless nights, his headaches, the pains in his side and his stomach), along with the writing, revision and copying of poems, new and old.

Dorothy's journal for spring 1802 is contained within one of the richest manuscripts in the entire corpus of English literature.[1] It was the very same little notebook that her brother had used in Germany in 1798: it contains his notes on his conversations with Klopstock and his early drafts for his autobiographical poem, including such key incidents as the infant memory of bathing in the Derwent, the boat-stealing and raven's-nest episodes and the boy blowing mimic hootings to the silent owls. The notebook was only half filled. In February 1802, Dorothy turned it upside down and started writing from the other end.

Each entry is a mark of her gift for living in the moment and then recovering her impressions at the end of the day, with minute details exquisitely remembered: favourite places, local people, food, housework, weather, sounds, letters from the Hutchinsons, from Coleridge and from Annette in France. Always she is writing out, rewriting, stitching up William's poems. Sometimes she tries her hand at verse herself.

Wednesday 17 March is a representative entry. William went up into the orchard behind the cottage and finished a poem. Some neighbours called, and Dorothy was offered manure for the garden. Then she sat with William and 'walked backwards and forwards in the orchard till dinner time':

He read me his poem. I broiled beefsteaks. After dinner we made a pillow of my shoulder – I read to him, and my Beloved slept . . . A sweet evening as it had been a sweet day, a grey evening, and I walked quietly along the side of Rydale lake with quiet thoughts – the hills and the lake were still – the Owls had not begun to hoot, and the little birds had given over singing. I looked before me and saw a red light upon Silver How as if coming out of the vale below,

There was a light of most strange birth,
A light that came out of the earth,
And spread along the dark hill-side.

Thus I was going on when I saw the shape of my Beloved in the road at a little distance.

The light faded; owls hooted as they sat on the wall at the foot of White Moss. The moon broke through and 'When we came in sight of our own dear Grasmere, the vale looked fair and quiet in the moonshine, the Church was there and all the cottages. There were huge slow-travelling clouds in the sky, that threw large masses of shade upon some of the mountains.' They walked backwards and forwards till Dorothy was tired, at which point 'William kindled, and began to write the poem.' So they 'carried cloaks into the orchard, and sate a while there'. Dorothy, 'tired to death', went to bed before him. Soon, though, William 'came down to me, and read the poem to me in bed'. That same day, a sailor passed through, begging, on his way to Glasgow. 'He spoke chearfully in a sweet tone.' Dorothy is unashamed to record everything from manure and broiled beefsteaks to poetry and intimacy to a passing victim of the war.

Most days, it was just the two of them. Sometimes, though, Coleridge walked down from Keswick and they were a trinity again, as at Alfoxden. On 23 April, Shakespeare's birthday, a beautiful morning, they left the cottage at eleven, 'intending to stay out of doors'. They headed for Nab Scar, the gentle mountain overlooking Rydal Water. The sun shone and they 'were lazy':

> Coleridge pitched upon several places to sit down upon, but we could not be all of one mind respecting sun and shade, so we pushed on to the foot of the Scar. It was very grand when we looked up, very stony, here and there a budding tree. William observed that the umbrella yew tree, that breasts the wind, had lost its character as a tree, and had become something like to solid wood. Coleridge and I pushed on before. We left William sitting on the stones, feasting with silence, and C. and I sat down upon a rocky seat . . . He was below us, and we could see him.

William came up to them and recited his poems 'The Waterfall and the Eglantine' and 'The Oak and the Broom'. They looked out over the vale, and in writing up the day Dorothy captured the scene in prose of astonishing precision and emotion:

> After we had lingered long, looking into the vales, – Ambleside vale, with the copses, the village under the hill, and the green fields – Rydale, with a lake all alive and glittering, yet but little stirred by breezes, and our own dear Grasmere, first making a little round lake of nature's own, with never a house, never a green field, but the copses and the bare hills enclosing it, and the river flowing out of it. Above rose the Coniston Fells, in their own shape and colour – not man's hills, but all for themselves, the sky and the clouds, and a few wild creatures. C. went to search for something new. We saw him climbing up towards a rock. He called us, and we found him in a bower – the sweetest that was ever seen.

When the Goslar notebook was full, she turned to another one, in which her brother had written his draft of 'Michael'. On Thursday 6 May, 'a sweet morning', they gardened together, putting the finishing touches to their bower. Then they sat in the orchard. William had been building a wall and Dorothy brought him an apple. They heard small birds singing, 'lambs bleating, cuckow calling'. A thrush sang 'by fits' and neighbour Thomas Ashburner's axe was 'going quietly (without passion) in the orchard', while 'hens are cackling, flies humming, the women talking together at their doors, plum and pear trees are in blossom – apple trees greenish – the opposite woods green, the crows are cawing'. Dorothy was at one with place and time, wholly attuned to the ecosystem: 'We have heard ravens, the ash trees are in blossom, birds flying all about us. The stitchwort is coming out, there is one budding lychnis, the primroses are passing their prime, celandine, violets, and wood sorrel for ever more, little geraniums and pansies on the wall.'

That evening they walked out to 'inquire about hurdles for the orchard shed'. They looked up: 'The moon was a perfect boat, a silver boat, when we were out in the evening. The birch tree is all over green in *small* leaf, more light and elegant than when it is full out. It bent to the breezes, as if for the love of its own delightful motions. Sloe-thorns and hawthorns in the hedges.'[2]

★

Their principal poetic task was the further working up of 'The Pedlar' so as to form part of *The Recluse*. With his increasing confidence in the autobiographical voice he had found in Goslar, Wordsworth also wrote more personal material intended for the project that was growing ever wider in scope, ever less likely to be completed. During the Dove Cottage years he decided that his epic should begin with his return to the Lake District. The fair-copy manuscript is headed:

THE RECLUSE – PART FIRST

BOOK FIRST

HOME AT GRASMERE

It begins with a childhood memory of seeing the vale of Grasmere:

> Once to the verge of yon steep barrier came
> A roving school-boy; what the Adventurer's age
> Hath now escaped his memory – but the hour,
> One of a golden summers holiday,
> He well remembers, though the year be gone –

Alone & devious from afar he came;

And, with a sudden influx overpowered

At sight of this seclusion, he forgot

His haste, for hasty had his footsteps been

As boyish his pursuits; &, sighing said,

'What happy fortune were it here to live?'[3]

Milton's cosmic epic was called *Paradise Lost*. Wordsworth's plan was to write a personal epic in which the vale of Grasmere would be his paradise found. At the climax of the planned 'Part first Book first' was a hymn of love addressed to the place, in which the valley surrounded by its low mountains is made the centre of his world, the embodiment of what Coleridge called the one life within us and abroad:

Embrace me then, ye Hills, and close me in;

Now in the clear and open day I feel

Your guardianship; I take it to my heart;

'Tis like the solemn shelter of the night.

But I would call thee beautiful, for mild

And soft and gay and beautiful thou art,

Dear Valley, having in thy face a smile

Though peaceful, full of gladness.

Grasmere is imagined as a place where there is a perfect harmony among the natural phenomena and between the environment and the buildings. The word 'pleased', ascribed to the vale itself rather than the poet's perception of it, suggests this sense of everything being well fitted:

Thou art pleased,

Pleased with thy crags and woody steeps, thy Lake,

Its one green Island and its winding shores,
The multitude of little rocky hills,
Thy Church and Cottages of mountain stone –
Clustered like stars, some few, but single most,
And lurking dimly in their shy retreats,
Or glancing at each other cheerful looks,
Like separated stars with clouds between.

Out of this harmony comes a sustaining sense of a world where the self and its surroundings are blended, creating a feeling of wholeness and of happiness, of 'Perfect Contentment, Unity entire'. Wordsworth begins with his surroundings:

What want we? Have we not perpetual streams,
Warm woods and sunny hills, and fresh green fields,
And mountains not less green, and flocks and herds,
And thickets full of songsters, and the voice
Of lordly birds . . .

He then proceeds to the 'sensation' inspired by those surroundings:

'Tis (but I cannot name it), 'tis the sense
Of majesty and beauty and repose,
A blended holiness of earth and sky,
Something that makes this individual Spot,
This small abiding-place of many men,
A termination and a last retreat,
A Centre, come from wheresoe'er you will,
A Whole without dependence or defect,
Made for itself and happy in itself,
Perfect Contentment, Unity entire.[4]

These lines, themselves the very 'Centre' of Wordsworth's poetic vision, were not published until 1888, nearly forty years after their creator's death.

They are the lines of a poet now fully confident in his vocation. That buoyancy was setting Wordsworth on the opposite path to Coleridge. Lifted by Dorothy's daily ministration, he did not allow his aches and pains and moments of darkness to impede his creativity, whereas for Coleridge declining health, despair over his love for Sara Hutchinson and a sense of inferiority to Wordsworth were drying up his muse and leading him to ever-increasing reliance on opium.

A mark of Wordsworth's growing confidence in his vocation was that when *Lyrical Ballads* was reprinted in 1802 he explained his poetic theory afresh without the assistance of Coleridge. He added an appendix developing his account of what he meant by 'poetic diction' and he altered the text of the Preface to further clarify that the 'principal object' of the collection was not merely to 'choose incidents and situations from common life' but 'to relate or describe them, throughout, as far as was possible in a selection of language really used by men, and, at the same time, to throw over them a certain colouring of imagination, whereby ordinary things should be presented to the mind in an unusual aspect'.[5] This emphasis on 'ordinary things' made 'The Ancient Mariner' seem even more marginal to the project.

★

In November 1801 Mary Hutchinson came to stay with William and Dorothy in Grasmere. She remained with them until New Year's Eve. For the last few days of her visit, the three of them were guests at Eusemere, the spacious and comfortable dwelling of Thomas and Catherine Clarkson, with its beautiful views of

Ullswater. A long two-storey house with large windows, it resembled the Wordsworths' childhood home in Cockermouth (though it was built of local stone, not brick). It could hardly have been a greater contrast to the dark little cottage at Town End.

William and Dorothy spent a further three weeks with their friends, with Mary coming and going, sometimes bearing letters from Coleridge and her sister Sara. There was a fond parting towards the end of January: 'Dear Mary! there we parted from her', wrote Dorothy in her journal, 'I daresay, as often as she passes that road she will turn in at the gate to look at this sweet prospect.'⁶ Just over a week later, Dorothy wrote to Mary and William to Annette. The letters are lost, but their content can be guessed at: William and Mary were becoming closer than they had ever been during their long years of friendship. The peculiar intensity of Dorothy's journal entries describing her life with William at this time may well have sprung from her knowledge that soon it would no longer be just the two of them.

On St Valentine's day 1802 William and Dorothy woke to a fine sunny morning after a hard night's frost. Snowdrops were just beginning to come into bloom. Leaving Dorothy to alter some passages of 'The Pedlar', William went out into the orchard. It was the moment for him to make a decision. 'The fine day pushed him on to resolve' is how Dorothy put it, focusing on the weather rather than the traditions of 14 February. He came back into the house and said that he would go to Penrith, where Mary Hutchinson was staying with an aunt. Dorothy finished her work on his poem and gave him some letters for her. He set off, wearing his fashionable blue 'spencer' jacket and 'a pair of *new* pantaloons fresh from London'. Towards sunset, Dorothy walked out alone to the Wishing Gate that was one of their favourite spots. Once in view of Rydal Water, she looked up to the hills. The sky was white, portending snow, but she was confident that her brother would have made a safe passage over the Kirkstone pass. Back in the cottage, after their servant Molly had left for the night, she wrote to Coleridge. She went to bed at midnight. 'Slept in Wm.'s bed and I slept badly, for my thoughts were full of William.'[7]

The next day it snowed and a letter came from Annette. The day after, William returned at teatime, after a rough journey – 'his mouth and breath were very cold when he kissed me'. He reported that he had walked out with Mary for no more than a couple of hours. Dorothy's journal is reticent on the subject of their conversation, but within a matter of days Coleridge was telling his wife that 'Wordsworth will marry soon'.[8] William wrote again to Annette.

Her reply came nearly a month later. It is unclear how much detail about her life she gave in this and other letters. She would have been wary of the possibility of her correspondence being intercepted, because she had become an active member of the counter-revolutionary resistance. The term is not an exaggeration: in a surviving police file, she is described as 'Widow Williams at Blois; gives shelter to Chouans' – that is, to counter-revolutionary insurgents. The house that she shared with her sisters in Blois was indeed searched by the authorities in January 1800. Years later, after the Bourbon restoration of the monarchy, a petition was launched proposing that the king should reward Annette, who by then had moved to Paris, with a pension for life in recognition of her courageous devotion to the royalist cause.[9]

'We resolved to see Annette, and that Wm. should go to Mary', wrote Dorothy.[10] Wordsworth owed it to Annette to tell her that he was going to marry, and he owed it to Mary to tell her what he was going to do about his former lover and his child in France. Following Nelson's victory at the Battle of Copenhagen a year before, there had been a suspension of hostilities, and the British government was now in the final stage of the lengthy process of negotiating a peace treaty with Napoleon, which was duly signed at Amiens two days after the Wordsworths resolved to try to see Annette. The opening of the border meant that over the coming months some 10,000 English visitors made their way to France.

First, though, for Wordsworth there was the delicate matter of going to Mary. He went on his birthday, 7 April. He was back within a week, the surprise of his sudden return shooting through Dorothy like a bolt. The next day, William slept in till dinner time. Dorothy was 'ill, out of spirits, disheartened'.[11] They took a long walk in the rain. They were staying with the Clarksons at Eusemere again. They left the following day, which was mild but very windy. The lake was rough; a boat that had become detached from its mooring bobbed alone in the middle of the bay. In the woods beyond Gowbarrow Park, they saw a few daffodils close to the waterside:

We fancied that the sea had floated the seeds ashore, and that the little colony had so sprung up. But as we went along there were more and yet more; and at last, under the boughs of the trees, we saw that there was a long belt of them along the shore, about the breadth of a country turnpike road. I never saw daffodils so beautiful. They grew among the mossy stones about and above them; some rested their heads upon these stones, as on a pillow, for weariness; and the rest tossed and reeled and danced, and seemed as if they verily laughed with the wind, that blew upon them over the lake; they looked so gay, ever glancing, ever changing.[12]

Wordsworth in 1798,
the year of *Lyrical Ballads*,
portrait by William Shuter

Jean Duplessis-Bertaux, *Storming of the Tuileries Palace on 10 August 1792*: Wordsworth witnessed the aftermath

Wordsworth in 1817, portrait by Richard Carruthers

Wordsworth in Benjamin Robert Haydon's *Christ's Entry into Jerusalem*, beside Newton and Voltaire, with Keats behind

The New School: detail from James Gillray's caricature *New Morality*

Dorothy as a young
woman, miniature portrait

Dorothy in old age, portrait
by Samuel Crosthwaite,
photographed in the early
twentieth century by
Christopher Wordsworth

Annette, presumed miniature portrait

The lost children: presumed drawing of Thomas and Catharine

Samuel Taylor
Coleridge, portrait
after James Northcote

Charles Lamb by
William Hazlitt

The Quantocks today,
with thorn tree, lonesome
road and view towards
the Bristol Channel, from
where it was feared that the
French might invade

Symonds Yat today, a few
miles above Tintern Abbey,
with woods, sylvan river,
steep and lofty cliffs

Wordsworth around the time of
the completion of *The Prelude*,
pencil drawing by Henry Edridge

'Perfect Contentment, Unity entire': the vale of Grasmere

Wordsworth's skates

Alfoxden as it is today

Birthplace: the family home in Cockermouth as it is today

Rydal Mount in Wordsworth's time

Dove Cottage as it was when Wordsworth lived there

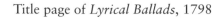
Title page of *Lyrical Ballads*, 1798

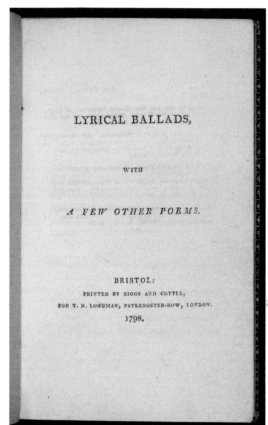

LYRICAL BALLADS,

WITH

A FEW OTHER POEMS.

BRISTOL:
PRINTED BY BIGGS AND COTTLE,
FOR T. N. LONGMAN, PATERNOSTER-ROW, LONDON.
1798.

Sir George Beaumont's
painting of Piel Castle

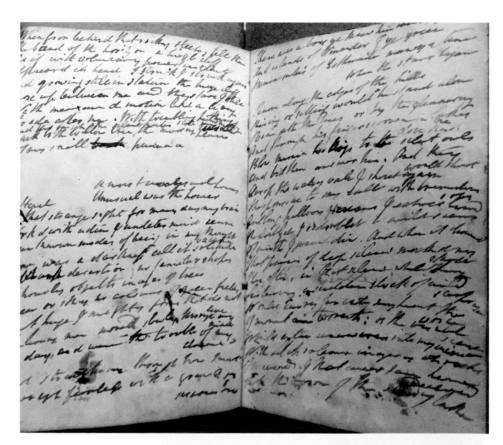

Original Goslar
manuscript of
'There was a Boy'

The wedding ring and
Dorothy's journal
entry for her brother's
wedding day

William and Mary in old age

THE PRELUDE;

OR,

GROWTH OF A POET'S MIND.

An Autobiographical Poem.

BY

WILLIAM WORDSWORTH.

NEW-YORK:
D. APPLETON & COMPANY, 200 BROADWAY.
PHILADELPHIA:
GEO. S. APPLETON, 164 CHESNUT-ST.
1850.

Title page of first American
edition of *The Prelude*, 1850

Max Beerbohm, *Wordsworth in the
Lake District, at Cross-purposes*

Wordsworth on Helvellyn, painted by
Benjamin Robert Haydon in 1842

This diary entry of Dorothy's would eventually give Wordsworth raw materials for a poem, written two years later, in which the memory of the movement of the daffodils as they walked together flashes upon his imagination – his 'inward eye' – in moments of contemplative solitude:

> For oft, when on my couch I lie
> In vacant or in pensive mood,
> They flash upon that inward eye
> Which is the bliss of solitude;
> And then my heart with pleasure fills,
> And dances with the daffodils.[13]

There is no reason to doubt that he remembered the daffodils when he lay alone on his couch, but the famous line that begins the lyric is a poetic conceit: he did not wander 'lonely as a cloud', since Dorothy was with him, on the way home to Grasmere. That night, they spent a cheerful evening at an inn with a reasonably stocked library. They read from a poetry anthology and a volume of Congreve's comedies over glasses of warm watered-down rum. They 'wished for Mary'.[14]

Back at Dove Cottage, they read a poem called 'The Glow-worm'. William explained that he had written it while riding his horse back from seeing Mary in County Durham. It begins:

> Among all lovely things my Love had been;
> Had noted well the stars, all flowers that grew
> About her home; but she had never seen
> A Glow-worm, never one, and this I knew.[15]

When riding on a stormy night, the 'I' of the poem spots a single glow-worm, leaps down from his horse, lays it on a leaf, takes it to 'the Dwelling of my Love', places it beneath a tree in the orchard and, to his love's great joy, shows it to her the following night. Wordsworth wrote out the whole poem in a letter to Coleridge, adding that the incident which inspired it 'took place about seven years ago between Dorothy and me'.[16] That same day, Dorothy wrote to Mary, addressing her as 'my dear Sister' and expressing anxiety at William's report of how thin she had grown.[17]

Wordsworth, then, wrote a poem that reads as a love-offering while he was riding from his fiancée back to the sister with whom he had once joyfully shared the sight of a glow-worm. In the version of the poem copied in the letter to Coleridge, he calls the beloved 'my Emma', the name that in other poems he used for Dorothy. But a copy of the poem in a notebook written out by Sara Hutchinson calls her 'my Mary'.[18] And when it was published in his 1807 collection, she has become 'my Lucy' (the association of the name with 'light' being especially appropriate for a poem about a glow-worm). This provides as good an answer as any to the riddle of Lucy's identity: she is a composite creation, the archetype of a beloved. At the same time, Dorothy's special fondness for the glow-worm poem would seem to have stemmed from her recognition that William's deep spiritual love for her now existed alongside a love for Mary that had grown from friendship into passion.

For brother and sister, it was as if something was coming to an end. Thursday 29 April was a beautiful morning. The first cuckoo of spring was heard. William composed a short poem about a tinker and Dorothy wrote it down. Then they went to the grove that they had named for their brother John. They sat for a while and

Afterwards William lay, and I lay in the trench under the fence – he with his eyes shut, and listening to the waterfalls and the birds. There was no one waterfall above another – it was a sound of waters in the air – the voice of the air. William heard me breathing and rustling now and then but we both lay still, and unseen by one another – he thought that it would be as sweet thus to lie so in the grave, to hear the *peaceful* sounds of the earth and just to know that ones dear friends were near.[19]

In this moment, or at least in Dorothy's remembering and recording of it in her journal, they have turned themselves into Lucy in the grave, rolled round with rocks and stones and trees. But together.

Paradoxically, they wanted to be both a secluded couple and the centre of what we would now call a 'friendship group'. A few days later, they spent a hot early May day with Coleridge on the road between Grasmere and Keswick. Dorothy was 'in heaven': it was Alfoxden Revisited. They went to a rock which they had christened 'Sara's Crag'. Coleridge had once carved the initials SH upon it. More recently, he had added STC and DW. Dorothy kissed all the initials and William took Coleridge's penknife and deepened the T.[20]

Ten days later, Dorothy inscribed her own imaginary rock of names on the blotting paper in her journal:

S. T. Coleridge

Dorothy Wordsworth   William Wordsworth

Mary Hutchinson   Sara Hutchinson

William   Coleridge   Mary

Dorothy   Sara

16th May

1802

John Wordsworth

In Dorothy's imagination, they are all together, except perhaps John the mariner, whose name is separated by the date. Coleridge is top and centre. Dorothy and William have the second line to themselves, but then the Hutchinson sisters intervene. Soon the trinity will be William, Coleridge and Mary, with Dorothy and Sara relegated – perhaps in the role of amanuenses rather than muses – to the line below.

In late May, Wordsworth began work on what he called his poem on 'Going for Mary'. It was eventually published under the title 'A Farewell'. Curiously, since the plan was to bring Mary to the cottage in Grasmere and incorporate her into their life there, it has an elegiac air of parting:

> Farewell, thou little Nook of mountain ground,
> Thou rocky corner in the lowest stair
> Of Fairfield's mighty Temple that doth bound
> One side of our whole vale with grandeur rare,
> Sweet Garden-orchard! of all spots that are
> The loveliest surely man hath ever found,
> Farewell! we leave thee to heaven's peaceful care,
> Thee and the Cottage which thou dost surround.[21]

As the poem recalls the simple possessions that William and Dorothy had gathered in the little house that was later named Dove Cottage, and the tenderness with which they plucked wild flowers from the fellsides and planted them in their garden, one realizes that it is a farewell not to the house but to the private bond of brother and sister.

★

Prudent marriage, as Jane Austen's novels reminded readers of the time, was always bound up with money. In this regard,

Wordsworth had a rare stroke of luck. Towards the end of May, news came that James Lowther, Earl of Lonsdale, had died. He had no son, so his vast wealth and huge estates were left to a distant cousin who had a reputation as an honourable gentleman. There was a genuine opportunity that the long-standing debt owed to the Wordsworth family might at last be paid. One of the things that had made Wordsworth hesitate about proposing to Mary had been his lack of financial means, especially in the light of his need to provide continued support to Annette and Caroline in France. The Calvert legacy of £70 a year together with his meagre literary earnings would hardly have sufficed to keep Mary and raise a family. She was bringing a dowry of only about £400. There was also the question of Dorothy. The plan was that she would continue to live with William and Mary, maintaining her habits of extreme frugality and being given a small allowance by her other brothers. Despite these worries, William had made his proposal and Mary had accepted. Now there was a glimmer of hope that the finances might ease. Action to recover the debt was recommenced and in early 1803 news came that the legal representatives of the new earl had agreed that a sum of about £8,000 (roughly eighty per cent of the debt and its interest) would be paid to the Wordsworth family.

★

Very early on the clear warm morning on 29 July 1802, Dorothy and William Wordsworth mounted the Dover coach at Charing Cross. As they crossed Westminster Bridge, they looked out at the city, St Paul's Cathedral and the river with its 'multitude of little boats'. In Dorothy's words, 'The houses were not overhung by their cloud of smoke, and they were spread out endlessly, yet the sun shone so brightly, with such a fierce light, that there was even something like the purity of one of nature's own grand spectacles'.²² William turned this thought into a sonnet, which he seems to have written up when they returned to London just over a month later:

> Earth has not any thing to shew more fair:
> Dull would he be of soul who could pass by
> A sight so touching in its majesty:
> This City now doth like a garment wear
> The beauty of the morning; silent, bare,
> Ships, towers, domes, theatres, and temples lie
> Open unto the fields, and to the sky;
> All bright and glittering in the smokeless air.
> Never did sun more beautifully steep
> In his first splendor valley, rock, or hill;
> Ne'er saw I, never felt, a calm so deep!
> The river glideth at his own sweet will:
> Dear God! the very houses seem asleep;
> And all that mighty heart is lying still!²³

Wordsworth's usual move is to contrast the deep calm of the countryside to the frenetic noise and commerce of the city, but at this dawn moment he and Dorothy find peace in the heart of London.

The coach took them through rural Kent. Everything was new to Dorothy. It was nearly dark when they reached Dover. The packet boat was about to sail, so they went quickly through Customs, drank tea with a travelling gentleman and his tutor, and sailed overnight, arriving at Calais at four in the morning. The weather was hot, their lodgings badly furnished and smelly. They stayed for a month, in the company of Annette and Caroline, who had travelled to the coast to meet them.

After their return to England, Dorothy gave a brief retrospective account of the visit. They had walked on the long sandy beach almost every evening, sometimes with Annette and Caroline, at other times William and Dorothy alone. She had a bad cold and could not bathe at first, but William did – along with 'perhaps a hundred people' enjoying the new fashion for sea-bathing. During their walks in the cool of the evening, they saw 'far off in the west the Coast of England like a cloud crested with Dover Castle'. Dorothy especially remembered one night when

the day had been very hot, and William and I walked alone together upon the pier – the sea was gloomy for there was a blackness over all the sky except when it was overspread with lightning which often revealed to us a distant vessel. Near us the waves roared and broke against the pier, and as they broke and as they travelled towards us, they were interfused with greenish fiery light.[24]

On the calm hot nights, they saw 'little boats row out of the harbour with wings of fire'. The fiery track which the vessels cut as they went along closed up 'with a hundred thousand sparkles, balls shootings and streams of glow-worm light'. 'Caroline was delighted', Dorothy recorded – her only reference to William's daughter. Her journal says nothing of his conversations with Annette.

For William, it was a time of conflicting emotions. He was meeting his nine-year-old daughter for the first time. Having missed her childhood, he knew that he would also miss her adolescence. Annette, meanwhile, had to be told about his impending marriage. Money would certainly have been discussed, but we do not know how much she told him about her work for the monarchist resistance. The return to Calais also brought back memories: it was now that he wrote the sonnet to Jones commemorating the first time he had set foot on French soil, in such different personal and political circumstances.

Those evening walks along the sands and to the end of the pier, with the white cliffs of Dover clearly visible and the light-ships gleaming from the English coast, together with the knowledge that the peace treaty with Napoleon was fragile, had him thinking about patriotism. In Grasmere, he and Dorothy had been reading the sonnets of Milton.[25] From this time on, the Miltonic sonnet – a balance of octave and sestet, as opposed to the three quatrains plus closing couplet of the Shakespearean variety – became one of his favourite forms. He would write over 500 of them. Like those of Milton, some were personal and others political. Those written in Calais and then in Kent on his return are both at once:

> *Composed by the Sea-side, near Calais, August, 1802*
> Fair Star of Evening, Splendor of the West,
> Star of my Country! on the horizon's brink
> Thou hangest, stooping, as might seem, to sink
> On England's bosom; yet well pleas'd to rest,
> Meanwhile, and be to her a glorious crest
> Conspicuous to the Nations. Thou, I think,
> Should'st be my Country's emblem; and should'st
>   wink,
> Bright Star! with laughter on her banners, drest
> In thy fresh beauty. There! that dusky spot
> Beneath thee, it is England; there it lies.
> Blessings be on you both! one hope, one lot,
> One life, one glory! I, with many a fear
> For my dear Country, many heartfelt sighs,

Among Men who do not love her linger here.[26]

Some years later, John Keats would take that image of a 'Bright
Star' and make it his own.

Near Dover, on the day of landing back in the country of his
birth, Wordsworth was overwhelmed with a sense of Englishness:
the cock crowing from a farmyard, smoke curling over a cottage,
church bells ringing, boys in white-sleeved shirts playing in a
meadow:

> All, all are English. Oft have I look'd round
> With joy in Kent's green vales; but never
>   found
> Myself so satisfied in heart before.
> Europe is yet in Bonds; but let that pass,
> Thought for another moment. Thou art free
> My Country! and 'tis joy enough and pride
> For one hour's perfect bliss, to tread the grass
> Of England once again, and hear and see,
> With such a dear Companion at my side.[27]

Dorothy, who had been seasick all through the return crossing,
was the companion by his side. Not his daughter Caroline. He
could say nothing in public about her. But he allowed himself
to fix his memory of her on the Calais sands in another sonnet,
which begins 'It is a beauteous Evening, calm and free'.
Wordsworth compares the peaceful evening to the quietness of
a nun. The tranquillity of the scene puts him into a spiritual
mood:

> Listen! the mighty Being is awake
> And doth with his eternal motion make

A sound like thunder – everlastingly.
Dear Child! dear Girl! that walkest with me here,
If thou appear'st untouch'd by solemn thought,
Thy nature is not therefore less divine:
Thou liest in Abraham's bosom all the year;
And worshipp'st at the Temple's inner shrine,
God being with thee when we know it not.[28]

Perhaps under the influence of Annette's staunch Catholicism, in blessing his child he overtly invokes the Judaeo-Christian God for one of the first times in his mature poetry: the 'mighty Being' of this sonnet is at one and the same time the nature spirit of 'Tintern Abbey' and something more orthodox. The allusion to Abraham is one of only two in the entire corpus of his poetry.[29]

★

After three weeks in London, they went north to the Hutchinsons, who were now living in Yorkshire at a house called Gallow Hill in the village of Brompton-by-Sawdon near Scarborough on the coast of the North Sea. Mary met them in the avenue that led to the house. She had put on weight and looked well. The rest of the Hutchinson family followed. Brother Tom was standing on a corn cart with a long fork in hand. Dorothy looked on 'with tranquillity and happiness' but for the remainder of their stay she was ill.

Her diary entry for the day when William and Mary went down to the village church is written in an uncharacteristically spare style, devoid of her habitual bright-eyed observation of nature:

On Monday, 4th October 1802, my brother William was married to Mary Hutchinson. I slept a good deal of the night,

and rose fresh and well in the morning – at a little after eight
o clock I saw them go down the avenue towards the Church.
William had parted from me up stairs. I gave him the wedding
ring – with how deep a blessing! I took it from my forefinger
where I had worn it the whole night before – he slipped it
again onto my finger and blessed me fervently.

During their absence for the ceremony, Sara the maid prepared
the wedding breakfast. Dorothy kept herself as quiet as she could,
but when she saw 'the two men', presumably Mary's brothers,
'running up the walk', coming to tell them that 'it was over',
she 'could stand it no longer' and threw herself on the bed,
where she 'lay in stillness, neither hearing nor seeing any thing'.[30]
'She neither hears nor sees', Wordsworth had written of the dead
Lucy. Consciously or not, Dorothy is making herself into Lucy.
This time, she is alone in her metaphoric grave, not lying in
stillness with William as she had done in that trench in the vale
of Grasmere that summer. Her only consolation was the symbolic
marriage that had taken place before William tied the legal knot,
that early morning exchange of the wedding ring she had worn
all through the previous night.

The maid came upstairs and told her that the bride and groom
were coming: 'This forced me from the bed where I lay and I
moved, I knew not how, straight forward, faster than my strength
could carry me till I met my beloved William, and fell upon his
bosom.' Together with John Hutchinson, William led her back
to the house, where she waited to welcome her 'dear Mary'.
The married Wordsworth had crossed his new wife's threshold
in the company not of his bride but of his sister.

After the wedding breakfast, the three of them left for Grasmere.
Stopping on the way for the horses to be fed, they sauntered in
a churchyard and read the gravestones. Along the way, which

William and Dorothy had travelled before, they pointed out their favourite sites to Mary. Dorothy had a particular affection for Stavely, near Windermere, because it was 'the first mountain village that I came to with Wm when we first began our pilgrimage together'.[31]

15

THE CHILD IS FATHER
OF THE MAN

Coleridge gave William and Mary a curious wedding present in the form of a poem published in the *Morning Post* on the day of their marriage, which was also his own wedding anniversary. Entitled 'Dejection: an Ode', it was a shortened and redacted version of a very personal poem that he had written back in the spring. The private history behind it, invisible to the readers of the *Morning Post*, reveals the growing gulf between the two poets.

One evening back in March 1802, as Dorothy was getting ready for bed, Wordsworth wrote a short poem that she called 'The Rainbow':

My heart leaps up when I behold
   A Rainbow in the sky:
So was it when my life began;
So is it now I am a Man;
So be it when I shall grow old,
   Or let me die!
The Child is Father of the Man;
And I could wish my days to be
Bound each to each by natural piety.[1]

His hope is that the 'natural piety' of childhood, manifested in the leap of the heart at the sight of a rainbow, will remain with him all his life. The next day over breakfast, even though it was what Dorothy called 'a divine morning', he began to have doubts.[2] He 'wrote part of an Ode', in which the 'was' of childhood is *contrasted* to the poet's feelings in the 'now' of manhood:

There was a time when meadow, grove, and
   stream,
The earth, and every common sight,
    To me did seem
   Apparell'd in celestial light,
The glory and the freshness of a dream.
It is not now as it has been of yore; –
   Turn wheresoe'er I may,
    By night or day,
The things which I have seen I now can see
   no more.[3]

'The Rainbow comes and goes', he continues. The rose is lovely. So are the moon and the lake on a clear night. But, somehow, for the adult as opposed to the child, 'there hath pass'd away a glory from the earth'. It is this recognition that infuses so much of Wordsworth's poetry with an elegiac tone, a sense of loss. Yet he also recognizes that the 'timely utterance' of poetry ('My heart leaps up') can relieve the mind from this 'thought of grief' and make the doubting self 'strong' again by directing us back to the joys of childhood and of nature in the springtime of the year. At this point, Wordsworth set his ode aside, the two conflicting thoughts unresolved.

The next day, William and Dorothy went to stay with the Coleridges in Keswick. Wordsworth showed Coleridge his fragmentary ode. A week later, Coleridge sent Sara Hutchinson a verse letter that darkens the vision. 'There *was* a time when tho' my path was rough, / The Joy within me dallied with Distress', he writes, echoing Wordsworth's sense that there can be moments in adult life when the unmediated joy of childhood is not altogether lost. Now, however, the things that restore Wordsworth – notably the landscapes surrounding them in the Lake District – no longer restore Coleridge:

> These Mountains too, these Vales, these Woods, these
>   Lakes,
> Scenes full of Beauty and of Loftiness
> Where all my Life I fondly hop'd to live –
> I were sunk low indeed, did they *no* solace give;
> But oft I seem to feel, and evermore I fear,
> They are not to me now the Things, which once they
>   were.[4]

Furthermore, he finds himself questioning Wordsworth's sense of the reciprocal relationship between mind and nature, the belief that there is a life in things that is a gift to the willing human respondent:

O Sara! we receive but what we give,

And in *our* Life alone does Nature live.

Our's is her Wedding Garment, our's her Shroud . . .

Ah! from the Soul itself must issue forth

A Light, a Glory, and a luminous Cloud

Enveloping the Earth!

And from the Soul itself must there be sent

A sweet and potent Voice, of it's own Birth,

Of all sweet Sounds the Life and Element.

Wordsworth's 'celestial light' and 'glory from the earth' are seen as mere projections from within the mind. Nature is dead without them. The 'one life' is now solely 'within us', not 'within us and abroad'.

Coleridge's poem for Sara contains several scarcely veiled hints as to the reasons for this gloomy turn of thought. He imagines her joining William, Dorothy and Mary in their home at Grasmere:

When thou, and with thee those, whom thou lov'st best,

Shall dwell together in one happy Home,

One House, the dear *abiding* Home of All.

The implication is that he is to be excluded from this happy place. 'But now ill Tidings bow me down to earth', he writes, at exactly the time that Wordsworth was bringing glad tidings of plans for his wedding to Sara's sister. Coleridge, meanwhile, was stuck with the Sara he no longer loved. Furthermore, each time Wordsworth arrives with new poems and ideas for poems (the verse letter alludes explicitly to the ballads *Peter Bell* and 'Lucy Gray'), Coleridge feels a sense of his own inferiority, a drying up of his art:

But oh! each Visitation

Suspends what Nature gave me at my Birth,

My shaping Spirit of Imagination!

Later in April, as William and Dorothy sauntered in their cottage garden back in Grasmere, Coleridge came to them and 'repeated the verses he wrote to Sara'. Dorothy 'was affected with them and was on the whole, not being well, in miserable spirits'. She absorbed the sentiments of the poem: 'The sunshine – the green fields and the fair sky made me sadder; even the little happy sporting lambs seemed but sorrowful to me.'[5]

Wordsworth as well as Coleridge had episodes of what they called dejection and we would now call depression. But he was determined to use his poetry to fight rather than to indulge the feeling of joylessness. Two weeks after Coleridge read him the verse letter to Sara, he wrote a poem recollecting an encounter that had taken place some eighteenth months earlier, when he and Dorothy were walking back to Grasmere from Ambleside, after saying goodbye to his college friend Robert Jones, who had been visiting. They met an old man bent almost double. Under his coat he carried a bundle. He was wearing an apron and a nightcap. He was Scottish, from an army family; had married and been blessed with ten children. Now, though, his wife was dead, as were nine of his children. The survivor was a sailor from whom the old man had not heard for years. 'His trade', Dorothy recorded, 'was to gather leeches':

but now leeches were scarce, and he had not strength for it. He lived by begging, and was making his way to Carlisle, where he should buy a few godly books to sell. He said leeches were very scarce, partly owing to this dry season, but many years they have been scarce – he supposed it owing to their being much sought after, that they did not breed fast, and were of slow growth. Leeches were formerly 2s. 6d. [per] 100; they are now 30s. He had been hurt in driving a cart, his leg broken, his body driven over, his skull fractured. He felt no pain till he recovered from his first insensibility.[6]

Wordsworth summoned this figure back from the pages of Dorothy's journal and used him as an admonition. He began a poem with the same stormy weather as that of the opening of Coleridge's dejected letter to Sara: 'There was a roaring in the wind all night / The rain came heavily and fell in floods'. But the next day is fine and the speaker of the poem walks out on the moor. At first, he responds to a running hare and the roar of distant waters 'as happy as a Boy'. Then, however, his mood swings, for no apparent reason:

> But as it sometimes chanceth from the might
> Of joy in minds that can no farther go
> As high as we have mounted in delight
> In our dejection do we sink as low,
> To me that morning did it happen so
> And fears and fancies thick upon me came
> Dim sadness and blind thoughts I knew not nor could
> name.[7]

Even though he is at this moment 'a happy child of earth', he cannot stop himself thinking of how he may on other days have to face 'Solitude pain of heart distress and poverty'. It then occurs to him – and here he is clearly recalling Coleridge's poem of dejection – that poets are unusually susceptible to such thoughts:

I thought of Chatterton the marvellous Boy
The sleepless Soul who perished in its pride
Of Him who walked in glory and in joy
Behind his Plough upon the mountain's side
By our own spirits we are deified
We Poets in our youth begin in gladness
But thereof comes in the end despondency and madness.[8]

Suddenly, though, perhaps by some 'peculiar grace', he comes to the 'borders of a Pond' 'By which an Old man was, far from all house or home'. Propped on his staff, the figure is motionless, like a natural object. Then he stirs the water with his staff, hoping to flush out some leeches for sale to the medical profession (he would have caught them by allowing them to attach themselves to his legs). They strike up a conversation and his spare, dignified story of hardships endured gives the poet 'human strength, and strong admonishment'.[9] Despite the decay of the leech population, he perseveres, finding them where he can. Wordsworth concludes that whenever he is tempted to think of 'mighty Poets in their misery dead', of cold and pain and 'fleshly ills' (a half-recollection of Hamlet's 'thousand natural shocks / That flesh is heir to'), he will think about the leech gatherer on the moor. The old man becomes an exemplar of – as Wordsworth entitled the poem when he published it five years later – 'Resolution and Independence'.

Sara Hutchinson was not persuaded. She did not like the latter part of the poem (in manuscript, it was simply called 'The Leech Gatherer'). Wordsworth defended himself in a letter offering a prose explanation of his feeling in writing the poem. First, 'I describe myself as having been exalted to the highest pitch of delight by the joyousness and beauty of Nature and then as depressed, even in the midst of those beautiful objects, to the lowest dejection and despair'. Then, 'I am rescued from my dejection and despair almost as an interposition of Providence':

> A person reading this Poem with feelings like mine will have been awed and controuled, expecting almost something spiritual or supernatural – What is brought forward? 'A lonely place, a Pond' 'by which an old man *was*, far from all house or home' – not stood, nor sat, but '*was*' – the figure presented in the most naked simplicity possible . . . I can *confidently* affirm, that, though I believe God has given me a strong imagination, I cannot conceive a figure more impressive than that of an old Man like this, the survivor of a Wife and ten children, travelling alone among the mountains and all lonely places, carrying with him his own fortitude, and the necessities which an unjust state of society has laid upon him.[10]

Even as his poverty is an indictment of social injustice, the old man is made into a figure of existential authenticity, of pure 'being': 'not stood, nor sat, but "*was*"' (when Wordsworth revised the poem for publication he weakened it by replacing 'was' with 'He stood alone'). Where a more conventional – or a more Coleridgean – poem might have introduced some 'spiritual or supernatural' epiphany, the leech gatherer is the very opposite. He is extraordinary by virtue of being ordinary.

That summer, Coleridge wrote a long letter to a friend – the poet, dramatist and translator William Sotheby – laying out the '*radical* Difference' between his own and Wordsworth's theoretical opinions on poetry. In the course of the letter, he suggested that many of the ideas in the Preface to *Lyrical Ballads* were his own, implying that they had been distorted by Wordsworth.[11] Be that as it may, to understand the radical difference between their poetic practice, one only has to turn from the supernatural solicitings of 'The Ancient Mariner' to the sublime stoicism of 'The Leech Gatherer'.

★

What was the relevance of the other poets to whom Wordsworth alludes: 'Chatterton the marvellous Boy' and 'Him who walked in glory and in joy / Behind his Plough'?

Thomas Chatterton was born in Bristol in 1752 and raised in humble circumstances. He was an astonishingly precocious genius – a Mozartian wunderkind, as it were – who began publishing accomplished poetry at the age of eleven. He passed off his work as that of an invented fifteenth-century bard called Thomas Rowley. Failing to find a patron in the provinces, when he was seventeen he moved to London, scribbling away in his garret in dire poverty, first in Shoreditch, then in Holborn. There is a story that one day he was walking with a friend in St Pancras Old Churchyard, so absorbed in inward communion with his Muse that he fell into a newly dug grave. His companion helped him out and joked that he was glad to assist in the resurrection of a genius, to which Chatterton replied, 'My dear friend, I have been at war with the grave for some time now.'[12] Three days later, he took home a portion of arsenic, tore up his literary remains and drank the poison. Though it has been suggested that the arsenic was bought as a cure for syphilis and that the overdose was accidental,[13] Wordsworth and his contemporaries had no reason to doubt the verdict of the inquest that the cause of death was suicide in a fit of madness. After all, even the supremely classical poet John Dryden had said that great wits are to madness near allied. Robert Southey lamented that

Chatterton's sad story is well known; his life the wonder, his death the disgrace of his country. That a boy of seventeen years should have afforded a subject for dispute to the first criticks and scholars of his time is scarcely to be credited: who then shall believe that this prodigy of nature should be left a prey to indigence and famine![14]

The idea, espoused by Shelley and others, that John Keats was killed by the sheer malice of his critics had its origins in this image of the neglected Chatterton. He served as an avatar for the Romantics: Coleridge wrote a 'monody' for him; Keats dedicated his longest poem, *Endymion*, to his memory; in France, Alfred de Vigny dramatized his life and death in a play; Henry Wallis enshrined him in Pre-Raphaelite art, his body swooned in his London garret, manuscripts littering the floor. Chatterton, then, embodied the image of the struggling artist that in France would come to be called 'bohemianism', not to mention the cult of youth and early death, together with the reaction against the polished classicism of eighteenth-century poetry and the desire to return to the populist energies of medieval ballads.

Robert Burns held a similar place in the imagination of Wordsworth and his fellow poets. Born in 1759, the son of a self-educated tenant farmer in Ayrshire, he had little schooling and became a farm labourer in his teens. He gained a reputation as a womanizer. Unable to subsist 'behind his plough', he accepted an offer to take up a position on a sugar plantation in Jamaica. In order to pay his passage, he published a volume of *Poems, chiefly in the Scottish Dialect*. This led to him being taken up in Edinburgh literary society, saving him from exile to the West Indies. But with success came depression and alcoholism. He died at the age of thirty-seven.

When Wordsworth was reunited with Dorothy during his summer vacations from Cambridge, he borrowed a copy of Burns's *Poems, chiefly in the Scottish Dialect* from a lending library

in Penrith. He and Dorothy would read the poems as they walked
the hills together. Many years later, Wordsworth remarked that
familiarity with the dialect of the border counties made it easy
for him both to understand Burns and to *feel* his poems. As
William Cowper was his favourite for blank-verse meditation,
Burns was the strongest influence on his ballad-writing and 'songs'
addressed to the simple things of nature. Writing to Coleridge
in Germany in 1800, Wordsworth said that everywhere in Burns
'you have the presence of human life'. At the same time, he
added, 'His Ode to Despondency I can never read without the
deepest agitation'.[15] Anticipating Wordsworth, Burns maps a
decline from the untrammelled joys of youth:

> Oh, enviable, early days,
> When dancing thoughtless Pleasure's maze,
>   To Care, to Guilt unknown!
> How ill exchang'd for riper times,
> To feel the follies, or the crimes,
>   Of others, or my own![16]

The choice of the word 'despondency' in Wordsworth's poem
about the leech gatherer was clearly an allusion to this ode by
Burns.

But neither Chatterton nor Burns actually went mad. The
idea of the poet's madness is perhaps more generic than particular. In giving 'The Leech Gatherer' to Sara Hutchinson,
Wordsworth was clearly responding to the 'Dejection' letter that
Coleridge had sent her. Knowing what he did about Coleridge's
feelings for her, the idea of a young poet being driven mad by
unrequited love would also have been in his mind. The archetype
for such a narrative was Goethe's early novel *The Sorrows of Young
Werther* – which happens to include a scene in which the narrator

meets a strange old man who is failing to gather medicinal herbs and who then tells the story of his life, including a period confined in a lunatic asylum.[17]

The mature Goethe, who may reasonably be described as the creator of classical German culture, renounced Romanticism when it was in full flow: he said that it embodied everything that was sick. But the young Goethe's thinly disguised autobiographical novel of lovesickness was one of the absolute foundational works of the movement. Written in the much-used epistolary style of letters to a friend in which the narrator pours out his heart, the novel tells of how young Werther moves into a rural community and is enchanted by the simple ways of the peasantry. He falls in love with a girl called Charlotte, but she is engaged to another man. He tries to sustain the relationship as a mere friendship, but cannot bear this constraint. He is driven mad and in the end he blows his brains out. Late in his own life, Goethe said that everybody has a time in their life when they feel as though *Werther* had been written exclusively for them. Napoleon Bonaparte certainly thought so: he wrote a monologue inspired by *Werther* and carried a copy of the book in his pocket on his military campaigns. Across Europe, young men dressed in Werther's clothes. Images from the novel were marketed as engravings, as silhouettes, on Meissen pottery. One could even buy a perfume called Eau de Werther. Stories began to circulate of young men with broken hearts, all across Europe, committing suicide in imitation of their hero. It is in fact hard to track down any genuinely documented cases, but the panic stirred by the media was such that in some cities, such as Copenhagen and Leipzig, the novel was banned. Psychologists still speak of 'the Werther effect', the idea that the will to suicide can be a kind of contagion among groups of alienated or unhappy young people.

Read in the light of *Werther's* extraordinary popularity at the time, 'Resolution and Independence' may be seen as both Wordsworth's attempt to stave off the black dog of depression and his voicing of the fear that Coleridge's unrequited love for Sara Hutchinson, coinciding as it did with the fruition of Wordsworth's own love for her sister Mary, might lead to madness and even suicide.

★

Coleridge's anguish at being married to one Sara and in love with another was heightened by his powerful paternal instincts. His poem 'Frost at Midnight', written in the Nether Stowey cottage when Hartley was a baby, is for many readers the most exquisitely realized poem of fatherly love in the English language. A separation would do unknown damage to Hartley, who was now nearly six, and Derwent, not yet two. He was accordingly seeking to shore up his marriage: in close proximity to the writing of the letter to Sara Hutchinson, Sara Coleridge became pregnant again. In December 1802, she gave birth to a daughter, unsurprisingly named Sara, who would grow up to edit her father's works and become a poet herself. Coleridge was sacrificing his own desires for the sake of his family.

One may wonder in this regard whether there is a certain pointedness in his allusion to Wordsworth's ballad 'Lucy Gray' in the verse letter to Sara. 'Lucy Gray' is a narrative ballad, very different in style to the enigmatic 'Lucy' lyrics, though written in Goslar around the same time. 'It was founded on a circumstance told me by my Sister, of a little girl, who not far from Halifax in Yorkshire was bewildered in a snow-storm', Wordsworth explained: 'Her footsteps were traced by her parents to the middle of the lock of a canal, and no other vestige of her, backward or forward, could be traced. The body however was found in the canal.'[18] The poem ends with a superstition that her ghost walks the 'lonesome Wild' like a 'living Child':

> O'er rough and smooth she trips along,
> And never looks behind;
> And sings a solitary song
> That whistles in the wind.[19]

It is intriguing that Coleridge alluded to this poem about a lost girl child at exactly the time when he was trying to stay true to his family as Wordsworth was planning to travel to France to see his own daughter for the first time in her life, and to tell her mother that he was about to marry someone else.

Wordsworth, meanwhile, saw in Hartley Coleridge an image of the 'happy Child' of nature, 'exquisitely wild' in his freedom of spirit. He feared, though, for the clouds that might gather in the future:

> O blessed Vision! Happy Child!
> Thou art so exquisitely wild,
> I think of thee with many fears
> For what may be thy lot in future years.[20]

The fears proved to be well grounded: Hartley grew up to live a wretched life as an alcoholic.

As with so many of Wordsworth's poems, the verses addressed 'To H. C., Six Years Old' have a personal origin but also enter into a literary tradition. Let us return for a moment to the self-image that inaugurates *The Prelude*: Wordsworth himself as a four-year-old child bathing unclothed in the river Derwent at the bottom of his garden and standing in the rain alone like 'a naked savage' framed against crag, hill, wood and 'distant Skiddaw's lofty height'.[21] 'Naked', 'savage', 'wild' and 'child': each of these words had very particular associations. They carried heavy political baggage.

Wordsworth was born into a Britain in which bodies were always covered in public: frock coats, stiff collars, breeches and boots. People did not wear shorts to hike the hills, let alone strip off to sunbathe. In the early 1780s, when Wordsworth was entering puberty, Mary 'Perdita' Robinson was what we would now call a leading fashion icon of the day. She was the first to import a new style of garment from France: the figure-hugging chemise, flowing with the contours of the female body. In a world of hoops and stays, this was perceived to be revolutionary and dangerous. Liberty of dress could all too easily lead to sexual freedom. A similar charge would have been laid against the celebration of naked youthful bodies in the art of William Blake. For Wordsworth, as for Blake, the naked child denoted a state of innocence free from the oppression and control that came with swaddling clothes, dogmatic lessons and the discipline of the whip.

Three years before Wordsworth was born, Henry Fuseli – an artist, like Blake, who rebelled against the conventions of the age and relished the naked human body – published, with the aid of the radical bookseller Joseph Johnson, a brief anonymous treatise entitled *Remarks on the Writings and Conduct of J. J. Rousseau*. It was perhaps the first work in English to offer a defence of Rousseau's much-maligned answer – 'known to all, read by few, understood by less'[22] – to the question 'what is the origin of inequality among mankind and does the law of nature authorize it?' In a discourse submitted to the academy of Dijon, Rousseau had undertaken the thought experiment of imagining a society without inequality and found it in the 'savage' or natural man. The hunter-gatherer was not, however, Rousseau's only example of an idealized figure with no notion of property: his other instance of humankind uncorrupted by the divisive inequality of social institutions was the young child. Fuseli saw the connection and described Rousseau's man in the state of nature by way of language that could equally well have been applied to the infant at the mother's breast. Rousseau, he explains,

> traced man to the nipple of nature, found him wrapped up in instinct, – taught his lore by appetite and fear – harmless because content – content because void of comparative ideas – solitary, because without wants, – snatching the moment on the wing, from the past and future ones.[23]

When Wordsworth begins his poetic autobiography by representing himself as a 'naked boy' and then 'A naked savage in the thunder-shower', living in the moment, at one with nature, he is identifying as a 'natural man' of the kind evoked here. This is a political idea as well as a philosophical one because in the 'wilderness of nature' mankind is 'free, improveable, compassionate'. The nakedness of both boy and savage is a sign that they have not yet been chained into an unequal social system through a process of chastisement, education and submission to authority. The child and the 'noble savage' are thus linked to the ideology of the French Revolution. Wordsworth's overt politics would twist and turn, but his best poetry would always be Rousseauistic insofar as – to use Fuseli's terms – it traces man to the nipple of nature, relishes *instinct*, and snatches the moment on the wing.

Fuseli's metaphor of man at the nipple of nature, which anticipates Wordsworth's imagery of 'Drinking in / A pure organic pleasure from the lines / Of curling mist', was also shaped by the argument of Rousseau's highly controversial and influential *Emile, or On Education.* Both a novel and a treatise, it developed the idea that humankind and the human individual start out in purity and goodness, but degenerate through the process of socialization. Here Rousseau argued that children should be fed at the breast of their mothers, not farmed out to wet nurses as was the custom in polite society. And he railed against the constriction of babies in swaddling clothes. Breastfeeding was 'natural' and should be the beginning of an education among the beauties of nature – nature's beauty being the only proof of God's existence, as Rousseau went on to argue in a section of *Emile* called 'The Profession of Faith of the Savoyard Vicar', which led to the book being banned and burned by the Catholic Church. Swaddling clothes, by contrast, were the beginning of that process whereby man was born free but enchained by social convention.

The pervasive influence of the Rousseauistic idea of a 'child of nature' explains why there was enormous interest across Europe when a 'wild boy', aged about twelve, was discovered in the Aveyron in 1800. He appeared to have spent his whole life in the woods and had no language. He was taken up by a doctor, Jean Marc Gaspard Itard, who named him 'Victor', placed him in a school for deaf-mutes, and duly wrote a book about the case, which was soon translated into English. There is consider-able uncertainty as to exactly where Victor came from and how long he had been in the woods, but the public perception was that this was a true case of a child in the state of nature.[24] Mary Robinson wrote a poem called 'The Savage of Aveyron' in which Victor is the epitome of solitude:

Such was the boy of Aveyron,
The tenant of that solitude,
Where still, by misery unsubdued,
He wander'd nine long winters, all alone.[25]

Coleridge followed the case with great interest and even suggested
that the story should be incorporated into Wordsworth's *Recluse*:
'A fine subject to be introduced in William's great poem is the
Savage Boy of Aveyron in Itard's account – viz – his restless joy
and blind conjunction of his Being with natural Scenery.'[26]

Wordsworth and Coleridge were equally fascinated by the idea
of a child prodigy. In 1803 an eleven-year-old actor took to the
Irish stage under the name 'Master Betty'. He was acclaimed for
his performance as Young Norval in the highly popular Scottish
tragedy *Douglas*, in which the character enters with sword drawn
and speaks the much-quoted lines

> My name is Norval; on the Grampian Hills
> My father feeds his flocks; a frugal swain,
> Whose constant cares were to increase his store,
> And keep his only son, myself, at home.[27]

As a child Norval was left to die on a hillside, but adopted and
raised by a kindly shepherd. He is really the son of Douglas by
the aristocratic Lady Randolph, with whom he is briefly reunited
before being killed by the heir whose inheritance is threatened
by his reappearance. His death leads Lady Randolph to throw
herself off a cliff in remorse. To have the part played by a child
actor added a special piquancy to the tragedy and word soon
spread of the native genius of Master Betty, who was dubbed,
in an allusion to the most famous actor of ancient Rome, 'the
Young Roscius'. He took on the role of *Hamlet*, toured through
Britain and finally made his debut at Covent Garden, causing a
near-riot as crowds queued for entrance. His fame was short-lived
and his later comeback attempts failed, but for a brief period in
1803 to 1804 his Young Norval was the epitome of the child as
father of the man.

'I hope the young Roscius if he go on as he has begun', Wordsworth wrote to his patron Sir George Beaumont in 1804, 'will rescue the English theatre from the infamy that has fallen upon it and restore the reign of good sense and Nature.'[28] Dorothy told Lady Beaumont that, if they had been within sixty miles of London, she and William would have done anything to see Master Betty on stage and that 'My Brother vows that if the boy grow up as he has begun he will write a play on purpose for him.' But she also recognized that all does not usually end well for young prodigies: 'I never heard of a very extraordinary child that lived to be a man', she wrote, adding that the few who do are either 'wasted by vanity' or 'their bodies and minds are enfeebled by too early and intense exercise of their faculties'. For this reason, she could not think of Master Betty with anything but 'melancholy feelings' and she was sure that if she ever saw him on stage she would weep with 'deep sadness'.[29]

★

All these influences coalesced when in 1804 Wordsworth returned to the ode that he had begun in 1802. He was feeling the loss of that innocence which had characterized his own favourite poems in the first edition of *Lyrical Ballads*: the ballad based on the encounter with the little girl in the churchyard in the Wye Valley, who had insisted that 'we are seven' despite the fact that two of her siblings were in the grave, and 'The Idiot Boy', the story of 'Johnny', the Down's syndrome child who rides out alone at night, to the consternation of his mother. The title of 'We are Seven' is a clever pun, in that it suggests not only the number of siblings but also the imagined consciousness of a child around the age of the little girl: she says that she is eight years old, but the lines spoken in her voice enable the reader to imagine the innocent way in which we might have seen the world when we were seven.[30] Johnny, meanwhile, is an idiot savant because, just as the girl in 'We are Seven' does not know death, he does not know the divisions of the rational mind that murders to dissect. Rational adults distinguish between night and day, owl and cock, but Johnny has a glorious unity of consciousness:

> And thus to Betty's question, he
> Made answer, like a traveller bold,
> (His very words I give to you,)
> 'The cocks did crow to-whoo, to-whoo,
> 'And the sun did shine so cold.'
>   – Thus answered Johnny in his glory,
> And that was all his travel's story.[31]

Now, however, Wordsworth is consumed by the thought of the adult's loss of the child's ability to live in the moment and be at one with nature. Johnny in 'The Idiot Boy' and the little girl in 'We are Seven' are entirely themselves, but as we grow up we find ourselves playing a series of parts. We become actors, as Shakespeare recognized. It was perhaps because of this recognition that William and Dorothy both expressed doubts about whether Master Betty would really have been up to the complexities of Shakespearean character.

> Behold the Child among his new-born blisses,
> A four year's Darling of a pigmy size!
> See, where mid work of his own hand he lies,
> Fretted by sallies of his Mother's kisses,
> With light upon him from his Father's eyes!
> See, at his feet, some little plan or chart,
> Some fragment from his dream of human life,
> Shap'd by himself with newly-learned art;

A wedding or a festival,

A mourning or a funeral;

  And this hath now his heart,

And unto this he frames his song:

  Then will he fit his tongue

To dialogues of business, love, or strife;

  But it will not be long

  Ere this be thrown aside,

  And with new joy and pride

The little Actor cons another part,

Filling from time to time his 'humorous stage'

With all the Persons, down to palsied Age,

That Life brings with her in her Equipage;

As if his whole vocation

Were endless imitation.

Wordsworth subsequently revised the age of the child in this stanza from four to six, making it coincide with the title of 'To H. C., Six Years Old'. The child with his 'dream of human life', lit by his father's gleaming eye, is Hartley. But it is also Wordsworth himself and every one of us who grows into the compromises, the disillusionment, the 'dialogues of business, love, or strife' in adult life.

Wordsworth said that the structure of the poem rested upon the feeling or experience of his own mind that 'Nothing was more difficult for me in childhood than to admit the notion of death as a state applicable to my own being.'[32] A psychoanalyst might well detect a strong element of denial in this claim, given the fact of his mother's death when he was a child. Be that as it may, he saw it as the task of the poem to assist his adult self, and that of his readers, in coming to terms with the inevitability of death by evoking the child who does not know death in order

to gain an intimation of immortality. The recollection of childhood, he hopes, as the poem comes towards its climax, will be
sufficient to stave off despondency and direct the self towards the
Christian virtues of faith, hope and charity:

> Though nothing can bring back the hour
> Of splendor in the grass, or glory in the flower;
> We will grieve not, rather find
> Strength in what remains behind,
> In the primal sympathy
> Which having been must ever be,
> In the soothing thoughts that spring
> Out of human suffering,
> In the faith that looks through death,
> In years that bring the philosophic mind.[33]

★

When Wordsworth wrote earlier in the ode of how 'Our Souls
have sight of that immortal sea', of seeing the 'children sport
upon the shore' and hearing 'the mighty waters rolling evermore',
he framed eternity via an image of pre-existence. He was criticized for this by orthodox Christians, for whom eternity was an
afterlife, but there is no doubt that in the ode his language was
becoming more biblical than it had been before. Around the
same time, he wrote another ode, addressing it 'to Duty'. 'Stern
daughter of the Voice of God!' it begins, naming Duty as 'a Light
to guide, a Rod / To check the erring, and reprove'.[34] At some
level, he was reproving himself for his own youthful errors of
pantheism, republicanism and fathering an illegitimate child.

Wordsworth was becoming respectable. He was in his mid-
thirties, married to an old friend from a solid farming family.
They had a son, not yet one year old, named John after his

father (and his seafaring brother); as he was writing the two
odes, Mary was pregnant with another child – their daughter
Dora, born in August 1804. Where once the word 'patriot'
meant a supporter of the French Revolution, now Wordsworth
had become a defender of his country as war with Napoleon
resumed: at this time he enlisted with the Grasmere Volunteers,
the equivalent of the Second World War Home Guard. He was
more financially secure, with not only the Calvert legacy and
his share of the Lowther debt, but also a wealthy patron in the
form of the cultivated and wealthy Sir George Beaumont, whom
he had met through Coleridge. Beaumont had even purchased
a small estate by Bassenthwaite Lake under Skiddaw, and
presented it to Wordsworth so that he could build himself a
house there. Wordsworth did not want to move away from
Grasmere, and asked if he could perhaps rent out the land
instead. Beaumont replied, with the grace and generosity that
characterized all his dealings with Wordsworth, 'Plant it, delve
it and build on it or not as it suits your convenience, but let
me live and die with the idea [that] the sweet place, with its
rocks, its banks, and mountain stream [is] in the possession of
such a mind as yours, and moreover let the particulars of the
transaction remain unknown to all but you, Coleridge, Lady
Beaumont and myself.'[35]

★

Although Wordsworth declined the opportunity to build his own
home by Bassenthwaite, he came to recognize that Dove Cottage
was too small for his growing family. A third child, Thomas, was
born in the summer of 1806. A temporary solution was provided
by another kind offer from the Beaumonts: the use of a farmhouse on their Coleorton estate in Leicestershire. That October,
they all went over from Grasmere to the nearby town of Kendal

to make arrangements to travel south. There they met up with Sara Hutchinson. They had seen a lot of her during the previous two years: as Mary went through her pregnancies and looked after the children, it was Sara, along with Dorothy, who transcribed William's poems, most notably his long verse autobiography, which had been his principal preoccupation during these years.

He had been working on it without the help of Coleridge, who, back in 1804, had left for the Mediterranean for the sake of his health and to take up a position as Acting Public Secretary on the island of Malta. So they had not seen him for nearly three years. Now he was back. He had put on weight and was addicted to opium and alcohol. Dorothy told a friend that the first sight of the utter change in his appearance was the greatest shock of her life.

He was at last in the process of ending his marriage. Sara Coleridge and the three children – Hartley now ten, Derwent six, and Sara not quite four – were still living at Greta Hall, the fine (rented) house in Keswick. They shared it with her sister Edith and her husband, Coleridge's former poetic collaborator. Robert Southey, author of the story of Goldilocks and the Three Bears, loved children, cherished his own babies and had acted as a substitute father during Coleridge's absence. Still magnetically drawn to Sara Hutchinson, Coleridge was determined to reject this household and join that of the Wordsworths instead. He had also come to realize that Wordsworth was a far greater poet than Southey.

After two nights in Kendal, Mary and Dorothy Wordsworth, together with servant Molly Fisher and the children, set off on a three-day journey by chaise to Coleorton. Wordsworth, Coleridge and Sara stayed on in Kendal for one more night. Wordsworth agreed that Coleridge could come to live with him and his family, at least for a time. First, though, Coleridge would have to confront his own family in Keswick.

Wordsworth and Sara travelled fast, catching up with the family. They all settled into Hall Farm, a new and comfortable three-storey farmhouse a few hundred yards from Coleorton Hall, which Sir George and Lady Beaumont had been rebuilding since 1804. In the early stages of the building work, they had stayed in the farmhouse themselves. The Beaumonts went off to their home in London, leaving William and Dorothy to plan the design and planting of a 'winter garden' in the grounds of the hall.

Sara wrote out a fair copy of William's poem *Peter Bell*, his equivalent of Coleridge's 'Ancient Mariner', but with a donkey standing in for the albatross. William himself prepared the printer's copy for a new anthology of his poems, to be published in two volumes. It was to be his first work in print since *Lyrical Ballads*. The publication of the new book was to be a make-or-break moment.

In late November, Wordsworth walked over to the nearest post office, at Ashby de la Zouch. He picked up a letter from Coleridge, bearing the news that the separation from his wife was going ahead, but that he intended to keep his sons with him. He said that he would soon be on his way to Coleorton. He procrastinated, as he always did, but just before Christmas he turned up at Hall Farm, with Hartley but without Derwent.

It was over the following nights that Wordsworth read aloud his 'Poem / Title not yet fixed upon / Addressed to S. T. Coleridge'.

★

Why didn't Wordsworth publish the poem after reading it to Coleridge and the women in his household that Christmas and New Year of 1806 to 1807? Perhaps there was a degree of apprehension about the chutzpah of devoting an entire epic to the subject of himself. But the main reason was that in Wordsworth's mind, it was only a prelude to the still longer poem 'On Man, on Nature, and on Human Life' that was to be called *The Recluse*.

The previous summer, he had turned his mind back to the larger task. Coleridge's return from Malta was a stimulus in this regard, because it had been he who had been urging his friend to write a philosophical epic ever since their time together in the West Country. 'Within this month I have returned to the Recluse, and have written 700 additional lines', Wordsworth informed Sir George Beaumont. 'Should Coleridge return, so that I might have some conversation with him upon the subject, I should go on swimmingly.'[36]

In particular, Coleridge had suggested that a key theme should be the question of how society might be improved in the light of the knowledge that revolution on the French model was not the answer: 'I wish you would write a poem, in blank verse, addressed to those, who, in consequence of the complete failure of the French Revolution, have thrown up all hopes of the amelioration of mankind, and are sinking into an almost epicurean selfishness.'[37] *The Prelude* was such a poem, written from Wordsworth's personal point of view. The plan for *The Recluse* was to broaden the scope by creating a character suffering from political disillusionment – he would be called The Solitary – and putting him into debate with other characters. But although Coleridge spent many weeks with the Wordsworths in the next few years, *The Recluse* proceeded only in fits and starts, often stalling.

The interim would be filled by the new collection of Wordsworth's shorter poems. At Coleorton, Coleridge, Dorothy, Mary and Sara all helped to make the selection and prepare the work for the press. *Poems, in Two Volumes, by William Wordsworth,*

Author of The Lyrical Ballads was published by Longman and company in May 1807, in an edition of 1,000 copies, 230 of which would be remaindered seven years later. It began with a section called 'The Orchard Pathway', which included a similar mixture of poems to that of *Lyrical Ballads*: there were lyrics addressed to flowers such as the daisy and the hitherto unsung lesser celandine, a few ballads, another 'Lucy' poem ('I travell'd among unknown Men'), the poem for Hartley Coleridge and, to round off the section, the 'Ode to Duty'. Then there was a grouping of a handful of 'Poems composed during a Tour, chiefly on Foot', including an address to a skylark contrasting the bird's joyous flight with the poet's plodding step. This section ended with the leech-gatherer poem, now given the title 'Resolution and Independence'. The remainder of the first volume was given over to sonnets, divided into two sections. First there was a 'Miscellaneous' group that included 'Composed upon Westminster Bridge' and some of the Calais sonnets such as 'It is a beauteous Evening' with its address to the (unidentified) 'Dear Child' Caroline. The second group collected Wordsworth's fourteen-line political and patriotic compositions under the title 'Sonnets dedicated to Liberty'.

The second volume began with 'Poems written during a Tour in Scotland'. Back in 1803, William had left Mary, recuperating well from the birth of their first child, and gone on a Scottish tour in the company of Dorothy and Coleridge. Where his previous travels had been undertaken largely on foot, this time they bought 'a Horse, aged but stout and spirited, and an open vehicle called a Jaunting Car'.[38] William and Dorothy had been happy travellers, whereas Coleridge was 'in bad spirits, and somewhat too much in love with his own dejection'.[39] They visited the grave of Scotland's most famous dead poet, Robert Burns, and the home of the man who was rapidly becoming its most famous living poet, Walter Scott. The title of the section is not strictly accurate: most of the poems, notably the haunting lyrics 'Stepping Westward' and 'The Solitary Reaper', were written not 'during' the tour, but when Wordsworth was remembering it two years afterwards. Furthermore, the latter poem was based not on a direct experience but on a passage in a guidebook. It is a beautifully executed versification of a prose recollection which reads 'Passed a female who was reaping alone: she sung in Erse as she bended over her sickle; the sweetest human voice I ever heard: her strains were tenderly melancholy, and felt delicious, long after they were heard no more.' This was Thomas Wilkinson in his *Tours to the British Mountains* which was read in manuscript by Wordsworth, who visited the author on his farm near Penrith and wrote a much-mocked poem, also in the 1807 volume, addressed to Wilkinson's spade. A footnote to 'The Solitary Reaper', which ends 'The music in my heart I bore, / Long after it was heard no more', acknowledges the debt. The origin of the poem is a reminder that the 'I' of Wordsworth's poems is not always the autobiographical self.

The rainbow and daffodils poems, both untitled, appeared in the next section, entitled 'Moods of my own Mind'. Volume two then continued with a very varied grouping (in both style and quality) called 'The Blind Highland Boy; with other poems', at the end of which there was a separate one-word title page, inserted by the printer late in the day on Wordsworth's instructions: 'ODE'. Its verso carried an epigraph: '*Paulò majora canamus*', 'let us sing of things a little more elevated', a quotation from Virgil's *Eclogues*. There followed the 'Ode' that began 'There was a time when meadow, grove, and stream'. In this first edition, it had no title, but when Wordsworth rearranged his work for the collected edition of 1815, he gave it the title 'Intimations of Immortality from Recollections of Early Childhood' and replaced

the Virgilian quotation with an epigraph of his own in the form
of a repetition of the last three lines of 'My heart leaps up' (the
short poem which he also repositioned for his 1815 collection,
placing it at the head of the very first section, 'Poems referring
to the Period of Childhood'):

> The Child is Father of the Man;
> And I could wish my days to be
> Bound each to each by natural piety.

Whereas 'Tintern Abbey' had become the climax of the first
volume of *Lyrical Ballads* by sheer chance of timing, the 'Ode'
was very deliberately made into the summation of *Poems, in Two
Volumes*.

★

They waited for the reviews.

A minor journal called *Monthly Literary Recreations* was first
out of the blocks. It began well, by pointing out that *Lyrical
Ballads* had 'not undeservedly met with a considerable share of
public applause', but then expressed disappointment that the
author had allowed his 'genius' to descend to trivial subjects 'in
language not simple, but puerile'. 'What will any reader or
auditor, out of the nursery, say to such namby-pamby as "Lines
written at the foot of Brother's Bridge"?' – a poem that begins
'The cock is crowing, / The stream is flowing, / The small birds
twitter, / The lake doth glitter'.[40] The anonymous reviewer is
incredulous that such lines could come from an author capable
of writing the ode and the best of the sonnets in the collection.
He was a nineteen-year-old Cambridge undergraduate who kept
a pet bear in his rooms at Trinity College: George Gordon, sixth
Baron Byron.

The *Critical Review* weighed in the following month: 'A silly book is a serious evil; but it becomes absolutely insupportable when written by a man of sense . . . he debases himself to the level of his own "ideot-boy" . . . lost in the vortex of false taste and puerile conceit.'[41] Then there was *Le Beau Monde, or, Literary and Fashionable Magazine.* For its reviewer, *Lyrical Ballads* had been bad enough: 'like a hysterical school-girl he had a knack of feeling about subjects with which feeling had no proper concern'. But these poems were worse: 'We really begin to think that the new school of poets, as they think fit to call themselves, suppose folly to be feeling, and consider nature as synonymous with nonsense.' The assault was relentless: 'childish effusions . . . drivels out her puerilities . . . pathetic lines'. As for the sonnets:

> The first is far-fetched, and the second leads to nothing; the third is unintelligible; and the fourth, sixth, and seventh dull; the fifth, eighth and ninth unmeaning; the eleventh, though not his own, common-place . . . the thirteenth, fourteenth, and fifteenth to no purpose; the sixteenth incomprehensible; the eighteenth and nineteenth nonsense.[42]

Then there was *The Satirist or Monthly Meteor.* 'Instead of occupying two duodecimo volumes of wire-wove and hot-pressed paper, with a beautiful type and a large margin, these poems would have been more appropriately invested with a fine gilt wrapping, adorned with wooden cuts, and printed and bound uniformly in all respects with Mother Bunch's tales and Mother Goose's melodies.' The 'occasional exhibitions of talent' in the volumes made it all the more 'inexcusable' that Wordsworth had 'obtruded so much miserable trash upon the public'.[43]

The following year, an anonymous poem called *The Simpliciad: a Satirico-Didactic Poem containing Hints for the Scholars of the New*

School was dedicated to 'Mssrs. W–ll--m W–rdsw–rth, R–b–rt S--th–y, and S. T. C–l–r–dg–.' It savaged the new poems of the 1807 volume as vigorously as the old ones of *Lyrical Ballads*:

> Poets, who fix their visionary sight
> On Sparrow's eggs in prospect of delight,
> With fervent welcome greet the glow-worm's flame,
> Put it to bed and bless it by its name;
> Hunt waterfalls, that gallop down the hills:
> And dance with laughing dancing daffodils;
> Or measure muddy ponds from side to side,
> And find them three feet long and two feet wide.[44]

Wordsworth was not amused at the time, but many years later he found it droll to find himself and the author of this, one Richard Mant, who later became a bishop, as guests at the same dinner party in Windermere.[45]

The Simpliciad launched a tradition of Wordsworthian parody that would extend through the pre-publication mockery of his *Peter Bell* to Lewis Carroll's reworking in *Through the Looking Glass* of 'Resolution and Independence' as a hunt for 'haddocks' eyes' to Max Beerbohm's affectionate caricature of 'We are Seven' as 'William Wordsworth in the Lake District, at cross-purposes'. It might be said in response that in order to be readily parodied a poet must be memorable.

Lady Beaumont had heard word in London literary circles that the poems might come under attack. In his reply to her letter of anticipatory commiseration, Wordsworth fortified himself for the onslaught by looking to posterity:

> Trouble not yourself upon the present reception of these
> poems; of what moment is that compared with what I trust

is their destiny, to console the afflicted, to add sunshine to daylight by making the happy happier, to teach the young and the gracious of every age to see, to think and feel, and therefore to become more actively and securely virtuous; this is their office, which I trust they will faithfully perform long after we (that is, all that is mortal of us) are mouldered in our graves.[46]

Poetry as consolation. Poetry as a means of teaching the young *to see, to think and feel.* He knew that, as he would put it in a later preface, he was in the process of creating the taste by which he would one day be enjoyed. He intimated the immortality of his own work.

EXCURSION

The downfall of the French school of poetry has of late been increasing in rapidity; its cold and artificial compositions have given way, like so many fantastic figures of snow; and imagination breathes again in a more green and genial time . . . . This has undoubtedly been owing, in the first instance, to the political convulsions of the world, which shook up the minds of men, and rendered them too active and speculative to be satisfied with their common-places. A second cause was the revived inclination for our older and great school of poetry, chiefly produced, I have no doubt, by the commentators on Shakspeare, though they were certainly not aware what fine countries they were laying open. The third, and not the least, was the accession of a new school of poetry itself, of which Wordsworth has justly the reputation of being the most prominent ornament, but whose inner priest of the temple perhaps was Coleridge.

(Leigh Hunt, Preface to *Foliage;*
or Poems original and translated, 1818)

16

FROM NEW SCHOOL
TO LAKE SCHOOL

We spend all our lives talking to ourselves. Every thought that is turned into words becomes part of the narrative of our own lives. An idea hatches. We word it inwardly and then we speak or act or write. Our consciousness flows, in the metaphor of the psychologist William James, in a stream. In describing who we are, whether to ourselves or to others, we rely on names, memories, narratives about relationships, stories of the evolution and education (in the broadest sense) of the self. We select the things that matter to us; we forgot those that don't – and sometimes our subconscious edits out or represses or displaces some of those that do. Each of us is our own autobiographer.

A new form of literature was born when Jean-Jacques Rousseau took it upon himself to share with his readers the story of the growth of his own self – not just his spiritual journey, in the manner of a long tradition of religious writing that began with St Augustine's *Confessions*, but his loves and fears, his perambulations and his politics, the everyday stuff of his life. Rousseau was perhaps the first to attempt such a thing systematically. He opened his *Confessions*, published in 1782, with the words 'I have resolved on an enterprise which has no precedent and which, once complete, will have no imitator. My purpose is to display to my kind a portrait in every way true to nature, and the man I shall portray will be myself.'[1] The claim to complete originality was, inevitably, an exaggeration: two centuries earlier, Michel de Montaigne had attempted something similar, also in French, albeit not in sequential narrative but in quirky, sporadic, fragmentary recollections, observations and opinions in a new form that he called the *essai*. Charles Lamb, William Hazlitt and Thomas De Quincey would develop this art of the autobiographical essay, prose musings that uncannily parallel Wordsworth's poetic endeavour.

It is, however, not an exaggeration to say that the first person to attempt a complete self-portrait in verse as opposed to prose, and in English as opposed to French, was William Wordsworth in the poem that he read to his wife, his sister, his sister-in-law and his friend that Christmas and New Year. It was, he had written to his patron Sir George Beaumont some time before, 'a thing unprecedented in literary history that a man should talk so much about himself'.[2]

Talking about himself: a cynic might blame Rousseau and Wordsworth for the culture of narcissism that afflicts our own age. Or rather, blame the cultural revolution through which Wordsworth lived and which has become generally known as 'Romanticism'. Let us step back for a moment and consider what exactly is meant by the term, where it originated, and how it fits with Wordsworth.

Lady Morgan, one of the most popular novelists of the early nineteenth century, remarked in 1821 upon 'the vehemence with which the question of Romanticism has been debated'.[3] As Coleridge discovered when immersing himself in contemporary German thought, the word 'Romanticism' was originally used by the Schlegel brothers in Jena. It was picked up by their most gifted disciple, Georg Philipp Friedrich von Hardenberg, who composed mystical poems, aphoristic philosophical fragments and unfinished novels under the pen name Novalis, before dying of tuberculosis at the age of twenty-eight. 'The world must be romanticized', wrote Novalis, 'In this way its original meaning will be rediscovered. Romanticization is nothing but a qualitative realization of potential . . . Insofar as I give a higher meaning to what is commonplace, and a mysterious appearance to what is ordinary, the dignity of the unknown to what is known, a semblance of infinity to what is finite, I romanticize it.'[4]

The term then spread to France and Italy as shorthand for the art of the present that set itself against the 'classicism' that had long dominated European culture, thanks in large measure to the formidable influence of such French writers as Voltaire, who believed that good writing should follow the prescriptions of the ancient Greeks and Romans. 'The French Academy', observed a London journalist in 1823, 'has determined never to receive within its bosom any one polluted by the dramatic heresy of romanticism.'[5] Leigh Hunt's preface to his poetry collection *Foliage*, quoted as epigraph to this chapter, attributed the rejection of the 'French school' of poetry to the 'political convulsions' of the age, the cult of Shakespeare, and the emergence of the 'new school' of Wordsworth and Coleridge.[6]

Later in the nineteenth century, literary historians gave the name 'Romantics' to the writers and artists in the various 'new schools' that had emerged around the time of the French revolution: those German thinkers and poets based in Jena in the 1790s; the writers, artists and composers, such as Stendhal, Victor Hugo and Hector Berlioz, who in the 1820s sought to break the stranglehold of classicism in its very Parisian bastion; and in Britain, the 'Lake School' of Wordsworth, Coleridge and Southey; the 'Cockney School' of Hunt, Hazlitt and Keats; the 'Satanic School' of Byron and Percy Shelley; the 'Gothic' fiction of Ann Radcliffe, M. G. Lewis and Mary Shelley; in Scotland, the 'North Britons' Robert Burns, Walter Scott and James Hogg; and the 'Hibernians' of Ireland, Tom Moore (who collected folk melodies) and Lady Morgan (who wrote novels under the influence of Rousseau and Goethe's *Sorrows of Young Werther*).

Possibly the first person to group together 'the Romantics' and name them as such was the French critic Hippolyte Taine, in a history of English literature published in 1864. There he tells of how 'On the eve of the nineteenth century began in Europe the great modern revolution. The thinking public and the human mind changed, and underneath these two collisions a new literature sprang up.' Taine was thinking of a triple revolution: not only the political one in France, but also the industrial one in Britain ('The steam-engine and spinning-jenny create in England towns of from three hundred and fifty thousand to five hundred thousand souls') and the philosophical revolution that began in Germany. As he put it,

Then was manifested the disease of the age, the restlessness of Werther and Faust . . . I mean, discontent with the present, the vague desire of a higher beauty and an ideal happiness, the painful aspiration for the infinite. Man suffered from doubt, yet he doubted; he tried to seize again his beliefs, they melted in his hand; he would sit down and rest in the doctrines and the satisfactions which sufficed his predecessors, and he does not find them sufficient. He expends himself, like Faust, in anxious researches through science and history, and judges them vain, dubious, good for . . . pedants of the academy and the library. It is the beyond he sighs for.[7]

By the end of the nineteenth century it had become commonplace to use the word 'revolution' to describe the literary innovations that had occurred at the dawn of that century. So, for example, in another history of English literature, by the biographer and scholar Edmund Gosse, we read of 'the romantic revolution of 1798' – that is to say, the 'revolution' of *Lyrical Ballads*. Gosse went on to argue that by the early 1820s,

the romantic revolution was complete: the new spirit had penetrated every corner of literary production, and the various strains introduced from Germany, from Celtic sources, from the resuscitated study of natural landscape, from the habit of contemplation of radical changes in political, religious, and social ideas, had settled down into an accepted intellectual attitude.[8]

In the twentieth century, the idea that there was a 'romantic revolution' in the late eighteenth and early nineteenth centuries broadened to the extent that the intellectual historian Isaiah Berlin could write:

The importance of romanticism is that it is the largest recent movement to transform the lives and thought of the Western world. It seems to me to be the greatest single shift in the consciousness of the West that has occurred, and that all the other shifts which have occurred in the course of the nineteenth and twentieth centuries appear to me in comparison less important, and at any rate deeply influenced by it.[9]

Politically, 'romanticism' was more of a paradox than a movement: the 'new schools' of thinking and writing were associated with the idea of revolution but also with the idea of nationalism, with the radical theory of anarchism but also with the conservative theory of the organic state. A 'Romantic' could be a freedom fighter on the streets or a hiker in the mountains (Lord Byron aspired to be both). Among those labelled Romantics, there were abolitionists, vegetarians, advocates for women's rights and animal rights and for what we would now call an environmental ethic, but one did not have to be a Romantic poet or novelist to be an abolitionist or a believer in an ever-widening circle of rights. Among the Romantic writers we find the simultaneous spirit of atavism and progress, of nostalgia and utopianism, of looking back and looking forward.

More generally, liberation from traditional constraints was apparent in the advent of short hair for women and long hair for men, along with the vogue for naturalness in dress: no powdered wig, 'Perdita' Robinson's figure-hugging chemise. With freedom from constraint came risk and soul-searching: the alarming notion that it might be glamorous to take drugs or commit suicide – or at the very least to live hard and die young. *Weltschmerz* and ennui, the rebel and the outsider: these are inventions of the 'Romantic' age. So too are new ideas that emerged or grew in the artistic realm: the full-scale development of a conception of 'the aesthetic', which is to say a philosophical theory of beauty; the modern meanings of the words 'imagination', 'creativity', 'genius' and 'literature'; a public appetite for sensation; the vampire story and the science fiction novel; the worship of Shakespeare as the icon of Western culture alongside a new fascination with Eastern, especially Hindu and Buddhist, thought; and, as Taine discerned, the transformation of artistic expression into a yearning for eternity at a time when traditional religious beliefs were being called into question.

All these cultural developments give warrant to Isaiah Berlin's high claim that Romanticism was a movement that transformed 'the lives and thought of the Western world'. Academics have (very properly) long been demanding that we distinguish between different strands of Romanticism, or perhaps Romanticisms, or maybe that we should abandon the term altogether.[10] Yet the metaphor of a revolution remains well grounded: as we have seen, commentators at the time – notably William Hazlitt, the sharpest English observer of the culture of the age – saw the work of Wordsworth and Coleridge in 1798 as a translation into the literary sphere of the spirit of the French Revolution of 1789. Furthermore, Hazlitt's conviction that there *was* a 'spirit of the age' demonstrates that thinking men and women believed that a profound transformation of culture and values was under way.

Talk of revolution should not, however, allow us to fall into the trap of setting up an easy opposition between Classic and Romantic, or the Age of Reason and the Age of Feeling, or the era of Dr Johnson and that of Wordsworth. Enthusiasm for nature, one of the traditional hallmarks of Romanticism, can be traced back to the mid-eighteenth century: indeed, in 1740 an eighteen-year-old Oxford student called Joseph Warton composed a long poem called *The Enthusiast, or The Lover of Nature*, which would have been a perfectly apt description of Wordsworth in the Lake District sixty years later.[11]

★

It is tempting to portray the Wordsworth of the 1790s as the utopian radical welcoming the French Revolution's spirit of liberty, equality and fraternity, and the Wordsworth of the 1800s as the nostalgic lover of the lakes and mountains in full retreat from his own earlier idealism. The talk of youthful errors in the 'Ode to Duty' and the shift in the direction of Christian faith in the 'Intimations of Immortality' ode support such a view. But the true picture was more complicated: Wordsworth idealized the 'statesmen' of the Lake District because their way of life and form of land ownership embodied a 'democratic' ideal not unlike that of the Swiss cantons – and it was the invasion of Switzerland that, as much as the Terror, turned him against the French Revolution. Equally, he was still regarded by some as a 'republican' well into the new century.[12]

The connection between the two images of Wordsworth as political radical and Lake Poet becomes clear when one recognizes that both conceptions of him came principally from the same source. Although William Hazlitt claimed that when he met Wordsworth and Coleridge in Somerset in 1798, he sensed that they were creating a poetic revolution on 'French' principles, he was writing with the benefit of hindsight twenty-five years later. The first person to go into print with an account of Wordsworth as a leading exponent of what Canning and Gillray had satirized as the 'new morality' in poetry was a much less sympathetic critic.

In the autumn of 1802, a group of Edinburgh intellectuals with backgrounds in the law and moral philosophy launched a quarterly magazine called the *Edinburgh Review, or Critical Journal.*

Featuring much longer and more intellectually rigorous essays and reviews than those in the plethora of monthly and quarterly magazines coming out of London, the *Edinburgh* would rapidly take centre stage in the political and cultural debates of the age. The very first issue included an essay, following hard on the heels of a consideration of 'Irvine's Inquiry into the Causes and Effects of Emigration from the Highlands and Western Islands of Scotland', by one of the founding fathers of the magazine, Francis Jeffrey. He had been commissioned by the editor, Sydney Smith, 'to barbecue a poet or two'.[13]

The piece was purportedly a review of *Thalaba the Destroyer*, the latest epic poem by Robert Southey (in contrast to Wordsworth and Coleridge, Southey was able to knock out lengthy verse narratives with alarming facility). But Jeffrey had little to say about the poem. Instead, he used the piece as an opportunity to attack 'a sect of poets, that has established itself in this country within these ten or twelve years'. Jeffrey alleges that these poets had a 'peculiar' set of doctrines that made them 'dissenters from the established systems in poetry and criticism'. The word 'dissenter' was a red flag: the whole thrust of Canning's and Gillray's attack on the 'new morality' had been the supposedly toxic connection between religious dissent and revolutionary politics. Jeffrey continued with a deliberately provocative use of religious language: 'Though they lay claim, we believe, to a creed and a revelation of their own, there can be little doubt, that their doctrines are of German origin, and have been derived from some of the great modern reformers of that country.' In other words, as the religious Reformation of the sixteenth century that began with Martin Luther in Germany had assaulted the hierarchical Roman Catholic Church, so these poetic reformers were subverting the established order of literary culture. 'Some of their leading principles, indeed, are probably of an earlier date, and seem to have been borrowed from the great apostle of Geneva': here Jeffrey converts John Calvin into the latter-day scourge of traditional values, Rousseau, whose 'anti-social principles and distempered sensibility' is taken to be the chief influence on the 'new sect'.[14] Their poetry, he argues, is infected with Rousseau's 'discontent with the present constitution of society − his paradoxical morality, and his perpetual hankerings after some unattainable state of voluptuous virtue and perfection'.

Southey and his circle are also said to be under the influence of questionable modern German literature − 'The simplicity and energy (*horresco referens*) of Kotzebue and Schiller' − and to be engaged in an attempt to combine 'The homeliness and harshness of some of Cowper's language and versification' with an odd mixture of milksop pastoralism and obscure poetic theologizing in the vein of the 'metaphysical' poets of the seventeenth century. Furthermore, their 'great love of nature' had led them to 'an affectation of great simplicity and familiarity of language' and what Jeffrey regarded as an indecorous mimicking of the language of 'low-bred heroes and interesting rustics'. Poetry, he believed, should elevate itself far above 'the ordinary language of conversation in the inferior orders of society'. 'In making these strictures on the perverted taste for simplicity that seems to distinguish our modern school of poetry', Jeffrey concludes,

we have no particular allusion to Mr Southey, or the production now before us: on the contrary, he appears to us to be less addicted to this fault than most of his fraternity; and if we were in want of examples to illustrate the preceding observations, we should certainly look for them in the effusions of that poet who commemorates, with so much effect, the chattering of Harry Gill's teeth, tells the tale of the one-eyed huntsman who had a cheek like a cherry, and beautifully warns his studious friend of the risk he ran of 'growing double'.

Though unnamed, Wordsworth was the one under fire. Jeffrey was the first to brand him as a Rousseauist who had succumbed to the influence of the excessive 'sensibility' of modern German literature, as exemplified by the torrid plays of August von Kotzebue – whose *Lovers' Vows*, which would bring illicit sexual entanglement to the world of Jane Austen's *Mansfield Park*, was a hit on the London stage in the year of the first edition of *Lyrical Ballads*.[15]

It was also Francis Jeffrey who gave prominence to the association of Wordsworth and his circle with the Lake District. Five years after writing about *Lyrical Ballads* in his notice of Southey's *Thalaba*, the publication of *Poems, in Two Volumes* gave him the opportunity to review Wordsworth directly. His treatment in the *Edinburgh* proved to be more balanced than the other reviews. There was the usual mockery of the 'simple' poems, but also a recognition of Wordsworth's qualities. Indeed, the argument of Jeffrey's essay was that Wordsworth was bad when he was following the prescriptions of the 1800 Preface (said to lead to 'vulgarity, affectation, and silliness'), but good when he abandoned them and wrote with 'originality, pathos, and natural feeling': 'in point of fact, he does always write good verses, when, by any accident, he is led to abandon his system, and to transgress the laws of that school which he would fain establish on the ruin of all existing authority'.[16] Jeffrey's legal background was in play here: though a progressive Whig, he believed that the stability of society depended on a legal system based on 'authority' and precedent. He was accordingly threatened by the attempt of the 'new school' to overthrow the authority of the poetic tradition.

His review of *Poems, in Two Volumes* began 'This author is known to belong to a certain brotherhood of poets, who have haunted for some years about the Lakes of Cumberland'. Suspicion of revolutionary *fraternité* lurks in the word 'brotherhood', but the association of the 'new school' with lakes remote from the urban centres of Edinburgh and London also hints once more at allegiance to the revolutionary thinker who hailed from Geneva and sparked the flames of passion between Julie and Saint-Preux by locating *La nouvelle Héloïse* in a lakeland landscape. Jeffrey might well have labelled the 'new sect' as 'the English Rousseauists', but he chose instead, when reviewing *The Excursion* in 1814, to call them 'the Lakers'. By this time, the nomenclature 'Lake Poets' was in circulation. Three years after that, another reviewer coined the phrase 'the Lake School'.[17]

Rousseau bequeathed to Romanticism not only reverence for nature but also a belief in the free expression of the self both in writing and in what we would now call 'lifestyle'. For the 'Lake Poets', the two ideas coexisted. Coleridge and Southey's abortive 'Pantisocratic' dream of creating an idealistic commune was anchored to the rural setting of the banks of the romantic-sounding Susquehanna river in Pennsylvania. Wordsworth once visited the 'Ladies of Llangollen', two wealthy Irish women, Sarah Ponsonby and Lady Eleanor Butler, who openly lived together in intimate friendship in the Welsh hills. He wrote a not very good sonnet in their honour, yoking their bond to their landscape, their particular secluded 'spot':

> the *Vale of Friendship*, let *this* spot
> Be named; where, faithful to a low-roofed
>   Cot,
> On Deva's banks, ye have abode so long;
> Sisters in love – a love allowed to climb

Even on this Earth, above the reach of
  Time.[18]

In the generation after Wordsworth and Coleridge, Percy
Shelley, who was sent down from Oxford for writing a pamphlet
called *The Necessity of Atheism*, espoused the cause of 'free love'
outside the constraints of marriage in both an essay 'On Love'
and a long poem called 'Epipsychidion'. He found that this
was easier to practise among the mountains of Switzerland
(Rousseau country) and the hills of Italy than in London, under
the prying eyes of the scandalmongering press and a censorious
family.

As for self-expression in writing, the Romantic epoch can
indeed be described as the first age of autobiography and autobiographical literary creation. This was the time when poets and
memoirists began writing self-consciously and unapologetically
about themselves. In the words of François-René, vicomte de
Chateaubriand, who came to be regarded as the father of French
Romanticism: 'We are convinced that great writers put their
own story into their works. The only thing that can be painted
well is one's own heart, ascribed to another, and the best part
of genius consists of memories.'[19] The great writers have told
their own story in their works: as far as the English language is
concerned, it was Wordsworth who was the first to do so with
absolute self-consciousness, in his autobiographical epic poem.
For Chateaubriand, one only truly describes one's own heart
by attributing it to another: Wordsworth pulled off an unprecedented double act in describing his own heart by simultaneously
attributing it to himself (the 'I' who speaks so many of his
poems) and to others (among them, his sister Dorothy, his friend
Coleridge, and a vast assortment of observed or invented Lakeland
shepherds, vagrants, discharged military personnel, not to

mention birds and beasts and flowers and indeed the very forms of nature, lakes and mountains and clouds). *Genius is composed of memories*: the words should perhaps have been carved on Wordsworth's grave.

★

If Rousseau was the most influential progenitor of Romantic ideas and Goethe's *The Sorrows of the Young Werther* the prototype of the Romantic novel, what was the poem that could be said to have captured the imagination of the age of 'sensibility' in which the seeds of Romanticism were sown? It was without question the work that Werther reads to Charlotte in their last and most romantic moment. Goethe introduces it into the novel in a letter written by Werther as he is being seized by the madness of his passion:

> To what a world does the illustrious bard carry me! To wander over pathless wilds, surrounded by impetuous whirlwinds, where, by the feeble light of the moon, we see the spirits of our ancestors; to hear from the mountain-tops, mid the roar of torrents, their plaintive sounds issuing from deep caverns, and the sorrowful lamentations of a maiden who sighs and expires on the mossy tomb of the warrior by whom she was adored. I meet this bard with silver hair; he wanders in the valley; he seeks the footsteps of his fathers, and, alas! he finds only their tombs.[20]

In Werther's final meeting with Charlotte, after which he walks into a dark and stormy night to prepare for his self-willed journey to his own tomb, he reads her a long passage from this work in his own translation – that is to say, Goethe's translation. With eyes full of tears, he begins to read:

Star of descending night! fair is thy light in the west! thou
liftest thy unshorn head from thy cloud: thy steps are stately
on thy hill. What dost thou behold in the plain? The stormy
winds are laid. The murmur of the torrent comes from afar.
Roaring waves climb the distant rock. The flies of evening
are on their feeble wings: the hum of their course is on the
field. What dost thou behold, fair light? But thou dost smile
and depart. The waves come with joy around thee: they bathe
thy lovely hair. Farewell, thou silent beam! Let the light of
Ossian's soul arise![21]

On and on he reads, until the force of the words falls upon him
and he flings himself at Charlotte's feet, seizes her hands and
presses them to his forehead. She in turn draws his hands to her
bosom and they kiss passionately, the world disappearing from
their eyes. Collecting herself, 'with disordered grief, in mingled
tones of love and resentment', she says his name and pushes him
away: '"It is the last time, Werther! You shall never see me any
more!" Then, casting one last, tender look upon her unfortunate
lover, she rushed into the adjoining room, and locked the door.'
He calls to her but she does not answer: 'He stopped, and listened
and entreated; but all was silent. At length he tore himself from
the place, crying, "Adieu, Charlotte, adieu for ever!"'[22] And off
he goes to commit suicide.

This flood of passion was stimulated by the poetry of Ossian,
a legendary Gaelic bard, whose works were discovered and translated — or were they forged, invented from pure imagination?
— by James Macpherson in the early 1760s. The cult of Ossian,
and the debate over the material's authenticity, has been the
subject of whole books in itself. Modern scholarship has suggested
that Macpherson did find many fragments of ancient Gaelic
poetry — ballads and the like — and that he got help with his

translation, but that the organization of his epic tales and huge swathes of the texts were indeed of his own making.²³ Whether or not Ossian was historically real, the age of sensibility needed to reinvent him.

Ossian was the embodiment of the impassioned Bard amidst the mighty forms of nature. He was seen as – Wordsworth's phrase in a poem inspired by a visit to his supposed grave during his Scottish tour – the 'last of all his race'.²⁴ That is to say, Ossian was imagined as the vestige of a primitive age of heroism in a sublime setting that was the very antithesis of increasingly domestic, urbanized and commercialized modernity. From the point of view of the emerging nationalisms of the age, the Ossian myth gave the north a foundational epic equivalent to that of Homer in the Mediterranean south. *Fingal* and Macpherson's other *Fragments of Ancient Poetry, collected in the Highlands of Scotland, and translated from the Gaelic or Erse Language* answered a yearning for scale, for vicarious adventure and danger. The equivalent in our time would be *Lord of the Rings* or *Game of Thrones*. Just as 'Visit New Zealand' has profited from the desire of fans to seek out the locations where Tolkien's epic was turned into film, so the cult of Ossian had as great an effect on tourism as on literature: 'Fingal's Cave' in the Hebrides became the destination of choice for Romantic travellers.

Poets and readers across Europe were inspired by Macpherson's corpus of Ossianic poetry. A translation by a Viennese Jesuit called Michael Denis had a huge influence not only on the young Goethe, but also on works by Klopstock and Herder that were formative of German national literature. Within a few years, there were also translations into Danish, Swedish, Spanish, Russian, Dutch, Polish, Czech and Hungarian. Napoleon admired the Ossian poems as much as he did *Werther*. He even suggested that his godson – to whose father he gave a Scandinavian crown – should be named after one of the characters, a prince called Oscar. The boy eventually became King Oscar I of Sweden and Norway.

For a Londoner such as William Blake, the sublime northern landscape of Macpherson's sprawling prose poems opened a theatre of the imagination that took him far from the chartered streets and dark satanic mills of his immediate environment. His own epics such as *Milton* and *Jerusalem* are replete with Ossianic vocabulary. For Wordsworth, by contrast, mountains and vales, wind and rain, were his own domain. He accordingly thought that the poetry of Ossian was not only ridiculously overblown, but also wholly lacking in accuracy of description:

> Open this far-famed Book! – I have done so at random, and the beginning of the 'Epic Poem Temora', in 8 Books, presents itself. 'The blue waves of Ullin roll in light. The green hills are covered with day. Trees shake their dusky heads in the breeze. Grey torrents pour their noisy streams. Two green hills with aged oaks surround a narrow plain. The blue course of a stream is there . . .' Precious memorandums from the pocket-book of the blind Ossian!

As far as Wordsworth could tell, Macpherson could offer only basic colours (blue, green, grey) and undifferentiated hills, trees and streams. 'Having had the good fortune to be born and reared in a mountainous Country,' writes Wordsworth, 'from my very childhood I have felt the falsehood that pervades the volumes imposed upon the World under the name of Ossian':

> From what I saw with my own eyes, I knew that the imagery was spurious. In nature every thing is distinct, yet nothing defined into absolute independant singleness. In Macpherson's

work it is exactly the reverse; every thing (that is not stolen) is in this manner defined, insulated, dislocated, deadened, – yet nothing distinct. It will always be so when words are substituted for things.[25]

This is both a devastating critique that nails the difference between good and bad poetry, and an illumination of Wordsworth's own art. In stark contrast to 'blind Ossian', Wordsworth sees into the 'distinct' life of things. His poetic eye singles out the singularity of things. He names the particular places that have inspired him and relives the moments when he has felt the elements upon his skin and in his heart. Wordsworth had no time for the Ossianic sublime because – unlike any previous English poet – the environment in which he was born and raised enabled him to write from first-hand experience of how, as he put it in the Preface to *Lyrical Ballads*, 'the passions of men' may be 'incorporated with the beautiful and permanent forms of nature'.

This privilege of birth and first-hand experience also gave him the opportunity to reinvent another literary genre that was also wholly characteristic of the age: the tour guide.

★

In 1726 Daniel Defoe published the third volume of *A Tour through the Whole Island of Great Britain*. He had begun the project four years earlier, describing a series of journeys, purportedly eyewitness accounts of the state of the nation from the pen of a man who could be described as the first modern journalist. There is in fact some uncertainty as to whether he undertook all the tours himself – some of his reports appear to be second-hand. But whether his source was his eyes, his ears or his reading, Defoe was unequivocal in his attitude to the English Lake District. He pronounced Westmorland to be a county 'eminent only for being the wildest, most barren and frightful of any that I have passed over in *England*, or even in *Wales* it self'. Worse even than Wales: imagine! 'The West side, which borders on *Cumberland*,' he continued, 'is indeed bounded by a Chain of almost unpassable Mountains, which, in the Language of the Country, are called *Fells*'. There was, said Defoe, but one word to sum up the landscape: 'Horror'.

These Lakeland fells, he wrote, have 'no rich pleasant Valleys between them, as among the *Alps*; no Lead Mines and Veins of rich Oar [ore], as in the *Peak*; no Coal Pits, as in the hills about *Hallifax*, much less Gold, as in the *Andes*, but all barren and wild, of no use or advantage either to Man or Beast'.[26] Those terms 'use' and 'advantage' are revealing: Defoe was a man who believed in what we would now call the bourgeois or capitalist idea of getting on in the world, whether that meant mining for lead, coal and gold, or building a shelter and a fledgling economy like his Robinson Crusoe, or using your sex appeal to survive in a patriarchal society like his Moll Flanders.

The Life and Strange Surprizing Adventures of Robinson Crusoe, one of the foundational texts of the modern novel, had been published a few years earlier, in 1719. Crusoe is often described as the exemplar of economic man: with the assistance of a little slave labour from Friday, he shows that the bourgeois virtues of resilience, enterprise and hard work may enable a man to build a functioning economy even in the inhospitable environment of a desert island. Crusoe introduces British technology and agriculture to the island, and sets up a political structure with himself at the top. In the words of James Joyce, Crusoe is 'the true prototype of the British colonist', embodying the 'whole Anglo-Saxon spirit': 'the manly independence, the unconscious cruelty, the persistence, the slow yet efficient intelligence, the sexual apathy, the calculating taciturnity'.[27] The Lake District, implies

Defoe – a Londoner and a businessman – in his *Tour*, has no such economic potential, indeed no value at all. Fast-forward two centuries and now nearly 20 million visitors per year visit the Lake District National Park, spending £1.4 billion and supporting nearly 20,000 jobs.[28] How did we get from there to here?

A clue as to the change in sensibility that led to the transformation of attitudes to the lakes and mountains of the north may be found in a different aspect of *Robinson Crusoe*, namely the way in which it works as a spiritual autobiography. Crusoe's solitude among the forms of nature on his island leads him to contemplate God. As a Puritan, Defoe believed that revealed faith, the personal encounter with Jesus, was paramount; he did, however, recognize that, thanks to 'natural religion' (the 'deist' idea of finding God in nature), even 'savages' such as Friday may have a sense of the divine. Crusoe makes it his business to build on this potential and convert Friday to his 'revealed' Christianity. Deism gathered pace as the eighteenth century unfolded, often as a middle-class reaction against the perceived danger that Nonconformist zeal – Puritanism and, later, Methodism – might lead to disruption of the social order. Add to this the aesthetic revolution associated with the theory of the 'sublime' – the idea that 'horror' in the face of the awe-inspiring power of mountains, storms and wilderness might be both mentally stimulating and indeed an encounter with a divine force – and we find ourselves on the road to that aspect of Romanticism which has sometimes been described as 'spilt religion'.[29]

In 1753, a Cambridge-educated clergyman called John Brown, who came from Wigton in Cumberland, wrote a letter to Lord Lyttelton, which was published some years later under the title *Description of the Lake and Vale of Keswick*. 'The full perfection of KESWICK', he wrote 'consists of three circumstances, *Beauty*, *Horror*, and *Immensity*, united'. 'To give you a complete idea of these three perfections, as they are joined in KESWICK,' he continued, 'would require the united powers of *Claude, Salvator, and Poussin.*'[30] Claude Lorrain would 'throw his delicate sunshine over the cultivated vales, the scattered cots, the groves, the lake, and wooded islands'; Salvator Rosa would 'dash out the horror of the rugged cliffs, the steeps, the hanging woods, and foaming water-falls': it would later become commonplace to associate Salvator with the wild sublime and Claude with the gentler idea of the beautiful. Poussin — Brown was probably thinking of Gaspard, not the more famous Nicolas — would fill in the mountains. As shorthand, we may say that this was the first occasion on which the Lake District was praised in the language of the sublime. And it was perhaps also the first occasion in which the Lake District was represented by means of an artistic comparison: renowned landscape painters are invoked in order to suggest that it might be worth visiting the Lakes because the experience would be like looking at a real-life three-dimensional example of a great painting. And implicitly, the painter of the scenery is God. The aesthetic of the sublime, the connoisseurship of artistic taste, and the comfort of deism thus come together.

John Brown supplemented his modest clergyman's stipend by serving as tutor to a gentleman in Carlisle called John Bernard Gilpin. Both Dr Brown and Mr Gilpin had artistic aspirations, which they duly passed on to one of the latter's sons, a boy called William Gilpin, who would grow up to develop a hugely influential theory for which he coined a name. In his *Observations on the River Wye* of 1782 — the book that inspired Wordsworth to make the tour of the Wye that led him to write 'Tintern Abbey' — Gilpin proposed a 'new object of pursuit' for tourists: instead of inquiring into the culture of soils or the manners of men in the places they visited, they should 'examine the face of a country *by the rules of picturesque beauty*'. William Gilpin had defined his term some years earlier, in an essay on prints and engravings: by 'picturesque' he meant, of course, 'expressive of that peculiar kind of beauty, which is agreeable in a picture'.[31] In 1786, he published *Observations relative to Picturesque Beauty made in 1772, on several parts of England; particularly the Mountains and Lakes of Cumberland and Westmoreland* in which his principles were applied to the landscape of the Lake District, thus encouraging more and more fashionable tourists to venture north.

Another key figure in the story was Thomas Gray. In his account of the Grande Chartreuse, which so inspired Wordsworth on his walking tour with Jones in 1790, he wrote that 'There are certain scenes that would awe an atheist into belief, without the help of other argument': 'Not a precipice, not a torrent, not a cliff, but is pregnant with religion and poetry.'[32] The elision of religion and poetry sows a seed for Matthew Arnold's claim, in the face of science's assault upon the old biblical certainties about the age of the earth and the evolution of man, that there would come a time when the only remains of religion would be the poetry of it.

Back in England, Gray read Dr Brown's essay on the glories of Keswick and decided to take a trip to the Lakes himself, in order to find closer to home some sublimity akin to that of the Alps. He was duly impressed by Borrowdale and the craggy fells, but he also found gentler landscapes, approximating to what Edmund Burke called the beautiful as opposed to the sublime. Nowhere more so than in the vale of Grasmere:

> The bosom of the mountains spreading here into a broad basin discovers in the midst Grasmere-water, its margin is hollowed into small bays, with bold eminences; some of them rocks, some of soft turf, that half conceal, and vary the figure of the little lake they command: from the shore a low prom-

ontory pushes itself far into the water, and on it stands a
white village with the parish church rising in the midst of
it: hanging inclosures, corn-fields, and meadows green as an
emerald, with their trees and hedges, and cattle, fill up the
whole space from the edge of the water: and just opposite to
you is a large farm-house at the bottom of a steep smooth
lawn, embosomed in old woods, which climb half-way up
the mountain's side, and discover above them a broken line
of crags, that crown the scene. Not a single red tile, no flaring
gentleman's house, or garden-walls, break in upon the repose
of this little unsuspected paradise; but all is peace, rusticity,
and happy poverty in its neatest, most becoming attire.[33]

Wordsworth would sympathize with many aspects of Gray's
description: the paradise-like quality of the vale of Grasmere
does indeed come from the harmony of its elements, the sense
of a manageable scale to its mountain beauty, its blended colours
and the integration of its buildings with their environment.
But he dissented with a passion from the notion of 'happy
poverty' – of the rural poor as no more than part of the
picturesque scene. It was in reaction against such complacency
that he sought in his poetry to find a voice for the vagrant,
the old leech gatherer, the destitute widow, the hill farmer on
the breadline.

   Brown's influential description of the vale of Keswick, Gray's
journal of his Lakeland tour, and other key texts were gathered
together in an appendix to the second edition of a book well
known to Wordsworth: Thomas West's *A Guide to the Lakes in
Cumberland, Westmorland and Lancashire*, published in 1778 and
expanded in 1780. This became *the* volume for fashionable travellers to pack in their baggage. Between them, Gilpin and West
wrote the rulebook for Lake District tourists of the kind that

today outnumber those who go to walk the rugged fells: the day-tripper, the beauty-spot photographer. West provided a list of so-called 'stations', elevated points where you could stop your carriage and take in a view that was composed like a picture with a dark foreground, a sharp middle distance and a hazy horizon. When he came to the vale of Grasmere, he quoted Gray's description of the 'little unsuspected paradise', but then added:

> Mr *Gray's* description is taken from the road descending from *Dunmail-raise*. But the more advantageous station, to view this romantic vale from, is on the fourth end of the western side. Proceed from *Ambleside* by *Clappersgate*, along the banks of the river *Brathay*, and at *Scalewith-bridge*, ascend a steep hill called *Loughrig*, that leads to *Grasmere*, and a little behind its summit you come in sight of the valley and lake lying in the sweetest order.[34]

West adds that, in terms of the sweetness and order of the compositional effect, this has a great advantage over the aspect from Dunmail-raise because 'Mr *Gray* has omitted the island in his description, which is a principal feature in the scene.'

Gilpin, meanwhile, developed more fully the notion of turning a landscape into a 'scene' by recommending the use of a 'Claude glass', an oval-shaped pocket mirror to which various filters could be applied, so that you could turn your back on the landscape and capture the scene in such a way as to make it resemble a painting by Claude Lorrain. There is little difference between this and the modern phenomenon whereby a tourist coach will stop at a Lake District 'viewpoint' or 'beauty spot', and the party will tumble out, turn their backs on the view and picture themselves by means of their selfie-sticks.

The popularity of Lake District tourism was such that by 1797 a gentleman called James Plumptre was moved to write a play satirizing the phenomenon. *The Lakers* includes assorted local rustics (including a beggar and his dog), a pair of hikers (known as 'pedestrians' because they insist upon travelling on foot, not by carriage) and, in the central role, Miss Beccabunga Veronica, an avid amateur botanist. Little wonder that early in the second volume of *Lyrical Ballads*, published just over three years later, Wordsworth would write, adopting the voice of a local vicar:

These Tourists, Heaven preserve us! needs must live
A profitable life: some glance along,
Rapid and gay, as if the earth were air,
And they were butterflies to wheel about
Long as their summer lasted; some, as wise,
Upon the forehead of a jutting crag
Sit perch'd, with book and pencil on their knee,
And look and scribble, scribble on and look,
Until a man might travel twelve stout miles,
Or reap an acre of his neighbour's corn.[35]

What kind of economy do we now have, these lines ask, in which some people have the wealth and time to sit and idly sketch while others must go about their business and their labour? And what kind of 'profit' does such indulgence avail the human soul? Is picturesque tourism merely a middle-class indulgence? As W. H. Auden would put it in a poem written over a hundred years later, 'Am I / To see in the Lake District, then, / Another bourgeois invention like the piano?'[36] What Wordsworth sought to articulate was an alternative response to his native region from that espoused by the likes of Gilpin and West.

He did so in prose as well as poetry. In 1807, Lord and Lady Holland, aristocrats of a literary disposition, were staying at the Low Wood Hotel on Windermere, on their way to Scotland for the shooting season. Lady Holland recorded in her diary that they 'sent an invitation to Wordsworth, one of the Lake poets, to come and dine'. In the course of a lively evening's conversation, they discussed the vogue for the 'picturesque'. Wordsworth rode one of his hobby horses: the way that the whitewashing of buildings on the side of the mountains spoiled the green scene. Lady Holland disagreed. Wordsworth then mentioned that 'he was preparing a manual to guide travellers in their tour amongst the Lakes'.[37] In order to research this further, he and Mary took an autumn tour of the wilder west side of Cumberland. They visited the remote valleys of Ennerdale and Wasdale, where scree slopes descend precipitously into Wastwater, while also taking the opportunity to revisit the Cockermouth of his birth. But on their return, a depressive lethargy blocked Wordsworth from writing, and the project stalled.

A visitor the following year asked whether he would consider writing a book descriptive of his sublime environment, but Wordsworth replied to the effect that one could be too familiar with a place to be able to describe it for an outsider. He did, however, agree a year later to write an introduction and a set of accompanying texts for a folio of (not very good) engravings of Lake District scenes by a Norfolk clergyman called Joseph Wilkinson, who was an acquaintance of Coleridge's. *Select Views in Cumberland, Westmoreland, and Lancashire* was published in monthly parts in 1810, with no mention of the fact that Wordsworth had written the text. It appeared under his own name only in 1820 in a book mostly written in verse: *The River Duddon, A Series of Sonnets: Vaudracour & Julia: and Other Poems.*

To Which is annexed, A Topographical Description of the Country of the Lakes, in the North of England. This edition carried an explanatory advertisement:

> This Essay, which was first published several years ago as an Introduction to some Views of the Lakes, by the Rev. Joseph Wilkinson, (an expensive work, and necessarily of limited circulation,) is now, with emendations and additions, attached to these volumes; from a consciousness of its having been written in the same spirit which dictated several of the poems, and from a belief that it will tend materially to illustrate them.

'The same spirit which dictated' is a lovely phrase that half-suggests an external force – a Muse – creating Wordsworth's poems, and indeed this essay on the Lakes, with him playing the role of mere scribe. As John Milton imagined himself as only a vessel and the Holy Spirit as the true author of *Paradise Lost*, which in his blindness he duly dictated to his amanuenses, and as William Blake imagined the spirit of Milton entering him (via the left foot), so Wordsworth implies that the spirit of the Lake District itself wrote 'several of his poems' and that his role was to be an accompanying guide.

He began his *Guide* by taking the reader to an imaginary station on a cloud midway between Great Gable and Scafell, from where the eight valleys of the Lake District may be seen stretched out like spokes from the nave of a wheel. By substituting an imaginary station for an actual one, Wordsworth differentiates his *Guide* from those intended only for the practical use of tourists; with the image of the wheel, he introduces the idea of a unified place with a common centre. Mountains, vales, and lakes all work together; even the humble tarn makes a necessary contribution to the whole: 'In the economy of Nature these are useful, as auxiliars to Lakes;

for if the whole quantity of water which falls upon the mountains in time of storm were poured down upon the plains without intervention . . . the habitable grounds would be much more subject than they are to inundation.'[38] Thomas West never seemed to notice tarns, presumably because he did not deem them either picturesque or sublime. Where other guides concerned themselves with how the more majestic lakes contributed to the charm of a scene, Wordsworth's was interested in the function performed within the ecosystem by the smaller and higher bodies of still water.

Throughout the *Guide*, people are seen firmly in relation to their material environment. Among Wordsworth's chief concerns are the management of trees and the architecture of rural buildings. The native inhabitants of the district are seen to share in a natural unity. 'The economy of Nature' and the human economy are brought together as the hand of man is 'incorporated with and subservient to the powers and processes of Nature'. Man works in partnership with his environment. Thus Lakeland cottages may be said rather 'to have grown than to have been erected; — to have risen, by an instinct of their own, out of the native rock'; the buildings 'in their very form call to mind the processes of Nature' and thus 'appear to be received into the bosom of the living principle of things'. Not even the places dedicated to Christian worship violate the *religio loci*, the spirit of place. A consequence of such integration with nature is an integrated social structure: until recently there has been 'a perfect Republic of Shepherds and Agriculturists, among whom the plough of each man was confined to the maintenance of his own family, or to the occasional accommodation of his neighbour'. There was no nobleman, knight, or squire; the ruling power was nature, not some human overlord. Here Wordsworth, alert to the region's distinctively democratic form of land tenure, describes the district of the Lakes as an 'almost visionary mountain republic'.[39]

But all this has changed as a result of influx and innovation. New residents who are not rooted in the land have brought dissonant new building styles; worse, in accordance with the 'craving for prospect', their new houses have been built on obtrusive sites where they do not 'harmonize with the forms of Nature'. The rage for picturesque 'improvement' has even resulted in the alteration of the contours of the principal island on Windermere lake: 'Could not the margin of this noble island be given back to Nature?' asks Wordsworth, very much in the tone of a modern conservationist.[40] Worst of all is the introduction of larch plantations. Wordsworth makes a powerful distinction between the way in which nature forms woods and forests, a gradual and selective process shaped by conditions of soil, exposure to wind, and so on, and the environmentally and aesthetically harmful practices of artificial planting.

Wordsworth's book was, then, unlike earlier guides in that it did far more than offer what he called tedious 'guide matter': it used the popular guidebook format to put his own concerns across to the public. In particular, whereas West and his followers all wrote exclusively for visitors to the Lakes, Wordsworth aimed to show what it meant to dwell there. It is symptomatic that in writing of the rootedness of Lakeland cottages Wordsworth included some lines of verse from the unpublished manuscript of *Home at Grasmere*, that poem which was so central to his sense of himself as a dweller in Westmorland. Where earlier guide writers adopted the picturesque tourist's point of view and rarely descended from their stations, Wordsworth's approach was holistic: he moved from nature to the natives, exploring the relationship between land and inhabitant; then in laying out a manifesto for the future preservation of the distinctive environment he considered the evolving and increasingly disruptive influence of modern, mobile man.

He knew that the new proprietors and tourists would not go away; he saw the function of the *Guide* as being to educate them to care for the delicate ecosystem, as we would now call it, of the Lakes. 'In this wish,' Wordsworth concludes, 'the author will be joined by persons of pure taste throughout the whole island, who, by their visits (often repeated) to the Lakes in the North of England, testify that they deem the district a sort of national property, in which every man has a right and interest who has an eye to perceive and a heart to enjoy.'[41] It was, we will discover, not least via the after-history of this idea that Wordsworth may be said to have changed the world.

PART TWO

1807–1850:
WORDSWORTH'S
HEALING POWER

But where will Europe's latter hour
Again find Wordsworth's healing power?
Others will teach us how to dare,
And against fear our breast to steel;
Others will strengthen us to bear –
But who, ah! who, will make us feel?

(Matthew Arnold, 'Memorial Verses'
on the poet's death)

17

SURPRISED BY GRIEF

The epic 'Poem to Coleridge' reached its moment of full achievement on those winter nights as 1806 turned to 1807. His poetry had been building to the climax of this moment. Though he would have vehemently denied the fact, nearly all his writing after that moment was anticlimactic. The second half of Wordsworth's life was the longest, dullest decline in literary history. Paradoxically, though, it was in the second half of his life that his fame grew and grew.

The test for an enduring poem is memorability: many lines in the poems written between 1797 and 1807 are unforgettable, whereas hardly anyone can remember a single line of late Wordsworth. When Nobel laureate Seamus Heaney published a selection of Wordsworth's best poems, he included only three written after the year 1806: the sonnet 'Surprised by joy', another sonnet that formed the conclusion of the sequence *The River Duddon*, and a late elegy called 'Extempore Effusion on the Death of James Hogg'. Heaney was an unerring judge of poetry as well as a formidable poet: many readers of Wordsworth would agree that these are indeed among the few later poems that are as powerful and memorable as so many of the earlier ones. All three of them are about death. It was as if, having suffered a kind of poetic death, Wordsworth could recapture his gift only when he wrote of death.

★

On 24 January 1805, Captain John Wordsworth wrote to his brother: 'I have the pleasure to inform you that the *Abergany* [sic] is arrived safe at Portsmouth and if the Wind continues fair which it is at present I shall expect to leave this place tomorrow.'[1] His 1,200-ton vessel was set for Bengal and Canton. On board were 402 people – passengers and troops as well as crew – together with supplies for the employees of the East India Company and silver dollars to be exchanged in China for tea, silk and porcelain that would be brought home. A captain's primary source of income would, however, be the smuggled cargo that was regularly taken on board in Calcutta and offloaded in Canton: opium.

The sea war with France had resumed (Nelson would win the Battle of Trafalgar later that year), so there was a risk of ambush in the English Channel. The *Abergavenny* was accordingly to go in convoy with other East Indiamen and two whaling vessels, under the escort of a forty-four-gun Royal Navy frigate. They gathered, waited on the wind, and sailed early on the morning of 1 February, only to be delayed further by a collision between the frigate and one of the East Indiamen. The commander of the frigate signalled an order that the passage out of harbour and past the Isle of Wight would be through the narrow Needles Channel. This made John Wordsworth nervous: he knew it was a hazardous route. Having set sail, they were unlucky with the weather. The wind changed direction and blew a squall. The frigate was separated from the convoy. A storm was brewing, so it was decided that they should return to port. The *Abergavenny* took on a pilot to steer them past Chesil Beach and around Portland Bill. They had to avoid the hazard of a notorious offshore shoal known as the Shambles. The pilot miscalculated and the ship was struck by a massive wave, swung round and driven onto the Shambles. John Wordsworth was heard to say 'Oh pilot! pilot! You have ruined me' – by which he seems to have been thinking of financial ruin, because the Wordsworth family had made a private investment of the huge sum of £20,000 in the voyage, in the hope of a very large return courtesy of the highly profitable illegal opium trade.

She floated off the shingle bank, but the hull had been breached. They pumped to no avail and Captain John decided that the only course of action would be to run her aground on Weymouth Sands. They did not make it to the shore: too much water had been taken in. The chief mate went to John Wordsworth, who was standing on the poop, and said 'We have done all we can, Sir – she will sink in a moment.' He replied, 'It cannot be helped. God's will be done.' The fourth mate survived to write a memorandum for the East India Company, describing the circumstances of the wreck. He also spoke to Charles Lamb, who worked as a clerk in the East India House, and at his behest wrote to Wordsworth in Grasmere, telling of how at the last he had seen 'several men hanging by ropes, fast to the mizzen mast amongst which was Capt. Wordsworth'. He tried to throw a rope, but John was 'motionless and insensible'.[2] The waves bore him away. About 260 of the 402 people on board perished with him. The

tragedy became a national news story, including some unsub-
stantiated bad press to the effect that John Wordsworth was 'in
a state of intoxication at the time of the calamity'.[3]

Sara Hutchinson was the first to get the news, probably from
a newspaper report. She collected the post in Ambleside and
took it to the Wordsworths' cottage in Grasmere. There was a
brief letter from brother Richard, telling William to break the
news to Dorothy gently. But Dorothy was the only one who
was home when Sara arrived. William and Mary were out for
a walk. They returned to find her weeping. That evening,
Wordsworth wrote to Sir George Beaumont, describing his late
brother as 'meek, affectionate, silently enthusiastic, loving all quiet
things, and a Poet in every thing but words'.[4] It would be more
than two months before he felt able to return to his own poetry,
or Dorothy to transcribing it. On May Day, he told Beaumont
that he had tried to write a poem in his brother's memory: 'I
began to give vent to my feelings, with this view, but I was
overpowered by my subject and could not proceed.'[5] It was not
until early June that he managed an elegy, inspired by a return
to Grisedale Tarn, where they had said their last goodbye. A
shepherd boy whistled, startling a buzzard from a rock:

> Lord of the air, he took his flight;
> Oh! could he on that woeful night
> Have lent his wing, my Brother dear,
> For one poor moment's space to Thee,
> And all who struggled with the Sea,
> When safety was so near.[6]

A year later, Wordsworth was staying with the Beaumonts in
their grand house in Grosvenor Square, London. Beaumont made
a point of not showing Wordsworth his painting *Peele Castle in*

a Storm.† It was there awaiting public exhibition in the summer Royal Academy show, to which Beaumont was also contributing another dark, windswept-looking canvas, number 96 in the catalogue, listed as 'The thorn. – See Lyrical Ballads, by W. Wordsworth, vol. I the Thorn'.

Beaumont knew that the image of a ship approaching the rocks would awake painful memories. But Wordsworth looked hard at the painting and composed 'Elegiac Stanzas suggested by a Picture of Peele Castle', which he published as the penultimate piece in his 1807 volume. The poem begins with his memory of the summer of 1794, when he had stayed for a few weeks in the village of Rampside, looking out over the 'glassy sea' to Piel Castle on calm, sunny days. There was a time, he is thinking, when even the sight of a ruined castle was apparelled in celestial light. But now 'A power is gone, which nothing can restore; / A deep distress hath humaniz'd my Soul'. It is the sentiment of 'Tintern Abbey' revisited, but with an overlay of Christian stoicism:

> But welcome fortitude, and patient chear,
> And frequent sights of what is to be borne!
> Such sights, or worse, as are before me here. –
> Not without hope we suffer and we mourn.

The poet of mourning is reaching for the 'hope' of life beyond the grave. In the 1807 volume, the reader is expected to turn the page and glimpse in the 'Ode' not the stormy waves that took John to his death but 'that immortal sea'.

★

---

† Piel Castle, off the Furness peninsula on the extreme south-western edge of the Lake District. Beaumont and Wordsworth spelt it 'Peele'.

In 1808, returning to *The Recluse,* Wordsworth wrote a new sequence lamenting some of the changes that had occurred in Grasmere during his time in the south at Coleorton – trees cut down, cottages fallen into disrepair, new houses that did not harmonize with the landscape. Ironically, it was at exactly this time that he moved into a new build that was one of the worst examples. He had complained about it in a letter when it appeared three years earlier:

> Woe to poor Grasmere for ever and ever! A wretched Creature, wretched in name and Nature, of the name of *Crump* . . . has at last begun to put his long impending threats in execution; and when you next enter the sweet paradise of Grasmere you will see staring you in the face upon that beautiful ridge that elbows out into the vale (behind the church and towering far above its steeple) a temple of abomination, in which are to be enshrined Mr and Mrs Crump. Seriously this is a great vexation to us as this House will stare you in the face from every part of the Vale, and entirely destroy its character of simplicity and seclusion.[7]

The house was called Allan Bank. When the Crumps decided to let it out, Wordsworth and Dorothy moved there. The Town End cottage was proving just too cramped. But they hated the new place: the chimneys smoked, coal was expensive and the larger size of the house meant they needed two servants rather than one. The loyal Molly Fisher had retired by this time, so they now employed two younger local women.

One of them, Sally Green, came from a large but very poor family in Easedale. William, Mary and Dorothy were deeply affected by a tragedy that struck her family this same year: returning from a farm sale in Langdale late on a snowy March afternoon, her parents George and Sarah Green set off across the fells and disappeared. Their bodies were found at the foot of a precipice two days later. Six children, ranging from an eleven-year-old to a baby, were left alone. At the funeral, Thomas De Quincey heard Dorothy say 'that the grief of Sarah's illegitimate daughter was the most overwhelming she had ever witnessed'. Mary Wordsworth and other local women clubbed together in order to find homes for the children, Dorothy circulated a 'Narrative' of the story, and William wrote to everyone he knew who had money, seeking donations. In due course, as De Quincey put it, 'A regular distribution of the children was made amongst the wealthier families of the vale.'[8] The Clarksons later encouraged Dorothy to publish her narrative of the tragedy; she refused, primarily because it would be an invasion of the children's privacy, but also because she was reluctant to go into print: 'My reasons are entirely disconnected with myself, much as I should detest the idea of setting myself up as an Author.'[9]

In order to write at his best, Wordsworth needed not only to have Dorothy and Coleridge by his side. He also needed to feel at home. That had been the key to his flowering at Racedown, Alfoxden and above all the snug home in Town End that is now known as Dove Cottage. Allan Bank was large, dreary and draughty. And something similar may be said of the poetry he composed there: this was the house in which, between 1808 and 1812, he wrote the bulk of the part of *The Recluse* that would be published in 1814 under the title *The Excursion*.

At the same time, inspired by the unprecedented success of the poetry of Sir Walter Scott, with whom he had struck up a warm friendship conducted largely by correspondence, he worked on a long narrative poem called *The White Doe of Rylstone*.[10] This led to a quarrel. First Wordsworth entrusted Coleridge with overseeing its publication by Longman, but then, mindful of the bad reviews of his 1807 volume, he asked Longman not to go ahead, without telling Coleridge first. This seemingly trivial matter was the surface manifestation of tensions that were brewing as a result of Coleridge's opium addiction and his obsession with Sara Hutchinson.

Despite this, they still worked together, though now in a more journalistic, less poetic, way. Together with Thomas De Quincey, Coleridge helped in the preparation of a long pamphlet attacking the Convention of Cintra, which was signed in 1808 after British troops under Sir Arthur Wellesley, later the Duke of Wellington, defeated the French in Portugal. Like many others on the home front, Wordsworth was outraged that the agreement allowed the French to retreat into Spain with their weapons. He felt that this was a shocking betrayal of the Spanish freedom fighters. His conception of liberty was closely tied to the idea of national independence: that had been the argument of the sonnet sequence in the 1807 volume, in which, as well as expressing his love for the liberty of his native England, he had denounced 'The Extinction of the Venetian Republic' and 'The Subjugation of Switzerland'. His vision was of a Europe of independent nations, free from the yoke of both Napoleonic imperialism and 'corrupt princedoms and degenerate nobility'. If Spain could one day be free, then other nations might follow:

The stir of emancipation may again be felt at the mouths as well as the sources of the Rhine. Poland perhaps will not be insensible; Kosciusko and his compeers may not have bled in vain. Nor is Hungarian loyalty to be overlooked. And, for Spain itself, the territory is wide: let it be overrun; the torrent will weaken as the water spreads.[11]

The title of Wordsworth's contribution to the public debate was *Concerning the Relations of Great Britain, Spain, and Portugal, to each other, and to the common enemy, at this crisis; and specifically as affected by the CONVENTION OF CINTRA: The whole brought to the test of these Principles, by which alone the Independence and Freedom of Nations can be Preserved or Recovered*. Revisions, delays and changes of plan over publication format meant that by the time it went to press, the controversy over the decision of the generals, and the ensuing inquiry, had long passed.

Wordsworth in turn helped Coleridge with his new weekly magazine, *The Friend*. Being Coleridge, he didn't manage to bring it out every week and the paper folded after fewer than thirty issues. Some passages from the unpublished *Prelude* and *Excursion* were published here, among them the skating scene, included in the Christmas 1809 issue under the title 'Growth of Genius from the Influences of Natural Objects, on the Imagination in Boyhood, and Early Youth'. Coleridge introduced it as an extract from a 'Poem on the growth and revolutions of an individual mind, by WORDSWORTH'.[12] It is not clear whether the suggestive inclusion of 'and revolutions' in the prospective title of the autobiographical epic came from Wordsworth or Coleridge.

A couple of months later, *The Friend* carried an 'Essay upon Epitaphs' in which Wordsworth argued that epitaphs inscribed upon the marking-places of the dead were among the earliest forms of writing. The essay turns some of the ideas of the 'Ode' into thoughtful prose, exploring the 'intimation or assurance within us, that some part of our nature is imperishable': 'Without the consciousness of a principle of Immortality in the human soul, Man could never have had awakened in him the desire to live in the remembrance of his fellows.' As in the Ode, he explores the question through the figure of the child. He had four of his own by now: Johnny, Dora and Tommy had been joined by Catharine, born in September 1808. He walked with them by the streams, through the woods and on the hills above Grasmere, listening to their unceasing prattle and questionings.

Children, he proposes, though they may not have had 'contact with a notion of death', are characterized by an 'early, obstinate, and unappeasable inquisitiveness' upon 'the subject of origina-tion'. They are always asking where things come from. This must mean that they also want to know where things go to. 'Origin and tendency are notions inseparably co-relative.' A child will stand by the side of a running stream and wonder, 'what power was the feeder of the perpetual current, from what never-wearied sources the body of water was supplied'. The correlative question must therefore be 'Towards what abyss is it in progress? what receptacle can contain the mighty influx?'

> And the spirit of the answer must have been, though the word might be Sea or Ocean, accompanied perhaps with an image gathered from a Map, or from the real object in Nature – these might have been the *letter*, but the *spirit* of the answer must have been *as* inevitably, a receptacle without bounds or dimensions, nothing less than infinity.

The reference to 'Sea or Ocean' reveals that, as in the elegiac stanzas on Beaumont's painting, Wordsworth was at some level thinking of John's death and comforting himself with the ancient image of eternity as a sea. The 'infinity' with which he closes the thought is 'the sense of Immortality'. And from that sense, he argues, 'the human affections are gradually formed and opened out'. For the Wordsworth of early 1810, it was 'inconceivable' that our 'sympathies of love towards each other' could survive after one had confronted death if our 'internal Being' did not have this primal intimation of immortality. 'I confess, with me the conviction is absolute that, if the impression and sense of death were not thus counterbalanced, such a hollowness would pervade the whole system of things . . . that there could be no repose, no joy.'[13]

Two years later, his conviction and the concomitant capacity for repose and joy would be tested to the extreme. In the meantime, though, he was feeling the 'sympathies of love' to the full. Another baby, William Jr, was born at Allan Bank in May 1810. Six weeks later, William and Dorothy returned to Coleorton, home of the Beaumonts. After a sojourn there, Sir George and William, both keen landscape gardeners, went off to visit the Leasowes in Shropshire, home of the eighteenth-century poet William Shenstone, renowned for its gardens. They also went to the theatre together in Birmingham before Wordsworth headed west to the Welsh borders, where Mary's brother Tom had taken a farm.

During his six weeks' absence from home, he and Mary wrote each other a series of letters, which after being lost for many years were discovered in a large cache of family papers in 1977, along with a further exchange from the summer of 1812, when William was staying with the Beaumonts in London. The correspondence reveals the depth of the couple's love. William remembers their reunion at Racedown after not having seen each other for many years, revealing that when she departed he was on the brink of taking her in his arms and proposing. He expresses their love sometimes with great simplicity – 'O Mary I love you with a passion of love which grows till I tremble to think of its strength' – and sometimes with a language of intense sensibility, attuned to her body:

Oh my beloved – but I ought not to trust myself to this senseless and visible sheet of paper; speak for me to thyself, find the evidence of what is passing within me in *thy* heart, in thy mind, in thy steps as they touch the green grass, in thy limbs as they are stretched upon the soft earth; in thy own involuntary sighs and ejaculations, in the trembling of thy hands, in the tottering of thy knees, in the blessings which thy lips pronounce, find it in thy lips themselves, and such kisses as I often give to the empty air, and in the aching of thy bosom, and let a voice speak for me in every thing within thee and without thee.'[14]

Mary's responses had equal fervour: 'O My William! it is not in my power to tell thee how I have been affected by this dearest of all letters . . . so new a thing to see the breathing of thy inmost heart upon paper that I was quite overpowered.'[15]

By contrast, that other deep bond of love, with Coleridge, was under great strain.

★

The jealousy would not go away. In the autumn of 1808, Coleridge complained to his notebook that Sara Hutchinson always seemed restless after just five or ten minutes sitting with him. He found her feelings for Wordsworth 'incomprehensible' and agonized over her 'evidently greater pleasure in gazing on' him.[16]

Coleridge, his marriage in a state of collapse, lived with the Wordsworth family at Allan Bank for an extended period. Hartley and Derwent came down from Keswick at weekends during the school holidays. Dorothy found it exhausting to clean his parlour, light his fire, prepare gruel or toast and water for him at irregular hours and make up his bed in the middle of the day as a consequence of his wildly fluctuating sleep patterns. He would lie in dejection on the sofa one day and write manically at his desk the next. He was also getting into the habit of lying, saying he had written the material for the latest *Friend* when he had not. Sara devoted herself to transcribing not only William's long poem but also the copy for the magazine.

Eventually, Coleridge's demands became too much for her. She left to visit her brother Tom on his farm in Radnorshire. In a letter to Catherine Clarkson, Dorothy reported her relief: 'He harassed and agitated her mind continually, and we saw that he was doing her health perpetual injury.' Expressing some remorse for her own candour, Dorothy went on to say that Coleridge's love for Sara was 'no more than a fanciful dream' and furthermore that 'He likes to have her about him as his own, as one devoted to him, but when she stood in the way of other gratifications it was all over.'[17]

With Sara gone, Coleridge left Allan Bank for Greta Hall. That autumn, Basil Montagu arrived in Grasmere. He stayed with the Wordsworths for a month, along with his third wife – a widow who had formerly been his housekeeper. During this time, he also paid visits to the Coleridges in Keswick. Mrs Coleridge was worried about a hare-brained scheme of her husband's to take himself off to live in Edinburgh. Impulsively, Montagu offered to bring him into his home down in London and put him under the care of his own highly regarded doctor. Consciously or not, he was attempting to return the favour that Wordsworth had done him by taking in young Basil back in the 1790s. Wordsworth felt, however, that he had no choice but to warn Montagu of what it had been like to live with Coleridge over the past two years, as his behaviour had become increasingly erratic, largely because of the opium and alcohol. The Kendal Black Drop was consumed, it must be remembered, in a tincture of brandy.

Wordsworth's fears were immediately justified. Montagu wrote to say that, even on the journey south, he had seen enough of Coleridge's habits to be convinced that 'he should be miserable under the same roof with him'. He had accordingly decided to lodge Coleridge in nearby rooms, not in his home. This had not been what Coleridge was expecting. There had been an awkward scene upon their arrival in town. Furthermore, to Wordsworth's mortification, at a dinner party the following evening Montagu had 'repeated to C what William had said to him and C had been very angry'.[18] Coleridge had stormed out and checked into a hotel. He vowed never to speak to Montagu again.

The Wordsworths did not hear from Coleridge for nearly a year. That was not unusual. They were unaware of the resentment that was festering in Coleridge, who in a letter to Daniel Stuart, the newspaperman, broke off from a request for work into an explanation that he could not possibly return to Grasmere, since 'so deep and rankling is the wound which Wordsworth has wantonly and without the slightest provocation inflicted in return for 15 years' most enthusiastic, self-despising and alas! Self-injuring Friendship'.[19] When they did find out about his feelings, via Mrs Coleridge, Wordsworth tried to get her to mediate, but she was reluctant. Coleridge remained resentful for another year.

We only have second-hand accounts of what Wordsworth actually said to Montagu. Coleridge's version was that Montagu had begun by reporting that Wordsworth had 'commissioned' him to say 'first that he has no hope of you' and secondly that Coleridge had been 'an ABSOLUTE NUISANCE in the family', who had 'rotted his entrails out' with drunkenness.[20] Wordsworth later denied much of this, but it is almost certain that he did use the phrase 'no hope of [him]', because Dorothy had said the same of Coleridge in her letter to Catherine Clarkson. Their friends at Greta Hall were divided: Southey, who knew Coleridge's habits, felt that it had been reasonable for Wordsworth to give the warning to Montagu and that it was the latter who was to blame for breaching the confidence, whereas Mrs Southey and her sister Mrs Coleridge blamed Wordsworth. When he tried to 'make excuses', the habitually timid Edith Southey shouted at him, 'it is *you*, Sir! *you* – not the things said, true or false!'²¹ The accusation of disloyalty after fifteen years' friendship struck to the quick.

In early 1812, Coleridge returned to the Lakes. He picked up his children, Hartley and Derwent, from their school in Ambleside, then drove through Grasmere. The Wordsworths had moved from Allan Bank to the old rectory in the village (which they found less draughty, but unbearably damp). Coleridge drove straight past it without stopping. Back at Greta Hall, Hartley 'turned as white as lime' when his mother told him that 'Mr W. had a little vexed his father by something he had said to Mr Montagu.' The children, who had so loved their visits to Grasmere and the opportunity to play with the Wordsworth children, 'could not comprehend how these things were'.²²

There was no contact over the coming weeks. In April, Coleridge returned to London. Wordsworth decided that the only thing to do was to go there in order to patch things up. That was why he was staying with the Beaumonts in Grosvenor Square, writing those loving letters to Mary.

Wordsworth believed that either Coleridge was misrepresenting what Montagu had said or Montagu had misrepresented what he had said. He proposed that the three of them should meet. Coleridge refused to be in the presence of Montagu, but agreed to meet Wordsworth. Charles Lamb did all he could to mediate, but matters were exacerbated when Wordsworth demanded that Coleridge should stop talking to people about the affair. Coleridge responded with a long and deeply hurt letter. Wordsworth declined to read it. He did, however, give a statement to another intermediary, Henry Crabb Robinson, in which he denied that he had ever used, or would ever use, such phrases as 'rotten drunkard' and 'rotted his entrails out'. He granted, though, that he might have used the word 'nuisance' in reference to 'certain habits', but that 'he never employed it as the result or summary of his feelings towards Coleridge'.[23] Coleridge responded with his version of what Montagu had said. Wordsworth in turn replied with 'a most solemn denial' that he had 'commissioned' Montagu to say such things.[24]

This was enough to make Coleridge relent with a letter that began 'My dear Wordsworth / I declare before God Almighty that at no time even of my sorest affliction did even the *possibility* occur to me of ever doubting your word.'[25] Wordsworth was able to report to Mary that 'The business between C – and me is settled by a Letter.'[26] Coleridge, meanwhile, was distracted by his newspaper duties: on the very evening that he had posted his letter of reconciliation to Wordsworth, the prime minister, Spencer Perceval, was assassinated by gunshot in the lobby of the House of Commons. The shocking news was a helpful distraction for them all. In the weeks that followed, Wordsworth went along to some of Coleridge's public lectures on literature and expressed gratification that he was being well looked after by his kindly friend John Morgan. Mostly, they saw each other only in the company of others, but once they went for a walk together on Hampstead Heath. They both knew in their hearts that, despite the patching up, there was no way back to the intense friendship that had existed for so long.

Mary, meanwhile, had gone to visit her sister Joanna and brother Tom at the farm in Radnorshire. From there, they took a tour down the Wye Valley: she was at last able to visit a place that had meant so much to her husband. 'With a beating heart did I greet the Wye – O Sylvan Wye thou Wanderer thro the

Woods!' she wrote to him from Hereford on Sunday 31 May, quoting 'Tintern Abbey'.[27] Two days later, she was revelling in the sight of the abbey ruin. By the end of the week she was back at the Hutchinson farm. She did not know that at home in Grasmere, 180 miles to the north, Catharine Wordsworth, not yet four years old, had been struck with a 'seizure'.

★

Thomas De Quincey, only five feet tall and with a childlike aspect, was obsessed with the poetry of Wordsworth. Shortly before going up to study at Worcester College, Oxford, he wrote a fan letter in which he said that the pleasure he had been afforded by *Lyrical Ballads* far outweighed that offered by the accumulated works of every other poet he had ever read. Wordsworth's name would be 'for ever linked to the lovely scenes of nature'. His poetry was the only thing that could rouse De Quincey from 'the lethargy of despair'; it was his 'only refuge' from 'many many bitter recollections'. Though he did not reveal as much at the time, the most bitter of those recollections was the death of his beloved nine-year-old sister Elizabeth in the summer of 1792, just before his seventh birthday. The day after she died, and before the body had been taken away, he stole into her bedroom at noon. It was a cloudless day, the bright blue sky making him think of infinity and of life. He turned to the angelic corpse and seemed to feel a wind blowing, uncannily, 'the one sole *audible* symbol of eternity'.[28] The memory never left him.

Wordsworth answered De Quincey's fan letter with a kindly, but stiff and paternalistic response, in which he offered a luke-warm invitation to Grasmere. De Quincey wrote again, explaining that his first encounter with the poetry had been 'We are Seven', the ballad about the child who does not give in to death. It was being handed around in manuscript when he was on holiday in

Bath. From there, he went on to devour the whole of *Lyrical Ballads*. His only consolations in life, he claimed, were 'Love of Nature' and Wordsworth's poetry, which was his guide and tutor in 'new feelings'.[29] In two successive summers, De Quincey went to the Lake District with the intention of knocking on the door in Grasmere, but each time he was too nervous to go through with his plan. However, in the summer of 1807 he managed to obtain an introduction to Coleridge, when the latter was temporarily back in the West Country. They shared a voracious and eclectic love of books, a gift for serpentine sentences, and an addiction to opium. Coleridge was short of money, as usual, and De Quincey, who had just come into an inheritance, made him a 'loan' of £300. A few weeks later, De Quincey accompanied Sara Coleridge and the children on their journey home to Greta Hall. They stopped off at the cottage in Town End, and De Quincey at last had the opportunity to meet his hero, who held out his hand and greeted him warmly. De Quincey never forgot his first entrance into the cottage and the sight of Mary – 'a tall young woman, with the most winning expression of benignity upon her features that I had ever beheld' – and Dorothy, shorter, slighter, dark-skinned and with 'some subtle fire of impassioned intellect' burning within her, yet checked by 'an air of embarrassment and even of self-conflict'.[30]

Back at Worcester College after his short visit to the Lakes, De Quincey prepared for his final examinations, choosing a concentration in Greek tragedy. On the first day, he wrote a stellar set of answers, but then he lost his nerve and left Oxford for London, never to complete his degree. He made himself useful to Wordsworth by seeing the *Convention of Cintra* pamphlet through the press and then, in the autumn of 1809, following the Wordsworths' move to Allan Bank, he filled the vacancy in the cottage at Town End. It was a dream fulfilled to be living in the house where Wordsworth had written so much of his greatest poetry, sleeping in the bed where his hero had once slept. He became a great favourite among the Wordsworth children. Little Catharine, not quite four years old, was the one he loved best, almost as if his long-lost sister had come back to life. But he was overspending his income. In June 1812, he left the cottage for London with the intention of reading for the bar at Middle Temple.

★

Catharine had never been a well child. There was 'something peculiar' in the cast of her face, a curiously comic look about her, the 'funniest laugh' peeping through her eyes even when she was a baby.[31] At eighteen months, she suffered convulsions and lost the use of her right side. When she recovered, she retained a limp and her parents would massage her along the spine and down the weak side for hours at a time, to help her to walk and to regain feeling in her arm. They took her to the seaside for a cure, but she was always subject to bouts of vomiting, to whooping cough, ear infections, fevers. It has been suggested, ironically in the light of 'The Idiot Boy', but not entirely persuasively, that she may have been a Down's child.[32]

She died on 4 June 1812, aged three and three-quarters. The cause seems to have been hydrocephalus or possibly meningitis: 'The disease lay in the Brain, and if it had been possible for her to recover, it is much to be feared that she would not have retained the Faculties of her Mind.'[33]

Dorothy had to write the most difficult letters of her life. First to William, who, after settling matters with Coleridge, had gone to Essex to stay with his clergyman brother Christopher. She advised him to go straight to Wales and give the news to his wife in person. Then she wrote to De Quincey:

I am grieved to the heart when I write to you – but you must bear the sad tidings – Our sweet little Catharine was seized with convulsions on Wednesday night . . . The fits continued till ¼ after 5 in the morning, when she breathed her last. She had been in perfect health, and looked unusually well – her leg and arm had gained strength – and we were full of hope. In short, we had sent the most delightful accounts to her poor Mother. It is a great addition to our affliction that her Father and Mother were not here to witness her last struggles, and to see her in the last happy weeks of her short life. She never forgot Quincey – dear Innocent, she now lies upon her Mother's bed, a perfect image of peace.[34]

Dorothy was not to know the particular agony that last image would have caused to the man who was so haunted by the trauma of his own sister's death in childhood. Wordsworth passed through London on his way to Wales. He met with De Quincey and Henry Crabb Robinson, who thought that Wordsworth was bearing himself with gentlemanly stoicism, whereas 'Mr De Quincey burst into tears on seeing Wordsworth, and seemed to be more affected than the father.'[35]

De Quincey's reply to Dorothy reveals the extremity of his feelings for his hero's little girl:

Nobody can judge from her manner to me before others what love she shewed to me when we were playing or talking together alone. On the night when she slept with me in the winter, we lay awake all the middle of the night – and talked oh how tenderly together: When we fell asleep, she was lying in my arms . . . Many times on that night – when she was murmuring out tender sounds of endearment, she would lock her arms with such passionateness round my neck – as if she had known that it was to be the last night we were ever to pass together.[36]

Wordsworth ended the 'Intimations of Immortality' ode with the thought that the 'meanest flower that blows' – the brevity of a flower's life being an ancient poetic symbol of mortality – could bring him 'Thoughts that do often lie too deep for tears'. After Catharine's death, he closed in on himself, his emotions too deep for tears. De Quincey was the one who released a spontaneous overflow of powerful feelings. On his return to Grasmere, he spent many nights lying on the little girl's grave in the village churchyard, trying, perhaps, to make himself believe, like the child in 'We are Seven', that there is no division between the living and the dead.

★

Eight-year-old Dora behaved badly that summer, struggling to cope with her sister's absence and the fraught atmosphere in the house. Johnny, nine, was a worry: slow at school, seeming to be in a world of his own. Willy, just learning to talk, was too young to understand. Tommy was everyone's comfort. He had the sweetest temper; the other children quarrelled with each other, but never with him. His sixth birthday came a few days after his sister's death. He was beginning to show a love of books and learning. His father loved him with what Dorothy called 'a peculiar tenderness'.[37] Wordsworth was hoping that this might be the son who would follow in his poetic footsteps. He would describe his boy as 'of heavenly disposition, meek, simple, innocent, unoffending, affectionate, tender-hearted, passionately fond of knowledge, ardent in the discharge of his duty, but in everything else mild and peaceful'.[38]

Dorothy was away from home when there was an outbreak

of measles in Grasmere. On 1 December 1812, just six months after Catharine's death, it was William's turn to write to De Quincey with heartbreaking news:

My very dear Friend,

We have had measles in the house, and I write under great affliction. Thomas was seized a few days ago, i.e. last Thursday. He was held most favourably till eleven this morning, when a change suddenly took place; and, with sorrow of heart I write, he died, sweet innocent, about six this afternoon. His sufferings were short, and I think not severe. Pray come to us as soon as you can.[39]

The following evening, Wordsworth wrote to Southey: 'For myself dear Southey I dare not say in what state of mind I am; I loved the Boy with the utmost love of which my soul is capable, and he is taken from me.' Having reflected for a day, it struck him that, though it was a relief that six-year-old Tommy 'did not appear to suffer much in body', he had recently grown into consciousness of death – in sharp contrast to the little girl in 'We are Seven' and indeed the image of Hartley Coleridge at six. 'I fear', Wordsworth added, that he did suffer 'something in mind as he was of an age to have thought much upon death a subject to which his mind was daily led by the grave of his Sister.'[40]

When Dorothy returned, she said that her brother had instantly aged by ten years. Over the following weeks, he and Mary lost weight, almost lost the will to live. Their other boys caught the measles, but survived. Just after Christmas, he wrote to Basil Montagu with this reassuring news. He was mindful of the fact that Tommy had died at the very age of Basil Jr during the time when he and Dorothy had cared for him in Somerset and watched the lively ways of childhood. The quarrel with Coleridge, and

Montagu's role in provoking it, seemed trivial now. Indeed, one compensation in these dark days was the warmest of condolence letters from Coleridge: 'Oh dearest friend! What comfort can I afford you? What comfort ought I not to afford, who have given you so much pain? . . . Again and again my dearest Wordsworth!!! I am affectionately and truly yours S. T. Coleridge.'[41]

They needed a fresh start. In the New Year, Dorothy wrote to her friends with the news that they were determined to quit Grasmere and had every reason to expect that they would get a house called Rydal Mount. She explained that it was 'most delightfully situated – the very place which in happier days we longed for'. The only objection was that from the garden they would be able to see the Grasmere hills, with all the associated memories. But they wanted to be within walking distance of Grasmere, in order 'to keep up that bond betwixt the living and the dead by going weekly to the parish Church, beside which their bodies are laid'. Dorothy did not think there would be 'anything unkindly in the sadness produced by the sight of those dear hills, except in Mary's mind'. She hoped that her sister-in-law's 'chearfulness may return when those familiar objects connected with the daily goings-on of the children are no longer before her eyes – objects which are to all of us perpetual sources of melancholy and of frequent anguish'. 'Thomas', she hardly needed to add, 'was the darling of the house and of everyone who looked at him'.[42]

Dorothy was the last person to leave the old rectory that had been their temporary home. She had been to the graves of Catharine and Thomas in the churchyard. There she comforted herself with thoughts of immortality. But the house reminded her only of 'desolation, gloom, emptiness, and chearless silence'.[43]

★

When a loved one dies, especially a child, you believe that you will never be happy again. But time is the healer of all things. One day, there will be a moment of lightness. You turn to share the joy, and then are brought up short because the person you want to share it with is no longer beside you. Then you feel guilty because to have been happy again seems like a betrayal of their memory. How is it possible to go on living and yet preserve their memory and your grief, your love? Wordsworth knew the answer: he had reached it in the essay suggesting that the epitaph was among the earliest forms of human utterance. The remembrance of the dead: that was one of the primary functions of poetry, perhaps its very origin. As he had remembered his dead parents and lost childhood in the elegiac blank verse of the opening books of his poem on his own life, and as he had remembered his brother John in the 'Elegiac Stanzas' on Sir George Beaumont's painting of the ship in the storm, so now he wrote the most elegiac of all his sonnets. Ostensibly a remembrance of Catharine, it is an epitaph for both his dead children:

> Surprized by joy – impatient as the Wind
> I wished to share the transport – Oh! with whom
> But thee, long buried in the silent Tomb,
> That spot which no vicissitude can find?
> Love, faithful love recalled thee to my mind –
> But how could I forget thee? – Through what
>   power,
> Even for the least division of an hour,
> Have I been so beguiled as to be blind
> To my most grievous loss? – That thought's return
> Was the worst pang that sorrow ever bore,
> Save one, one only, when I stood forlorn,

Knowing my heart's best treasure was no more;
That neither present time, nor years unborn
Could to my sight that heavenly face restore.[44]

The extreme emotion of parental bereavement was 'recollected in tranquillity' months after the double loss. Wordsworth never again wrote a poem filled with such powerful feelings.

18

THIS WILL NEVER DO

Slowly, Wordsworth got over his bereavement by immersing himself in what Dorothy repeatedly called his 'great poem'. 'Part first Book first' had not got far beyond 'Home at Grasmere', but Part Second, developed from 'The Ruined Cottage' and 'The Pedlar', was nearly ready for publication. Its mood became solemn. The 'argument' of the later sections, put into the mouth of a village pastor, moved from 'Graves of unbaptized Infants' and 'Funeral and sepulchral observances' to 'a female Infant's grave' by way of 'Profession of belief in the doctrine of Immortality'. It was published – 500 copies only – in August 1814 under the title *The Excursion, being a Portion of The Recluse, A Poem.*

It begins with the story of Margaret and her ruined cottage. The Pedlar is now renamed the Wanderer. In the second book, together with 'the Author', he travels through the valleys and deep into the hills until they reach his friend 'the Solitary', who in the third book tells his story, which runs from 'dejection' to his being 'roused by the French Revolution' to 'disappointment and disgust' at its turn to violence and imperialism. The book concludes with the Solitary's 'languor and depression of mind, from want of faith in the great truths of Religion, and want of confidence in the virtue of Mankind'. In the fourth book, 'Despondency Corrected', the Wanderer tries to cheer up the Solitary by arguing that 'Rural Solitude' leavened by 'bodily exertion and communion with Nature' can restore the mind to health. He suggests, in Rousseauistic fashion, that 'Apathy and destitution' were 'unknown in the infancy of society' thanks to early humankind's close kinship with nature.

The Wanderer and the Author then move on to meet the Pastor, who spends the next four books sermonizing to them upon the ways of Christian orthodoxy. The final book ('Discourse of the Wanderer, and an Evening Visit to the Lake') is an attempt to reconcile the Christianity of the Pastor, reflecting the later Wordsworth, with the pantheism of the Wanderer, a vestige of the earlier Wordsworth. Its opening lines, drafted back in the late 1790s, are strongly reminiscent of 'Tintern Abbey':

'To every Form of Being is assigned,'
Thus calmly spake the venerable Sage,
'An *active* principle: – howe'er removed
From sense and observation, it subsists
In all things, in all natures, in the stars
Of azure heaven, the unenduring clouds,
In flower and tree, in every pebbly stone
That paves the brooks, the stationary rocks,
The moving waters, and the invisible air.[1]

The sequences of greatest poetic intensity are without question those written in the earlier years: the heart-rending story of Margaret in book one, a vision of a heavenly city among the clouds in book two, which reads like an overflow from the Simplon Pass and Snowdon passages of *The Prelude*, and a sequence in which the Wanderer finds a sense of the infinite among the mountains:

> A Herdsman on the lonely mountain tops,
> Such intercourse was his, and in this sort
> Was his existence oftentimes *possessed* . . .
> But in the mountains did he *feel* his faith;
> There did he see the writing; – all things there
> Breathed immortality, revolving life
> And greatness still revolving; infinite;
> There littleness was not; the least of things
> Seemed infinite; and there his spirit shaped
> Her prospects, nor did he believe, – he *saw*.[2]

There is an awkward disjunction between passages such as this and the lengthy discourses of the Pastor in the second half of the poem. It is also noticeable that there is little differentiation between the language of the Pedlar, the Solitary and the Pastor, despite their very different social status. For most readers today, *The Excursion* is likely to induce the response of a character in *The Romany Rye*, the autobiographical novel by George Borrow, the Victorian observer of Romany life:

> It was written in blank verse, and appeared to abound in descriptions of scenery; there was much mention of mountains, valleys, streams, and waterfalls, harebells and daffodils. These descriptions were interspersed with dialogues, which, though

they proceeded from the mouths of pedlars and rustics, were
of the most edifying description; mostly on subjects moral or
metaphysical, and couched in the most gentlemanly and unex-
ceptionable language, without the slightest mixture of
vulgarity, coarseness, or pie-bald grammar. Such appeared to
me to be the contents of the book; but before I could form
a very clear idea of them, I found myself nodding, and a
surprising desire to sleep coming over me.[3]

★

Wordsworth explained the relationship of *The Excursion* to the
larger never-finished *Recluse* in a preface: 'it belongs to the second
part of a long and laborious Work, which is to consist of three
parts'. Had he finished the first part, he would have 'preferred
the natural order of publication, and have given that to the world
first', but 'as the second division of the Work was designed to
refer more to passing events, and to an existing state of things,
than the others were meant to do, more continuous exertion
was naturally bestowed upon it, and greater progress made here
than in the rest of the poem'. Since this middle part did not
'depend upon the preceding to a degree which will materially
injure its own peculiar interest', it was now being published.
Wordsworth went on to explain that in order to prepare himself
for the undertaking of *The Recluse*, his intended 'literary Work
that might live', he had felt it necessary to undertake a 'review
of his own mind, and examine how far Nature and Education
had qualified him for such employment'. This had led to the
'subsidiary' record of 'the origin and progress of his own powers,
as far as he was acquainted with them'.

'That Work', Wordsworth continued his 1814 preface,
announcing in print for the first time the existence of his autobiographical poem and its intimate relationship with Coleridge,

was 'addressed to a dear Friend, most distinguished for his know-ledge and genius, and to whom the Author's Intellect is deeply indebted'. It 'has been long finished', he added, 'and the result of the investigation which gave rise to it was a determination to compose a philosophical poem, containing views of Man, Nature, and Society; and to be entitled, *The Recluse*; as having for its principal subject the sensations and opinions of a poet living in retirement'. He went on to explain that the 'preparatory' poem was 'biographical', conducting 'the history of the Author's mind to the point when he was emboldened to hope that his faculties were sufficiently matured for entering upon the arduous labour which he had proposed to himself'. It was a kind of 'ante-chapel . . . to the body of a Gothic church'. By the same account, the shorter poems, those 'minor Pieces, which have been long before the Public, when they shall be properly arranged, will be found by the attentive Reader to have such connection with the main Work as may give them claim to be likened to the little cells, oratories, and sepulchral recesses, ordinarily included in those edifices'.[4]

As a 'prospectus' for the unfinished *Recluse*, he then added to his preface a passage of verse intended for the end of its first part. Written in the elevated style of an invocation to the Muse, it makes high claims for a personalization of the epic tradition. Wordsworth writes that he will pass over the territory of Milton's *Paradise Lost* 'unalarmed' and reach instead 'Into our Minds, into the Mind of Man'. Why should paradise, he asks, be 'A history only of departed things / Or a mere fiction of what never was?' If the 'individual Mind' and the 'external World' are 'exquisitely' fitted to each other in 'love and holy passion', then paradise may be found to be 'A simple produce of the common day'. This, says Wordsworth, is his 'high argument'.[5]

William Blake was a very different sort of visionary, for whom

the poetic imagination existed in stark opposition to the physical – he called it the 'vegetable' – world. He had no time for
this argument: he told Crabb Robinson that reading the preface
to *The Excursion* gave him a bowel complaint that nearly killed
him and he scrawled in the margin of his copy of the poem,
'You shall not bring me down to believe such fitting & fitted
I know better & Please your Lordship.' For Blake, who was
deeply influenced by Gnosticism, the very idea of a separation
between mind and world was a sign of the Fall from the
original unity of the human and the divine. Nature was the
work of the Devil and he accordingly considered Wordsworth's
worship of nature to be a form of atheism. 'Natural Objects
always did & now do obliterate Imagination in me', he wrote
in another annotation, 'I see in Wordsworth the Natural Man
rising up against the Spiritual Man Continually & then he is
No Poet but a Heathen Philosopher at Enmity against all true
Poetry or Inspiration.'[6] Wordsworth in turn said of Blake,
according to their mutual friend Crabb Robinson: 'There is
no doubt that this man is mad, but there is something in this
madness which I enjoy more than the Sense of W: Sc[ott] or
Lord B[yron].'[7] Charles Lamb took the view that Blake was
actually a 'mad Wordsworth'.[8]

★

At the time of publication of *The Excursion*, Wordsworth was on
his second tour of Scotland with Mary and Sara Hutchinson.
Mountain sightseeing was mingled with literary encounters.
Wordsworth enjoyed the company of James Hogg, the 'Ettrick
Shepherd'. He also went to Abbotsford, the home of Sir Walter
Scott, but found him absent, though he was welcomed by Scott's
wife and daughter.

His friendship with Scotland's most celebrated writer had

begun on his first visit north of the border back in 1803, and been cemented two years later when Scott visited Grasmere and the two poets climbed Helvellyn together. Scott was a phenomenal commercial success: his narrative poem *Marmion* had raced through eight editions, its follow-up *The Lady of the Lake* had turned the Trossachs into a tourist destination almost overnight, and a few weeks before the appearance of *The Excursion* he had made his fiction debut with *Waverley*, one of the foundations of the historical novel. Although published anonymously, many people knew that it was by Scott. The reviews were immediate and highly complimentary. Two reprints followed in a matter of months. For Wordsworth, whose poetry had never sold in high numbers, there was inevitably a degree of jealousy, albeit mixed with a sense that Sir Walter was a little too much the follower of fashion in the interests of sales. Whatever its reception might be, *The Excursion* was at least true to Wordsworth's high vision of the poet's calling. A shrewd observer of the literary scene, comparing the two authors, said that Scott's developing character could be 'traced to the effect of Success operating on a genial temperament, while Wordsworth's takes its rise from the effect of unjust ridicule wounding a deep self-estimation'.[9]

Nothing would wound him more than the response of Francis Jeffrey to *The Excursion*, in a lengthy review which appeared that autumn in the *Edinburgh*. Continuing the attack that he had begun in his reviews of Southey's *Thalaba* and Wordsworth's 1807 poems, Jeffrey began with one of the most devastating opening sentences of any review ever written: 'This will never do.'

It was no more encouraging to read on to the end of the first paragraph. The poem was 'longer, weaker, and tamer, than any of Mr Wordsworth's other productions; with less boldness of originality, and less even of that extreme simplicity and lowliness of tone which wavered so prettily, in the Lyrical Ballads, between silliness and pathos'. There were 'imitations of Cowper, and even of Milton', engrafted upon 'the natural drawl of the Lakers – and all diluted into harmony by that profuse and irrepressible wordiness which deluges all the blank verse of this school of poetry, and lubricates and weakens the whole structure of their style'.[10]

Occasional moments of praise punctuated the review, but most of it was a tirade against the poem's 'truisms more cloudy, wordy, and inconceivable prolix, than any thing we ever met with'. As before, Jeffrey took against the idea of putting high thoughts into a low-born mouthpiece: 'Why should Mr Wordsworth have made his hero a superannuated Pedlar?' And – ironically, in the light of Wordsworth's drift towards Anglican orthodoxy – he associated the language of the poem with the dissenting tradition that was regarded by many in the middle and upper classes as a threat to the established order of things: 'a tissue of moral and devotional ravings . . . the mystical verbiage of the methodist pulpit is repeated, till the speaker entertains no doubt that he is the elected organ of divine truth and persuasion'. 'The case of Wordsworth', Jeffrey concluded, was 'now manifestly hopeless'. His poetry was 'incurable', 'beyond the power of criticism'. The phrasing was especially painful to Wordsworth because it applied to his poetry the word that he had applied to Coleridge as a person: a 'hopeless' case.[11]

Jeffrey surpassed himself a year later when Wordsworth published his long-delayed narrative poem, *The White Doe of Rylstone*. This time he began: 'This, we think, has the merit of being the very worst poem we ever saw imprinted in a quarto volume.'[12]

★

Fortunately for Wordsworth, other voices were emerging on the London literary scene. Paradoxically, at the very time when he was moving most markedly to the political right, the reputation of his poetry was saved by a group of writers from the political left.

In 1808, two London-based journalist brothers, John and Leigh Hunt, launched a new weekly magazine. They called it *The Examiner*, taking the title from a periodical produced by Jonathan Swift and his fellow Tories a century before, though coming from the opposite end of the political spectrum. Their aim was 'to assist in producing Reform in Parliament, liberality of opinion in general (especially freedom from superstition), and a fusion of literary taste into all subjects whatsoever'. 'Freedom from super-stition' was code for religious scepticism. Hunt would make himself unpopular with conservatives by peopling his poems with pagan gods and even writing a mini-epic called *The Story of Rimini* that glorified the adulterous couple Paolo and Francesca whom Dante had placed in the second circle of hell.

Within months of its first issue *The Examiner* was prosecuted for publication of an article entitled 'Military Depravity', which attacked the corrupt, bribery-ridden system of promotions in the army. To say anything negative about the armed forces at the height of the Peninsular War was considered dangerously seditious. The case was dropped, but another one ensued a couple of years later when the magazine reprinted an article that had been published in a provincial paper under the title 'One Thousand Lashes!!' It condemned the practice of flogging soldiers for minor disciplinary infractions. This time, they were found not guilty of seditious libel, thanks to a powerful case for the defence mounted by the lawyer Henry Brougham. But in 1813 the Attorney General was able to press a case successfully. Provoked by an article in the *Morning Post* that praised the newly anointed Prince Regent as an 'Adonis in loveliness', *The Examiner* noted that George was actually 'a corpulent gentleman of fifty' who, moreover, was 'a violator of his word, a libertine over head and ears in debt and disgrace, a despiser of domestic ties, the companion of gamblers and demireps, a man who has just closed half a century without one single claim on the gratitude of his country or the respect of posterity!'[13] This cost the Hunt brothers their two years' sentence in separate prisons. Leigh Hunt decked out his cell with flowers and continued to edit the paper from behind bars.

From 1810 to 1811, Leigh Hunt edited not only the weekly *Examiner*, but also a quarterly literary and political magazine called *The Reflector*. He used it as a vehicle for the publication of his own poems, including a satire on the contemporary poetical scene called *The Feast of the Poets*, in which he mocked Coleridge for 'his idling, and gabbling, and muddling in prose'. The next couplet read: 'And as to that Wordsworth! He'd been so benurst, / Second childhood with him had come close on the first'. Apollo, god of poetry, says to the Lakers 'Depart and be modest, ye driv'llers of the pen'.[14]

Hunt was basing his opinion of Wordsworth solely on the drubbing that the 1807 volume had received from the reviewers and in *The Simpliciad*. When he actually read the poems, while he was in prison, he came to the conclusion that Wordsworth had all the elements 'not only of a good, but of a great poet'.[15] Accordingly, when he revised *The Feast of the Poets* for publication in book form, he changed tack. Now, Apollo acknowledges that instead of 'becoming a joke to half-thinkers and wits', Wordsworth should have been 'the first man' at his table.[16]

In order to flesh out his poem to book length, Hunt added a series of explanatory notes. His gloss on the sequence in the poem when Robert Southey is introduced at Apollo's feast may have been the first appearance in print of the phrase 'the Lake Poets'. Leigh Hunt uses the note to attack Southey, Wordsworth and Coleridge as political turncoats: in their youth, they had 'public as well as private integrity', by which Hunt meant that their actions as well as their poems were true to their liberal politics. 'Mr Southey, and even Mr Wordsworth,' he writes, 'have both accepted offices under government, of such a nature, as absolutely ties up their independence'. Mr Coleridge, meanwhile, 'in pamphlets and newspaper, has done his best to deserve likewise'. They will all tell you, says Hunt, that 'they have not diminished their free spirit a jot'. And yet they are now 'violent and intolerant against their old opinions'.[17] For Hunt, independence from government influence was the key to the role of the writer as conscience of the nation. The Lake Poets had abnegated that role, which they had taken on so enthusiastically back in the 1790s. 'Like most Revolutionists', Hunt would add when reviewing Keats's poems, 'the Lake Poets' went to 'an extreme', then turned volte-face.[18]

Hunt was some months into his prison sentence when, following the death of the Poet Laureate, Henry James Pye, one of the worst versifiers ever to hold the office, a successor was appointed in the form of Robert Southey, who back in the early 1790s had written an inflammatory play called *Wat Tyler* that welcomed the French Revolution. The Prince Regent had originally wanted Scott to accept the post but the canny Sir Walter recognized that it would prove a poisoned chalice and nominated instead his friend Southey, who needed the money. As for Wordsworth, in this same year of 1813 he was appointed Distributor of Stamps for the County of Westmorland.

His job was to oversee the sending out of stamps to post offices in the region and the imposition of impressed duty stamps, a tax on legal transactions such as insurance policies and the preparation of documents for use in court. Hence the conception of 'stamp duty' when buying a house. The position gained him financial security in the form of a salary of £400 a year for not very much work, but the opprobrium of Leigh Hunt for his acceptance of an office of the Establishment, a job dished out, moreover, by his patron, the Tory landowning coal magnate Lord Lonsdale. Southey as Laureate and Wordsworth as purveyor of the royal head on the stamps were now in the service of that 'corpulent gentleman of fifty' the Prince Regent. Coleridge, meanwhile, was writing for the right-wing press.

To Leigh Hunt's credit, he did not allow his disappointment at this collective political apostasy to cloud his judgment of the poetry. The note on Wordsworth in *The Feast of the Poets* deplores the fact that the man has become 'government property' – perhaps, Hunt speculates, it is the fate of all revolutions to go from one extreme to the other – but this does not diminish the profundity of the best of his writing. Hunt makes the high claim that no writer since the days of Spenser and Milton has seen further into 'the sacred places of poetry'. Indeed, 'Mr Wordsworth is capable of being at the head of a new and great age of poetry; and in point of fact I do not deny that he is so already, as the greatest poet of the present.'[19] Wordsworth's patron Sir George Beaumont took considerable satisfaction in this encomium. Lord Byron, who always had mixed views about the Lake Poets ('Wordsworth – stupendous genius! Damned fool!'[20]), told Hunt that he thought the notes were of a very high order, especially the one on Wordsworth. Hunt suggested, late in life, that Byron had accused him of making Wordsworth popular in town.[21]

Byron's own view was that Sir Walter Scott was the 'Monarch of Parnassus', the king of contemporary poets. He graded his contemporaries by drawing a pyramid in his journal:

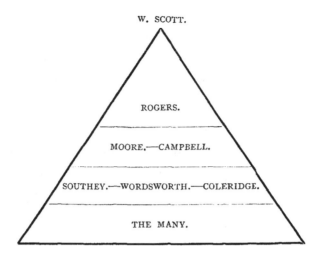

Leigh Hunt changed the ranking. When he revised *The Feast of the Poets* for a second edition the following year, he added a passage in which the other poets admitted to Apollo's table – Scott, Thomas Campbell, Robert Southey, Thomas Moore and Lord Byron himself – raise a toast to Wordsworth:

> And all cried at last, with a passion sublime,
> 'This, this is the Prince of the Bards of his Time!'

Apollo then twitches Coleridge by the ear and says, 'There, you lazy dog, sit you down too.'[22]

★

In the spring of 1814, not long after the publication of *The Feast of the Poets*, the Hunts hired William Hazlitt as a columnist. His subject matter would range from painting to philosophy to politics to poetry to prizefighting. His prose was always filled with what he called 'gusto' – 'power or passion defining any object'. Gusto gives 'the truth of character from the truth of feeling'.[23]

Hazlitt's writing always began from the feeling evoked, the gut instinct for liberty and fairness, the emotional response in the viewer of a painting or a landscape, the reader of a poem or a novel, the spectator of a Shakespeare play (or a parliamentary debate or a boxing match or an Indian juggling act). This emphasis on *power* and on *feeling* was in some considerable measure derived from Wordsworth's famous remark in the Preface to *Lyrical Ballads* about poetry being the spontaneous overflow of *powerful feeling*.

It was Hazlitt whom Leigh Hunt commissioned to write the *Examiner* review of Wordsworth's *Excursion*, which was so long that it appeared in three instalments. The choice of reviewer created a challenge because there was a complicated backstory to the relationship between the critic and the poet.

Hazlitt always looked back with joy on that visit to Coleridge in Nether Stowey in 1798 when he first met Wordsworth, which he immortalized twenty-five years later in his essay 'My First Acquaintance with Poets'. But then there had been a disastrous encounter in the Lakes in 1803. Wordsworth and Coleridge had both agreed to sit for portraits by him. Though an amateur (his brother John was a professional), Hazlitt was a stylish portraitist. The following year he executed a painting of Charles Lamb, in a black doublet modelled on that in Velazquez' rendition of Philip IV of Spain, that has the air of a latter-day Titian – Hazlitt's favourite artist. The crabby diarist Henry Crabb Robinson said, however, that it was not a good likeness of Lamb. Soon after painting it, Hazlitt put away his brushes and became instead the most accomplished pen–portraitist of the age.

During the sittings in Grasmere, Wordsworth read from recent work, but he and Hazlitt disagreed over politics. They disagreed over Sir Isaac Newton, over Shakespeare, over Milton. When they went boating together on the lake, Wordsworth was offended by Hazlitt's suggestion that the local inscriptions in the 'Poems on the Naming of Places' that immortalized favourite spots around the lake might have owed a debt to *Paul and Virginia*, a Rousseauistic French novel that had been translated by Helen Maria Williams, that poet whom Wordsworth so admired in his early years. Hazlitt may even have made the mistake of proposing to Dorothy: 'Miss Wordsworth had several offers; amongst them, to my knowledge, one from Hazlitt; all of them she rejected decisively.' Such was the testimony of Thomas De Quincey, albeit not the most reliable witness.[24]

It was then that William, Dorothy and Coleridge departed for their first Scottish tour. Hazlitt went back to Manchester with his two paintings. He returned in October to finish his portraits of the two poets. This time he stayed with Coleridge at Greta Hall. Wordsworth arrived for dinner and they all debated the existence of God. Coleridge was frenzied by Hazlitt's atheism. Then came the incident. The exact circumstances are hard to reconstruct, since there was no disinterested telling of the tale, but events seem to have been as follows.

Hazlitt escaped the bad atmosphere at Greta by going to a local tavern. A girl flirted with him. He misread flirtation as desire for sex and made an advance. She called him a black-faced rascal and everyone started laughing at him and making snide remarks. He made the fatal error of taking the girl on his knee, lifting her petticoats and spanking her on the bottom. We would now say: he committed a sexual assault. The locals threatened to beat him up. He scurried back to Greta Hall with an angry mob in pursuit, threatening to give him a ducking (Coleridge later numbered them at 200, on horseback, but that must be an exaggeration). Coleridge smuggled Hazlitt out of the back door and he escaped to Grasmere, wearing a pair of Coleridge's shoes. Wordsworth kindly sheltered him for the rest of the night, gave him clothes and money. He left for Ambleside at dawn, never to return to the Lakes.

He seems to have destroyed the portrait of Wordsworth, which, like that of Lamb, was painted in the style of Titian. Southey saw it and said that it made Wordsworth look like a man 'At the gallows – deeply affected by his deserved fate – yet determined to die like a man.' Little Hartley Coleridge, by contrast, thought that it was a good likeness, though 'Wordsworth is far handsomer'.[25]

Hazlitt also did a sketch of Hartley, which Wordsworth admired 'as representative of a Child whom we wish to remember'. He wrote to Hazlitt about this picture the following spring, signing the letter 'very affectionately yours' and saying how much he would have liked to show Hazlitt the 'mountain brook scenery' above Rydal, near a spot on Nab Scar that Hazlitt had sketched.[26] This would suggest that, initially at least, Wordsworth had no intention of disowning Hazlitt as a result of the incident with the young woman. Yet on a visit to London four years later, when Wordsworth called on Charles Lamb in order to read out his latest poem, *The White Doe of Rylstone*, he told Coleridge that upon discovering that Hazlitt and his wife were present he refused to share his work. Hazlitt always believed that Napoleon was the sword-arm, not the extinguisher, of the principles of the revolution. His was a minority view that Wordsworth and Coleridge strongly opposed. Perhaps his presence reminded Wordsworth of the political differences that had been exposed during the portrait sittings.

Hazlitt was as fierce a believer as Hunt in liberty and independence. He was as disappointed as his editor at the turn to the right in the politics of the Lake Poets. What, then, would he make of *The Excursion*? The first impression was hardly favourable: turning over the title page, he would have been confronted

by a nauseatingly sycophantic dedicatory sonnet addressed to Lord
Lonsdale. But, like Hunt, Hazlitt did not allow his politics to
distort his literary-critical opinion. The review began: 'In power
of intellect, in lofty conception, in the depth of feeling, at once
simple and sublime, which pervades every part of it and which
gives to every object an almost preternatural and preterhuman
interest, this work has seldom been surpassed.' If it had felt fully
finished and properly selected, Hazlitt asserts, it would have been
a national monument. As it was, the poem had some of the nakedness and confusion of the Lakeland landscape − 'the rude chaos
of aboriginal nature'.[27] The poet's mind was 'coeval with the
primary forms of things, holds immediately from nature': his focal
points were 'a stone, covered with lichens, which has slept in the
same spot of ground from the creation of the world', or a thunder-
cracked fissure between two mountains, or a 'cavern scooped out
by the sea'. No one, he suggests, had written about stones before.

Hazlitt praised *The Excursion* as a 'philosophical pastoral poem'
− something different from, and superior to, the descriptive procession that was typical of earlier pastoral poems. Everything in
Wordsworth, he argued, was the result of the poet's own reflections
on the forms of nature: 'his thoughts are his real subjects'. Hence
the solitude of his own heart, as he lived in the deep silence of
thought. Hence the indisputable conclusion that 'The recluse, the
pastor, and the pedlar are three persons in one voice.' Hence
Hazlitt's conclusion when he repurposed his review as a lecture
on the Lake School: 'so that the only thing remarkable left in the
world by this change, would be the persons who had produced
it. A thorough adept in this school of poetry and philanthropy is
jealous of all excellence but his own . . . His egotism is in some
respects a madness.' Egotism: that was the perennial criticism of
Wordsworth, the poet who wrote an epic about himself.

In the second instalment, Hazlitt turned to Wordsworth's

treatment of the French Revolution. Here, their political differences become explicit. Hazlitt recognized that 'The loss of confidence in social man' (that is to say, in systemic political change) which Wordsworth attributes to the Solitary belonged to Wordsworth himself.[28] He dissented from Wordsworth's view that 'virtue and liberty' would one day triumph through *individual* renewal alone. And he brilliantly turned the words of the 'Intimations of Immortality' ode back onto Wordsworth by reanimating the spirit of youthful joy at the revolution that had been captured in the sonnet addressed to Jones, which Hazlitt had read in the *Poems* of 1807:

> But though we cannot weave over again the airy, unsubstantial dream, which reason and experience have dispelled –
>
> > What though the radiance, which was once so bright,
> > Be now for ever taken from our sight,
> > Though nothing can bring back the hour
> > Of glory in the grass, of splendour in the flower: –
>
> yet we will never cease, nor be prevented from returning on the wings of imagination to that bright dream of our youth; that glad dawn of the day-star of liberty; that spring-time of the world, in which the hopes and expectations of the human race seemed opening in the same gay career with our own; when France called her children to partake her equal blessings beneath her laughing skies; when the stranger was met in all her villages with dance and festive songs, in celebration of a new and golden era.[29]

The trajectory of these first two instalments of the review swerved from high praise to political disillusionment. The latter mood led Hazlitt to think negatively about Wordsworth, with the result that when it came to the third part of his review – published just over a month later, and reading more like a self-contained essay than a continuation of the earlier analysis – he could not resist dredging up the painful memory of his humiliation among the Lake folk. Personal animus undid the work of critical acclamation: 'All country people hate each other . . . They hate all strangers . . . There is a perpetual round of mischief-making and backbiting for want of any better amusement.' When Mary Wordsworth read this, she wrote to Dorothy saying that Hazlitt's multi-part review would surely benefit the sales of the book, but that the attack on 'the Mountaineers' (a neat phrase for the local people) was most ungrateful, given that Wordsworth had protected him on the night when he was run out of town.[30]

Hazlitt himself gave an account, at second hand, of Wordsworth's reaction to his review. An unsolicited copy of *The Examiner* arrived in the mail at Rydal Mount. The politics of the paper were 'rascally' and the expense an annoyance – postage at this time was usually paid by the receiver, not the sender. The Scottish gentleman John Wilson, who lived on an estate above Windermere and aspired to be a Lake Poet himself, was present. 'Oh,' he said (or so he said that he said when he told Hazlitt the story – or so Hazlitt reported his report), 'let us see what there is in it. I dare say they have not sent it you for nothing. Why here, there's a criticism upon the *Excursion* in it.' Wordsworth expostulated: 'What did they know about his poetry? What could they know about it? It was presumption in the highest degree for these cockney writers to pretend to criticise a Lake poet.' 'Well,' said Wilson, 'at any rate let us read it':

So he began. The article was much in favour of the poet and the poem. As the reading proceeded, 'Ha,' said Mr Wordsworth, somewhat appeased, 'there's some sense in this fellow too: the Dog writes strong.' Upon which Mr Wilson was encouraged to proceed still farther with the encomium, and Mr Wordsworth continued his approbation; 'Upon my word very judicious, very well indeed.' At length, growing vain with his own and the *Examiner*'s applause, he suddenly seized the paper into his own hands, and saying 'Let me read it, Mr Wilson,' did so with an audible voice and appropriate gesture to the end, when he exclaimed, 'Very well written indeed, Sir, I did not expect a thing of this kind,' and strutting up and down the room in high good humour kept every now and then wondering who could be the author, 'he had no idea, and should like very much to know to whom he was indebted for such pointed and judicious praise' – when Mr Wilson interrupt[ed] him with saying, 'Oh don't you know; it's Hazlitt, to be sure, there are his initials to it.[31]

At which, Wordsworth expressed 'outrageous incredulity to think that he should be indebted for the first favourable account that had ever appeared of any work he had ever written' to Hazlitt, a man as 'rascally' in his personal conduct as in his politics.

Despite their personal and political differences, and notwithstanding frequent barbs in later reviews, essays and public lectures, Hazlitt, picking up and running with the instinct expressed by Leigh Hunt in *The Feast of the Poets*, argued again and again that 'Mr Wordsworth's genius is a pure emanation of the Spirit of the Age'. His 'levelling muse' spoke better than any other to the levelling age of revolution. In his summative essay on Wordsworth in *The Spirit of the Age*, published in 1825, Hazlitt argued that in the best of his poetry each object of nature is 'connected with a thousand feelings, a link in the chain of thought, a fibre of his own heart'; each object is, furthermore, linked to the poet's birthplace or to the key moments in his life. To Wordsworth, he says, 'nature is a kind of home': 'There is no image so insignificant that it has not in some mood or other found the way into his heart: no sound that does not awaken the memory of other years.' A daisy, a cuckoo, an old withered thorn, 'a grey cloak, seen on some wild moor, torn by the wind, or drenched in the rain': each *thing* 'becomes an object of imagination to him'. Even 'the lichens on the rock have a life and being in his thoughts':

> He has described all these objects in a way and with an intensity of feeling that no one else had done before him, and has given a new view or aspect of nature. He is in this sense the most original poet now living, and the one whose writings could the least be spared: for they have no substitute elsewhere. The vulgar do not read them, the learned, who see all things through books, do not understand them, the great despise, the fashionable may ridicule them: but the author has created himself an interest in the heart of the retired and lonely student of nature, which can never die.[32]

Here the critic becomes a prophet. Hazlitt recognizes that Wordsworth's true reputation has yet to be established, but he predicts that his genius will never die. The poems would live, waiting to create, as Wordsworth himself put it in his 1815 'Essay, supplementary to the Preface', the taste by which they were to be enjoyed.

19

AMONG THE COCKNEYS

On the morning of 11 June 1815, the forty-five-year-old poet sat in a dressing gown in a lodging house in Great Marlborough Street, London. His hands were folded, his manner 'sedate, steady and solemn'. His face was covered in plaster.

Wordsworth had arrived in London a few weeks before. He and Mary travelled by coach via Oxford, where they dropped off Hartley Coleridge, now of university age, with his tutor. The main purpose of the trip was to see Lord Lonsdale in order for Wordsworth to tell his patron in person that he did not wish to accept the position of Collector of Customs at Whitehaven. He already had one Civil Service post, thanks to His Lordship. Although the Customs position would have been a great deal more lucrative, it would have required him to move to the large port town of Whitehaven. He did not wish to leave Rydal Mount. The Distributor of Stamps position was sufficient; he enjoyed being based in a local office in Ambleside, periodically riding around the beautiful countryside appointing and overseeing the 'subs' who sold stamps around the county, and receiving reasonable remuneration for a not unreasonable amount of work, allowing him time to sit in his upstairs study at Rydal Mount, looking out over the vale of Grasmere and getting on with his poetry.

Six weeks in town also provided an opportunity to meet old literary friends: tea with Charles Lamb, conversation with Henry Crabb Robinson, breakfast with Walter Scott. Lamb's exceptional combination of warmth and wit meant that he could tease Wordsworth and criticize his poetic failings without ever causing offence. The tragic circumstance of his sister Mary's mental illness, which meant that he could never marry because he had to watch carefully over her at home in order to keep her out of the lunatic asylum, might easily have made him jealous of Wordsworth for having the constant adoration of both a wife and a sister, but it never did. He was the epitome of loyalty to both the man and the work. Just before heading to London, Wordsworth had received a letter from him praising to the skies his two volumes of collected *Poems*, in which the poems were rearranged into categories, such as 'Poems referring to the Period of Childhood', 'Poems of the Fancy' and 'Poems of the Imagination'. The distinction between the two latter terms, favourites of Coleridge's, was explained, rather imprecisely, in another preface.

Now he was about to meet a magazine editor called John Scott who had written a review the previous summer describing Wordsworth as 'the greatest poetical genius of the age'.[1] He had been invited to join the poet for breakfast. The host, who owned the dressing gown and had applied the plaster cast, invited Scott to take a peep so that 'he might say the first sight he ever had of so great a poet was such a singular one as this'. They saw him sitting there, 'unable to see or to speak, with all the mysterious silence of a spirit'. He had the aura of one of his own poems, in which the mundane and the bizarre take on a dignity and a sublimity. Once the plaster cast had set and been removed, Wordsworth came into breakfast 'with his usual cheerfulness'.[2]

He was introduced to editor Scott, giving delight and awe to the company through his turns of phrase and 'bursts of inspiration'. He talked impressively about his plans for the epic philosophical poem *The Recluse*, of which a foretaste had been provided by the publication of *The Excursion* the previous year. 'Wordsworth's faculty', wrote the host in his diary, was in describing all the 'intense feelings & glimmerings & doubts & fears & hopes of Man'. His weakness was his egotism: he 'did not possess the power of wielding these feelings to any other purpose but as referring to himself'. That egotism was, however, modified by the power of his poetry to create analogous feelings in the reader by way of 'personal sympathy'. All in all, the account of this breakfast meeting concludes, 'I don't know any man I should be so inclined to worship as a purified being.' He could not agree with the people who found fault with Wordsworth 'for speaking of his own genius'.[3] Years later, the author of these words would name one of his sons in honour of the poet, who would stand as godfather. The child was called Frederick Wordsworth Haydon.

Wordsworth's host was Benjamin Robert Haydon. Born in Devon in 1786, he studied the art of painting at the Royal Academy so ardently that fellow-artist Henry Fuseli wondered how he had time to eat. Haydon spent his career toiling at grand history paintings in the Renaissance style and failing to sell them.

He also kept a diary, which offers a wonderfully lively day-by-day record of the cultural life of London in the years of the Regency and beyond. He loved nothing more than to share evenings of food, wine and conversation with writers. The occasions would often prove inspirational.

The morning after one such evening in 1816, at Leigh Hunt's, a young poet wrote to Haydon:

My dear Sir –
Last Evening wrought me up, and I cannot forbear sending you the following – Your's unfeignedly John Keats –

Great Spirits now on Earth are sojourning
    He of the Cloud, the Cataract the Lake,
    Who on Helvellyn's summit wide awake
Catches his freshness from Archangel's wing
He of the Rose, the Violet, the Spring,
    The social Smile, the Chain for freedom's sake:
    And lo! – whose stedfastness would never take
A Meaner Sound than Raphael's Whispering.
And other Spirits there are standing apart
    Upon the Forehead of the Age to come;
These, These will give the World another heart,
    And other pulses – hear ye not the hum
Of mighty Workings in a distant Mart?
    Listen awhile ye Nations, and be dumb![4]

Haydon would have been very flattered by the comparison to Raphael. The second of the 'great spirits' was Leigh Hunt, champion of freedom and author of numerous poems arrayed with floral imagery. But first and foremost was the poet whose hallmark was 'the Cloud, the Cataract, the Lake'. The reference to Helvellyn may be Keats's recollection of one of the 'Poems on the Naming of Places' in *Lyrical Ballads*,[5] but it could be that Haydon had shared with Keats the manuscript of a recent as yet unpublished Wordsworth poem called '*To* – – – , ON HER FIRST ASCENT TO THE SUMMIT OF HELVELLYN', which begins

> Inmate of a mountain Dwelling,
> Thou hast clomb aloft, and gaz'd,
> From the watch-towers of Helvellyn;
> Awed, delighted, and amazed![6]

The poem continues with a series of biblical references, then ends with an image of the 'majesty' of what Wordsworth calls 'the power of hills'. In Keats's allusion to the archangel's wing there may also be a witty nod to the pastoral 'Michael'. Michael was the only angel named in the New Testament as an archangel, so there is a suggestion of divine inspiration, but Keats may be hinting that the 'freshness' of Wordsworth comes from his innovation of giving tragic dignity to ordinary people.

Wordsworth was the inspiration for Keats's sonnet in another sense, too. He had recently published a slender volume of very overblown poetry in celebration of the end of the Napoleonic Wars, entitled *Thanksgiving Ode, January 18, 1816, with other short pieces, chiefly referring to recent public events*. One of the few pieces that was not inspired by 'public events' was a sonnet addressed to 'R. B. Haydon, Esq.' (Wordsworth or his printer got the initials the wrong way round). The poem extolled the high calling of 'Creative Art', both writing and painting, with its demand for strenuous work 'of mind and heart' and its mission to fashion something enduring despite the neglect and distress suffered by the creative artist.

Just over a year later, Haydon would introduce the two poets to each other.

★

Coleridge was a little aggrieved that Wordsworth had a way of making use of his ideas, often without proper acknowledgment, while failing to listen to his advice. He told Lady Beaumont that he thought *The Excursion*, though it showed that Wordsworth's genius had not entirely deserted him, was not up to the standard of 'the Work on the Growth of his own spirit' – except, that was, for the story of the ruined cottage, which he had 'ever thought the finest Poem in our Language'.[7] The problem with *The Excursion* was that it contained too many commonplaces and truisms. When Wordsworth heard of this criticism, he asked Coleridge to explain. This elicited a long and critical letter, the main thrust of which was disappointment that *The Recluse* had not unfolded as the 'philosophical poem' that Coleridge had told Wordsworth he should write.

Meanwhile, there was the question of how to respond to Francis Jeffrey. After years of remaining publicly silent over the repeated battering he had received from his critics, Wordsworth rose to the bait of the *Edinburgh*'s assaults on *The Excursion* and *The White Doe of Rylstone*. A chance came with a request to write a pamphlet in posthumous defence of Robert Burns. Wordsworth's task was to direct readers towards the greatness of the ploughman's poetry and away from the gossip about drunkenness and womanizing in the biographies of the man. Along the way, he veered into some uncharacteristic language. Jeffrey had also written a takedown of Burns. Wordsworth argued that this revealed him to be an 'infatuated slanderer', the possessor of 'a mind obtuse, superficial, and inept'. He accused Jeffrey (without actually naming him) of 'intellectual deformity', 'self-conceit', vanity that is 'restless, reckless, intractable, unappeasable, insatiable', even of being an 'intoxicated despot' who could only be compared to Robespierre.[8] One senses a good deal of satisfaction on Wordsworth's part at his finally having had the opportunity to fight back. This intervention would, however, draw his name into an even more bitter literary dispute that began two years later and ended in tragedy.

Coleridge was also furious with Jeffrey, not least because he knew, as did others in the literary world, that the attacks (like many negative reviews down the ages) were really motivated by an egotistic desire to show off and an editor's knowledge that the way to sell papers was to create controversies. Jeffrey actually had a very high regard for many of Wordsworth's poems. Sir Walter Scott, with his usual combination of impeccable judgment and an eye to where money was to be made, observed that in private he had seen the editor of the *Edinburgh* 'weep warm tears over Wordsworths poetry' but that in print he 'mounted into the Scorner's chair' in order to create sales, which would in turn serve the paper's progressive Whig political agenda.[9]

It was partly in order to offer a fairer assessment of his sometime collaborator that in 1817 Coleridge published his *Biographia Literaria; or Biographical Sketches of my Literary Life and Opinions.* This was originally drafted two years earlier, as a preface for a proposed collection of Coleridge's poems. The intention was to give his version of the story of the *Lyrical Ballads* collaboration, correcting and refining the arguments of Wordsworth's 1800 Preface. However, in order to explain his own theory of the poetic imagination Coleridge felt the need to outline the philosophical development whereby he had rejected as being too passive the Hartleian model of the mental association of impressions received through the senses, and embraced instead the 'idealism' of Kant and Schelling, in which the mind actively shapes the process of cognition. The book accordingly took two years in the writing and grew to two volumes in bulk, baffling its readers as it began as a literary manifesto, veered into German philosophy, developed Wordsworth's distinction between 'fancy' and 'imagination' into a full-scale theory of the imagination as 'a repetition in the finite mind of the eternal act of creation in the infinite I AM', then swung back into a detailed account of the strengths and weaknesses of Wordsworth's poetry.

The climax of the book was a riposte to Jeffrey and a defence of Wordsworth on the grounds of his 'verbal precision', the *freshness* of his observation, 'the sinewy strength and originality of single lines and paragraphs', and 'the perfect truth of nature in his images and descriptions as taken immediately from nature'.[10] Coleridge supported his argument with ample quotation. 'By what principle of rational choice', he asks, could Jeffrey have described the following magnificent lines in *The Excursion* as 'a proof and example of an author's tendency to *downright ravings*, and absolute unintelligibility?'

> O then what soul was his, when on the tops
> Of the high mountains he beheld the sun
> Rise up, and bathe the world in light! He looked –
> Ocean and earth, the solid frame of earth,
> And ocean's liquid mass, beneath him lay
> In gladness and deep joy. The clouds were touch'd,
> And in their silent faces did he read
> Unutterable love. Sound needed none,
> Nor any *voice* of joy; his spirit drank
> The spectacle! sensation, soul, and form,
> All melted into him. They swallowed up
> His animal being: in them did he live,
> And by them did he live: they were his life.[11]

This was indeed part of a sequence that Jeffrey had described as a 'raving fit'. Part of his point had been that the poem represented these elevated feelings as the reaction to a sunrise of a six-year-old who will grow up to be a pedlar. Taken literally, this does seem somewhat implausible, giving Jeffrey grounds for his attack. For Coleridge, on the other hand, the passage is a prime example of Wordsworth's imagination at work. Elsewhere in the *Biographia*, he wrote of 'that willing suspension of disbelief for the moment, which constitutes poetic faith': he understood that readers need to suspend their disbelief in the possibility of a six-year-old child having such a vision when beholding a sunrise from a mountaintop.[12] Of course the thought belongs to the poet Wordsworth, not an imaginary Pedlar, and of course it is a symptom of his longing for the time of unmediated oneness with nature that he has lost, but the point is that the poet has the capacity to direct readers to the possibility that the feeling might be regained and their lives thus enriched.

'I have not read Mr Coleridge's *Biographia*, having contented myself with skimming parts of it', Wordsworth casually remarked two months after the book's publication.[13] This may be disingenuous: some of the revisions he made to his poems when preparing a new collected edition in 1820 do seem to have been made in response to Coleridge's criticisms, but then again he had the habit of tinkering with his texts every time there was a new edition. There is no record of his expressing gratitude for Coleridge's defence against the strictures of Jeffrey, just as he never thanked Hazlitt for his positive review. Several friends were beginning to notice a tendency towards vanity and pomposity in the middle-aged Wordsworth.

Two days after Christmas 1817, there was an awkward dinner party at the home in Queen Anne Street of Tom Monkhouse, a man who took pleasure in literary company. Coleridge and

Hartley were invited, and Crabb Robinson, and Charles and Mary Lamb, along with Wordsworth. It was the first face-to-face meeting of the former partners since the quarrel five years before. Wordsworth was unduly cold, contradicting everything that Coleridge said.

★

There was a very different atmosphere at Haydon's the following night.

He had been working away for years at the vast canvas of his *Christ's Entry into Jerusalem*, portraying his living friends and the famous dead as figures in the crowd. 'Poor Keats' is shouting, unheard; Hazlitt is 'scrutinizing Christ' (when he saw his own likeness, he quoted Wordsworth to Haydon, 'His face was keen as is the wind / That cuts along the hawthorn fence'); the atheist Voltaire 'sneers'; and Wordsworth is there, head bowed and hands clasped in reverence, beside Newton, 'among the believers'.[14] Hazlitt said that this was the best likeness of Wordsworth, capturing 'his drooping weight of thought and expression'.[15] To paint his face, Haydon had him sit again, when he was back in London. He began with a drawing, during which Wordsworth recited 'Tintern Abbey' and some passages of *Paradise Lost*. Haydon concluded that 'in moral grandeur of Soul and extension of scope, he is equal to Milton'. Three weeks later, Wordsworth sat again and Haydon began to put his head in the picture. This time, the poet read the entire fourth book of *The Excursion*, 'Despondency Corrected'.

A few days later, Haydon took his protégé Keats to meet the great poet at Monkhouse's. Wordsworth received the young man kindly and after a few minutes asked him what he had been writing. Haydon said that Keats had 'just finished an exquisite ode to Pan'. He begged Keats to recite it to Wordsworth, which the shy twenty-two-year-old poet did from memory, in a chant, walking up and down the room. When he finished, Wordsworth drily said that his lines were 'a very pretty piece of Paganism', Haydon thought that 'this was unfeeling, and unworthy of his high Genius to a young Worshipper'.[16]

As Haydon remembered it, 'Keats felt it *deeply*'. John Keats felt everything deeply. Born in 1795, the son of a Moorgate stable-keeper, he was introduced to poetry by Charles Cowden Clarke, a close friend of the Lambs and son of the head teacher of the small school in the London suburb of Enfield where Keats was educated before beginning his training as a medical student at Guy's Hospital. The knowledge of the human body that he gained at Guy's was one of the factors that made his poetry so sensuous. His letters and his poetry are rich in breathing and in blushes. 'Axioms in philosophy are not axioms until they are proved upon our pulses', he wrote to a friend in a letter about his attitude to Wordsworth, 'We read fine things but never feel them to the full until we have gone the same steps as the Author.'[17] Proving on the pulses and feeling to the full: that was one of his missions as a poet. 'Tintern Abbey' was his touchstone because it was, as Wordsworth put it, 'Felt in the blood, and felt along the heart'.

In this same letter, written a few weeks after meeting Wordsworth, Keats compared human life to 'a large Mansion of Many Apartments'. The first he called 'the infant or thoughtless Chamber'. This was his equivalent of Wordsworth's idea of the child's unmediated oneness with nature. Then we enter 'the second Chamber, which I shall call the Chamber of Maiden-Thought', where 'we become intoxicated with the light and the atmosphere, we see nothing but pleasant wonders, and think of delaying there for ever in delight': this is the time of the 'glad animal movements' that Wordsworth associated with his first visit to Tintern Abbey. Keats continues:

However among the effects this breathing is father of is that tremendous one of sharpening one's vision into the heart and nature of Man – of convincing one[']s nerves that the World is full of Misery and Heartbreak, Pain, Sickness and oppression – whereby This Chamber of Maiden Thought become gradually darken'd and at the same time on all sides of it many doors are set open – but all dark – all leading to dark passages – We see not the ballance of good and evil. We are in a Mist – *We* are now in that state – We feel the 'burden of the Mystery,' To this point was Wordsworth come, as far as I can conceive when he wrote 'Tintern Abbey' and it seems to me that his Genius is explorative of those dark Passages. Now if we live, and go on thinking, we too shall explore them. [H]e is a Genius and superior [to] us, in so far as he can, more than we, make discoveries, and shed a light in [*sic*] them – Here I must think Wordsworth is deeper than Milton.[18]

For Keats, Wordsworth had gone beyond Milton and it was his own vocation to seek to go beyond Wordsworth. He believed – and in this he was much influenced by Hazlitt, whose public lectures he attended – that the problem with what he called 'the Wordsworthian' was the 'egotistical Sublime', the perpetual writing from the point of view of the *self*.[19] As he matured as a poet and thinker, Keats sought to combine Wordsworth's poetry of feeling with a counter-model that was the antithesis of egotism: the art of 'negative capability' and the dissolution of the authorial self into a full gamut of dramatic characters. The example, that is to say, of Shakespeare.

Wounded as he was by Wordsworth's condescension towards the lines that he had recited from his long romance *Endymion*, Keats joined Lamb and others at Haydon's dinner party presided over by the painting of *Christ's Entry into Jerusalem*, in which he was placed immediately behind his flawed hero. The painting made it look as if he was standing on the shoulder of the poet whom Coleridge had called 'the Giant Wordsworth'.

The man himself was 'in fine cue' that evening and they had what Haydon called 'a glorious set-to – on Homer, Shakespeare, Milton and Virgil'. Charles Lamb 'got exceedingly merry and exquisitely witty; and his fun in the midst of Wordsworth's solemn intonations of oratory was like the sarcasm and wit of the fool in the intervals of Lear's passion'. 'Now,' said Lamb, 'you old lake poet, you rascally poet, why do you call Voltaire dull?' Everyone else defended Wordsworth and agreed that 'there was a state of mind when Voltaire would be dull'. Lamb then jokingly abused Haydon for putting Newton in the picture beside Wordsworth: 'A fellow', he said, 'who believed nothing unless it was as clear as the three sides of a triangle.'

Keats ventured to agree with Lamb that 'all the poetry of the rainbow' – they were thinking not least of Wordsworth's 'My heart leaps up' – was destroyed by Newton's 'reducing it to the prismatic colours'. The exchange seeded some lines that Keats would later include in his 'Christabel'-influenced poem 'Lamia':

> Do not all charms fly
> At the mere touch of cold philosophy?
> There was an awful rainbow once in heaven:
> We know her woof, her texture; she is given
> In the dull catalogue of common things.
> Philosophy will clip an Angel's wings,
> Conquer all mysteries by rule and line,
> Empty the haunted air, and gnomed mine –
> Unweave a rainbow.[20]

As they spoke of Newton, Wordsworth no doubt thought back
to his undergraduate days at Cambridge, when he had looked
down from his room and seen the statue of the great math-
ematician with his prism next door in Trinity College. Having
enjoyed his mathematical studies, he hesitated to join in the
banter. But he went with the flow of the evening. 'It was
delightful to see the good humour of Wordsworth in giving
in to all our frolics without affectation and laughing as heartily
as the best of us', wrote Haydon in his diary. It was impossible
to resist the wit and warmth of Charles Lamb in his cups.
They all drank 'Newton's health, and confusion to mathematics'.[21]

'I am convinced that there are three things to rejoice at in
this Age', Keats told Haydon in the new year: 'The Excursion,
Your Pictures, and Hazlitt's depth of Taste.' Haydon replied that
there was a fourth: '*John Keats's genius!*'[22] But there remained the
problem of Wordsworth's political apostasy. When the summer
came, Keats walked north. He ventured into the vale of Grasmere.
He went to Rydal Mount, admiring its beautiful setting. None
of the Wordsworths were at home, so he wrote a note and left
it on the mantelpiece, leaning against a portrait of Dorothy (both
are, alas, lost). But he was shocked by the local news, picked up
in the inns. For one thing, 'Lord Wordsworth, instead of being
in retirement, has himself and his house full in the thick of
fashionable visitors.' So much for his resemblance to the Solitary
of *The Excursion*. Worse still, he was out campaigning – and even
writing election materials – on behalf of the candidate for the
Tory Lowther interest, who was locked in a bitter fight against
Henry Brougham, Leigh Hunt's brilliant defence attorney, star
of the liberal Whig front bench.

★

The Edinburgh press, meanwhile, had not fallen silent. A publisher called William Blackwood decided that there was a market for a Tory monthly to rival the Whig *Edinburgh Review*. Its editors, John Wilson and J. G. Lockhart, took a leaf out of Jeffrey's book: publishing slashing reviews of contemporary writers in order to gain attention for the paper. The first issue of *Blackwood's Edinburgh Magazine* included an article attacking Wordsworth for his attack on Jeffrey in the pamphlet defending Burns. This was curious not only because of its deference to the magazine that the new publication was supposed to be rivalling, but also because it was by Wilson, the sometime disciple of Wordsworth who had gone to live by Windermere and set himself up as a Lake Poet. 'We wish to have done with this lyrical ballad-monger', he now wrote, albeit under the veil of anonymity.[23] Even more curiously, the second number of the magazine contained a reply defending Wordsworth that was also written anonymously by Wilson: 'with all the fearlessness of original genius, he has burst and cast away the bonds which were worn very contentedly by many great writers . . . Posterity will hail him as a regenerator and a creator.'[24]

The October 1817 issue of *Blackwood's* also contained something far more damaging, an anonymous diatribe, signed Z, entitled 'On the Cockney School of Poetry':

WHILE the whole critical world is occupied with, balancing the merits, whether in theory or in execution, of what is commonly called THE LAKE-SCHOOL, it is strange that no one seems to think it at all necessary to say a single word about another new school of poetry which has of late sprung up among us. This school has not, I believe, as yet received any name; but if I may be permitted to have the honour of christening it, it may henceforth be referred to by the designation of THE COCKNEY SCHOOL. Its chief Doctor and

Professor is Mr Leigh Hunt, a man certainly of some talents, of extravagant pretensions both in wit, poetry, and politics, and withal of exquisitely bad taste, and extremely vulgar modes of thinking and manners in all respects. He is a man of little education.[25]

Why 'Cockney', other than to provide a London name to contrast with the 'Lake School' of the rural north? The word was, of course, the nickname given to the citizens of London, or persons born within the sound of Bow Bells.[26] This was a full-scale assault on the grounds of class. Great poets, it is said, have always been country gentlemen. Z sneers at the false representation of nature in these upstart urban and suburban writers: Hunt is 'the ideal of a Cockney Poet. He raves perpetually about "green fields," "jaunty streams," and "o'er-arching leafiness," exactly as a Cheapside shop-keeper does about the beauties of his box on the Camberwell road'. Wordsworth, meanwhile, was reclaimed for the political right:

How such an indelicate writer as Mr Hunt can pretend to be an admirer of Mr Wordsworth, is to us a thing altogether inexplicable. One great charm of Wordsworth's noble compositions consists in the dignified purity of thought, and the patriarchal simplicity of feeling, with which they are throughout penetrated and imbued . . . Mr Hunt praises the purity of Wordsworth as if he himself were pure, his dignity as if he also were dignified.[27]

Taking as his primary exhibit the sexual matter of *The Story of Rimini* (the Paolo and Francesca poem), Z brands Leigh Hunt's 'polluted muse' with 'odious and unnatural harlotry'. His poetry is said to be the 'kept-mistress of a demoralizing incendiary'. 'We tore off her gaudy veil and transparent drapery, and exhibited the painted cheeks and writhing limbs of the prostitute': how dare such a writer presume to admire the lofty tones of *The Excursion?*

Inevitably, it was only a matter of time before Keats was caught in the crossfire. Another Tory newspaper, William Gifford's *Quarterly Review*, picked up the Cockney moniker and published an excoriating review of his romance *Endymion.* Z then weighed in with an attack on the sonnet addressed to Haydon:

> In this exquisite piece it will be observed, that Mr Keats classes together WORDSWORTH, HUNT, and HAYDON, as the three greatest spirits of the age, and that he alludes to himself, and some others of the rising brood of Cockneys, as likely to attain hereafter an equally honourable elevation. Wordsworth and Hunt! what a juxtaposition! The purest, the loftiest, and, we do not fear to say it, the most classical of living English poets, joined together in the same compliment with the meanest, the filthiest, and the most vulgar of Cockney poetasters.[28]

★

John Scott, the editor who first saw Wordsworth when he was shrouded in Haydon's plaster cast, was a close associate of Leigh Hunt. He started his career editing another radical newspaper for him, *The Statesman*, before establishing a sequence of liberal magazines of his own, notably *The Champion*. In January 1820, as the influence of *The Examiner* was waning, he launched a new monthly, the *London Magazine*. He worked indefatigably, writing about a third of the paper himself, giving a new platform to Hazlitt and providing a forum for two other London-based prose writers, Thomas De Quincey and Charles Lamb. The former's

Confessions of an English Opium Eater and the latter's *Essays of Elia* were first published in serial form in the *London*.

Scott's editorials began to make hits at 'the mean insincerity, and vulgar slander of Z' in *Blackwood's*.[29] What kind of artistic judgment was being shown in references to Haydon's greasy hair and the fact that Keats had walked the hospitals as a trainee apothecary? In November 1820, he launched a full-scale assault in a long article headed 'Blackwood's Magazine'. It was a 'poisonous infection', a 'threatening plague', 'the most foul and livid spot, indicative of an accursed taint in the literature of the day'. Scott dared to use a word loaded with risk: 'The *honour* of the literature of the present day we consider as now at stake.' In particular, he pointed to the great Sir Walter Scott's connections to the Tory *Blackwood's* circle in Edinburgh, demanding that 'the brightest ornament of his country's modern literary history' should be cleared of 'a diseased, false, affected, profligate, whining, and hypocritical character' by means of a clear announcement as to the identity of Z, in order to reassure the public that Sir Walter was not implicated.[30]

There was no response from Edinburgh, so in the next issue John Scott upped his game. An article called 'The Mohock Magazine' accused *Blackwood's* of infamy, cowardice, selfishness, stupidity, antisocial enormities, insensibility, insensitivity, spite, 'and when the poisonous stimulus exercises its full strength, treachery and malignity darken the aspect, and corrupt the influence of what may be termed the literary pleasures of general society . . . Iscariot treachery, and Iago malice'. He set his sights on the contributor and co-editor 'Christopher North', the pseudonym of John Wilson, who was now libelling Wordsworth, having earlier eulogized him in both poetry and prose. Then there was the accusation that Coleridge was 'a still greater quack than Leigh Hunt', not to mention the unauthorized publication by *Blackwood's* of one of his private letters.[31] Naturally, John Scott also sprang to the defence of Keats, letting it be known how profoundly the young poet, who was by now at death's door, had been affected by the Cockney School essays.

On Wednesday 10 January 1821, John Scott received a call from a gentleman acting on behalf of J. G. Lockhart, who everyone in the literary world suspected, correctly, was Z. Only a year older than Keats, Lockhart had been a brilliant student. Too good for school, he was sent to Glasgow University at the age of twelve, became Snell Exhibitioner at Balliol College, Oxford at fourteen, and took a first-class degree in Greats at nineteen. During a continental tour, he had paid homage to Goethe and obtained permission to translate into English Friedrich Schlegel's lectures on the history of literature. Back in Edinburgh, he had become one of the editors of *Blackwood's*, with the support of Sir Walter Scott, whose biography he would write and whose daughter he married at exactly the time the Cockney controversy blew up.

John Scott of the *London* had named Lockhart as 'an understood, though unavowed, conductor of BLACKWOOD'S MAGAZINE'. Lockhart's London friend, a Mr J. H. Christie, now asked John Scott if he was the author of a series of three articles discussing the conduct and management of *Blackwood's* which Lockhart considered 'offensive to his feelings, and injurious to his honour'. That key word, honour. Scott said that he would reply within a couple of hours. He did so, with the cautious undertaking that if Lockhart's motives in putting the inquiry should 'turn out to be such as gentlemen usually respect' he would give an explicit answer.[32]

Christie came back and said that Lockhart did not intend to commence legal proceedings, but wished for a public apology. Scott replied that if he were to admit that he was editor of the

London, would Lockhart admit that he was editor of *Blackwood's?* He also said that Lockhart should have come to London and confronted him face to face. He then sent a further note, questioning whether Lockhart was really offended since the most damning article had been in print for over a month without any complaint and asking whether he was acting as 'a *gentleman*, assailed in his honourable feelings by the indecent use of his name in print; or as a *professional scandal-monger*, who had long profited by fraudulent and cowardly concealment'.

To and fro the correspondence went, with Christie continuing to act as proxy for Lockhart. Neither side backed down. This was a far more bitter and public dispute than that between Wordsworth and Coleridge. With honour at stake, there was no alternative to the traditional gentleman's resolution. Christie would stand as proxy for Lockhart, who remained in Edinburgh.

Scott and Christie were ill met by moonlight on the night of Friday 16 February 1821, in a wooded knoll on Primrose Hill, not far from the Chalk Farm Tavern, where the editor of the *London* had left a third of a bottle of wine, saying that he would return to finish it later. The pistols were primed and loaded. Christie called out 'Mr Scott, you must not stand there; I see your head above the horizon; you give me an advantage.' The seconds consulted with each other. Adjustments were made. All was ready. Both men fired. Both missed. The seconds should have declared that honour had been duly satisfied. But Christie's second, James Traill, was a stickler for the etiquette of the duel (which was by this time illegal, which is why they were meeting at night). Christie had deliberately fired wide, whereas Scott had taken aim at Christie. How could one be sure that he had missed deliberately, and was not just a bad shot? For honour to be satisfied, there would have to be a second shot on equal terms. Traill spoke: 'Gentlemen, before this proceeds, I must insist on one thing. You, Mr Christie, must give yourself the usual chances, and not again fire in the air, or fire away from Mr Scott.' 'What,' said Scott, 'did not Mr Christie fire at me?' P. G. Patmore, his second, replied, 'You must not speak; 'tis now of no use to talk; you have now nothing for it but firing.'[33] The signal was given.

Scott took the ball between his ribs and his hip bone. It passed through into the stomach. The attending surgeon took one look at the wound and fled. The other three men got Scott back to the tavern, then ran away to avoid arrest. For two days, Scott lay in the tavern, his family watching over, together with their doctor, George Darling (who was also doctor to John Keats and John Clare). The bullet was removed from the abdomen, and there was hope for a few days. But then Scott's fever returned and he died on the night of Tuesday 27 February 1821.

And what of Keats? All through that January and February of 1821, as literary crossfire escalated towards real bullets, he lay desperately ill in Rome. He, too, was on his deathbed. His stomach, like Scott's, was ruined, but in his case due to the ravages of tuberculosis. He asked for a bottle of opium to kill himself. He wrote, 'I shall soon be laid in the quiet grave – thank God for the quiet grave – O! I can feel the cold earth upon me – the daisies growing over me – O for this quiet – it will be my first'.[34] He died at 11 p.m. on 23 February, four nights before the editor who had defended the honour of the Cockneys. He was laid to rest in the English Protestant cemetery. Keats supposedly wanted nothing but some enigmatic words on the gravestone: 'Here lies one whose name was writ in water', a suggestion of being forgotten, not living, as he had said he hoped to live, 'among the English Poets after my death'. But his friends chose instead (and later regretted) words that allude to the wounding articles in *Blackwood's* and the *Quarterly*:

> This grave contains all that was Mortal, of a Young English Poet Who, on his Death Bed, in the Bitterness of his Heart at the Malicious Power of his Enemies, Desired these Words to be engraven on his Tomb Stone: *Here lies One Whose Name was writ in Water.*

When the news reached Rydal Mount of the death of John Scott in London and John Keats in Rome, Mary Wordsworth connected the two events and wrote 'God forgive those who have been the hasteners of their untimely fate.'[35] Wordsworth considered Scott's appalling and unnecessary death to be a sign of the terrible decline of the times in both the nation and the 'republic of letters':

> Poor Scott! living in this solitude we have thought more about him, and suffered more anxiety and sorrow on his account, than you among the many interruptions of London can have leisure to feel. I do not recollect any other English Author's perishing in the same way. It is an Innovation the effect of others which promise no good to the Republic of Letters or to the Country. We have had ribaldry, and sedition, and slanders enough in our Literature heretofore, but no epithet which those periods deserved is so foul as that merited by the present, viz. the *treacherous.*[36]

★

Percy Bysshe Shelley was not so forgiving as Mrs Wordsworth. In his poem *Adonais: An Elegy on the Death of John Keats*, he went so far as to imply, as others among Keats's friends explicitly said, that these assaults were the cause of Keats's death.

> Our Adonais has drunk poison – oh!

What deaf and viperous murderer could crown
Life's early cup with such a draught of woe?

The poem goes on to demand that 'The nameless worm' who
wrote the attacks in *Blackwood's* should 'now itself disown'. Shelley
voices a splendid curse: 'Thou noteless blot on a remember'd
name! . . . Remorse and Self-contempt shall cling to thee; /
Hot Shame shall burn upon thy secret brow'. But then the poem
turns beautifully to the idea of Keats's poetic immortality: 'He
has outsoar'd the shadow of our night; / Envy and calumny and
hate and pain'. Shelley does not imagine the dead poet's afterlife
in terms of the heavenly bliss of orthodox Christianity: this,
remember, was a man who was sent down from Oxford for
writing a pamphlet called *The Necessity of Atheism*. Immortality
comes instead in the form of a reunion with nature. 'He is a
portion of the loveliness / Which once he made more lovely':

He is made one with Nature: there is heard
His voice in all her music, from the moan
Of thunder, to the song of night's sweet bird;
He is a presence to be felt and known
In darkness and in light.[37]

The inclusion of 'night's sweet bird' – the nightingale – is a
delicate touch, a nod to the most musical of Keats's odes. But
the notion of being 'made one with Nature' and of the 'presence' of a spirit in nature that brings love, mental sustenance
and the kindling of creative life: these ideas are wholly
Wordsworthian, testimony to his shaping influence upon the
next generation of poets.

★

Wordsworth's reading of 'Despondency Corrected', the fourth book of *The Excursion*, as Haydon took the likeness of his head for inclusion in *Christ's Entry*, did not, alas, correct the painter's own despondency. Haydon endured depression for almost another thirty years until a June morning in 1846, when, after a life of debt and disappointment, he purchased a pistol, kissed his wife and shot himself in the head. The ball failed to pierce his unusually thick skull, so he slit a seven-inch gash in his throat. The twenty-sixth volume of his diary was left open at the last entry:

FINIS OF B. R. HAYDON

'STRETCH ME NO LONGER ON

THIS TOUGH WORLD' – *LEAR*

END – [38]

Four years earlier, Haydon had painted Wordsworth, now in his seventies, once more. He wanted to envision him among the mountains of the Lakes, but had to content himself with sittings in London and to supply the sublime scenery from memory. Wordsworth went into Haydon's studio and was measured to ensure accuracy: he was five feet nine and seven-eighths inches, which was very tall for the time (Lamb and De Quincey, one recalls, were barely five feet). The sitting did not go well: the aged Wordsworth had an inflamed eyelid, so had to sit with his back to the light, meaning that Haydon was directly facing the light, which strained his eyes. For a while, they reminisced about the immortal dinner. But it was a hot day and Wordsworth fell asleep. Haydon almost nodded off himself.

The painting showed Wordsworth standing on Helvellyn, head bowed in thought as he composes a sonnet inspired by Haydon's painting of the Duke of Wellington returning to the battlefield of Waterloo twenty years after the event. It has a profoundly elegiac quality, a sense of looking back as mortality beckons. This made it Wordsworth's favourite among all the likenesses that had been taken in his life.[39] The young poet Elizabeth Barrett of Wimpole Street, a devoted Wordsworthian, was inspired to write a sonnet:

Wordsworth upon Helvellyn! Let the cloud
Ebb audibly along the mountain-wind,
Then break against the rock, and show behind
The lowland valleys floating up to crowd
The sense with beauty. *He*, with forehead bowed
And humble-lidded eyes, as one inclined
Before the sovran thought of his own mind,
And very meek with inspirations proud, –
Takes here his rightful place as poet-priest
By the high altar, singing prayer and prayer
To the higher Heavens! A noble vision free,
Our Haydon's hand hath flung out from the mist!
No portrait this, with Academic air –
This is the poet and his poetry.[40]

To Victorians readers such as Elizabeth Barrett, this is what Wordsworth had become by the end of his life: a 'poet-priest', inseparable from the mountains of the Lake District, embodiment of both a new form of religion and the ability to search 'his own mind'. As Haydon was preparing for his suicide, he sent Miss Barrett the painting for safekeeping. It is now in the National Portrait Gallery in London.

20

THE LOST LEADER

In 'Michael', Wordsworth wrote that he wished to relate his stories 'of man, the heart of man, and human life' for 'the delight of a few natural hearts' and, 'with yet fonder feeling', for the sake 'Of youthful Poets' who would be 'my second Self when I am gone'.[1] The youthful poets of the Regency era were, in their various ways, his second selves. But, like many children, they revolted against their father.

Wordsworth's poetry made it possible for Shelley in *Adonais* to imagine the spirit of Keats being at one with Nature. Many of Shelley's other richest poems are suffused with Wordsworthian language. But, along with Hazlitt, Haydon and Keats, Shelley recognized that Wordsworth's 'egotistical sublime' was a problem. The first poem in which Shelley truly found his voice, *Alastor;*

or The Spirit of Solitude, published in 1816, tells of a young poet led by his imagination to 'contemplation of the universe'. He drinks deep of the beauties of the natural world. He joys in reaching for the infinite. But this 'self-centred seclusion' isolates him from friends, lovers, family, and 'citizens of the world'. The life of the Solitary can only end in misery. 'The good die first', Shelley writes at the end of the poem's preface, 'And those whose hearts are dry as summer dust, / Burn to the socket!' The quotation is from *The Excursion,* making clear to the informed reader whom he has in mind when writing of a secluded and self-centred poet.[2] Shelley had purchased a copy of Wordsworth's poem in 1814, upon returning (briefly) to London after eloping to the continent with Mary Godwin, daughter of philosopher William Godwin and feminist Mary Wollstonecraft. They started reading *The Excursion* together and were 'much disappointed'. Mary wrote their shared judgment on Wordsworth in her journal: 'He is a slave.'[3]

If readers of Shelley's *Alastor* volume (who were, admittedly, very few in number) had any doubts about his attitude to Wordsworth, they would have been dispelled by the sonnet that, thanks to the book's large print, fills the whole of page sixty-seven:

Poet of Nature, thou hast wept to know
That things depart which never may return:
Childhood and youth, friendship and love's first glow,
Have fled like sweet dreams, leaving thee to mourn.
These common woes I feel. One loss is mine
Which thou too feel'st, yet I alone deplore.
Thou wert as a lone star, whose light did shine
On some frail bark in winter's midnight roar:
Thou hast like to a rock-built refuge stood

Above the blind and battling multitude:
In honoured poverty thy voice did weave
Songs consecrate to truth and liberty, –
Deserting these, thou leavest me to grieve,
Thus having been, that thou shouldst cease to be.

Like Hazlitt, Shelley turns the 'Intimations of Immortality' ode back upon its author. He begins by acknowledging that Wordsworth is *the* 'Poet of Nature'. Shelley shares his sorrow at the passing of childhood joys, first love and even friendship (mention of which might have been inspired by London literary gossip about Wordsworth's falling-out with Coleridge). But he cannot forgive Wordsworth's rejection of his commitment to 'truth and liberty'. He honours the young poet who had high ideals and no money. The Distributor of Stamps for the County of Westmorland, in his gentleman's residence at Rydal, on the brink of campaigning for the Tories, has – as a poet – ceased to be.

In April 1819, Wordsworth finally published (after much hesitation and revision) his long narrative poem *Peter Bell*, which he had recited to Hazlitt two decades earlier, at the time of *Lyrical Ballads*. Before it even appeared, Keats's friend J. H. Reynolds published a parody of it, including such delicious stanzas as

I do doat on my dear wife,
On the linnet, on the worm,
I can see sweet written salads
Growing in the Lyric Ballads,
And always find them green and firm.[4]

The dig at Wordsworth's uxoriousness hints at insider knowledge. The squib was furnished, naturally, with a preface (and a 'supplementary essay') that mercilessly mocked Wordsworth's pretentiousness in writing analyses of his own work and the egotism that had become increasingly apparent to all the 'Cockneys'. Not to mention his poor sales:

It is now a period of one-and-twenty years since I first wrote some of the most perfect compositions (except certain pieces I have written in my later days) that ever dropped from poetical pen. My heart hath been right and powerful all its years. I never thought an evil or a weak thought in my life. It has been my aim and my achievement to deduce moral thunder from buttercups, daisies, celandines . . . Out of sparrows' eggs I have hatched great truths, and with sextons' barrows have I wheeled into human hearts, piles of the weightiest philosophy . . . My Ballads are the noblest pieces of verse in the whole range of English poetry: and I take this opportunity of telling the world I am a great man. Mr Milton was also a great man. Ossian was a blind old fool. Copies of my previous works may be had in any numbers, by application at my publisher.[5]

Keats relished the wit of this and wrote a skittish review of the parody for *The Examiner*, trying to be kind to both his mischievous friend Reynolds and his flawed idol Wordsworth.[6]

Reynolds took a swipe at Wordsworth's political sell-out by way of a reference to his 'independent stamp (of whch Stamps I am proud to be a Distributor)', but his primary target was the apparent banality (along with the jingling rhymes) of the real *Peter Bell*, which he must have glimpsed in proof.[7] The publication of the parody did indeed lead to some confusion among readers and reviewers as to which was the real poem and which the pretend. The sad truth is that Wordsworth was publishing the poem too late in the day. Back in the period of *Lyrical Ballads*, it was a bold experiment to write about the need for kindness and the bond between humankind and nature by way of a story about a man who beats an ass, then learns from the beast to feel that 'The heart of man's a holy thing'.[8] In the robust literary culture of the Regency – when boxing and satire were all the rage – it was asking for trouble to publish such stanzas as

> Towards the gentle Ass he springs,
> And up about his neck he climbs;
> In loving words he talks to him,
> He kisses, kisses face and limb, –
> He kisses him a thousand times![9]

Leigh Hunt called the poem 'another didactic little horror of Mr Wordsworth's, founded on the bewitching principles of fear, bigotry, and diseased impulse'.[10]

Shelley, meanwhile, could not resist writing a further parody, 'Peter Bell the Third', in which Peter is a double for Wordsworth himself. The first Peter is 'antenatal', a mocking of the 'Immortality' ode's idea of pre-existence. The second Peter is 'polygamic', a sharp thrust at Wordsworth's household of devoted women – Henry Crabb Robinson returned from a visit to Rydal Mount in 1816 and told Mary Lamb that 'he never saw a man so happy in *three wives* as Mr Wordsworth is'.[11] The third Peter is damned for his political servility: 'Lo, Peter in Hell's Grosvenor square, / A footman in the Devil's service!' This was hardly fair to Sir George Beaumont, at whose Grosvenor Square house Wordsworth often stayed when he was in London – his patronage was not predicated upon a political *quid pro quo* in the way that the Lowthers' gift of the stamp distributorship led to Wordsworth's electioneering *Addresses to the Freeholders of Westmorland*.

By the end of the poem, Peter is doubly damned as he receives his 'sinecure' from a cheating Lord. Shelley sent his satire to his publisher from Italy, but it did not appear in print, not least for fear of a libel action. The harshest aspect of the poem is not so much the political knockabout as the accusation that Wordsworth 'had as much imagination / As a pint-pot' because he could never 'fancy' any situation other than that in which he stood himself. Shelley's accusation is that Wordsworth's high claims for imagination, and his distinction between that faculty and the 'fancy', are just another example of his egotism. The poem also passes a cruel but just judgment on what Wordsworth's poetry was becoming:

> Peter was dull – he was at first
>   Dull – O, so dull – so very dull!
> Whether he talked, wrote, or rehearsed –
> Still with this dulness was he cursed –
>   Dull – beyond all conception – dull.[12]

★

Shelley's friend Lord Byron made a similar accusation that the later poetry of Wordsworth was boring. His attitude to Wordsworth was as paradoxical as everything else about him. *Childe Harold's Pilgrimage*, the poem that made Byron famous, would not have been possible without the Lake Poets. There are moments when Childe Harold, who is indistinguishable from Byron himself, sounds exactly like the Wanderer in *The Excursion*:

> I live not in myself, but I become
> Portion of that around me; and to me
> High mountains are a feeling, but the hum
> Of human cities torture.

Apart from the fact that 'The pure bosom of [the] nursing lake' that inspires the sentiment is located in Switzerland rather than Westmorland, lines such as the following are pure Wordsworth:

> Are not the mountains, waves, and skies, a part
> Of me and of my soul, as I of them?
> Is not the love of these deep in my heart
> With a pure passion?[13]

John Wilson, the maverick minor Lake Poet turned bruising critic, said that 'it was Wordsworth who first taught Byron to look at a mountain'.[14] When a correspondent asked Wordsworth about Byron's 'poetical obligations' to him, he replied that they were 'most apparent in the 3rd canto of Childe Harold; not so much in particular expressions, tho' there is no want of these, as in the tone (*assumed* rather than natural) of enthusiastic admiration of Nature, and a sensibility to her influences'. For evidence of the influence, which Wordsworth sometimes suggested amounted to actual plagiarism, he said that one would need to do no more than compare this section of *Childe Harold's Pilgrimage* with 'the blank verse poem on the river Wye'.[15]

When challenged, Byron acknowledged the debt, blaming Shelley for dosing him with Wordsworth, 'even to nausea', when they were in Switzerland together. Wordsworth, he said, 'had once a feeling for Nature, which he carried almost to a deification of it: – that's why Shelley liked his poetry'.[16] What was galling to Wordsworth was that *Lyrical Ballads* had sold fewer than 2,000 copies in nearly twenty years, whereas the first instalment of *Childe Harold* sold 13,000 in a year and the third canto was launched in an edition of 12,000, more than twice the sales of all his own publications put together.

While the Romantic Byron owed a considerable obligation

to Wordsworth, the anti-Romantic Byron pilloried him repeatedly. His satire *English Bards and Scotch Reviewers*, written out
of allegiance to the witty rhyming couplets of Dryden and
Pope, guyed the Lake Poets quite unmercifully: 'The simple
Wordsworth' was 'dull', an 'apostate from poetic rule' who 'both
by precept and example, shows / That prose is verse, and verse
is merely prose'.[17] As for Coleridge, he was the master of 'turgid
ode and tumid stanza'. This teasing vein of anti-Laker sentiment
continued in Byron's sprawling and hilarious comic epic *Don
Juan*, which began with an ironic dedication to Poet Laureate
Southey:

> Bob Southey! You're a poet – Poet Laureate,
>   And representative of all the race;
> Although 'tis true that you turn'd out a Tory at
>   Last, – yours has lately been a common case: –
> And now, my epic renegade! what are ye at,
> With all the Lakers in and out of place?[18]

'And Wordsworth has his place in the excise', Byron adds: he
too has become placeman.[19] He took to calling him 'Turdsworth
the grand metaquizzical poet'.[20] And in the first canto of *Don
Juan*, he set his sights on a passage in *The Excursion* that has the
eighteen-year-old Wanderer 'Communing with the glorious
universe' in the manner of an adolescent falling in love for the
first time ('Accumulated feeling pressed his heart . . . he was
o'erpowered / By . . . first virgin passion'). He parodied the
sentiment with laser-sharp wit:

> Young Juan wander'd by the glassy brooks,
>   Thinking unutterable things; he threw
> Himself at length within the leafy nooks

Where the wild branch of the cork forest grew;
There poets find materials for their books,
    And every now and then we read them through,
So that their plan and prosody are eligible,
Unless, like Wordsworth, they prove unintelligible.

He, Juan (and not Wordsworth), so pursued
    His self-communion with his own high soul,
Until his mighty heart, in its great mood,
    Had mitigated part, though not the whole
Of its disease; he did the best he could
    With things not very subject to control,
And turn'd, without perceiving his condition,
Like Coleridge, into a metaphysician.

He thought about himself, and the whole earth,
    Of man the wonderful, and of the stars,
And how the deuce they ever could have birth;
    And then he thought of earthquakes, and of wars,
How many miles the moon might have in girth,
    Of air-balloons, and of the many bars
To perfect knowledge of the boundless skies;
And then he thought of Donna Julia's eyes.

In thoughts like these true wisdom may discern
    Longings sublime, and aspirations high,
Which some are born with, but the most part learn
    To plague themselves withal, they know not why:
'Twas strange that one so young should thus concern
    His brain about the action of the sky;
If *you* think 'twas philosophy that this did,
I can't help thinking puberty assisted.

The parody is so deadly because it captures the essence of Wordsworth's language, from his taste for negatives ('unutterable things') to his delight in 'nooks' to the 'huge balloon' of the first stanza of *Peter Bell* to the 'longings sublime' of 'Tintern Abbey' and the 'mighty heart' of 'Westminster Bridge'. Byron also accused Keats's luxuriant verse of being a form of mental masturbation. For him, the poetry that we call 'Romantic' was simply not very grown-up.

'It is satisfactory to reflect', Byron told a friend, 'that where a man becomes a hireling and loses his mental independence, he loses also the faculty of writing well.'[21] Whether or not this is true as a general principle, it became a well-grounded consensus with regard to Wordsworth.

★

Byron died in 1824 at the age of thirty-six, on his way to fight for the freedom of Greece. Imagine an alternative history in which it had been Wordsworth who died at that age. Suppose that one day in January or February 1807, he woke early, while his 'three wives' were still asleep, put on his cherished skates, and cut his way across a pond on the Coleorton estate, only to misjudge the thickness of the ice, to hear a crack and to go down, like his brother, to a watery grave. The two-volume *Poems* of 1807 would have been safely at press, ready to join *Lyrical Ballads* in the public domain. Once they had overcome their initial grief, the 'three wives' would have seen the unpublished poems into print, as Mary Shelley would do with the work of her husband after his twin-mast schooner the *Don Juan* went down in the Gulf of La Spezia in 1822, drowning him a few weeks before his thirtieth birthday (with Leigh Hunt's copy of Keats's poems doubled open in his jacket pocket). Dorothy, Mary and Sara would have published the 1805 *Prelude*, instead of

Wordsworth spending nearly forty years revising it, almost always for the worse. And they would have retrieved the manuscripts of 'The Ruined Cottage', 'The Pedlar', 'Home at Grasmere' and 'Salisbury Plain'. The quarrel with Coleridge would never have happened, and Hazlitt and the Cockney School would have promoted these posthumously published works without any of the equivocations arising from the political apostasy.

What would be the downside of this hypothetical history? The sonnet 'Surprised by joy' would never have been written – but then Catharine would never have been born and Wordsworth would not have had the agony of witnessing Tommy's death. We would not have those swathes of *The Excursion* that were so soporific to George Borrow. We would not have the pumped-up patriotism of the 'Thanksgiving Ode': 'To Thee the *exterminating sword* is given. / Dread mark of approbation, justly gained!' We would not have the forced exclamations of the sequence of poems, mostly sonnets, published in 1822 as *Memorials of a Tour on the Continent*, undertaken with Mary and Dorothy two years before: 'Not (like his great compeers) indignantly / Doth DANUBE spring to life!' We would not have the sonnet sequence *Ecclesiastical Sketches*, published the same year: 'Diluvian truths, and patriarchal lore: / Haughty the Bard; – can these meek doctrines blight / His transports? wither his heroic strains?' ('Trepidation of the Druids'). We would not have the 1835 volume *Yarrow Revisited, and Other Poems, Composed (two excepted) during a Tour in Scotland, and on the English Border, in the Autumn of 1831*: 'Tradition, be thou mute! Oblivion, throw / Thy veil, in mercy, o'er the records hung / Round strath and mountain' ('In the Sound of Mull'). The damage to the annals of the best that has been thought and known in the world – Matthew Arnold's definition of culture – would not be great.

Other than 'Surprised by joy' and one or two elegiac poems

in *Yarrow Revisited*, the only genuine loss in our 'what if?' scenario would be certain parts of *The River Duddon*, which was published in 1820 along with 'Vaudracour and Julia' and the prose guide to the Lakes. This was Wordsworth's first genuine sonnet *sequence*; it follows the course of one of the lesser Lake District rivers from its source to the sea. It was his miniaturized version of Coleridge's never-written project 'The Brook', which was imagined back in the Somerset year as an attempt to improve upon Cowper's *The Task* by providing 'equal room for description, incident and impassioned reflections on men, nature, and society', but with greater 'connection to the parts and unity to the whole', achieved by tracing a stream from origin to end point.

The analogy between human life and a river had been a motif in the work of the poets who revived the sonnet form in the generation before Wordsworth and Coleridge: Thomas Warton addressed a sonnet 'To the River Lodon', while William Bowles's 'To the River Itchin' inspired Coleridge's sonnet on his 'sweet birthplace', 'To the River Otter'.[22] Wordsworth told Isabella Fenwick that he had many 'affecting remembrances' of times spent on the banks of the Duddon, but the sequence gives little sense of these.[23] In most of the poems, Wordsworth is in apostrophic and public mode, using the associations of various buildings beside the Duddon to evoke a history that veers from 'the imperial Bird of Rome' to the 'new rites' of the Reformation. He also describes various geographic features, local traditions, and customs such as sheep-washing; in one pairing of sonnets he swings from thoughts about the biblical deluge to the imagining of another, grander river, the Oroonoko: '*There* would the Indian answer with a smile / Aim'd at the White Man's ignorance, the while / Of the Great Waters telling, how they rose'.[24] Most of this is dispensable late Wordsworth. Just occasionally, though, the voice is quieter and there are glimmers of personal memory:

Whence that low voice? – A whisper from the heart,

That told of days long past when here I roved

With friends and kindred tenderly beloved;

Some who had early mandates to depart,

Yet are allowed to steal my path athwart

By Duddon's side; once more do we unite,

Once more beneath the kind Earth's tranquil light;

And smother'd joys into new being start.[25]

This sonnet ends with the relentless march of 'Time' stalled for a moment by the figure of 'Memory', who is personified as 'light and free, / As golden locks of birch': it has been suggested that this could be a veiled recollection of a real-life original for 'Lucy', a young woman, 'tenderly beloved' but with an 'early mandate' to depart her earthly life, encountered when the young Wordsworth wandered by the Duddon, perhaps during his first summer vacation from Cambridge.[26]

The real loss to the Wordsworth canon in our imaginary scenario would be the concluding sonnet of the *River Duddon* sequence. Here he recaptured the voice of the 'Immortality' ode, in which looking *backward* – to childhood, to his own past, to history – becomes a way of looking forward beyond the vanishing of death to the service that a human life and a body of spiritual ideas expressed in memorable words may offer to the future:

For *backward*, Duddon! as I cast my eyes,

I see what was, and is, and will abide;

Still glides the Stream, and shall for ever glide;

The Form remains, the Function never dies;

While *we*, the brave, the mighty, and the wise,

We Men, who in our morn of youth defied

The elements, must vanish; – be it so!

Enough, if something from our hands have power
To live, and act, and serve the future hour;
And if, as tow'rd the silent tomb we go,
Thro' love, thro' hope, and faith's transcendant dower,
We feel that we are greater than we know.[27]

In this sonnet, for almost the last time, Wordsworth was writing with a full complement of what Hazlitt called 'gusto', power or passion defining his object.

In the third of the 'Essays upon Epitaphs' written for Coleridge's *The Friend*, Wordsworth reflected on the power of language:

Words are too awful an instrument for good and evil to be trifled with: they hold above all other external powers a dominion over thoughts. If words be not (recurring to a metaphor before used) an incarnation of the thought but only a clothing for it, then surely will they prove an ill gift . . . Language, if it do not uphold, and feed, and leave in quiet, like the power of gravitation or the air we breathe, is a counter-spirit, unremittingly and noiselessly at work to derange, to subvert, to lay waste, to vitiate, and to dissolve.[28]

In the late 1790s and early 1800s, William Wordsworth incarnated his thoughts in words more powerful and aptly chosen than those of any other English poet save Shakespeare. His best poems uphold and feed and leave in quiet the spirit of the reader. His unremitting later voice, with rare exceptions such as this concluding Duddon sonnet, was a counter-spirit which laid waste his powers, subverted his ideals and vitiated his reputation among the creative spirits of the next generation.

★

What went wrong? It cannot be a coincidence that both Wordsworth and Coleridge started writing their best poetry when they met each other, and that their verse declined in quality when they fell out. It can legitimately be argued that 'To William Wordsworth, composed on the night after his recitation of a Poem on the Growth of an Individual Mind' was Coleridge's last memorable poem, just as it can be argued that after 1806 there passed away a glory from Wordsworth's verse. The rise and fall of the relationship with Coleridge cannot, however, be the whole answer. After all, Dorothy, the third member of the triumvirate, continued to be beside Wordsworth, inspiring him, giving him eyes.

There can be no simple answer to the question, but if we take seriously Wordsworth's claim that all *good* poetry comes from 'powerful feelings', a number of other factors become apparent. Wordsworth uncannily anticipates Sigmund Freud in all sorts of ways. Freud believed that desire and death, *Eros* and *Thanatos*, were the fundamental drivers of human psychology and especially of artistic creativity.

Thanatos: the deaths of Wordsworth's parents when he was a child, the deaths that he witnessed in Paris during the revolution, the death of his friend Raisley Calvert (which led to the legacy that freed him to write), the quasi-deaths of his separations – from Dorothy through most of his later childhood, from Annette when he left France, and from his daughter Caroline for the first ten years of her life. Freud would have said that the powerful feelings generated by these blows were *sublimated* into the intensely felt poetry of *The Prelude*, the Lucy and Mathew poems, 'The Ruined Cottage', 'Michael', 'Resolution and Independence' and the 'Immortality' ode.

Eros: for Wordsworth, France was a time of 'bliss' not only because of the revolution and the hope for a better world, but also because he was in love for the first time, and making love to Annette. As far as we know, he did not make love to another woman until he married Mary ten years later. For a man of strong passions to have gone from the age of twenty-two to that of thirty-two without having sex could not have been easy: Freud's analysis might have been that during these years Wordsworth *projected* his libido into his poetry. Once his desires were fulfilled in marriage – the intensity of the rediscovered love letters and the frequency of Mary's pregnancies suggests a very satisfactory sex life – the energy of his poetry was dissipated.

Could it have been that the price of a quiet life and a happy marriage was the extinction of those sparks of inspiration, moments of vision, spots of time, that had animated the decade between his time in France and the recollection of that time in the reading of *The Prelude*? More mundanely, perhaps he simply grew tired. He always had trouble sleeping. By 1810 there were five children under the age of seven in the house. Nights would often have been interrupted. And his legs were becoming wearied from all the walking, he had pains in his side and his stomach, headaches and failing eyesight. Besides, he had been writing poetry for so many years that it was easy to turn out line after line of pentameter, walking up and down the gravel path in a regular rhythm, as a matter of routine, not of 'powerful feeling'. And after John's death, then Catharine's and Tommy's, what was there left to say about love, about grief?

His muse returned one last time, again in the context of multiple losses. Sir George Beaumont died in February 1827. Wordsworth wrote to one of the good friends of his later life, the poet Samuel Rogers: 'nearly five and twenty years have I known him intimately, and neither myself nor my family ever received a cold or unkind look from him'.[29] Raisley Calvert's brother William, who had overseen the legacy, died two years later. Two years after that, in the company of his daughter Dora, Wordsworth visited Sir Walter Scott at Abbotsford for the last time. He knew that they would never meet again: the 'Wizard of the North', as Wordsworth called him, was severely ill and about to leave, as Keats had done in his last illness, for Italy. Wordsworth cranked out a ponderous sonnet 'On the Departure of Sir Walter Scott from Abbotsford, for Naples'. The great Scotsman died the next year.

Coleridge died in Highgate in July 1834. They had reconciled sufficiently to go on a tour of Germany, Belgium and the Netherlands together, also with Dora, in 1828, but they saw little of each other in the later years and their correspondence had long since dried up. Then in December 1834, Charles Lamb fell and grazed his face, contracting an infection that killed him. Felicia Hemans, one of the several women poets whom Wordsworth greatly admired, succumbed to dropsy the following year, in her early forties. A writer for whom the notion of an English 'home' was a recurring trope, she had published shortly before her death a 'Remembrance of Grasmere', in which the place is seen as an isle 'of the blest' because it was Wordsworth's home.[30]

On 23 June 1835, a month after Hemans' passing, Sara Hutchinson died of rheumatic fever. She had lived with the family for the best part of thirty years.[31] 'Her loss', Wordsworth wrote, is 'irreparable to us all. – It is astounding to me that she should have gone before my beloved sister who is very feeble and suffers much at times – Her departed friend had little or no acute pain after the fever left – O – What a heavenly expression was on her face after the breath had left her body.'[32]

The late autumn brought news of another poet's death, that of James Hogg, the 'Ettrick Shepherd' whom Wordsworth had met on his Scottish tour two decades earlier. Hogg had been a

visitor at Rydal Mount and a frequent subject in correspondence
with Scott. Within days, Wordsworth had composed an elegy in
memory of the procession of poets who had gone to the grave.
He remembered Hogg guiding him to the banks of the river
Yarrow. He remembered Scott – 'the mighty Minstrel' – taking
him to the same place on his later tour (in so doing, he was
nodding to his own poems about Yarrow unvisited, visited and
revisited). He remembered George Crabbe, with whom he had
once walked on Hampstead Heath. And Hemans. And Lamb,
'the frolic and the gentle'. And, of course, Coleridge, 'the rapt
one, of the Godlike forehead'.

> Like clouds that rake the mountain-summits,
> Or waves that own no curbing hand,
> How fast has brother followed brother,
> From sunshine to the sunless land![33]

This poem was indeed a 'spontaneous overflow of powerful feelings'. Wordsworth's niece Elizabeth (known as 'Ebba') Hutchinson
was staying at Rydal Mount when they read in the newspaper
that Hogg had died. Deeply affected, Wordsworth left the room.
Half an hour later, he came back with 'some lines which he had
just composed'. He asked her to transcribe them for him. The
working title was 'The Graves of the Poets'.[34] The transcript is
lost; the title was changed to 'Extempory Verses' for the publication of the poem at the end of the month, in the newspaper in
which Wordsworth had read of Hogg's death. When including
it in a new edition of his collected poems two years later,
Wordsworth called it 'Extempore Effusion upon the Death of
James Hogg'.

It was not, though, entirely extempore. The emotion was
recollected in tranquillity: Wordsworth put it through nine

manuscript versions and four published texts. Clearly, he cared a great deal about the poem. And yet, there is something detached about it. He was never close to Hogg, let alone Crabbe. The deaths of Coleridge and Lamb, who meant so much to him, are passed over very rapidly. There is an evasion at its core. Brother poets follow each other to the grave, Felicia Hemans becoming an honorary man. What Wordsworth could not confront was the death of his sister-in-law, Coleridge's Asra, his own most important amanuensis, and an occasional poet herself. The purpose of Ebba Hutchinson's stay at Rydal Mount was to comfort and support her aunt Mary, and Dorothy, who were both very ill in the months following Sara's death.

Another year passed before Wordsworth could write an elegy for Sara. It took the form of a sonnet, simply entitled 'November 1836'. It portrays Sara as 'Death's bride', her 'heaven-revealing smile' serving as a perpetual reminder of the hope of eternal life, a rekindling of 'the lamp of faith'. The sonnet closes:

And let my spirit in that power divine
Rejoice, as, through that power, it ceased to mourn.[35]

Somehow, though, the poem fails to move the reader in the way that we are moved by the powerful feeling of such lines as

few could know
When Lucy ceas'd to be;
But she is in her Grave, and oh!
The difference to me.

The pious assurance of salvation extrapolated from the corpse of Sara Hutchinson stifles the release of grief. The heart does not surge as it does at the end of 'Surprised by joy'. Shelley grieved

in his sonnet that Wordsworth should 'cease to be' as a result of his political turn. But perhaps the real reason why he 'ceased to be' as a poet of powerful feeling was that a time came when he 'ceased to mourn': he had suffered so many losses that a slumber sealed his spirit and his writing came to have no motion, no force.

★

The New Englander Ralph Waldo Emerson, on the brink of his career as philosopher of 'transcendentalism', visited Rydal Mount in 1832. He arrived to find 'a plain, elderly, white-haired man, not prepossessing, and disfigured by green goggles'. Wordsworth had for a long time worried about his eyes. He believed that he was going blind – perhaps it was his destiny, given that he was recognized by himself and many others as England's second Milton.

He was opinionated by now. He took it upon himself to lecture the American about his own country: 'they needed a civil war in America, to teach the necessity of knitting the social ties stronger'. Americans were vulgar, though that wasn't important. It came from 'the pioneer state of things'. No, the real problem with Americans was that they were 'too much given to the making of money'. The conversation turned to literature. Emerson was a great admirer of the work of Thomas Carlyle, whom he had just visited in Edinburgh. Wordsworth 'said he thought him sometimes insane'. The sage of Rydal continued to lecture the future sage of Concord. He heartily abused Goethe's novel *Wilhelm Meister*, which Carlyle had translated into English: 'It was full of all manner of fornication. It was like the crossing of flies in the air. He had never gone further than the first part; so disgusted was he that he threw the book across the room.' Carlyle was the most obscure of writers. 'Even Mr Coleridge wrote more clearly, though he

had always wished Coleridge would write more to be understood.'

Wordsworth then led Emerson out into his garden and showed
him the gravel walk upon which he had composed his verses in
his head. His eyes were very inflamed, but he said that it was
no loss, 'except for reading, because he never writes prose, and
of poetry he carries even hundreds of lines in his head before
writing them'. He then recited from memory three sonnets on
Fingal's Cave, which he had written upon returning from his
latest Scottish tour. Emerson told him that 'Tintern Abbey'
appeared to be the public favourite among his poems, but that
more philosophically minded readers preferred the first books of
The Excursion and the sonnets. 'Yes, they are better', said
Wordsworth, perhaps because he regretted the perceived pantheism
of the Wye Valley poem. 'He preferred such of his poems as
touched the affections, to any others; for whatever is didactic
– what theories of society, and so on – might perish quickly;
but whatever combined a truth with an affection was good today
and good forever': this at least was an opinion that would be
borne out by the afterlife of his voluminous output.

He walked with Emerson 'a good part of a mile, talking, and
ever and anon stopping short to impress the word or the verse'.
He parted 'with great kindness, and returned across the fields'.

Emerson was greatly disappointed in the old man, yet he held
fast to his belief that 'the genius of Wordsworth' was the 'exceptional fact of the period'. He regretted that Wordsworth's
'temperament was not more liquid and musical' and that 'he has
written longer than he was inspired'. 'But for the rest, he has
no competitor': 'He had no master but nature and solitude . . .
His verse is the voice of sanity in a worldly and ambitious age.'[36]

★

Southey died in 1843 and Wordsworth was offered the position
of Poet Laureate. More than a decade had passed since he had
written to Benjamin Robert Haydon saying that 'the Muse has
forsaken me'.[37] He attributed his drying-up to 'the villainous
aspect of the times', by which he meant the cause of Catholic
Emancipation and the progress towards the Great Reform Act
that widened the franchise, liberal political developments that he
heartily opposed (so vigorously indeed that his family feared for
his health). Initially, he declined to accept the Laureateship. He
had nothing left to write. When he was told that there would
be no obligation to write anything, and that Queen Victoria
particularly wanted him to accept, he did so. The previous year,
he had accepted a civil list pension. Now he was bowing his
knee before the throne of Majesty.

Robert Browning, a disciple of Shelley and the leading avant-
garde poet of the day, was disgusted. 'Just for a handful of silver
he left us', he wrote, 'Just for a riband to stick in his coat':

> We that had loved him so, followed him, honoured him,
>   Lived in his mild and magnificent eye,
> Learned his great language, caught his clear accents,
>   Made him our pattern to live and to die!
> Shakespeare was of us, Milton was for us,
>   Burns, Shelley, were with us, – they watch from their
>   graves!
> He alone breaks from the van and the freemen,
>   He alone sinks to the rear and the slaves![38]

The later Wordsworth 'boasts his quiescence'. He bids the masses
to crouch whereas Shelley and Byron bade them to 'aspire'. This
is not entirely fair. During the political turmoil of 1848, when
the Chartists were agitating for the rights of the working man,

Wordsworth (despite his opposition to the Great Reform Act
sixteen years earlier) said that he had a great deal of the Chartist
about him – by which he meant a desire for the common people
to have their voice.[39] But the old spirit of liberty and independence hardly ever comes across in his later writing. 'Blot out his
name', Browning laments, 'record one lost soul more'. Wordsworth
is made the epitome of all who turn from youthful idealism to
aged conservatism and complacency: 'Never glad confident
morning again!'

Browning called his poem 'The Lost Leader'.

A MEDICINE FOR
MY STATE OF MIND

For Wordsworth, the year after the Battle of Waterloo was marked by a death, a marriage, and a birth. His brother Richard, the lawyer who handled all the family's financial affairs, became ill and died. Sorting out his tangled affairs cost William considerable time and energy, though far less of the raw grief with which he had been afflicted by John's drowning a decade before.

There was a happier event in Paris. It had been difficult to keep in touch with Annette and Caroline during the long years of the Napoleonic Wars, but in 1812 Wordsworth received a letter from a prisoner-of-war camp in Oswestry, Shropshire. It came from a French officer called Eustace Baudouin, who had seen action at the siege of Tarragona, then been captured by

Spanish guerrillas and handed over to the British. He announced that his brother, Jean-Baptiste, was engaged to be married to Wordsworth's daughter Caroline, and he asked Wordsworth to try to secure his release from the camp. In June 1814, when the war seemed to be over, Eustace Baudouin was free to visit Rydal Mount. Wordsworth took him over to Greta Hall to visit Southey, who had a particular interest in the history of the Peninsular War. Southey considered him a charming young man, who 'had grace enough to acknowledge that the Spanish business was an unjust war'.[1]

During the visit to Rydal, plans were made for Dorothy to attend Caroline's wedding to Baudouin's brother in Paris – a presence that Annette and Caroline very much wanted. But Napoleon's escape from Elba and the resumption of hostilities meant that the wedding had to be postponed. It finally took place in the spring of 1816. A plan for Caroline to visit Rydal before her marriage was mooted, but proved impossible to arrange. Nor was Dorothy able to attend the wedding. Nine months later, however, when Caroline gave birth to a daughter, Wordsworth's first grandchild, she was named Dorothée. Wordsworth stood godfather, by proxy.

He gave Caroline a marriage settlement of £30 per year, the equivalent of about £3,000. The following year, he asked Southey to call on the family in Paris while en route to Italy. Southey arrived at the address that Wordsworth had given him and was greeted by a young woman who spoke no English and did not know his name. He explained in his broken French that he was a friend of Wordsworth's and she immediately said that she was his daughter. 'We had a tete a tete of about an hour long very much like a scene in a sentimental comedy', Southey reported to his wife; 'She is a very interesting young woman, with much more of natural feeling than of French manners, and intriguingly like John Wordsworth, much more than his own sister. The little French Dorothy is very like her mother, a sweet infant, in perfect health and good humour.'[2] Caroline wept a good deal in the course of their conversation.

Three years later, Wordsworth returned to France and retraced the steps he had taken with Jones thirty years before, this time in the company of his wife and his sister. On their way back from the Alps, they stayed in Paris for a month. Wordsworth finally got to meet Helen Maria Williams, whom he had narrowly missed upon his arrival in the early days of the revolution. And he revisited old haunts. The sometime revolutionary sympathizer wrote to his Tory patron Lord Lonsdale: 'The exterior of Paris is much changed since I last visited it in 1792. I miss many antient Buildings, particularly the Temple, where the poor king and his family were so long confined. That memorable spot where the Jacobin Club was held, has also disappeared.'[3]

The trip was also an opportunity to see Caroline and Annette, and to meet his granddaughters – a second baby girl had been born. They took lodgings in the street where the Baudouins lived. On their first morning in the city, they drank chocolate and tea in a café. Mary then returned to their lodgings, while William and Dorothy called on his French family at their home. Later, they all met at the Louvre. To judge from surviving accounts, it was a warm and happy visit, though Mary's diary is silent on the subject of her impression of Annette. Henry Crabb Robinson, who was with them, felt that it was inappropriate for Caroline constantly to refer to Wordsworth as father.

In 1837, Wordsworth would see his French family one final time, when he went on yet another tour, this time on the way to Italy, again with Crabb Robinson. He told Dorothy that the Baudouins were all well, and had made 'a thousand kind inquiries' after her.[4] It is doubtful that he would have told them what

Dorothy's condition was by then. Once again, Paris was a city
of memory, this time evoked via his recurring metaphor of a
river:

> What shall I say of Paris? Many splendid edifices and some
> fine streets have been added since I first saw it at the close
> of the year --91. But I have had little feeling to spare for
> novelties, my heart and mind having been awakened every-
> where to sad and strange recollections of what was then passing
> and of subsequent events, which have either occurred in this
> vast City, or which have flowed from it as their source.[5]

★

Dorothy wrote a lengthy journal account of the 1820 continental
tour. They seriously considered publishing some of her travel
writings. The plan faltered, so her extraordinary talent as a writer
remained unknown to the public for many years. That changed,
however, because of Thomas De Quincey.

There had been a falling-out during De Quincey's tenancy of
Dove Cottage in the Regency years. This was largely because
Wordsworth — for all his talk about the integrity of the ordinary
people of the dales — had taken the snobbish view that his sometime worshipper should not have begun a love affair with Margaret
Simpson, the (very beautiful) teenage daughter of a local farmer.
She became pregnant and bore him a son; De Quincey married
her the following year. They had seven further children and were
very happy together. Wordsworth's disapproval was, to say the
least, hypocritical in the light of his own relationship with Annette
Vallon.

By the 1830s, De Quincey, who was frequently in debt as well
as addicted to opium, was eking out a living as a journalist. In
1839, he published a series of biographical essays about Wordsworth

in *Tait's Edinburgh Magazine*. The first of them credited Wordsworth
with the 'regeneration of our national poetry' and told the story
of how De Quincey himself had become obsessed with his work
while he was an Oxford undergraduate, made his several attempts
to pluck up the courage to visit his hero, and eventually been
welcomed to the cottage in Town End.[6]

De Quincey went on to give the first detailed published account
of Wordsworth's life, including his time in France. Tactfully, he
did not mention Annette and Caroline. His account of the poetry
is a judicious balance of criticism and praise, including some
suggestions as to the reasons for Wordsworth's literary decline –
arrogance, too much money, marriage that got in the way of his
friendship with Coleridge and, by implication, with De Quincey
himself. For the Wordsworths, the unforgivable thing was the
revelation of certain personal details. The fact, for example, that
on one occasion Wordsworth 'became a martyr to some nervous
affection' and that the 'remedy, or palliation' of his friends and
family was to play cards with him. De Quincey could not forbear
to smile at the idea of the grand and earnest poet playing *cards*.
He had the information from Dorothy, so it must have been true.
But it was a breach of confidence to publish the story.

He made an even more indiscreet revelation about Dorothy.
From the beginning of their acquaintance, he wrote, 'Even her
very utterance and enunciation often, or rather generally, suffered
in point of steadiness or clearness, from the agitation of her
excessive organic sensibility, and, perhaps, from some morbid
irritability of the nerves.' Like Charles Lamb, she sometimes
stammered. He admired her immensely because it was she who
'couched' her brother's eye 'to the sense of beauty' and 'human-
ized' him into charity. But he also revealed that in later life she
suffered from severe 'nervous depression'.[7]

This, he suggested, was the consequence of her never having

become a published author, despite the great merits of her journals. Had her extreme 'sensibility', her talents and energies, been channelled into a professional career as a writer, she would have been fulfilled and healthy. Wordsworth took grave offence at this line of argument. He regarded his sister as a woman who wanted her life and her writings to remain private – perhaps forgetting that back in 1823, when Samuel Rogers proposed that her *Recollections of a Tour in Scotland* should be published, she had told him that she might be willing to 'sacrifice her privacy' if her earnings were in excess of £200.[8] More immediately, Wordsworth did not want the world to know that his sister was suffering from severe mental illness.

★

She had often been ill with migraine-like headaches, pains in the bowels, vomiting, hot and cold fevers. Increasingly, she came to rely on opium, taken in the form of around twenty drops of laudanum per day. In 1835, mental as well as physical symptoms began to appear. Early in the year she was left with Dora at Rydal when William and Mary went to London in order to sort out an employment opportunity for their youngest child, Willy, who was now twenty-four. Dorothy fell into a depression.

Then she was badly affected by Wordsworth's decision to stop paying the annual allowance to Caroline in France, releasing himself from his obligation by way of a single lump sum. Annette wrote to Dorothy, asking her to try to persuade her brother to change his mind. And then came Sara's death. Wordsworth said that it gave Dorothy a shock from which she never recovered. Since her sister-in-law's demise, he wrote that August, Dorothy had been 'so confused as to passing events, that we have no distinct knowledge of what she may actually have to support in the way of physical pain'.[9]

She became incontinent. She overate. She would burst into fits of rage that terrified strangers. She tore at the caps of her nurses and beat them in the face. Crabb Robinson was his habitual direct self: 'Entre nous,' he wrote to his brother in November 1835, 'poor Miss W: is sinking into imbecility.'[10] She lost her short-term memory, but could still recite swathes of poetry by heart. Here is Crabb Robinson again, after a visit to Rydal Mount in 1841:

> Her mind feeble but she talks nothing absolutely insane or irrational, but she has so little command of herself that she cannot restrain the most unseemly noises, blowing loudly and making a nondescript sound more shrill than the cry of a partridge and a turkey. From this she is to be drawn only by a request to repeat Verses which she does with affecting sweetness – She is fond of repeating her own pretty lines Which way does the wind blow?[11]

All her symptoms are those of dementia, almost certainly of the kind that is now identified as Alzheimer's.

The poem that Dorothy held in her brain through the darkness of her mental deterioration, 'What way does the Wind come?', was one of the very few among her verse compositions that was published in her lifetime. Wordsworth included it among the 'Poems referring to the Period of Childhood' that opened his two-volume collected works of 1815. It was given the title 'ADDRESS TO A CHILD, *During a boisterous Winter Evening. By a female Friend of the Author*'. He brought another of her poems, 'Floating Island', into print in his 1842 volume *Poems, chiefly of Early and Late Years*, over the initials 'D. W.' That volume also included a poem by Sara Hutchinson, addressed from her sickbed to a robin outside the window. Wordsworth added the attribution 'by a deceased female Relative'.

'Floating Island' is perhaps the best of Dorothy's poems. A manuscript version of it, with the fuller title 'Floating Island at Hawkshead, an Incident in the Schemes of Nature', is to be found in a sequence of lyrics that she wrote out in her commonplace book during a period of illness, under the heading 'Sick-bed Consolations composed during the Spring of the year 1832'.[12] It tells of a 'slip of earth' that, eroded by the lapping waves, has broken from the bank of Esthwaite Water and is seen floating on the surface of the lake, creating a little home for an array of creatures:

> Food, shelter, safety, there they find;
> There berries ripen, flowerets bloom;
> There insects live their lives, and die;
> A peopled world it is; in size a tiny room.[13]

We might describe the floating island as a miniature ecosystem. It is also a metaphor for the power of memory to create those imaginary ecosystems that we call poems. At the end of the lyric, the island has sunk, 'Yet the lost fragments shall remain / To fertilize some other ground'. The ground that they fertilize is the mind of Dorothy, as she lies on her sickbed. The recollection of the floating island is among her 'consolations', just as in another poem in her 1832 manuscript sequence, the memory of Tintern Abbey transports her from her confinement: 'No prisoner in this lowly room / I *saw* the green banks of the Wye'.[14]

Even as her dementia grew more severe, there would be flashes of clarity, in which she would remember the distant past, spontaneously recite lines of verse, or pick up from her brother as he spoke his poems aloud. Only rarely, though, was she able to write. Her last surviving letter from within the lifetime of her brother was addressed to the daughter whom he named after

her, but who was always known as Dora. It was written on 3
October 1837:

My dearest Dora

They say I must write a letter − and what shall it be? News
− news I must seek for news. My own thoughts are a wilderness − 'not pierceable by power of any star' − News then is
my resting-place − news! news!

　Poor Peggy Benson lies in Grasmere Church-yard beside
her once beautiful Mother. Fanny Haigh is gone to a better
world. My Friend Mrs Rawson has ended her ninety and two
years pilgrimage − and I have fought and fretted and striven
− and am here beside the fire. The Doves behind me at the
small window − the laburnum with its naked seed-pods shivers
before my window and the pine-trees rock from their base.
− More I cannot write so farewell! and may God bless you
and your kind good Friend Miss Fenwick to whom I send
love and all the best of wishes. − Yours ever more

Dorothy Wordsworth[15]

Her mind is a 'wilderness', possessed by thoughts of death, but
she is still able to recall a line of poetry from Spenser's *Faerie
Queene*. And to observe the laburnum and the pine trees outside
her window.

She lived for another seventeen years.

★

In the end, the only measure of a writer is their effect upon their
readers. Poetry was a palliative for Dorothy in her dementia, but
the therapeutic capacity of Wordsworth spread far beyond his family.

　John Stuart Mill was brought up on books, books and books.
His father, a noted economist and historian of British India,

sought to shape his child as a strict utilitarian in the mould of Jeremy Bentham. Mill's childhood was the very antithesis of Wordsworth's vision of an education in which books were forsaken for the knowledge that came from the vernal wood. Unsurprisingly, he suffered a nervous breakdown at the age of twenty. He seriously contemplated suicide.

The fifth chapter of his *Autobiography* gives a precise account of what psychiatrists now call a major depressive episode:

> In the autumn of 1826, I was in a dull state of nerves, such as everybody is occasionally liable to; unsusceptible to enjoyment or pleasurable excitement; one of those moods when what is pleasure at other times, becomes insipid or indifferent . . . In this frame of mind it occurred to me to put the question directly to myself: 'Suppose that all your objects in life were realized; that all the changes in institutions and opinions which you are looking forward to, could be completely effected at this very instant: would this be a great joy and happiness to you?' And an irrepressible self-consciousness distinctly answered, 'No!'[16]

The 'whole foundation' on which his education had been constructed fell down. He 'seemed to have nothing left to live for'. The clouds grew thicker as the months passed. Mill found himself in exactly the state described in Coleridge's 'Dejection', which he duly quoted when recording what he called the 'crisis in my mental history':

> A grief without a pang, void, dark and drear,
> A drowsy, stifled, unimpassioned grief,
> Which finds no natural outlet or relief
> In word, or sigh, or tear.

He struggled on with his life, fulfilling his day-to-day tasks 'mechanically, by the mere force of habit'.

But then he stumbled across a passage in a volume of memoirs in which the French writer Jean-François Marmontel told of how, when his father died and his family was distraught, he, though a mere boy, 'felt and made them feel that he would be everything to them – would supply the place of all that they had lost'. In imagining this scene, and the *feelings* of the family, Mill was moved to tears. It was a moment of catharsis. His mental burden grew lighter. He began to take pleasure again 'in sunshine and sky, in books, in conversation, in public affairs'. Though he had several relapses into melancholy, often lasting for several months, he was never quite so miserable as he had been during his crisis.

The lesson that he learnt from his moment of empathy with Marmontel was that 'among the prime necessities of human well-being' was 'the internal culture of the individual'. A utilitarian desire for what Jeremy Bentham called the 'greatest happiness of the greatest number' in society would never be enough to guarantee the happiness of each individual. For that, it was necessary to cultivate 'the feelings'. The instrument of that cultivation was 'poetry and art' – which had been singularly lacking when his father had drilled him in mathematics, logic, history, philosophy, politics and economics.

So it was that in the autumn of 1828 Mill read Wordsworth for the first time: 'I took up the collection of his poems from curiosity, with no expectation of mental relief from it, though I had before resorted to poetry with that hope'. He had read Byron during the worst period of his depression, but that had made him feel worse still: the poet's dark state of mind was too like his own. 'But while Byron was exactly what did not suit my condition, Wordsworth was exactly what did': his poetry redirected Mill to 'the love of rural objects and natural scenery' which had helped relieve him from one of his 'longest relapses into depression'. The key, however, was not merely the natural description; Mill thought that Scott was better at that. Rather, 'What made Wordsworth's poems a medicine for my state of mind, was that they expressed, not mere outward beauty, but states of feeling, and of thought coloured by feeling, under the excitement of beauty. They seemed to be the very culture of the feelings, which I was in quest of.'

Mill drew from Wordsworth's poems 'a source of inward joy, of sympathetic and imaginative pleasure, which could be shared in by all human beings; which had no connection with struggle or imperfection, but would be made richer by every improve-ment in the physical or social condition of mankind'. They identified for him 'the perennial sources of happiness', the 'real, permanent happiness' that could be found 'in tranquil contem-plation'. Not, though, as a retreat from the task of changing society and the Benthamite goal of creating greater happiness for the greatest number: 'Wordsworth taught me this, not only without turning away from, but with a greatly increased interest in, the common feelings and common destiny of human beings.' The result of reading Wordsworth, Mill concluded this chapter of his autobiography, 'was that I gradually, but completely, emerged from my habitual depression, and was never again subject to it'.

Mill went on to become the father of modern liberal philosophy and an advocate for the emancipation of women. His *On Liberty* is the classic defence of the freedom of the individual. It is unlikely that it would have been written had the poetry of Wordsworth not been there in his youth to guide him beyond his depression and introduce him to the very culture of the feelings.

★

John Stuart Mill's story is only the most famous example of how Wordsworth's poetry was 'a medicine' for the 'state of mind' of many nineteenth-century readers. Another compelling case is that of William Hale White, who was 'de-converted' from his strictly religious Congregational upbringing by his encounter with *Lyrical Ballads* when he was in training for the ministry in 1850. In his autobiography, written under the pseudonym Mark Rutherford, he described it as an experience akin to that of St Paul on the road to Damascus:

> I happened to find amongst a parcel of books a volume of poems in paper boards. It was called *Lyrical Ballads*, and I read first one and then the whole book. It conveyed to me no new doctrine, and yet the change it wrought in me could only be compared with that which is said to have been wrought on Paul himself by the Divine apparition.[17]

That change was from one kind of religion – a faith of dogma, discipline and denial – to another. Wordsworth was a believer, White acknowledges, 'but his real God is not the God of the Church, but the God of the hills, the abstraction Nature, and to this my reverence was transferred':

> Instead of an object of worship which was altogether artificial, remote, never coming into genuine contact with me, I had now one which I thought to be real, one in which literally I could live and move and have my being, an actual fact present before my eyes. God was brought from that heaven of the books, and dwelt on the downs in the far-away distances, and in every cloud-shadow which wandered across the valley.[18]

For William Hale White, Wordsworth's poetry was a force that 're-created' the 'Supreme Divinity', substituting 'a new and living spirit for the old deity', giving him the strength to go on living in a world in which the old verities were being challenged by the new knowledge that was emerging from the sciences of geology and astronomy and that would be capped by Charles Darwin's theory of *The Origin of Species*.

★

In 1848, Ralph Waldo Emerson paid a return visit to Wordsworth. By this time, he had developed his own philosophy of religion, nature and the human mind, his thinking profoundly shaped by Wordsworth and Coleridge; he, in turn, would shape the thinking of Henry David Thoreau, another avid reader of Wordsworth, who developed his distinctively American strain of Romantic retreat and engagement in what he called his own 'lake country' of Walden woods.

Emerson was staying with the pioneering sociologist and advocate for women's rights, Harriet Martineau. She had come to the mountains to recuperate from illness, and dedicated herself to the improvement of the lives of the local people. She lived in Ambleside and shared many friends with Wordsworth, who had advised her on the design of her garden.

When they arrived at Rydal Mount, they found Wordsworth asleep on the sofa. When he awoke, he 'soon became full of talk on the French news' – revolution was brewing in Paris once more. He was not sanguine about the prospects. From abusing the French, he turned to the Scots, speaking bitterly of Jeffrey and the *Edinburgh Review*. When the conversation turned to contemporary poetry, he expressed qualified admiration for Tennyson, the coming man of English poetry, who would soon succeed him as Poet Laureate and favourite of

Queen Victoria: 'a right poetic genius, though with some affectation'.

Back in Ambleside Harriet Martineau praised Wordsworth 'not for his poetry, but for thrift and economy; for having afforded to his country neighbours an example of a modest household, where comfort and culture were secured without any display'. In a double-edged compliment she said that 'in his early housekeeping at the cottage where he first lived, he was accustomed to offer his friends bread and plainest fare: if they wanted anything more, they must pay him for their board'. Emerson, meanwhile, reached his own conclusion: though Wordsworth 'had egotistic puerilities in the choice and treatment of his subjects', he was alone in his time in treating 'the human mind well, and with an absolute trust'. And his 'Ode on Immortality' was 'the high-water mark which the intellect has reached in this age'.[19]

★

Another visitor to Rydal in the revolutionary year of '48 was the eighth Duke of Argyll. He and his duchess found the old man languid and sleepy, by his fireside. But he became animated in conversation and then said that he would walk out with them. Beside the mount at the front of the house, the duchess asked Wordsworth if he would repeat some of his verses. He said that he hardly thought he could do so, but that he would be glad to read to them. At this point, Mary Wordsworth came outside and invited them back in for tea. The duke persuaded Wordsworth to reminisce about Coleridge and Southey, which he did vividly, though running off into 'irrelevant anecdotes'. After tea, they asked him to read again. 'Oh dear, that is terrible!' he said – but he asked them to choose a poem. They proposed either 'Tintern Abbey' or any part of The Excursion. He chose 'Tintern Abbey', telling them the circumstances of its composition exactly fifty years before.[20]

He read the opening descriptive lines 'in a low clear voice'. When he came to the 'thoughtful and reflective lines', his tones deepened and he spoke with 'a fervour and almost passion of delivery'. Towards the end, he gave particular emphasis to the phrases 'My DEAR, DEAR friend!' and 'In thy wild eyes'. When the duke and duchess had called at Rydal Mount earlier in the day, they had found no one at home save 'an invalid lady, very old, and apparently paralysed'. She was drawn in a bath chair by a servant. At this moment, as Wordsworth read the closing section of 'Tintern Abbey', addressed to his beloved sister, they realized who the old invalid was.

Mary Wordsworth told the duke and duchess that this was the first time Wordsworth had read his poetry aloud since the death from tuberculosis of his daughter Dora the previous year, which had broken his heart.

★

William Wordsworth died of pleurisy on 23 April 1850, the day traditionally marked as Shakespeare's birth and death day. It was just over two weeks after his eightieth birthday. The Rydal Mount cuckoo clock, a gift from Isabella Fenwick, to whom he had dictated his memories of the origin of his poems, was calling out the hour of twelve noon.

Precisely a month later, a storm broke over Helvellyn. Down in Ambleside, Harriet Martineau wrote to a friend: 'Cannot you fancy what it is to think of Wordsworth knowing nothing of these things – being under the sod. – vacating his place among these shows of nature?' They had all known that the end was near: 'but the feeling remains as fresh as it was that sunny afternoon, when the news spread that he was gone, and every body on the road looked grave, and the blinds were down in his cottage'.[21]

Wordsworth's son-in-law Edward Quillinan, Dora's widower, commissioned a young poet to write an elegy. Matthew Arnold was the son of Thomas Arnold, the famous headmaster of Rugby School. The family's summer holiday home was at Fox How, near Ambleside. The Arnolds had become close friends of the Wordsworths. Matthew's tribute appeared in *Fraser's Magazine* in June 1850. It lamented the loss, years before, of Europe's two most famous literary names, Goethe and Byron. Others would rise, Arnold argues, to replicate the wisdom of the former and the force of the latter. There could, however, be no substitute for the poet whom he had first encountered when he was playing in a child-built fort on the side of Loughrigg, the mountain above Rydal Water: 'But where will Europe's latter hour / Again find Wordsworth's healing power? . . . But who, ah! who will make us feel?'

RETROSPECT

Though but few have read the work by which he lives, and fewer know more of him than his name, he has changed the world . . . He has changed it by altering the chemical composition of the cultural air that all men breathe.[1]

A SORT OF
NATIONAL PROPERTY

Matthew Arnold became an inspector of schools and then Oxford Professor of Poetry. In 1879, he edited a selection of *The Poems of Wordsworth* for the publisher Macmillan. Its preface argued that Wordsworth was the only poet of the previous 200 years to rank with Shakespeare and Milton. More than any other modern poet, he teaches us 'how to live'. In particular, he shows us how to feel 'the joy offered to us in nature, the joy offered to us in the simple primary affections and duties'. At the level of the individual line, he created 'touchstones' of poetic excellence, none more 'true and characteristic' than the line from 'Michael' that reads 'And never lifted up a single stone': 'There is nothing subtle in it, no heightening, no study of poetic style, strictly so called at all; yet it is expression of the highest and most truly expressive kind . . . a style of perfect plainness.'[1]

At the same time, Arnold argued, 'work altogether inferior, work quite uninspired, flat and dull, is produced by him with evident unconsciousness of its defects, and he presents it to us with the same faith and seriousness as his best work'. Wordsworth wrote poetry for sixty years and yet 'it is no exaggeration to say that within one single decade of those years, between 1798 and 1808, almost all his really first-rate work was produced'. Arnold was the first to identify this period so specifically as what later critics would call Wordsworth's 'great decade'. He did not stop to speculate upon the reasons for the subsequent decline; his aim for the anthology was to dispose of 'a great deal of the poetical baggage which now encumbers him'. Only by rigorous selection would Wordsworth be valued at his 'real worth'. Otherwise he would survive only as a poet for 'the few'.[2]

At the time when Arnold wrote his preface, Wordsworth's most widely read work was not *Lyrical Ballads* or *The Excursion* or the collected poems that he had put through a series of editions in his lifetime. It certainly was not *The Prelude*, which had little impact when the family brought it into print soon after his death. Arnold recalled Wordsworth relating how one of the many pilgrims who made their way to Rydal Mount in his late years of fame 'asked him if he had ever written anything besides the *Guide to the Lakes*'.[3] The guidebook was his only bestseller. It was reprinted, in various forms and with various titles, no fewer than ten times in the first half-century of its life.

Having first appeared as an accompaniment to Joseph Wilkinson's engravings and then in the company of the river Duddon sonnets and the disguised account of the affair with Annette Vallon, it became a book in its own right in 1822, under the title *A Description of the Scenery of the Lakes in the*

North of England. This quickly sold out and was reprinted with revisions the following year. The 1822 edition included a new account of an excursion up Scafell Pike and the 1823 added an account of an excursion to Ullswater. Both were based closely and without acknowledgment on unpublished material by Dorothy Wordsworth. Then the *Guide* appeared in 1835 under the auspices of a local publisher, with the title *A Guide Through the District of the Lakes in the North of England, with a Description of the Scenery, etc. For the Use of Tourists and Residents. Fifth Edition, with considerable additions.* In this edition, the 'Directions and Information for the Tourist' became a separate prefatory division, set apart from the main body of the text. Wordsworth began this edition by saying that his purpose was 'to furnish a Guide or Companion for the *Minds* of Persons of taste, and feeling for Landscape, who might be inclined to explore the District of the Lakes with that degree of attention to which its beauty may fairly lay claim', but that he would begin by getting out of the way 'the humble and tedious Task of supplying the Tourist with directions'.[4]

Then in 1842 it became part of *A Complete Guide to the Lakes, Comprising Minute Directions for the Tourist, With Mr Wordsworth's Description of the Scenery of the Country, etc. And Three Letters on the Geology of the Lake District, by the Rev. Professor Sedgwick, Edited by the Publisher.* Wordsworth explained in a letter to Adam Sedgwick, the first Woodwardian Professor of Geology at the University of Cambridge, that in the tourist market his guide was being outsold by others which attended more to the needs of 'the *Body* of the Tourist', that he had tried to remedy this defect but found the work troublesome and '*infra dig.*', and that he had therefore turned the 'guide matter' over to the publisher, John Hudson of Kendal, who had undertaken to interweave it with further material compiled by himself, but to leave 'all that related to mind' entire and separate from the rest. In addition, Thomas Gough of Kendal would 'promote the Botany' (Gough furnished a table listing the woods and fells where some 250 species of plant could be found). Thus with Sedgwick's geological contribution, 'a Book would be produced answering every purpose that could be desired'.[5] This version went through five editions in seventeen years; Sedgwick added a fourth letter on geology to the 1846 edition and a fifth to that of 1853. There was a consonance between poet and scientist: for Sedgwick, as for Wordsworth, the mountains 'give back to us, as the earth's touch did of old to the giant's body, new spirits and enduring strength'. The allusion is to the ancient Greek myth of Antaeus, a story about the need to keep in touch with the earth.

The essays of a clergyman who was one of the crucial figures in the history of the science of geology were thus incorporated in a text that had begun its life accompanying the productions of a clergyman cashing in on the vogue for the picturesque. The evolution of the *Guide* is a fascinating index of the shift from the age of William Gilpin and Thomas West to that of Charles Lyell and Charles Darwin. Sedgwick actually used the opportunity provided by Wordsworth to educate the public about the principles of geology. The name and nature of the Silurian and Cambrian systems gained currency outside scientific circles chiefly because of Sedgwick's letters in the *Guide*. His contribution supplemented the Wordsworthian analysis of the surfaces of nature and the interaction between man and nature with an account of the depths of nature, of the fossil record which revealed 'countless ages before man's being' and taught 'of laws as unchangeable as the oracles of nature'.[6] By the time we reach this edition we have come a long way from West and his attempt to make a visit to the Lakes comparable to the composition of a landscape painting. The geologist's hammer has replaced the Claude glass.

For all this, the primary effect of the *Guide* was to bring more tourists to the Lake District. In the final decade of his life, Wordsworth began to regret his rallying call for his home territory to be deemed 'a sort of national property, in which every man has a right and interest who has an eye to perceive and a heart to enjoy'. In 1844, he sent a 'Sonnet on the projected Kendal and Windermere Railway' to the *Morning Post* newspaper, along with a letter objecting to the extension of a rail link into the heart of the Lake District. The poem begins with lines that would often be quoted in later campaigns: 'Is then no nook of English ground / Secure from rash assault?' It ends with a plea for the wind to 'protest against the wrong'.[7]

His anti-railway sentiment undoubtedly had an element of 'not in my back yard', but he was also motivated by the feeling that it was up to the individual to discover the beauties of nature in their own time and their own environment. His principal objection was to large-scale organized Sunday outings. He suggested that reform of factory hours would be a better contribution to the well-being of manufacturing labourers: 'Packing off men after this fashion, for holiday entertainment, is, in fact, treating them like children. They go at the will of their master, and must return at the same, or they will be dealt with as transgressors'. Instead, Wordsworth proposed, the factory owners should 'consent to a Ten Hours' Bill, with little or, if possible, no diminution of wages'. With the necessities of life provided, 'the mind will develop itself accordingly, and each individual would be more at liberty to make at his own cost excursions in any direction which might be most inviting to him'. There would then be no need for their masters to send them 'in droves scores of miles from their homes and families to the borders of Windermere, or anywhere else'.[8] Rural recreation, in other words, should be a matter of personal choice, not mass organization.

The argument is consistent with Wordsworth's broader development towards individualism.

His voice went unheeded. In 1847, a branch line of the newly
constructed Lancaster and Carlisle Railway was brought to a
terminus in the village of Birthwaite, soon to be renamed
Windermere, half a mile from the lake. One of the engineers
celebrated its opening with a poem replying to Wordsworth,
published in the local newspaper, the *Kendal Mercury*. The advent
of the railway would 'give to town-cramp'd souls the power to
soar, / And taste of pleasures never known before'. As for the
Bard of Rydal Mount,

> The mind will surely place his beauties higher
> When read 'mid scenes that did the thoughts inspire,
> We'll spread his fame: – what more can he require?
> Are not these motives good, and clear, and strong,
> Full satisfaction for the sons of song?
> Carrying conviction wheresoever read,
> Appealing to the heart, as well as head.
> Conscious from wrong our cause we have been clearing,
> We'll give the Plaintiff good Words, – worth the hearing.[9]

★

In Wordsworth's youth, genteel tourists came to the Lake District
in search of the picturesque. After the advent of the railway, the
urban middle and working classes came in search of Wordsworth.
Numerous guidebooks were published in the course of the second
half of the nineteenth century. Instead of pointing out picturesque
'stations' or viewpoints, they directed visitors to the settings of
Wordsworth's poems. The district began to be called not just
'the Lake country' but 'Wordsworth country' and even
'Wordsworthshire'.[10] Readers of *The Excursion* headed for Blea

Tarn in the Langdale Valley, in search of the Solitary's cottage. In 1860, a pocket-sized edition of the poem was published, with topographical notes for the benefit of footsteppers. Admirers of 'Michael' went up Greenhead Ghyll to look for the sheepfold. Along the way, they could take a diversion via the cottage that had been the Grasmere retreat of Mrs Hemans, the most commercially successful English poet of the age.

While Wordsworth was alive, Rydal Mount remained a place of pilgrimage; after his death, people flocked to his resting place. In 1852, a group of Manchester workers took the night train to Windermere and walked to the quiet churchyard of St Oswald that overlooks the river Rothay running through Grasmere. They offered a prayer at the poet's grave: 'We shall bear your spirit with us – that, and the influence you have imparted, shall continue beneficently to hover around us, mighty for good, and your memory shall be held by us as a precious legacy, triumphant over time and change.'[11]

One of the many pilgrims to Wordsworth's grave was a Scotsman called John Muir. He recorded his visit in his notebook, writing with an eye for natural detail that is worthy of Dorothy:

Grasmere small village, small lake reedy small island in the middle. All surrounded by rough but not jagged heathy slate mtns [mountains]. ice sculpt [sculpted] into bold plain forms remarkably massive . . . Have just come over on coach from Windermere[.] Charming ride. dull & slightly rainy day. Have visited Wordsworths & [Hartley] Coleriges graves. & Dorothy's & the childrens, – plain headstones Wordsworths, Coleriges [on] upright white marble cross Wordsworths plain upright slabs – graves covered by flat slabs. Maple, yew, pine & ash hold boughs over them. – A robin . . . came & sang on the maple as I stood with damp eyes & a lump in my throat.[12]

He picked some leaves from the branches leaning over Wordsworth's grave and kept them for his wife.

Muir wanted to pay homage at the graveside because it had been Wordsworth's vision of the sublimity of the mountains, together with the philosophy of Emerson and Thoreau, and a memory of his early love of Robert Burns, that had given him a language in which to articulate the feeling for nature that he developed as a boy growing up in Scotland and aggrandized as a wanderer in Canada and the United States. The year before his pilgrimage to Grasmere, he had become the inaugural president of the Sierra Club, which was established in California with a mission to 'explore, enjoy and render accessible the mountain regions of the Pacific Coast' and 'to enlist the support of the people and the government in preserving the forests and other natural features of the Sierra Nevada Mountains'.[13] Two years before that, Muir had been the primary mover behind a bill passed by Congress proposing that the Yosemite area of northern California that he had made his home should be preserved on the model of Yellowstone, the world's first formally designated National Park. Muir's advocacy before the Committee on Public Lands of the House of Representatives was rehearsed in a pair of essays in *The Century* magazine, where his rhetoric was suffused with the Wordsworthian sublime, a language of 'clouds, winds, rocks, waters, throbbing together as one'. Thus in 'The Treasures of the Yosemite':

> Lunar rainbows or spraybows also abound; their colors as distinct as those of the sun, and as obviously banded, though less vivid. Fine specimens may be found any night at the foot of the upper Yosemite Fall, glowing gloriously amid the gloomy shadows of the cañon whenever there is plenty of moonlight and spray, silent interpreters of the heart-peace of Nature in the stormy darkness.[14]

And in 'Features of the Proposed Yosemite National Park':

> The opposite wall of the cañon rises in precipices, steep and
> angular, or with rounded brows like those of Yosemite, and
> from this wall as a base extends a fine wilderness of moun-
> tains, rising dome above dome, ridge above ridge, to a group
> of snowy peaks on the summit of the range. Of all this sublime
> congregation of mountains Castle Peak is king: robed with
> snow and light, dipping unnumbered points and spires into
> the thin blue sky, it maintains amid noble companions a perfect
> and commanding individuality.[15]

As Muir was essential to the movement to preserve the 'wilderness' of the American west, so Wordsworth was essential to the
mind and writing of Muir.

The same year that Muir was campaigning for Yosemite to be
made a National Park, the little cottage in Town End where
Wordsworth had lived during the 'great decade' was turned into
a shrine. In 1889 an Irish-born churchman called Stopford Brooke,
a worshipper of Wordsworth who had published a book on the
theology of the English poets, visited Grasmere with his brother.
In the morning, they walked to Easedale Tarn, imagining that
they were following in the footsteps of William and Dorothy.
Then in the afternoon, they strolled down to Town End and
stood by the wooden gate of the cottage. 'And in our mind's
eye we saw the place as it was in his time': no houses between
the cottage and the lake, green fields stretching down to the
water, and a winding path 'across the fields to the fringe of stones
and reeds, which, bordering the lake, defines the little point
among the copse-wood that Wordsworth called Point Rash-
Judgment'. They looked up towards the terrace of Loughrigg
Fell 'where Wordsworth walked at eventide', and 'to the right

was Silverhow, and the white wedge of Eas[e]dale Fall among the tumbled hills'.[16] Entering the cottage and its garden was an equally romantic experience for Brooke, inspiring him to propose to the owner that the freehold, together with that of the neighbouring meadow which the Wordsworths had called Dora's Field, should be preserved for the nation, on the model of the Shakespeare birthplace house that had been opened to the public in Stratford-upon-Avon some forty years earlier. Brooke put his proposal to the Wordsworth Society, which had been established a decade before. The idea won immediate support. A national appeal was launched and the purchase price of £650 was raised in a matter of months. A trust was established and a name at last given to the place: Dove Cottage.

On the seventh anniversary of its opening to the public, Stopford Brooke could confidently write that this little home in the mountains occupied 'as a goal of pilgrimage, a place in this country second only to Stratford-on-Avon'.[17]

★

In the early 1880s there was another anti-railway campaign, this time against a proposal to build a link to the slate quarries above Buttermere. This would have driven a path through the Newlands Valley, one of the most untouched parts of the Lake District, and a place especially loved by Wordsworth. The campaign was led by Canon Hardwicke Rawnsley, a disciple of John Ruskin. The indefatigable Rawnsley composed sub-Wordsworthian sonnets about Lake District landmarks, wrote books with such titles as *Literary Associations of the English Lakes*, and gathered a collection of not always flattering *Reminiscences of Wordsworth among the Peasantry of Westmoreland* (in which he reproduced the words of his interviewees in the local dialect). He served on the county council and fought not only against the railway (successfully), but also for the proper signposting of public footpaths, the reduction of mining pollution, and the maintenance of the historic character of the ancient mountain passes such as Kirkstone, over which Wordsworth had walked so many times.

In May 1883, Rawnsley addressed the annual meeting in Westminster of the Wordsworth Society. He proposed the establishment of a Lake District Defence Society. He knew that the key to its success would be the support of the grandees of the society devoted to the memory of the most famous son of the Lakes. The aim was 'To protect the Lake District from those injurious encroachments upon its scenery, which are from time to time attempted from purely commercial or speculative motives, without regard to its claims as a National Recreation Ground.'[18] Rawnsley gained support from the social reformer Octavia Hill, to whom he had been introduced by Ruskin. Her chief preoccupation was the improvement of housing conditions for the urban poor, but she believed with Ruskin in the healing power of nature for all. For a decade, she had been agitating for the preservation of the natural environment for the benefit of the people, especially around the rapidly growing metropolis of London. She worked closely with a lawyer, Robert Hunter, who had campaigned successfully with the Commons Preservation Society to save open spaces from development, notably Parliament Hill Fields, Hampstead Heath and Epping Forest.

'Men, women and children want more than food, shelter and warmth', Octavia Hill argued, 'They want, if their lives are to be full and good, space near their homes for exercise, quiet, good air, and sight of grass, trees and flowers; they want colour, which shall cheer them in the midst of smoke and fog.'[19] This was the gospel of Ruskin, who in turn had been inspired by Wordsworth. Hill had sought to put the theory into practice through the establishment of a charity called the Kyrle Society for the Diffusion of Beauty, led by her sister Miranda.

In November 1893, Rawnsley seized an opportunity. A Lake District estate had gone up for sale. It included the Falls of Lodore, about which Southey had written a tumbling rhyme for children that had become his most popular poem. Grasmere was also under threat, as was land near the summit of Snowdon, where Wordsworth had beheld his vision in the clouds. Bringing together the interests of the Lake District Defence Society, the Kyrle Society and the Commons Preservation Society, Rawnsley met with Hill and Hunter at the offices of the CPS and proposed the formation of a 'National Trust for Places of Historic Interest or Natural Beauty'. He led a successful press campaign over the following months; Octavia Hill became the public face of the proposed Trust, and early in 1895 it was formally incorporated. They persuaded one of the greatest landowners in the nation, the Duke of Westminster, to become president. The first donation of land was in Wales, but Rawnsley ensured that the Trust became active in the Lake District, protesting against such innovations as the erection of telegraph poles on White Moss Common, where Wordsworth had met the Leech Gatherer, the building of an electric tram-line from Bowness to Ambleside, and a proposal to allow seaplanes to land on Windermere.

At the turn of the century Brandelhow Park, an estate of over a hundred acres below the beautiful mountain of Catbells by Derwentwater, came onto the market. There was talk of it being purchased by a property developer who intended to build holiday villas by the lake. Rawnsley launched an appeal to buy the land for the Trust, and the necessary funds were raised in a few months, with contributions from a large number of donors from diverse social backgrounds. It was officially opened, preserved for the public in perpetuity, by Queen Victoria's fourth daughter Princess Louise. She, Rawnsley, Hill and Hunter planted four oak trees at the ceremony. Four years later, the Trust acquired the 750 acres of the most iconic lakeside site of all: Gowbarrow Park by Ullswater, where Wordsworth and Dorothy had seen the daffodils.

The mountainsides around Grasmere and the other Cumbrian lakes are not naturally smooth and green. They have been nibbled into that lovely condition by generations of Herdwick sheep. Without the hill farmers they would swiftly revert to bracken and wildwood. The person who did more than anyone else to recognize that the beauty of the Lake District was dependent not just on geology but also on the way of life of its people – its hill farmers – was a friend of Canon Rawnsley: Beatrix Potter. She used her substantial inheritance and the royalties from her little 'Peter Rabbit' books, not to mention the merchandising that went with them, to purchase more and more parcels of land in the Lakes. She expanded the holding of her farm at Hill Top, located close to the village of Hawkshead where Wordsworth went to school; in 1923 she purchased Troutbeck Park Farm, which brought her 2,000 acres and a flock of prize Herdwick sheep. She duly became a prize-winning breeder and a hugely respected figure within the tough-minded Herdwick Sheep Breeders' Association. In 1930, she was able to afford the Monk Coniston estate, another 4,000 acres in the Langdale Valley going towards Coniston, Ruskin's home in the later years of his life. She passed on half the estate to the National Trust at cost price, and vowed to gift the rest of it in her will. A key stipulation when she died in 1943 and left all her land to the National Trust – including fourteen farms – was that it should not be parcelled out for bungalows and holiday homes.

By the end of the Second World War, the Trust held well

over 100,000 acres of the Lake District, forming a substantial part of the National Park that it became in 1951. In the course of the first half of the twentieth century, there were various attempts to establish National Parks in Britain, on the American model, with the Lake District always at the forefront of thinking. The Trust had advocated the idea of the area becoming a National Park as early as 1904, when its annual report quoted Wordsworth's phrase about the Lakes being 'a sort of national property'. The problem was that in a small country with intensive agriculture, areas of outstanding natural beauty could not be set aside as 'wilderness' in the manner of Yellowstone or Yosemite. It would have been impossible to purchase the entire Lake District for the nation.

During the war, Lord Reith, in his government role as First Commissioner of Works, began to think about post-war reconstruction of the environment, in which 'preservation of areas of natural or historic interest, and the reservation of national parks and coastal areas' would be achieved through planning controls on building and development.[20] Reith conceived of preservation and reservation as a public service in the environmental domain, analogous to the service via the airwaves which he had achieved through his vision as the first director general of the BBC in the years between the wars.

The practicalities were entrusted to a civil servant named John Gordon Dower, who began his work with the Lake District. In November 1943, a time of increasing confidence that the war would be won, he submitted a report to the Ministry of Town and Country Planning. Each National Park, Dower proposed, would be 'an extensive area of beautiful and relatively wild country in which, for the nation's benefit', the 'characteristic landscape beauty is strictly preserved', 'access and facilities for public open-air enjoyment, including particularly cross-country and foot-path walking, are amply provided', 'wildlife and places and buildings of historic, architectural or scientific interest are suitably protected', while 'established farming use is effectively maintained'.[21]

In 1949, Clement Attlee's Labour government passed the National Parks and Access to the Countryside Act, which might be considered as an environmental equivalent of the National Health Service that was established the previous year. Drawing together conservation, planning, and access, the Act followed the lines of the Dower report. Each element of its definition of a National Park may ultimately be traced back to the values of Wordsworth's *Guide to the Lakes*: the maintaining of the place for the benefit of the whole nation; the conception of landscape beauty, with a particular emphasis on wild (sublime) country; the belief in the importance of the open air; the respect for buildings that have a history in the place; and the recognition that traditional agricultural practices are integral to the identity of the place. Wordsworth would have been pleased that shepherds still work on the hills of Westmorland and Cumberland, since, in contrast to the American model, the English and Welsh National Parks do not consist of enclosed areas owned by the government; the land in them may be used for commercial activities such as farming and forestry, and remains privately owned – a considerable amount of it by the National Trust, which is still a private charity, not a government agency. Conservation is sought by means of planning rather than possession.

For all the differences between the National Parks in the United States and in Britain, it may legitimately be claimed that all who hike or simply gaze in the wild places are legatees of Wordsworth's poetry, his *Guide*, and his way of seeing – though the old conservative of Rydal Mount would have been horrified at the scale and commercialization of mountain recreation, and its consequences of soil erosion and pollution. The National Parks in the United States were described by the south-western writer Wallace Stegner as 'America's best idea'.[22] They were really Wordsworth's best idea.

LOVE OF NATURE LEADING TO LOVE OF MANKIND

'Poetry makes nothing happen', wrote W. H. Auden in his poem on the death of fellow poet W. B. Yeats. He was wrong. Sometimes poetry can change the world.

William Wordsworth was not merely the most admired English poet of the nineteenth century: his poetry made many things happen. Locally, the ecology and economy of the vale of Grasmere, and the wider Lake District, were changed as a result of his canonization. Nationally, he made new claims for the power of poetry that shaped the minds of the most influential thinkers in Victorian Britain. Globally, his influence extended to John Muir's passion for the preservation of Yosemite.

Auden did not in fact believe that poetry makes nothing happen. Poets often disagree with themselves, which is one of the things that makes them poets. Having said that poetry makes nothing happen, he went on, later in the same poem, to describe poetry as 'A way of happening, a mouth'.[1]

Wordsworth's poetry was a way of happening because of the new way in which he sought, as Keats put it, to 'think into the human heart' by means of an unprecedented examination of the development of his own mind and his sense of belonging in the world. He became the mouth of his generation for what Keats called 'the true voice of feeling'.[2] In Victorian England, and simultaneously in the young United States of America, Wordsworth came to be regarded as a central figure in the revolutionary shift in cultural attitudes that would eventually be called the Romantic movement. He and his fellow poets and philosophers changed forever the way we think about childhood, about the sense of the self, about the purpose of poetry, and especially about our connection to our surroundings.

Hazlitt believed that Wordsworth and Coleridge embodied the spirit of the age. Their imaginative cross-fertilization made them into, to adapt a phrase of Ralph Waldo Emerson's, a composite 'representative man'. Among the 'great men' of his own time, Emerson regarded Napoleon as the archetypal 'man of the world', the 'representative of the popular external life and aims of the nineteenth century', and Goethe as the philosopher of the 'multiplicity' of its inner life.[3] Yet Emerson's own capacious mind and his vision for American literature were shaped less by Goethe than by the poetry of Wordsworth and the ideas of Coleridge.

The composite Wordsworthian–Coleridgean identity began to fracture on that morning of Saturday 27 December 1806 when Coleridge saw, or thought he saw, Wordsworth in bed with Sara Hutchinson. It broke down almost irretrievably after Basil Montagu passed on the gossip about Wordsworth finding Coleridge impossible to live with because of the alcohol and the opium. Though Coleridge would be generous in writing of Wordsworth's gifts in *Biographia Literaria*, and Wordsworth would mourn Coleridge's passing in the 'Extempore Effusion on the Death of James Hogg', it would never be glad confident morning again.

As he settled into fame and a gentleman's life at Rydal Mount, Wordsworth's genius deserted him. Yet as his mortal powers waned, he began to achieve immortality: his spirit lived on by means of his inspiration upon the next generation of readers and writers, then far beyond. To use another phrase of W. H. Auden's in his elegy on the death of W. B. Yeats, Wordsworth *became his admirers*. Radical Wordsworth endured through the nineteenth century in the poetry of Keats and Shelley, John Clare and Felicia Hemans (and, by negative influence, Byron); in the art of Benjamin Robert Haydon and the prose of Thomas De Quincey, William Hazlitt and Charles Lamb; in the ideas of John Stuart Mill, Matthew Arnold, John Ruskin and George Eliot; in the deeds of Canon Rawnsley, Stopford Brooke and Beatrix Potter; and, across the Atlantic, in the visions of Emerson, Thoreau and John Muir. Radical Wordsworth survives today whenever a person walks for pleasure and takes spiritual refreshment in the mountains or when a heart leaps up at the sight of a rainbow in the sky or a tuft of primroses in flower.

★

Thirty years after Wordsworth's death, and twenty after the publication of Darwin's *On the Origin of Species*, Matthew Arnold recognized which way the wind had blown. Introducing an anthology of *The English Poets*, he argued, under the deep influence of Wordsworth, that the future spirit of humankind would depend on poetry. Religion had relied on supposed fact; the science of Lyell, Darwin and others had disproved those facts.

The only part of religion to endure would be 'its unconscious poetry'. More and more, society would 'have to turn to poetry to interpret life for us, to console us, to sustain us': 'Most of what now passes with us for religion and philosophy will be replaced by poetry.' Even science itself would appear incomplete without it, 'For finely and truly does Wordsworth call poetry "the impassioned expression which is in the countenance of all science"; and what is a countenance without its expression?'[4]

Arnold's prose then takes off from another phrase in the preface to *Lyrical Ballads*:

> Again, Wordsworth finely and truly calls poetry 'the breath and finer spirit of all knowledge'; our religion, parading evidences such as those on which the popular mind relies now; our philosophy, pluming itself on its reasonings about causation and finite and infinite being; what are they but the shadows and dreams and false shows of knowledge? The day will come when we shall wonder at ourselves for having trusted to them, for having taken them seriously; and the more we perceive their hollowness, the more we shall prize 'the breath and finer spirit of knowledge' offered to us by poetry . . . the best poetry will be found to have a power of forming, sustaining, and delighting us, as nothing else can.[5]

Out of Wordsworth comes a manifesto for the enduring value of poetry beyond even that of religion, philosophy and science.

There was an unprecedented market for biography in the Victorian era. A notably popular series of literary lives, published by Macmillan under the editorship of the prolific journalist-politician-bookman John Morley, was called 'English Men of Letters'. The volume on Wordsworth was published in 1881, the year after Arnold's essay on the importance of poetry. It made the startling claim that 'the maxims of Wordsworth's form of natural religion were uttered before Wordsworth only in the sense in which the maxims of Christianity were uttered before Christ':

> The essential spirit of the *Lines near Tintern Abbey* was for practical purposes as new to mankind as the essential spirit of the *Sermon on the Mount*. Not the isolated expression of moral ideas, but their fusion into a whole in one memorable personality, is that which connects them for ever with a single name. Therefore it is that Wordsworth is venerated; because to so many men – indifferent, it may be, to literary or poetical effects, as such – he has shown by the subtle intensity of his own emotion how the contemplation of Nature can be made a revealing agency, like Love or Prayer, – an opening, if indeed there be any opening, into the transcendent world.[6]

Thirty years after his death, the poet from an obscure nook of northern England, who in the first half of his life was mercilessly derided by the critics, was being compared to Jesus Christ.

The author of the book that made this comparison was Frederic William Henry Myers. The son of a Keswick clergyman who knew and revered Wordsworth, Myers was a bisexual ex-don from Cambridge who, like Matthew Arnold, had become an inspector of schools. A few years before writing the biography, he was deeply scarred by the gruesome suicide in the Lake District of his cousin's wife Annie Marshall, with whom he had fallen in love and was having a (very intense but almost certainly unconsummated) affair.

He had also been deeply affected by the novels of George Eliot, herself another Victorian sage with boundless admiration for Wordsworth. After reading the final instalment of *Middlemarch* in the late autumn of 1872, Myers wrote Eliot a long fan letter in which he especially singled out the 'noble lovemaking' of Ladislaw and Dorothea. The 'contact of noble souls', he suggested, was the only reason to go on living in a world where 'there is no longer any God or any hereafter or anything in particular to aim at'.[7] The following spring, Eliot visited Myers in Cambridge. On a rainy May day, they walked in the Fellows' Garden of Trinity College. She responded to the three negatives in his letter – no God, no hereafter, no earthly goal – in words that seemed to Myers positively oracular: 'taking as her text the three words which have been used so often as the inspiring trumpet-calls of men, – the words *God, Immortality, Duty,* – pronounced, with terrible earnestness, how inconceivable was the *first*, how unbelievable the *second*, and yet how peremptory and absolute the *third*. Never, perhaps, have sterner accents affirmed the sovereignty of impersonal and unrecompensing Law.'[8]

Myers published his account of this conversation in the same year as his biography of Wordsworth. In reflecting on the necessity of *Duty* and the unbelievability of *Immortality*, he would inevitably have turned his mind to the two odes that dominated the *Poems* of 1807. Neither Eliot nor Myers could believe in God: the findings of Lyell in geology, popularized in Robert Chambers' 1844 *Vestiges of the Natural History of Creation*, had cracked centuries of Creationist belief. And then there was Darwin. Yet Myers could not live without maintaining faith in some kind of spiritual realm. He had to believe in the possibility that he might one day be reconnected with Annie on, to use the words of the 'Intimations' ode, the shore of an 'immortal sea'. In his study of Wordsworth, he kept returning to those passages which hinted at some 'mystic relation' between the visible and the invisible world.[9] That was why he wrote of

Wordsworth's natural religion offering 'an opening, if indeed there be any opening, into the transcendent world'.

In the circumstances, it was almost inevitable that, like many late Victorians grappling with death in an age of uncertainty, Myers became interested in spiritualism. Two years after the publication of his biography of Wordsworth, he became one of the founding members of the Society for Psychical Research. He began visiting mediums, writing about apparitions, and engaging in research on clairvoyance and transmundane experience. He spent his later years developing a theory of the 'subliminal self' or 'subliminal consciousness', suggesting that paranormal and mystical events were the product of contact between the realm of the deep unconscious and what he called the 'metetherial world'. To describe these mysterious forms of contact, he coined a new word: 'telepathy'.[10]

Myers invoked Wordsworth as prime evidence for his theory. Turning to *The Prelude*, he found numerous instances of 'subliminal uprush' – those spots of time in which 'the light of sense / Goes out, but with a flash that has revealed / The invisible world'. Lines such as 'To hold fit converse with the spiritual world' convinced him that there was a 'telaesthetic' quality to Wordsworth's genius.[11] The poems' moments of heightened consciousness 'bring with them indefinite intimations of what I hold to be the great truth that the human spirit is essentially capable of a deeper than sensorial perception, of a direct knowledge of facts of the universe outside the range of any specialized organ or any planetary view'.[12] The word 'intimations' is a sign that he was thinking of the great ode and its hope that, contrary to the gloomy pronouncement of George Eliot, there *was* a form of immortality that allowed the human spirit to survive beyond bodily death.

When he died, Myers left a message with a friend in a sealed envelope. He explained that he would attempt to transmit the same message from beyond the grave. When a medium made contact, she should repeat his words. The envelope would then be opened, and if the words were the same, his intimation of immortality would be proved. Margaret Verrall, the crystal-gazing wife of Cambridge University's first King Edward Professor of English Literature, had taken up 'automatic writing'. She used this method to reveal the words received from Myers in the spirit world. To the disappointment of the members of the Society for Psychical Research, they bore no resemblance to the sentence in the envelope. Myers' only voice from beyond the grave came in the body of his writing: two years after his death, Longmans – Wordsworth's publisher – brought into print his two huge volumes on the subject of *Human Personality and the Survival of Bodily Death*.

The American philosopher William James was an admirer of Myers' work. He contributed to the *Proceedings of the Society for Psychical Research* first an obituary entitled 'Frederic Myers' service to psychology' and then a broadly favourable review of his post-humous magnum opus.[13] This was at the time when James was working on his Gifford Lectures on Natural Religion, delivered in Edinburgh and published as *The Varieties of Religious Experience: A Study in Human Nature*. James set himself the task of exploring the *psychology* of religious feeling.

Like John Stuart Mill, as a young man James had been 'restored to sanity' by a reading of Wordsworth: he said that his own 'despondency' was 'corrected' by book four of *The Excursion*. Later, in his essay 'On a certain blindness in human beings', he wrote of Wordsworth's 'authentic tidings' in celebrating 'the limitless significance in natural things'.[14] So it is not surprising that his definition of religious experience in the Gifford Lectures is recognizably Wordsworthian: '*The feelings, acts, and experiences of individual men in their solitude, so far as they apprehend themselves to stand in relation to whatever they may consider the divine . . .* Certain aspects of nature seem to have a peculiar power of awakening such mystical moods.'[15] James believed in 'the reality of the unseen'. He followed Myers in locating this unseen world in the 'subconscious self' or 'subliminal consciousness'.[16] In the post-Lyell, post-Darwin world, God was not dead, as Nietzsche had proclaimed, but rather buried within the deep strata of the human psyche – the territory that Wordsworth had excavated in *The Prelude.*

It was at this period, around the turn of the nineteenth century into the twentieth, that his autobiographical poem began to be regarded as his greatest achievement. The first person to make such a claim was a Frenchman. In 1896, a publisher on the Boulevard Saint-Germain in Paris brought out a 500-page book by a young academic called Émile Legouis, entitled *La Jeunesse de William Wordsworth 1770–1798: Étude sur le 'Prélude'.* Legouis later uncovered documents regarding Wordsworth's French love affair and the existence of his daughter Caroline, but his book was notable for being the first fully to appreciate not only the importance of *The Prelude* as a biographical document but also its profundity as a psychological self-analysis.

In the early years of the new century, Legouis became the Professor of English Language and Literature at the Sorbonne, where he shared his excitement over Wordsworth with the university's inaugural Professor of Music, a thinker of eclectic range called Romain Rolland. Over the years, Rolland kept returning to *The Prelude* – a pacifist, but also an enthusiast for the Russian Revolution, he was fascinated by Wordsworth's involvement in the French Revolution and subsequent rejection of its values after the Terror. Those passages of quasi-mystical experience in the face of nature, which had so attracted Myers, contributed to

Rolland's thinking about religious feeling. In 1927, he read Sigmund Freud's comprehensive debunking of religion, *The Future of an Illusion*. Rolland wrote the author a letter: 'Your analysis of religions is just', he began, 'But I would have liked to see you doing an analysis of *spontaneous religious sentiment* or, more exactly, of religious *feeling*.' Rolland suggested to Freud that his book had failed to take into account a 'simple and direct fact' that was true independently of belief systems, churches and sacred books, namely that human beings down the ages have had a feeling of the 'eternal'. And he found a term for this feeling of being at one with the external world as a whole: 'oceanic'.[17]

Freud was intrigued by this idea of an 'oceanic feeling'. He began his next book, *Civilization and its Discontents*, with an account of Rolland's letter. Freud agreed that the 'oceanic' was indeed the source of all religious feeling. But where did the feeling come from? And why is it only in particular moments of intensity that people feel it? Surely, Freud argued, it was a vestige of that early time in our lives when there was no separation between the self and the world: 'An infant at the breast does not as yet distinguish his ego from the external world as the source of the sensations flowing in upon him.'[18] As we grow up, the 'reality principle' takes hold and the primal unity is lost. For Freud, religious feeling is the attempt of the unconscious to recover it.

This was an idea that Wordsworth anticipated in *The Prelude* when he sought to 'trace / The progress of our Being' from the baby at the mother's breast, holding an unbroken connection with 'an earthly soul'. For Wordsworth, as for Freud, this is the moment of primal unity when we are 'eager to combine / In one appearance, all the elements / And parts of the same object, else detach'd / And loth to coalesce'. This, for Wordsworth, is the oceanic feeling, the origin of both poetry and the religious sense:

> Such, verily, is the first
> Poetic spirit of our human life;
> By uniform controul of after years
> In most abated and suppress'd, in some,
> Through every change of growth or of decay
> Pre-eminent till death.[19]

When Freud died eight months after Yeats, W. H. Auden wrote another of his elegies. Freud wasn't especially clever, the poem argues: 'he merely told / the unhappy Present to recite the Past / like a poetry lesson'. Freud changed the world, says Auden, 'simply by looking back with no false regrets; / all he did was to remember / like the old and be honest like children'.[20] Auden could equally well have written these lines about Wordsworth, the poet who changed the world not least – though the line of influence was circuitous – by clearing a path for Freud.

★

Why should we still care about Wordsworth today? Because he reminds us that we need to care for our children and to cherish a child's way of looking at the world. Because he wrote with unprecedented sympathy for the poor, the excluded and the broken. Because his poetry has been for many, and can still be for some, a medium of solace and an oasis of calm in a noisy and stressful world, even a medicine for mental illness. Because his elegiac poetry can speak to us when we are bereaved. Because he expressed humankind's longing for the infinite and our sense of 'something far more deeply interfused' – the 'oceanic feeling' – in a way that was not dependent on religious dogma. Because he changed the way we perceive, inhabit and preserve the wilder places of the natural world. But above all, on our fragile planet and with our uncertain ecological future, because, at the very beginning of the industrial era that scientists have christened the Anthropocene, he foresaw that among the consequences of modernity would be not only the alienation of human beings from each other, but also potentially irretrievable damage to the delicate balance between our species and our environment.

We preserve the things that we value. We will not save that which we do not love. With this in mind, we might do well to attend to the title of the eighth book of *The Prelude*: 'Retrospect: Love of Nature leading to Love of Mankind'.

The book begins with an image of belonging: a summer fair in Grasmere, during which there is harmony within the community and between the community and its surroundings. Exercising his 'pathetic fallacy' to the full, Wordsworth imagines the 'circumambient world' embracing his 'fellow-beings'. Each natural element – morning light glistening on silent rocks, reposing clouds, running brooks, the presiding mountain of 'old Helvellyn' itself, even 'the blue sky that roofs their calm abode' – is said to 'love' humankind. Wordsworth knows perfectly well that inanimate things are not capable of love: the whole point of the pathetic fallacy is to flip the thought. He imagines nature loving us in order to make us love nature. His great argument is that it is *our* task, our duty, to understand our dependence on our environment. If we so do, we will learn to love each other, to be kind, and to treat the stranger in our path as 'a brother of this world'.[21] The French revolutionary value of *fraternité* must be extended not only throughout the world but to the world itself.

At this point in *The Prelude*, Wordsworth exemplifies his argument with a memory of a childhood walk in the mountains, on a day when the sun was gradually breaking through the mist. 'Emerging from the silvery vapours', he sees a shepherd and his dog, 'girt round with mists', standing in the light as if they were 'inhabitants / Of an aerial island floating on', breathed forward by the wind. The halo effect makes these figures, man and beast, into a secular version of the biblical Good Shepherd.[22] Wordsworth then uses the skilled and loving communication between shepherd and sheepdog as an image of the necessary living bond between the human and the non-human.

The harmonious image of Grasmere Fair is a deliberate contrast to the chaos and squalor of Bartholomew Fair in the London memories earlier in *The Prelude*. Just as William Blake saw 'marks of woe' on the faces of the London crowd and heard the cry of the child chimney-sweeper and the curse of the girl reduced to prostitution,[23] so Wordsworth saw the city as the place devoted to money-making at the expense of love of nature. As he wrote in one of the powerful sonnets gathered in his *Poems* of 1807:

> The world is too much with us; late and soon,
> Getting and spending, we lay waste our powers:
> Little we see in nature that is ours;
> We have given our hearts away, a sordid boon!
> This Sea that bares her bosom to the moon;
> The Winds that will be howling at all hours
> And are up-gathered now like sleeping flowers
> For this, for every thing, we are out of tune;
> It moves us not.

The function of the poet, he implies, is to bring the inhabitants of the urban world, who have been deprived of the privilege of living with nature, back into tune with water, sky and wind. The 'world' of materialistic 'getting and spending' lays waste to our power to love and it will in time lay waste to the very world upon which we rely for our survival. The poet asks us instead to see into the life of things, to look with pre-industrial eyes, to imagine as 'pagans' once did that there are gods in nature:

> Great God! I'd rather be
> A Pagan suckled in a creed outworn;
> So might I, standing on this pleasant lea,
> Have glimpses that would make me less forlorn;
> Have sight of Proteus coming from the sea;
> Or hear old Triton blow his wreathed horn.[24]

★

No one in the nineteenth century perceived the enervating and environmentally destructive dimensions of modernity more clearly than Wordsworth's disciple John Ruskin.[25] Towards the end of his long life, he began collecting his thoughts about the nature of the good life and the needs of society in a series of pamphlets, manifestos in the form of newsletters, called *Fors Clavigera: Letters to the Workmen and Labourers of Great Britain*. The fifth letter, dated May 1871, was entitled 'The White-thorn Blossom', and here Ruskin wrote:

> There are three Material things, not only useful, but essential to Life. No one 'knows how to live' till he has got them.
> These are, Pure Air, Water, and Earth.
> There are three Immaterial things, not only useful, but essential to Life. No one knows how to live till he has got them.
> These are, Admiration, Hope, and Love.*

The asterisk cues a footnote that cites Wordsworth's *Excursion*:

> We live by admiration, hope, and love;
> And even as these are well and wisely fixed,
> In dignity of being we ascend.[26]

For centuries, the Christian church had taught that the three things by which we should live are faith, hope and love. With the long slow withdrawal of what Matthew Arnold called 'the Sea of Faith' from the shores of Victorian England, Wordsworthian 'Admiration', embodied in the wonders of nature, began to take its place. Arnold's prediction that the only part of religion to survive would be its poetry was beginning to be fulfilled.

Our only hope, Ruskin argues, is an admiration – we might now say a respect – for the raw elements without which we cannot live. He believed that modern 'political economy', the science of getting and spending, was not a means to life but a recipe for the death of the planet:

> You can vitiate the air by your manner of life, and of death, to any extent. You might easily vitiate it so as to bring such a pestilence on the globe as would end all of you. Everywhere, and all day long, you are vitiating it with foul chemical exhalations; and the horrible nests, which you call towns, are little more than laboratories for the distillation into heaven of venomous smokes and smells, mixed with effluvia from decaying animal matter, and infectious miasmata from purulent disease.

On the other hand, he wrote, we have the 'power of purifying the air, by dealing properly and swiftly with all substances in corruption; by absolutely forbidding noxious manufactures; and by planting in all soils the trees which cleanse and invigorate earth and atmosphere'. Similarly, we may either tend the soil with care or erode it through reckless overuse. And as for water management: 'You might have the rivers of England as pure as the crystal of the rock; beautiful in falls, in lakes, in living pools . . . Or you may do always as you have done now, turn every river of England into a common sewer.'[27] For Ruskin, then, there was a direct line from the Wordsworthian notion of love of nature leading to love of mankind to the practice of what we would now call 'sustainability'.

In this sense, Wordsworth's vision, and Ruskin's efforts at a practical implementation of that vision, answer to Shelley's high claim for the vocation of poetry: 'Poets are the hierophants of an unapprehended inspiration; the mirrors of the gigantic shadows which futurity casts upon the present . . . the influence which is moved not, but moves. Poets are the unacknowledged legislators of the world.'[28] Ruskin argued in his essay 'The Storm Cloud of the Nineteenth Century' that industrialized humankind was changing the climate. His darkly prophetic prose was a mirror of the gigantic shadow that the futurity of a carbon-warmed atmosphere cast upon his present. Wordsworth's poetry, meanwhile, is the unacknowledged pre-legislation of an alternative vision for the future in which love of nature and love of humankind are enmeshed in a sacred web. Or, in the closing words of *The Prelude*:

Prophets of Nature, we to them will speak
A lasting inspiration, sanctified
By reason and by truth: what we have loved
Others will love; and we may teach them how,
Instruct them how the mind of man becomes
A thousand times more beautiful than the earth

On which he dwells, above this Frame of things
(Which 'mid all revolutions in the hopes
And fears of men doth still remain unchanged)
In beauty exalted, as it is itself
Of substance and of fabric more divine.[29]

When Wordsworth was born two and a half centuries ago, it was reasonable to expect that the earth on which we dwell would 'remain unchanged' through 'all revolutions in the hopes / And fears of men'. The stability of nature was a solace to him as he saw the French Revolution turn to violence, war and Napoleonic imperialism. Science tells us that this stability can no longer be relied upon: the earth is changing at a rate unprecedented in its history. That is why, just as Wordsworth once invoked the great poet of political liberty and free speech by opening a sonnet with the line 'Milton! Thou shouldst be living at this hour', we might say *Wordsworth, thou shouldst be living at this hour*. And through his poetry, he is. It survives, a way of happening, a mouth, teaching us to love what he and his fellow poets loved:

      the pristine earth,
The planet in its nakedness . . .
Man's only dwelling.[30]

CHRONOLOGY

1770 William Wordsworth born (7 April) in Cockermouth in the English Lake District, to John and Ann (Cookson) Wordsworth, second of five children (older brother Richard, 1768–1816; beloved sister Dorothy, born Christmas Day 1771, died, after many years of dementia, 1855; younger brothers John, born 1772, died at sea 1805; and Christopher, 1774–1846, who became master of Trinity College, Cambridge).

1778 Mother dies.

1779 Goes to Hawkshead Grammar School.

1783 Father dies.

1785 Earliest surviving poems.

1787 Goes up to St John's College, Cambridge. First published poem.

1789 Finishes writing *An Evening Walk*, published 1793. Storming of the Bastille in Paris.

1790 Walking tour of France, Switzerland and Germany with college friend Robert Jones.

1791 Graduates. In London, then returns to France.

1792 In Paris and the Loire Valley. Is influenced by Michel Beaupuy. Affair with Annette Vallon and birth of (illegitimate) daughter Caroline (15 December). Composes *Descriptive Sketches*, published 1793. Witnesses aftermath of Tuileries massacre in Paris and returns to England to earn a living.

1793 Wanders on Salisbury Plain, then revisits Jones in Wales, travelling via the Wye Valley. Writes, but does not publish, seditious *Letter to the Bishop of Llandaff*. King Louis XVI executed in January; Robespierre and the Jacobins consolidate power. Possible brief return visit to Paris in October, when Girondins (and Marie Antoinette) are guillotined, but then Anglo-French War prevents his return to France until 1802. Publication of William Godwin's *Political Justice* and government crackdown on dissent in England.

1794 Stays at Windy Brow, Keswick, in the Lake District, with Dorothy; nurses Raisley Calvert. Robespierre executed in Paris.

1795 Inherits legacy of £900, paid at £70 per year, from Raisley Calvert. Moves in radical circles in London. Meets Robert Southey and Samuel Taylor Coleridge (who has been lecturing on politics, anti-slavery and religion) in Bristol. Moves with Dorothy to Racedown in Dorset; they take the child Basil Montagu into their household.

1797 Friendship with Coleridge intensifies. William and Dorothy move to Alfoxden, Somerset, near to Coleridge's cottage in Nether Stowey. Writing of poetry accelerates, including play *The Borderers* and long poem 'The Ruined Cottage'. Plans for collaborative writing with Coleridge.

1798 *Annus mirabilis* of creative activity, including most of the poems published in September in *Lyrical Ballads* (anonymously published poems mostly by Wordsworth, with some by Coleridge, including 'The Ancyent Marinere'). Visit from William Hazlitt. Summer tour of the Wye Valley and writing of 'Tintern Abbey'. Initial plans for epic poem *The Recluse*. William, Dorothy and Coleridge travel to Germany for the winter. Begins writing autobiographical fragments, sowing the seed for *The Prelude*.

1799 William and Dorothy return to England, and at the end of the year settle back in the Lake District at the small former inn at Town End, Grasmere, which would later be named Dove Cottage.

1800 Preparation of second edition of *Lyrical Ballads*, now attributed to Wordsworth, with some changes of content, a new second volume entirely by Wordsworth, and a preface. Works on *Home at Grasmere* and preface to *The Recluse*.

1802 Productive year of lyric poetry, especially sonnets. New edition of *Lyrical Ballads* published with revised preface. Peace of Amiens ends war with France and allows William and Dorothy to go to Calais, where they meet Annette and his daughter Caroline. After receiving much-delayed settlement of debt owed to his late father, on 4 October William marries family friend Mary Hutchinson (1770–1859).

1803 Eldest son, John, born. War against France resumes. Summer tours with Dorothy and Coleridge to Scotland, where they meet Sir Walter Scott. Coleridge's health declining, so he decides to move to a warmer climate.

1804 First daughter, Dorothy (Dora), born. Another productive year of poetry. Autobiographical poem eventually published as *The Prelude* is expanded from five books, mostly focused on childhood, to length comparable with an epic and including material on residence in France and attitude to the French Revolution. Completes 'Ode: Intimations of Immortality'. Coleridge sails for Malta. Napoleon is crowned emperor, adding to Wordsworth's disillusionment with France.

1805   Brother John, captain of ship the *Earl of Abergavenny*, is lost at sea. William and Dorothy distraught. *The Prelude* finished, though revised in later years.

1806   Second son, Thomas, born. Visits London. Gains patronage of Sir George Beaumont and, with Dorothy and Mary and her sister Sara (beloved by Coleridge), spends winter at Park Farm, Coleorton, Leicestershire. Coleridge arrives from Malta, in poor health. In days after Christmas, begins reading *The Prelude* aloud.

1807   *Poems in Two Volumes* published in April. Receives damning reviews. Returns to Dove Cottage in summer. *The White Doe of Rylstone* composed, but unpublished until 1815.

1808   Second daughter, Catharine, born. Moves from Dove Cottage to Allan Bank, a larger but draughty house in Grasmere. Thomas De Quincey visits.

1809   Publishes prose work *The Convention of Cintra*.

1810   Third son, William, born. Quarrel with Coleridge, following gossip spread by Basil Montagu Sr. *Guide to the Lakes* published anonymously as introduction to a book of engravings of views.

1812   Children Thomas and Catharine die. Move from Allan Bank to the old rectory, Grasmere.

1813   Moves to Rydal Mount, between Grasmere and Rydal Water, his home for the rest of his life. Appointed Distributor of Stamps for Westmorland, a post in the Revenue paying £400 per year. Finishes *The Excursion*. Robert Southey becomes Poet Laureate.

1814   *The Excursion* published, with plan for *The Recluse*. Further savage reviews. Tours Scotland, including visit to Yarrow.

1815 Publishes a first collected edition of *Poems*, arranged thematically, and with a preface and supplementary essay.

1816 Publishes *Letter to a Friend of Robert Burns*.

1817 Visits London and spends time with Leigh Hunt, Keats, Benjamin Robert Haydon, and other writers.

1818 Campaigns for the Tories, to the distress of the younger writers who admired his earlier, revolutionary work.

1819 Publishes 'The Waggoner' and *Peter Bell*, both written many years earlier.

1820 Publishes sonnet sequence *The River Duddon*, also an enlarged collected *Poems*. Tours Europe, revisiting sights of 1790.

1822 Publishes *Memorials of a Tour on the Continent* and *Ecclesiastical Sketches*.

1827 Publishes a further enlarged collected *Poems*.

1828 Tours the Rhineland with Coleridge and beloved daughter Dora.

1831 Resists Catholic Emancipation and parliamentary reform. Tours Scotland and sees Scott for the last time.

1832 Another collected *Poems* published.

1834 Coleridge dies.

1835 Publishes *Yarrow Revisited, and Other Poems*. Writes 'Extempore Effusion' lamenting the passing of fellow poets James Hogg, Coleridge, Scott, Charles Lamb, George Crabbe and Felicia Hemans.

1836 Another collected *Poems* published.

1837 Tours France and Italy.

1838 Gathers his sonnets into a single volume. Revises *The Prelude* for the last time. Receives honorary doctorate of civil law from Durham University.

1839 Receives honorary doctorate of civil law from Oxford University.

1840 Queen Adelaide visits Rydal Mount. Climbs Helvellyn, his favourite mountain, on his seventieth birthday.

1842 Publishes *Poems, Chiefly of Early and Late Years*, including early works and *The Borderers*. Resigns position as Distributor of Stamps.

1843 Becomes Poet Laureate, following the death of Southey. Dictates notes on his poems to Isabella Fenwick.

1844 Objects to the construction of a railway link into the heart of the Lake District.

1845 Another collected *Poems* published.

1847 Deeply affected by death of daughter Dora.

1849 Prepares a final collected edition of his *Poems* for publication.

1850 Dies on 23 April, aged eighty. His long poem on the growth of his own mind is posthumously published in July, overseen by his wife and his executors, who give it the title *The Prelude: An Autobiographical Poem*.

SUGGESTIONS FOR FURTHER READING

EDITIONS

Readers new to Wordsworth might begin with *William Wordsworth: Poems selected by Seamus Heaney* (2007, repr. 2016), then proceed to the fuller selection, including the complete 1805 *Prelude*, in *William Wordsworth: The Major Works*, ed. Stephen Gill (Oxford, 2008). The evolution of *The Prelude* can be traced in the Norton critical edition, *The Prelude: 1799, 1805, 1850*, eds Jonathan Wordsworth, M. H. Abrams and Stephen Gill (New York, 1979). *Lyrical Ballads 1798 and 1802* have been edited with excellent notes by Fiona Stafford (Oxford, 2013) and Dorothy's journals by Pamela Woof, *The Grasmere and Alfoxden Journals* (Oxford, 2008). Correspondence can be sampled in *Letters of William Wordsworth: A Selection*, ed. Alan G. Hill (Oxford, 1984) and *Letters of Dorothy Wordsworth: A Selection*, ed. Alan G. Hill (Oxford, 1981).

For serious readers seeking completeness, the final versions of all the poems published in Wordsworth's lifetime, with valuable notes including those of Isabella Fenwick, *The Poetical Works of William Wordsworth*, eds Ernest de Selincourt and Helen Darbishire (5 vols, Oxford, 1940–67), has never been replaced. For the evolution of the manuscripts, the Cornell Wordsworth, gen. ed. Stephen Parrish, 21 vols (Ithaca, 1975–2007) is one of the great achievements of modern literary scholarship. Especially valuable are: *Home at Grasmere*, ed. Beth Darlington (1977); *Lyrical Ballads, and other Poems, 1797–1800*, eds James Butler and Karen Green (1992); *Poems in Two Volumes and other Poems, 1800–1807*, ed. Jared Curtis (1983); *The Excursion*, eds Sally Bushell, James A. Butler and Michael C. Jaye (2007); *The Prelude, 1798–1799*, ed. Stephen Parrish (1977); *The Ruined Cottage and The Pedlar*, ed. James Butler (1979); and *The Thirteen-Book Prelude*, ed. Mark L. Reed (1991).

Mark L. Reed, *A Bibliography of William Wordsworth, 1787–1930* (Cambridge, 2013), is a comprehensive history of the publication of the works in the poet's own time and for eighty years after his death.

BIOGRAPHIES AND BIOGRAPHICAL STUDIES

My recommendation would be to begin with the eyewitness accounts in Hazlitt's 'My First Acquaintance with Poets', available in his *Selected Writings*, ed. Jon Cook (Oxford, 2009), and De Quincey's *Recollections of the Lakes and the Lake Poets*, ed. David Wright (Harmondsworth, 1970), then perhaps proceed to *Barron Field's Memoirs of Wordsworth*, ed. Geoffrey Little (Sydney, 1975) and the vignettes in *William Wordsworth: Interviews and Recollections*, ed. Harold Orel (Basingstoke, 2005). *William Wordsworth: The Critical Heritage 1793–1820*, ed. Robert Woof (2001) is a mine of golden material. Readers with an appetite for other full-scale biographies have an ample selection to choose from, including Juliet Barker, *Wordsworth: A Life* (2000); Stephen Gill, *William Wordsworth: A Life* (Oxford, 1989); Kenneth Johnston, *The Hidden*

Wordsworth (New York, 1998); Mary Moorman, *William Wordsworth: A Biography: The Early Years 1770–1803* (Oxford, 1957) and *The Later Years 1803–1850* (Oxford, 1965); John Worthen, *The Life of William Wordsworth* (Oxford, 2014); and Duncan Wu, *Wordsworth: An Inner Life* (Oxford, 2002).

Particular aspects of the life are studied most rewardingly in Tom Mayberry, *Coleridge and Wordsworth in the West Country* (Stroud, 1992); Lucy Newlyn, *William and Dorothy Wordsworth: All in Each Other* (Oxford, 2013); Adam Nicolson, *The Making of Poetry: Coleridge, the Wordsworths and their Year of Marvels* (2019); Nicholas Roe, *Wordsworth and Coleridge: The Radical Years* (Oxford, 1988, 2nd edn 2018); Adam Sisman, *The Friendship: Wordsworth and Coleridge* (2006); T. W. Thompson, ed. Robert Woof, *Wordsworth's Hawkshead* (1970); and John Worthen, *The Gang: Coleridge, the Hutchinsons and the Wordsworths in 1802* (New Haven, 2001).

The other members of the 'triumvirate' are exceptionally well served in Richard Holmes, *Coleridge: Early Visions* (1989) and *Coleridge: Darker Reflections* (1998); Robert Gittings and Jo Manton, *Dorothy Wordsworth* (Oxford, 1985); Frances Wilson, *The Ballad of Dorothy Wordsworth* (2008); and Pamela Woof, *Dorothy Wordsworth, Writer* (Grasmere, 1988). Belated justice has been done to Thelwall in Judith Thompson, *John Thelwall in the Wordsworth Circle: The Silenced Partner* (New York, 2012). Kathleen Jones brings alive the women in the Wordsworth circle in *A Passionate Sisterhood: The sisters, wives and daughters of the Lake Poets* (1997). The authoritative life of Southey is W. A. Speck, *Robert Southey: Entire Man of Letters* (New Haven, 2006). De Quincey has been fortunate in his recent biographers: Grevel Lindop, *The Opium Eater: A Life of Thomas De Quincey* (1981); Robert Morrison, *The English Opium Eater: A Biography of Thomas De Quincey* (2009); and Frances Wilson, *Guilty Thing: A Life of Thomas De Quincey* (2016). The Cockneys are brought alive in Jeffrey Cox's *Poetry and Politics in the Cockney School* (Cambridge, 1999) and Gregory Dart's *Metropolitan Art and Literature, 1810-1840: Cockney Adventures* (Cambridge, 2012).

CONTEXT

There are many excellent books on the rise of the picturesque, tourism and Wordsworth's place in the Lake District, for example Malcolm Andrews, *The Search for the Picturesque: Landscape Aesthetics and Tourism in Britain, 1760–1800* (Stanford, 1989); David McCracken, *Wordsworth and the Lake District: A Guide to the Poems and their Places* (Oxford, 1985); Ian Thompson, *The English Lakes: A History* (2010); Victoria and Albert Museum, *The Discovery of the Lake District: A Northern Arcadia and its Uses* (1984); Anne D. Wallace, *Walking, Literature, and English Culture: The Origins and Uses of Peripatetic in the Nineteenth Century* (Oxford, 1993); and Robert Woof and Stephen Hebron, *Towards Tintern Abbey* (Grasmere, 1998). For Victorian developments and the birth of 'Wordsworthshire', I especially recommend Saeko Yoshikawa, *William Wordsworth and the Invention of Tourism 1820–1900* (Aldershot, 2014).

On the idea of Romanticism, I would begin with Tim Blanning's admirably concise, *The Romantic Revolution: A History* (2010), then proceed to Isaiah Berlin, ed. Henry Hardy, *The Roots of Romanticism* (1999). For a wealth of illustrated material relating Wordsworth to his age, seek out Jonathan Wordsworth, Michael C. Jaye and Robert Woof, *William Wordsworth and the Age of English Romanticism* (Grasmere and New Brunswick, 1987). On the political side, I would go first to E. P. Thompson, *The Romantics: England in a Revolutionary Age* (New York, 1997), then return to Isaiah Berlin, ed. Henry Hardy, *Political Ideas in the Romantic Age: their Rise and Influence on Modern Thought* (2006). For hard facts about sales and reading habits, William St Clair's *The Reading Nation in the Romantic Period* (Cambridge, 2004) is indispensable.

CRITICISM

The academic literature is extensive. To survey its range, begin with the compendious *Oxford Handbook of William Wordsworth*, eds Richard Gravil and Daniel Robinson (Oxford, 2015), or, if intimidated by scale, the more modest *Cambridge Companion to Wordsworth*, ed. Stephen Gill (Cambridge, 2003). Among the literary critical works of the late twentieth century that helped to shape my sense of Wordsworth were: M. H. Abrams, *Natural Supernaturalism: Tradition and Revolution in Romantic Literature* (New York, 1971); David Bromwich, *Disowned by Memory: Wordsworth's Poetry of the 1790s* (Chicago, 1998); Hugh Sykes Davies, *Wordsworth and the Worth of Words* (Cambridge, 1986); David Ellis, *Wordsworth, Freud and the Spots of Time: Interpretation in The Prelude* (Cambridge, 1985); Stephen Gill, *Wordsworth and the Victorians* (Oxford, 1998); Gary Harrison, *Wordsworth's Vagrant Muse: Poetry, Poverty and Power* (Detroit, 1994); Geoffrey H. Hartman, *Wordsworth's Poetry 1787– 1814* (New Haven, 1964) and *The Unremarkable Wordsworth* (Minneapolis, 1987); Mary Jacobus, *Tradition and Experiment in Wordsworth's Lyrical Ballads 1798* (Oxford, 1976); Lucy Newlyn, *Coleridge, Wordsworth and the Language of Allusion* (Oxford, 1986); H. W. Piper, *The Active Universe: Pantheism and the Concept of Imagination in the English Romantic Poets* (1962); and Jonathan Wordsworth, *The Music of Humanity* (1969) and *The Borders of Vision* (Oxford, 1982).

Among twenty-first-century ventures, I have been impressed by: Simon Bainbridge, *British Poetry and the Revolutionary and Napoleonic Wars* (Oxford, 2003); Matthew Bevis, *Wordsworth's Fun* (Chicago, 2019); Sally Bushell, *Text as Process: Creative Composition in Wordsworth, Tennyson and Dickinson* (Charlottesville, 2009); Richard Cronin, *The Politics of Romantic Poetry: In Search of the Pure Commonwealth* (Basingstoke, 2000); Paul H. Fry, *Wordsworth and the Poetry of what we are* (New Haven, 2008); Brian Goldberg, *The Lake Poets and Professional Identity* (Cambridge, 2007); Richard Gravil, *Wordsworth and Helen Maria*

Williams; or, The Perils of Sensibility (Penrith, 2010); Mary Jacobus, *Romantic Things: A Tree, a Rock, a Cloud* (Chicago, 2012); Steven Matthews, *Ceaseless Music: Sounding Wordsworth's 'The Prelude'* (2017); Daniel Robinson, *Myself and some other Being: Wordsworth and the Life Writing* (Iowa City, 2014); Nicholas Roe, *The Politics of Nature: William Wordsworth and some Contemporaries* (2nd edn, Basingstoke, 2002); Fiona Stafford, *Local Attachments: The Province of Poetry* (Oxford, 2010); and Susan J. Wolfson, *Romantic Interactions: Social Being and the Turns of Literary Action* (Baltimore, 2010). Less overtly Wordsworthian, but profoundly true to his spirit, so most highly recommended, are John Felstiner, *Can Poetry Save the Earth?* (New Haven, 2009) and Susan Stewart, *Poetry and the Fate of the Senses* (Chicago, 2001).

ACKNOWLEDGMENTS

My thanks, long after his death, to my father for introducing me to Wordsworth and the Lake District, and to my teachers – notably the late Alan Hurd at Sevenoaks and the great Christopher Ricks at Cambridge – who shared my passion and helped me to understand the work more deeply. The suggestions for further reading should be regarded as further acknowledgments: to the many dedicated Wordsworth and Coleridge scholars, from whom I have learned so much. I think especially of those, several of them now departed, who have given me their friendship as well as their learning, among them John and Gillian Beer, David Bromwich, Frederick Burwick, Marilyn Gaull, Richard Gravil, Peter Larkin, Terry McKormick, Lucy Newlyn, Seamus Perry, Nicholas Roe, Bill Ruddick, Jane Stabler, Nicola Trott, Mary Wedd, and Duncan Wu.

They were my fellow walkers on Richard Wordsworth's Wordsworth Summer Conference during the 1980s, which so profoundly shaped my thinking about the relationship between writers and place. The academic side of that remarkable endeavour was overseen by two extraordinary men. One was Richard's cousin, Jonathan Wordsworth, an Oxford don who specialized in the work of his ancestor, to whom he bore a striking resemblance, and who did more than anyone else to help us understand the evolution of *The Prelude*. The other was Robert Woof, who looked after the Wordsworth Library across the road from Dove Cottage, where, by some miracle of preservation and legerdemain of purchasing, a huge repository of the poet's original manuscripts was held – there, in the very environment that he so cherished and out of which he created so much of his work. Both Robert and his library, with its piles of books and manuscripts in what seemed to be nothing more than an old barn, exuded an air of chaos that concealed an astonishing wealth of scholarship and local lore. Then there was Robert's wife, Pamela, who somehow seemed like Dorothy Wordsworth to his William and who duly became a distinguished and highly sensitive editor and reader of Dorothy. Fittingly, their daughter, Emily Woof, whom I remember as a teenage girl on those ascents of Scafell, Skiddaw and the Old Man of Coniston, became an actor and played the part of Dorothy in the movie *Pandaemonium* (screenwriter Frank Cottrell-Boyce took the title from an anthology of eyewitness accounts of the Romantic and industrial revolutions compiled by Humphrey Jennings, which was also his inspiration for the opening ceremony of the 2012 London Olympics, thus helping to keep the Wordsworthian heritage alive). The hikes were led by the redoubtable Molly Lefebure, a former Home Office pathologist's assistant who had endured the Blitz, hunted on foot with the Blencathra Foxhounds for half a century, and was now writing books about Coleridge's opium addiction and his dysfunctional marriage. Among the speakers who joined us on the hills were not only the world's leading scholars of Romanticism such as Geoffrey Hartman from Yale and Thomas McFarland from Princeton, but also such luminaries as Seamus Heaney (was he the Wordsworth of our time? we wondered) and Britain's last truly intellectual political party leader Michael Foot (there to speak up for Wordsworth's great opposite, Lord Byron). Without all the memories of that time, in which indeed it was very heaven to be a young scholar of Romanticism, this book would never have been started.

That it has been finished is due to the forbearance of Arabella Pike at William Collins and Jennifer Banks at Yale University Press, who waited so many years for final delivery of a project that went through several metamorphoses and endless delays caused by other calls, such as the scale and complexity of the Ted Hughes archive, the growth of my E. H. Gombrich lectures into a much bigger book than originally planned, and the small matter of running an Oxford college for eight years. For waiting so long, then editing and publishing me with such authority and speed, heartfelt thanks. I am also most grateful to my anonymous reader at Yale University Press, for encouragement, suggestions and corrections, and to the publishing teams on either side of the Atlantic: Iain Hunt, Jo Thompson, Abigail Storch and my superb copy editor David Milner and indexer Mark Wells.

The serendipity of the delay was that it has allowed the book to become a present for Wordsworth on his 250th birthday, accompanied by the further gift of three documentaries for BBC Radio 4, in which I had the pleasure of walking in the poet's footsteps in the Lakes, the Wye Valley, the Quantocks, Calais and Paris, in the company of my superb producer Beatrice (Beaty) Rubens, at the behest of commissioner extraordinaire James Runcie. For their participation, particular thanks are due to Simon Russell Beale (who voiced the poems to perfection), Melvyn Bragg (friend and lifelong Wordsworthian), Lynn Hunt (historian of the French Revolution), Alice Oswald (pre-eminent river poet of our time), James Rebanks (shepherd, author, dalesman), fellow author Adam Nicolson, actor and writer Emily Woof.

For assistance with manuscripts and illustrations, I am most grateful to Jeff Cowton, Rebecca Turner, Melissa Mitchell and John Coombe at the Jerwood Centre, Dove Cottage, and Emily and Matthew Heath at Rydal Mount. Thanks to Jim McCue for helping me to sort out the structure of the book's opening chapters.

I am also grateful to Gresham College for giving me the opportunity, during my tenure in the ancient position of Professor of Rhetoric in the City of London, to try out some of this material – along with more extended thoughts on Keats and Byron – in a series of public lectures on Wordsworth and the Romantics. The chapter 'Among the Cockneys' makes use of a lecture I gave as president of the Hazlitt Society, with thanks to Gregory Dart; it was published, giving a much fuller account of the subject, as 'Hazlitt on Wordsworth' in the admirable *Hazlitt Review*, 11 (2018), 5–22.

My treatment of the *Guide to the Lakes* and the origins of the National Trust draws on and develops the argument of my now prohibitively expensive slender volume *Romantic Ecology: Wordsworth and the Environmental Tradition* (Routledge, 1991). That book led to my work of 'ecopoetics', *The Song of the Earth* (Picador and Harvard University Press, 2000), and thence to my biographies of the two other English poets of nature who, in their very different ways, stand beside Wordsworth: John Clare and Ted Hughes. In one sense, then, this book completes a circle and is a kind of ending. At the same time, in returning me to poetry, and the arts more generally, as a way of engaging with what is now the biggest challenge facing humanity – the sustainability of our environment – it is also a new beginning, a springboard for my future work as Foundation Professor of Environmental Humanities in the College of Liberal Arts and the School of Sustainability at Arizona State University, an opportunity for which I owe profound gratitude to Jeffrey Cohen (an exemplary literary ecocritic himself), President Michael Crow, Gary Dirks, Provost Mark Searle, and especially my co-dedicatee Mark Lussier.

And what can I say to Paula, Tom, Ellie and Harry but thanks for coming on the adventure to other mountains with me, rattlesnakes, scorpions and all.

NOTES

All quotations from Wordsworth's autobiographical epic are from the Norton Critical Edition, *The Prelude: 1799, 1805, 1850*, eds Jonathan Wordsworth, M. H. Abrams and Stephen Gill (New York, 1979). The 1805 text is used, unless otherwise stated; citations are by line number. All other quotations from Wordsworth's poems are, unless otherwise stated, from *The Poems of William Wordsworth: collected reading texts from the Cornell Wordsworth series*, ed. Jared Curtis (Penrith, 2009), which generally prints Wordsworth's first and freshest versions, but frequent use is also made of *The Poetical Works of William Wordsworth*, eds Ernest de Selincourt and Helen Darbishire (5 vols, Oxford, 1940–67, cited as PW), which generally prints his revised final versions. His prose works are quoted from *The Prose Works of William Wordsworth*, eds W. J. B. Owen and Jane Worthington Smyser (3 vols, Oxford, 1974), cited as

PrW. Letters are quoted from *The Letters of William and Dorothy Wordsworth*, ed. Ernest de Selincourt, 2nd edn revised by Chester L. Shaver, Mary Moorman and Alan G. Hill (8 vols, Oxford, 1967–93), cited as LEY, LMY and LLY for *Early Years*, *Middle Years* and *Later Years*. The highly revealing notes on the circumstances of composition of the poems, dictated to Isabella Fenwick, are quoted from *The Fenwick Notes of William Wordsworth: A Revised Electronic Edition*, ed. Jared Curtis (Bristol, 2007), cited as FN. Dorothy's journals are quoted from *The Journals of Dorothy Wordsworth*, ed. Ernest de Selincourt (2 vols, 1941), cited as DWJ. The *Collected Letters of Samuel Taylor Coleridge*, ed. E. L. Griggs (6 vols, Oxford, 1956–71), are cited as STCL and *The Notebooks of Samuel Taylor Coleridge*, ed. Kathleen Coburn (5 double vols, New York, 1957–2002), as STCN (cited by entry number). For the day-to-day details of Wordsworth's life, I have relied heavily on Mark L. Reed's two volumes, *Wordsworth: The Chronology of the Early Years 1770–1799* (Cambridge, Mass., 1967), cited as CEY, and *Wordsworth: The Chronology of the Middle Years 1800–1815* (Cambridge, Mass., 1975). Where possible, early critical responses to Wordsworth are quoted from Robert Woof's compendious anthology, *William Wordsworth: The Critical Heritage 1793–1820* (2001), cited as CH. Place of publication of all works is London, unless otherwise stated.

PREFACE

1. 'Thought of a Briton on the Subjugation of Switzerland'.
2. Stephen, 'A Sonnet', in *Lapsus Calami* (1891).
3. Lady Caroline Lamb's much quoted characterization of Byron, recorded in her diary on first meeting him, and reported in the *Memoirs* of Lady Morgan.
4. Kenneth Johnson, *The Hidden Wordsworth: Poet, Lover, Rebel, Spy* (New York, 1998); Juliet Barker, *Wordsworth: A Life* (2000).
5. Byron, dedication to *Don Juan* (1819).

6. PrW 1. 182.

7. My select bibliography suggests these and other starting points for further reading.

8. Hazlitt, 'My First Acquaintance with Poets' (1823), in CH 43.

9. Text here from the earliest 'Two-Part' *Prelude*, 1. 288–94 (begun as such in 1799, though some passages composed in 1798).

10. *Prelude*, 11. 336.

CHAPTER 1. THE EPOCH

1. We cannot be certain that he read one book per night, but it would seem logical, especially given the coincidence with the twelve days of Christmas. Coleridge's response-poem, discussed below, tells of his silent listening 'Eve following eve', which suggests many evenings.

2. William Hazlitt, 'My First Acquaintance with Poets', in CH 42–3.

3. *Prelude*, 1. 1–4.

4. Ibid., 13. 442–52.

5. Samuel Taylor Coleridge, *Poems*, ed. John Beer (1993), pp. 392–9, in a parallel text beside the revised version, 'To a Gentleman, composed on the night after his recitation of a poem on the growth of an individual mind', published in *Sibylline Leaves* (1817).

6. STCN 2975.

7. Ibid., 3148 (13 Sept 1807).

8. Ibid., 3328 (May 1808).

9. Ibid., 3231, my translations.

10. See the excellent account of Adam Roberts, 'The Latin "Ad Vilmum Axiologum" (1807): Coleridge and Ariosto', http://samueltaylorbloggeridge.blogspot.com/2015/11/the-latin-ad-vilmum-axiologum-1807.html.

11. STCN 2975, Note.

12. Ibid., 4537 (May 1819). The words about her breasts are written in Greek.

13. Nor even for certain whether Wordsworth was actually in the bed: the passages might just fit the construction that he was sitting in the room, with Sara alone in bed. That would still have constituted a degree of intimacy that was too much for Coleridge.

14. 12 March 1811, STCL 3. 305.

CHAPTER 2. A VOICE THAT FLOWED ALONG MY DREAMS

1. 'The Two-Part *Prelude* of 1799', in *The Prelude 1799, 1805, 1850*, eds Jonathan Wordsworth, M. H. Abrams and Stephen Gill (New York, 1979), 1. 1–6.

2. Alexander Carlyle, *Anecdotes and Characters of the Times*, ed. J. Kinsley (1973), p. 213.

3. LEY 7.

4. Ibid., 562–3 – Wordsworth, after John's death.

5. PW 4. 395.

6. Christopher Wordsworth, *Memoirs of William Wordsworth* (2 vols, 1851), 1. 9.

7. According to the Wordsworth family Bible, William was baptized on 13 April 1770, six days after his birth (early baptism was the norm, to ensure salvation in the event of infant death), then christened (the public declaration of a Christian upbringing) on the day of Dorothy's baptism. CEY 39–40.

8. 'To a Butterfly'.

9. 1799 *Prelude*, 1. 17–26. In the 1805 version (1. 291–99) he is five years old – such very early memories are inevitably

imprecise.

10. 1850 *Prelude*, 13. 143–50. As so often, the movement of the verse mimics the thought: the crossing of the line-ending with 'crossed / The naked summit' and 'space / Boundless' is itself a kind of 'disappearing line', a breaking of boundaries into the space of imagination.

11. *Memoirs*, 1. 9.

12. 1799 *Prelude*, 2. 268–94.

13. Ibid., 2. 311–26. Some critics (e.g. Moorman, *The Early Years*, 44) have denied any association between these lines and the death of Wordsworth's mother, arguing that they refer to the way in which his relationship with nature was first supported by such 'props' as boyish sports and companionable adventures, but that it became a solitary affair. But Wordsworth did not record a single break from company to solitude; besides, whether the association is conscious or unconscious, it is made inevitable by the close proximity to the images of mother and baby.

CHAPTER 3. FOSTERED

1. Quoted, CEY, 46n.

2. LEY 663.

3. *Prelude*, 1. 305–9.

4. 'Wordsworth's Skates' in Heaney, *District and Circle* (2006, p. 22). To be pedantic, it would actually seem that the poem alludes to a second pair, in Dove Cottage itself, which are bootless runners with frayed leather ties.

5. *Prelude*, 2. 99–144.

6. Ibid., 1. 460–2.

7. Ibid., 1. 477–8; 1850 1. 450.

8. 1798–9 *Prelude*, 1. 75–83; 1805 1. 485–6.

9. Ibid., 1. 490–2.

10. *The Friend*, 28 Dec 1809; *Poems* (1815), in *Poetical Works*, ed. de Selincourt, 1. 248–9.

11. T. W. Thompson, *Wordsworth's Hawkshead*, ed. Robert Woof (1970), pp. 108–9.

12. See Jeremy Adler, 'On steely wings', *Times Literary Supplement*, 4 Dec 2018, https://www.the-tls.co.uk/articles/public/on-steely-wings-skating/.

13. 1799 *Prelude*, 1. 298.

14. *Eighteenth Century Collections Online*, a database of 200,000 volumes published between 1700 and 1799, has nearly 30,000 instances of the adjective 'memorable' and over 90,000 of the verb 'remember', but not one of 'rememberable'. The *Oxford English Dictionary* offers no eighteenth-century instances, but interestingly has early nineteenth-century examples from two members of the Wordsworth circle, Southey and Hazlitt.

15. 1799 *Prelude*, 2. 27–31. Again, *Eighteenth Century Collections Online* has no precedent for 'self-presence'.

16. Butler, *The Analogy of Religion Natural and Revealed, to the Constitution and Course of Nature* (5th edn, 1765), pp. 440–4, responding to Locke, *An Essay on Human Understanding*, 2. 27. 18.

17. 1799 *Prelude*, 1. 299–313. As often, there is an element of conflation in Wordsworth's memory: the Penrith murderer had actually killed a butcher; the man who poisoned his wife was probably a memory of a different execution, on a gibbet in the water-meadows near the home of Wordsworth's foster-mother Ann Tyson (*Norton Prelude*, p. 9n).

18. Ibid., 1. 316–27.

19. Ibid., 1. 277–9.

20. Ibid., 1. 361–70.

21. *The Standard Edition of the Complete Works of Sigmund Freud*, eds James Strachey and Anna Freud (24 vols, 1953–74), 3. 305–7. The analogy between Wordsworth and Freud in this regard has been discussed in several excellent books, including Richard Onorato, *The Character of the Poet: Wordsworth in 'The Prelude'* (Princeton, 1971); David Ellis, *Wordsworth, Freud and the Spots of Time: Interpretation in 'The Prelude'* (Cambridge, 1985); and Douglas Wilson, *The Romantic Dream: Wordsworth and the Poetics of the Unconscious* (Lincoln, Nebraska, 1993).

22. *Hamlet*, 1. 4. 24.

23. Quoted from *Prelude*, 1. 393–5.

24. MS JJ fragment (c), 1–46.

25. 1799 *Prelude*, 1. 130–2.

26. *Prelude*, 1. 429–42.

CHAPTER 4: THERE WAS A BOY

1. George Dyer, 'The River Cam', in his *Poems* (1801).

2. *Prelude*, 7. 93–104. See further, Thompson, *Wordsworth's Hawkshead* (to which this chapter is indebted), pp. 42–3.

3. Thompson, *Wordsworth's Hawkshead*, pp. 71–2.

4. *Prelude*, 4. 76–83.

5. 'The Two April Mornings', *Lyrical Ballads* (1800).

6. 'Poems on the Naming of Places I', *Lyrical Ballads* (1800).

7. P. B. Shelley, 'Ode to the West Wind' (1819).

8. On this, see my *Shakespeare and the English Romantic Imagination* (Oxford, 1986) and *Shakespearean Constitutions: Politics, Theatre, Criticism 1730–1830* (Oxford, 1989).

9. Jane Austen, *Mansfield Park* (1814), 1. 60.

10. *The Winter's Tale*, 4. 4. 169–71.

11. MS JJ fragment (a), 127–31 (in *The Prelude*, eds Wordsworth, Abrams and Gill).

12. By Lewis Bayly (1613), one of the bestselling Protestant books of the seventeenth and eighteenth centuries, going through over seventy editions by Wordsworth's time.

13. Henry Home, Lord Kames, *Elements of Criticism* (1762), I. 4–5.

14. Robert Lowell, 'Night Sweat', in *For the Union Dead* (1964).

15. Dove Cottage MS 19.7 (also known as MS JJ).

16. STCL I. 453.

17. 1799 *Prelude*, I. 13–15.

18. James Thomson, 'Autumn', lines 1352–3, in *The Seasons* (1730).

19. William Cowper, *The Task* (1785), I. 181–3, 749–53. Wordsworth frequently borrowed, or alluded to, Cowper's phraseology.

20. Preface of 1815, PrW 3. 28. Though 'satire' is not right for Wordsworth's philosophical vein.

21. Cowper, *The Task*, I. 182–210.

22. Joanna Baillie, *De Monfort: A tragedy*, act 5 scene 3, in her *A Series of Plays* (1799), p. 378.

23. Thomas De Quincey, *Recollections of the Lakes and the Lake Poets*, ed. David Wright (Harmondsworth, 1970), p. 194.

24. Closing lines of 'There was a Boy' in *Lyrical Ballads* (1800); further revised in 1805 *Prelude*, to begin 'This boy was taken from his mates, and died / In childhood ere he was full ten years old'.

25. De Quincey, *Recollections*, p. 160.

26. Reminiscence of Fletcher Raincock, in Thompson, *Wordsworth's Hawkshead*, pp. 211–15.

27. 1799 *Prelude*, I. 57–66; also 1805, I. 342–51.

28. *Prelude*, 3. 645–9.

29. Ibid., 7. 146–8.

30. Ibid., 4. 247–64.

31. As noted by Beth Lau, 'Wordsworth and current memory research', *Studies in English Literature 1500–1900*, 42 (2002), 675–92. In reading Antonio Damasio's masterly *The Feeling of What Happens: Body, Emotion and the Making of Consciousness* (2000), which argues that the human self is characterised by a core consciousness defined as 'the feeling of knowing a feeling' and an extended consciousness that depends on memory, I frequently found myself scribbling 'Wordsworth' in the margin.

32. *The Prelude* MS W (Dove Cottage MS 38), fos. 47^r–51^r, in *The Thirteen-Book Prelude*, ed. Mark L. Reed (2 vols, Ithaca, 1991): photographs 1. 415–23, transcriptions 2. 300–7. Seemingly intended for concluding sequence of a five-book version of *The Prelude*: see Jonathan Wordsworth, 'The Five-Book *Prelude* of early spring 1804', *Journal of English and Germanic Philology*, 76 (1977), 1–25.

33. *Prelude*, 11. 334–43.

CHAPTER 5: WALKING INTO REVOLUTION

1. LEY 37.

2. Published 1807; the notebook Wordsworth had with him in France (Dove Cottage MS 38) dates the poem 'August 1st', the day he arrived in Calais. This is corrected to August 7th in the printer's copy for the 1807 volume.

3. LEY 3.

4. Ibid., 7.

5. *Prelude*, 7. 424–7.

6. These two lines are among the (few) truly great insertions in the later version of *The Prelude* (1850, 3. 62–3). Other quotations in this paragraph and the next are from Book 3.

7. *Prelude*, 3. 124–9, developed and personalized from a passage in

'The Ruined Cottage' manuscript, discussed in chapter 9, below.

8. These lines are an addition in the 1850 *Prelude* (4. 6–11): the older Wordsworth became, the stronger his attachment to the Lakes, here projected backward onto his first summer return from Cambridge. As always, we cannot be sure that his feelings at the time were quite so strong.

9. *Prelude*, 5. 95–9.

10. The Arab dream is told in *Prelude*, 5. 49–165 and 1850, 50–167.

11. *Prelude*, 6. 64–75. 'Encouraged' is changed to 'emboldened' in 1850.

12. Ibid., 5. 180–2.

13. This case is made in detail in David Chandler's superb article, 'Robert Southey and *The Prelude*'s "Arab dream"', *Review of English Studies*, 54 (2003), 203–19, which also condenses prior scholarship on the subject.

14. *Wordsworth at Cambridge: A Record of the Commemoration Held at St John's College, Cambridge in April 1950* (repr. Cambridge, 2009), pp. 31–2. See further, B. R. Schneider, *Wordsworth's Cambridge Education* (Cambridge, 1957).

15. *Prelude*, 6. 93–8.

16. LY 1. 169, Wordsworth to his brother Christopher.

17. Gray to his mother, 13 Oct 1739, in *The Poems and Letters of Thomas Gray with Memoirs of his Life and Writings by William Mason* (1775, repr. 1820), p. 62.

18. Wordsworth's earliest surviving letter to Dorothy, LEY 33.

19. *Descriptive Sketches* (1793), note to line 347.

20. Ibid., 690–5.

21. *Prelude*, 6. 446–65.

22. It took him some time in the compositional process to have the confidence to jump-cut straight from the remembered moment of disappointment to the paean to 'Imagination': the

draft in MS WW has a transitional passage, later moved to book 8 (711–27), involving an extended simile of a traveller going into a cave and being confused by the shifting play of light and darkness, shadow and substance.

23. *Prelude*, 6. 534–6.

24. Ibid., 6. 538–42.

25. *Paradise Lost*, 5. 164–5.

26. *Prelude*, 6. 556–72.

27. *Descriptive Sketches*, 249–50.

28. LEY 34.

29. *Prelude*, 6. 577–80.

30. DWJ 2. 259.

31. 6 Sept 1790, LEY 35.

32. From the Greek 'the many', this was the lowest class of pass degree, below the first-class Wranglers, the second-class Senior Optime and the third-class Junior Optime. Those at Wordsworth's level – without Honours, we might say – were known as 'poll men'.

33. *Prelude*, 7. 163–4, 612–23.

34. Dorothy to Jane Pollard, 26 June 1791, LEY 51.

35. Jones to Wordsworth, Dove Cottage WLMS A/Jones, Robert/1 (11 Oct 1815).

36. Some scholars have suggested that the ascent took place during Wordsworth's second visit to Jones in Wales, two years later, but the weight of evidence strongly favours the 1791 tour (CEY 315).

37. *Prelude*, 13. 1–65.

38. Ibid., 13. 66–73.

39. Ibid., 2. 336–7.

40. Thomas Pennant, *A Tour in Wales* (1784), 2. 164.

41. *An Evening Walk* (1793), notes to lines 173, 317, 187, 83.

42. James Beattie, *Dissertations Moral and Critical* (1783), p. 87.

43. 'The Vale of Esthwaite', 274–83.

CHAPTER 6: TWO REVOLUTIONARY WOMEN

1. 30 Nov 1791, LEY 62.

2. See Loraine Fletcher's excellent *Charlotte Smith: A Critical Biography* (Basingstoke, 1998), p. 55.

3. *Ethelinde; or, The Recluse of the Lake* (5 vols, 1789), I. 58.

4. *Desmond: A Novel* (3 vols, 1792), Preface, I. ii.

5. Thomas Lowes, comment added to a letter from Charlotte Smith to his wife, quoted, Fletcher, *Charlotte Smith*, p. 159.

6. *Poems*, I. 65.

7. Ibid., I. 66.

8. *Peru*, 'Canto the Sixth', 216ff., 247–50.

9. *Letters written in France* (1790), pp. 1–2.

10. Ibid., p. 14.

CHAPTER 7: BUT TO BE YOUNG WAS VERY HEAVEN

1. *Prelude*, 9. 48–9.

2. Ibid., 9. 65–7.

3. Ibid., 9. 156–61, 178–9, 195–200, 218–49.

4. Ibid., 9. 328–36.

5. Ibid., 9. 511–34.

6. Samuel Johnson, *Dictionary of the English Language* (1755); Joseph Priestley, 'Of Memory', in his *Hartley's Theory of the Human Mind, on the Principle of the Association of Ideas* (1775), p. 211; Joseph Berington, *Letters on Materialism and Hartley's Theory of the Human Mind, addressed to Dr Joseph Priestley* (1776), p. 144.

7. *Prelude*, 9. 555.

8. FN 55.

9. Émile Legouis, *William Wordsworth and Annette Vallon* (1922), p. 25.

10. 'Vaudracour and Julia', 95–101, *Poetical Works*, 2. 62.

11. Ibid., 171–84.

12. Ibid., 253–61.

13. Ibid., 278–80, 302, 283.

14. Published in Coleridge's *Fears in Solitude* (1798).

15. *Prelude*, 10. 1–8.

16. James Watt Jr to his father, 5 Sept 1792, quoted in Nicholas Roe's indispensable *Wordsworth and Coleridge: The Radical Years* (Oxford, 1988), p. 72.

17. *Prelude*, 10. 46–53.

18. Ibid., 10. 57–66.

19. Ibid., 10. 70–7.

20. Johnson's *Dictionary of the English Language*, 'revolution', senses 1 & 5.

21. Quoted, J. R. MacGillivray, 'Wordsworth and J.-P. Brissot', *Times Literary Supplement*, 29 Jan 1931.

22. *Barron Field's Memoirs of Wordsworth*, ed. Geoffrey Little (Sydney, 1975), p. 26.

23. *Prelude*, 10. 95–100.

24. *Memoirs of William Wordsworth*, 1. 76–7.

25. See J. G. Alger, *Englishmen in the French Revolution* (1889), pp. 325–8.

26. Henry Salt, 'Walking Stewart' (1849), repr. in *Temple Bar*, 93 (1891), 578; De Quincey, 'A Peripatetic Philosopher', in *The Note Book of an English Opium-Eater* (Boston, Mass., 1864), p. 248.

27. Paul Henri Thiry, Baron d'Holbach, *System of Nature; or, the Laws of the Moral and Physical World* (1797), vol. 1, p. 25.

28. *The Apocalypse of Nature* was published as volume two of Stewart's *Travels over the most Interesting Parts of the Globe: to*

Discover the Source of Moral Motion: Communicated to lead
Mankind through the Conviction of the Senses to Intellectual
Existence, and an Enlightened Sense of Nature: In the Year of Man's
Retrospective Knowledge, by Astronomical Calculation 5000 (1790).
Quotations from pp. 10, 22, 55.

29. Ibid., p. 193.
30. *Prelude*, 10. 690–1, 689, 701–2, 692–3.

CHAPTER 8: STEPPING WESTWARD

1. Legouis, *William Wordsworth and Annette Vallon*, pp. 127–33. My
   translations.
2. Ibid., p. 129.
3. Ibid., p. 126.
4. FN 49–50.
5. *An Evening Walk* (1793), 195–206.
6. FN 50.
7. *Prelude*, 10. 253–5.
8. *Prose*, 1. 47.
9. Letter to his friend Mathews, 8 June 1794, LEY 125–6.
10. From Richard Wordsworth, 23 May 1794, letter in Wordsworth
    Library, Dove Cottage, WLMS 2/47.
11. *Prelude*, 10. 457.
12. Ibid., 10. 565–6.
13. Ibid., 10. 931–5.
14. FN 39, 70.
15. Thomas Carlyle, *Reminiscences*, ed. Charles Eliot Norton (2
    vols, 1887), 2. 303.
16. Quoted, Nicholas Roe, *Wordsworth and Coleridge: The Radical
    Years* (2nd edn, Oxford, 2018), p. 53, with acknowledgment to
    Peter Swaab for noting the annotation.
17. *Prelude*, 10. 375–7.

18. A. Watts, *Alaric Watts: A Narrative of his Life* (2 vols, 1884), 2. 286.

19. Edmund Burke, *Reflections on the Revolution in France* (1790), para. 15.

20. Ibid., para. 126.

21. Thomas Paine, *Rights of Man: being an Answer to Mr Burke's Attack on the French Revolution* (1791), pp. 26–7.

22. *Prelude*, 10. 805–29.

23. Ibid., 11. 240.

24. Coleridge's phrase, in the prefatory note to *The Fall of Robespierre*, the verse drama that he and Southey dashed off in the immediate wake of Robespierre's execution in 1794.

25. *Prelude*, 10. 825–9.

26. *The Borderers*, 3. 5. 24–33.

27. '[On the Character of Rivers]' in Wordsworth, *The Borderers*, ed. Robert Osborn (Ithaca, 1982), p. 62.

28. *Poems, chiefly of Early and Late Years; including The Borderers, A Tragedy* (1842), p. 405.

29. *The Borderers*, 3. 5. 60–5.

30. John Frederick Pinney to William Coker, 9 April 1762, http://www.discoveringbristol.org.uk/slavery/learning-journeys/john-pinney/young-pinney/

31. 10 July 1793, LEY 97.

32. LEY 98.

33. Ibid., 101.

34. Ibid., 102–3.

35. 30 Nov 1795, EY 161.

36. Quotations from the final version, 'Guilt and Sorrow' (published, as was *The Borderers*, in Wordsworth's 1842 collection, *Poems, chiefly of Early and Late Years*), lines 491–2, 611–12.

37. Coleridge, *Biographia Literaria* (1817), chap. 4.

38. 'The Old Cumberland Beggar', lines 188–9, in *Lyrical Ballads* (1800).

39. *Specimens of the Table Talk of the late Samuel Taylor Coleridge* (2 vols, 1835), 2. 69.

40. Fair copy by Coleridge of the closing section of the original draft, in a letter of 10 June 1797, in *The Ruined Cottage and The Pedlar*, ed. James Butler (Ithaca, 1979), p. 95.

41. Ruskin's 'Of the Pathetic Fallacy' is in his *Modern Painters*, vol. 3 (1856), 5. 204–5.

42. Letter of 18 Jan 1816 to Archdeacon Francis Wrangham, explaining the technique of the poem *The White Doe of Rylstone*, LMY 2. 276.

43. Manuscript A and Coleridge transcription, *The Ruined Cottage and the Pedlar*, pp. 81, 83, 95.

44. Racedown Notebook: MS 13M, fo. 3ᵛ.

CHAPTER 9: A NEW SPIRIT IN POETRY

1. *The Poetical Works of S. T. Coleridge*, eds Derwent and Sara Coleridge (1852; repr. New York, 1857), p. vi.

2. LEY 188–9.

3. Coleridge to Poole, Dec 1796, STCL 1. 271.

4. STCL 1. 181.

5. LEY 189.

6. Lamb to Coleridge, 27 May 1796, in *The Letters of Charles and Mary Anne Lamb*, ed. Edwin W. Marrs (Ithaca, 1975), 1. 3–4.

7. 'This Lime-Tree Bower my Prison. – A Poem addressed to CHARLES LAMB, of the India-House, London', in *The Annual Anthology*, 2 (1800), pp. 140–4.

8. LEY 190–1.

9. Coleridge to Thelwall, 13 May 1796, STCL 1. 215–16.

10. Coleridge, *Table Talk*, 24 July 1830.

11. FN 44.

12. Letter of 18 July 1797, in '"Yours, A True Sans Culotte": Letters of John Thelwall and Henrietta Cecil Thelwall, 1794–1838', in *Presences that Disturb: Models of Romantic Identity in the Literature and Culture of the 1890s*, ed. Damian Walford Davies (Cardiff, 2002), p. 296. For Thelwall's importance to Wordsworth and Coleridge, see further, Judith Thompson's excellent *John Thelwall in the Wordsworth Circle: The Silenced Partner* (New York, 2012).

13. Jane Austen, *Northanger Abbey* (begun 1797, published 1818), chap. 24.

14. Quoted, George W. Meyer, 'Wordsworth and the Spy Hunt', *American Scholar*, 20 (1950–1), 50–6.

15. Letter from Dr Lysons of Bath to Duke of Portland (Home Secretary), reporting the suspicions of Mogg. These and subsequent quotations from Home Office correspondence were discovered and first published by A. J. Eagleston, 'Wordsworth, Coleridge, and the Spy', in *Coleridge: Studies by Several Hands on the Hundredth Anniversary of his Death*, ed. Edmund Blunden and Earl Griggs (1934), pp. 73–87.

16. Coleridge, *Biographia Literaria* (1817), chap. 10.

17. See Jonathan Israel's masterly study *Radical Enlightenment: Philosophy and the Making of Modernity 1750–1850* (Oxford, 2001).

18. Coleridge, *Poems on Various Subjects* (1796), pp. 98–9.

19. Coleridge to Thelwall, 21 Aug 1797, STCL 1. 343–4.

20. See the whole sequence at *Prelude*, 10. 635–58.

21. Manuscript B (1798) of 'The Ruined Cottage', lines 70–85.

22. Save, perhaps, Ovid in the *Metamorphoses*. And there is a fascinating history of 'geophilia', notably in the middle ages: see Jeffrey Jerome Cohen's rich study *Stone: An Ecology of the Inhuman* (Minneapolis, 2015).

23. LEY 212.

24. *Biographia Literaria*, chap. 10.

25. We do not know exactly when she started doing so. Her Alfoxden journal is lost, but fragments of it, beginning in January 1798, survive at second hand.

26. DWJ 1. 3.

27. Ibid.

28. Ibid., 1. 6.

29. Alfoxden journal, 25 Jan 1798.

30. Entitled 'A Fragment' in Wordsworth's 1798 Alfoxden notebook; published in *Poems* of 1815 as 'A Night-piece'.

31. STCL 1. 331.

32. Ibid., 2. 775 (to William Godwin, Nov 1801).

33. Dove Cottage MS 14. In her excellent book on the shared writing life of brother and sister, Lucy Newlyn argues that 'confluence' is the best term for their collaborative work: *William and Dorothy Wordsworth: All in Each Other* (Oxford, 2016). See also her article 'Confluence: William and Dorothy Wordsworth in 1798', *Journal of Eighteenth Century Studies*, 34 (2011), 227–45.

34. *Prelude*, 10. 904–29.

35. To Southey, July 1797; to Cottle, March 1798: STCL 1. 334, 391.

36. Hazlitt, 'My First Acquaintance with Poets', in his *Complete Works*, ed. P. P. Howe (1930–4), 17. 116–17. Subsequent references from same essay.

CHAPTER 10: THE BANKS OF THE WYE

1. Joseph Cottle, *Early Recollections: Chiefly relating to the late Samuel Taylor Coleridge* (1837), 1. 320.

2. FN 66.

3. Letter from Duke of Argyle to Rev. T. S. Howson (Sept 1848): 'taking four days to compose it, the last 20 lines or so being composed as he walked down the hill from Clifton to Bristol' (quoted, PW 2. 517).

4. My italics; change introduced in *Poems* (1815).

5. All 'Tintern Abbey' quotations from *Lyrical Ballads* (1798).

6. http://www.wyevalleyaonb.org.uk/images/uploads/general/Wordsworth-Walk.pdf.

7. Strong support for Symonds Yat as the location is offered in David Miall's fine article 'Locating Wordsworth: "Tintern Abbey" and the Community with Nature'.' *Romanticism on the Net*, 20 (November 2000), http://www.erudit.org/revue/ron/2000/v/n20/005949ar.html. Miall notes that in Wordsworth's time there was iron smelting along the banks of this part of the Wye, which would account for the 'wreathes of smoke' sent up from among the trees.

8. *Observations on the River Wye, and Several Parts of South Wales, &c.* (2nd edn, 1789), p. 39.

9. Coleridge to Thelwall, 14 Oct 1797, STCL 1. 349.

10. 'The Tuft of Primroses', 478–90.

11. Cottle, *Malvern Hills: A Poem* (1793), Preface, v–vi.

CHAPTER 11: THE EXPERIMENT

1. Quoted from 'Advertisement' in Wordsworth and Coleridge, *Lyrical Ballads*, eds R. L. Brett and A. R. Jones (1963), p. 7. This remains my favourite edition of *Lyrical Ballads*, with excellent endnotes.

2. Full title: *Manual of the Theophilanthropes, or Adorers of God, and Friends of Men. Containing the Exposition of their Dogmas, of their Morals, and of their Religious Practices; with Instruction respecting the Organization and Celebration of Their Worship. Arranged by certain*

Citizens, and adopted by the Theophilanthropic Societies established in Paris. Translated by John Walker, Author of Elements of Geography, and Universal Gazetteer. London 1797.

3. Though 'and Co' clearly means 'and Cottle', this interpretation is still not recognized by most commentators; some have even proposed that the fifth bard might be Wordsworth.

4. The word 'communistic' was used in the nineteenth century for the idea of holding property in common: see, for example, a scathing review of the *Life and Letters of Southey* in the right-wing *Quarterly Review*, 88 (1851), 214, referring to his 'republican and communistic ditties' (which Canning delighted in parodying).

5. STCL 1. 412.

6. Cottle was in financial difficulty at the time, so he very quickly sold on to a London publisher most of the copies that he had printed – Wordsworth had hoped that the volume would go to Joseph Johnson, but by the time that he made the request Cottle had committed it elsewhere. On the complicated publishing history of the book, see D. F. Foxon, 'The Printing of *Lyrical Ballads*, 1798', *The Library*, 5th series, 9 (1954), 221–41.

7. By the Swiss polymath Salomon Gessner (1758), translated into English by Mary Collyer (1761). It was a major influence on the prophetic books of William Blake.

8. Coleridge, Prefatory Note to 'The Wanderings of Cain', in *The Poetical Works of S. T. Coleridge* (1834), 2. 99-100.

9. FN 40.

10. Ibid., 41.

11. Ibid., 42.

12. Ibid., 64.

13. DWJ 1. 13.

14. 1799 *Prelude*, 1. 196–7.

15. 'The Tables Turned'.

16. Though it should be remembered that the effect of anonymous publication was that readers of the first edition did not know which poems were by Wordsworth and which by Coleridge. Indeed, the general assumption was that the entire collection was by a single author.

17. Alexander Pope, *An Essay on Man* (1733), 1. 289.

18. William Hazlitt, *Lectures on the English Poets* (1818), *Complete Works*, 5. 161–2.

19. Ibid., 5. 163.

20. See Robert Mayo, 'The Contemporaneity of the *Lyrical Ballads*', *PMLA*, 69 (1954), 486–522.

21. Blake, 'The Human Abstract', in *Songs of Innocence and of Experience* (1795).

22. Thelwall, *The Tribune*, 2 (1796), no. xvi, 16–17.

23. E. P. Thompson (who goes on to contrast Thelwall with Wordsworth), *The Romantics: England in a Revolutionary Age* (New York, 1997), p. 9.

24. *Prelude*, 12. 161–71.

25. These and many other examples are noted in Mayo's seminal article.

26. See further discussion of Hazlitt in chap. 19.

CHAPTER 12: LUCY IN THE HARZ WITH DOROTHY

1. Hazlitt offers a marvellous pen portrait of him in 'My First Acquaintance with Poets': 'This Chester was a native of Nether Stowey, one of those who were attracted to Coleridge's discourse as flies are to honey, or bees in swarming-time to the sound of a brass pan. He "followed in the chace like a dog who hunts, not like one that made up the cry." He had on a brown cloth coat, boots, and corduroy

breeches, was low in stature, bow-legged, had a drag on his walk like a drover, which he assisted by a hazel switch, and kept on a sort of trot by the side of Coleridge, like a running footman by a state coach, that he might not lose a syllable or sound that fell from Coleridge's lips. He told me his private opinion that Coleridge was a wonderful man. He scarcely opened his lips, much less offered an opinion the whole way: yet of the three, had I to choose during the journey, it would be John Chester. He afterwards followed Coleridge into Germany, where the Kantean philosophers were puzzled how to bring him under any of their categories.' (*Complete Works*, 17. 118.)

2. DWJ 24–5.

3. Quoted, F. H. Adler, *Herder and Klopstock* (Chicago, 1913), p. 3.

4. J. G. Herder, *Sämmtliche Werke*, ed. Bernhard Suphran (Berlin, 1877–1913), 2. 42.

5. Friedrich Schlegel, *Athenäums-fragmente* (1798), # 116, translated by Peter Firchow. On irony: # 51.

6. A. W. Schlegel, *A Course of Lectures on Dramatic Art and Literature* (English trans., repr. 1840), p. 380.

7. *The Friend*, in *The Collected Works of Samuel Taylor Coleridge: The Friend*, ed. Barbara Rooke (Princeton, 1969), 1. 115.

8. 22 Jan 1802, STCL 2. 782–4.

9. Ibid., 2. 782.

10. STCN 2. 2670 (1805).

11. FN 112–13.

12. Dec 1798, LEY 236.

13. Notably Dove Cottage manuscripts 15, 16, 19 (also known as MS JJ, with the earliest drafts of *The Prelude*), 25, 33.

14. Feb 1799, LEY 247.

15. Initial passages were drafted in MS JJ (Dove Cottage MS 19), October to November 1798; two further notebooks, with more

developed versions of Part 1 of the two-part 1799 *Prelude*, also belong to the Goslar months (Dove Cottage MSS 15, 16).

16. Dec 1798, STCL 1. 453.
17. Ibid., 1. 452.
18. LEY 142.
19. 6 April 1799, STCL 1. 478.
20. Ibid., 1. 478–9.
21. Ibid., 1. 479–80.
22. Letter to his publisher John Taylor, 27 Feb 1818, *The Letters of John Keats 1814–1821*, ed. H. E. Rollins (Cambridge, Mass., 1958), 1. 238.
23. FN 62. Late 1798 is a more likely date.
24. Joint letter of William and Dorothy to Coleridge, Dec 1798, LEY 236.
25. Ibid., 237.
26. On Mary Joyce, see my *John Clare: A Biography* (2003), especially pp. 137–8, 233–4, 391–6, 442–3, 457–60.
27. De Quincey, 'William Wordsworth', *Tait's Edinburgh Magazine*, April 1839, 247, but deleted when his essays on Wordsworth were reprinted in *Recollections of the Lakes and the Lake Poets* (1854).
28. 'Three years she grew', published in 1800 *Lyrical Ballads*, but not grouped with 'Strange fits of passion', 'She dwelt among' and 'A slumber'.
29. March 1799, CH 58.
30. Jeffrey to Robert Morehead, ibid.
31. Summer 1799, LEY 268.
32. Unsigned review, *Critical Review*, 24 (Oct 1798), 197–204, CH 66–7.
33. Unsigned review, *Monthly Review*, 29 (June 1799), 202–10, CH 74–8.
34. Jan 1799, CH 71.

35. June 1799, LEY 264.

36. Nov 1799, LEY 272.

37. STCN 1575.

38. 'Home at Grasmere', 219–34.

CHAPTER 13: BY W. WORDSWORTH

1. LEY 274.

2. Thomas De Quincey, *Recollections of the Lakes and the Lake Poets*, ed. David Wright (Harmondsworth, 1970), p. 128.

3. LEY 275. William and Dorothy both spelt the name of the lake 'Rydale', not Rydal.

4. Dorothy to Lady Beaumont, 29 Nov 1805, LEY 649.

5. Dorothy to Lady Beaumont, June 1805, LEY 598.

6. Catherine Clarkson to Priscilla Lloyd, 12 Jan 1800, CH 92–3.

7. Thomas Clarkson, *A Portraiture of Quakerism* (1806), 2. 146–50.

8. In *Poems, in Two Volumes* (1807).

9. See, for example, J. R. Oldfield's two books, *Popular Politics and British Anti-Slavery: The Mobilisation of Public Opinion against the Slave Trade 1787–1807* and *Chords of Freedom: Commemoration, Ritual and Transatlantic Slavery* (Manchester, 1995, 2006).

10. Everyone believed that Toussaint was a slave at the time of the uprising, but he had in fact been enfranchised over twenty years before.

11. 'To Toussaint L'Ouverture', in *Poems, in Two Volumes* (1807).

12. Wordsworth's concern for the rights of authors led to one of the public interventions of his later life, when, together with his friend Thomas Noon Talfourd, he played a major role in the passage of the 1842 Copyright Act, which extended the duration of copyright from twenty-eight years or the lifetime of the author to forty-two years or seven years after the author's death.

13. My account of Mary Robinson is much indebted to Paula Byrne, *Perdita: The Life of Mary Robinson* (2004). See also Heidi Thomson's very informative *Coleridge and the Romantic Newspaper: The Morning Post and the Road to 'Dejection'* (New York, 2016), especially chapters 7 and 8.

14. *Morning Post*, 2 April 1800. Coleridge later thanked Daniel Stuart for his support for *Lyrical Ballads*, so it is possible that the latter wrote (or suggested the writing of) this note, but its style is characteristic of his poetry editor.

15. Jan 1800, STCL 1. 562.

16. Mary Robinson, 17 June 1800, letter in Garrick Club Library.

17. Sept 1800, STCL 1. 627.

18. 1800 Preface to *Lyrical Ballads*, quoted (here and in subsequent paragraphs) from PrW 1. 118–59, which helpfully prints the 1800 text in parallel with final version of 1850, together with textual notes indicating additions that Wordsworth made when *Lyrical Ballads* was reprinted in 1802.

19. Quoted, PrW 1. 154.

20. *Lyrical Ballads* (1798), p. 110.

21. PrW 1. 176.

22. Ibid., 1. 177.

23. 'Now it is remarkable that, excepting the nocturnal Reverie of Lady Winchilsea, and a passage or two in the Windsor Forest of Pope, the poetry of the period intervening between the publication of the Paradise Lost and the Seasons [of Thomson] does not contain a single new image of external nature' – 'Essay, Supplementary to the Preface' (1815), PrW 3. 73.

24. PrW 1. 138.

25. John Dryden, *Of Dramatick Poesie, An Essay* (1668), p. 47.

26. 'For the sake of variety and from a consciousness of my own weakness I have again requested the assistance of a Friend who contributed largely to the first volume and who has now

furnished me with the ~~long and beautiful~~ Poem of Christabel, without which I should not yet have ventured to present a second volume to the public' – 1800 MS of Preface, transcribed in *Lyrical Ballads, and Other Poems, 1797–1800*, eds James Butler and Karen Green (Ithaca, 1992), p. 741.

27. DWJ 1.64.

28. To Davy, 9 Oct 1800, STCL 1. 631; to Wedgwood, 1 Nov 1800, STCL 1. 643.

29. Some of Coleridge's biographers have regarded this moment as a great betrayal on Wordsworth's part and a turning-point in the relationship between the two poets: see, for example, Richard Holmes, *Coleridge: Early Visions* (1989), p. 285 ('it was little short of a catastrophe'). I share the view of John Worthen, *The Gang: Coleridge, the Hutchinsons and the Wordsworths in 1802* (New Haven, 2001), pp. 6–12, that the evidence does not support this interpretation.

30. Letter to James Tobin, Sept 1800, STCL 1. 623.

31. Wordsworth's *Peter Bell* and Coleridge's 'To a Young Ass' were key texts. Cowper's poetry was also a favoured point of reference, as in the seminal contribution of Thomas Erskine, *Cruelty to Animals: the Speech of Lord Erskine, in the House of Peers, on the second reading of the Bill preventing malicious and wanton cruelty to animals* (1809), p. 4. See further, David Perkins, *Romanticism and Animal Rights* (Cambridge, 2003) and Christine Kenyon-Jones, *Kindred Brutes: Animals in Romantic-Period Writing* (Aldershot, 2001). On vegetarianism, Tristram Stuart, *The Bloodless Revolution: A Cultural History of Vegetarianism from 1600 to Modern Times* (2007), and Timothy Morton, *Shelley and the Revolution in Taste* (Cambridge, 1995).

32. *Lyrical Ballads* (1800), 2. 19. 'Westmoreland', not Westmorland, was the common spelling of the name of Grasmere's county.

33. To Fox, Jan 1801, LEY 312–15.

34. His reply was printed in the *Memoirs* of Wordsworth compiled by his nephew in 1851 (I. 17).

35. For sales figures, drawn from the Longman archive, see Appendix 9 of William St Clair's authoritative *The Reading Nation in the Romantic Period* (Cambridge, 2004).

CHAPTER 14: HOME AT GRASMERE

1. Dove Cottage MS 19.

2. DWJ I. 112, 121–2, 125–6, 143–4.

3. MS D, copied by Mary Wordsworth in 1806, in *Home at Grasmere: Part First, Book First of The Recluse*, ed. Beth Darlington (Ithaca, 1977), p. 413.

4. *Home at Grasmere*, lines 129–70.

5. PrW I. 123.

6. DWJ I. 99.

7. Ibid., I. 113–14.

8. STCL 2. 788, 24 Feb 1802 (he actually writes '. . . soon after my return' – his return from London to the Lakes, that is).

9. Printed in Legouis, *William Wordsworth and Annette Vallon*, pp. 137–40.

10. 22 Mar 1802, DWJ I. 128.

11. Ibid., I. 131.

12. 15 April 1802, ibid.

13. Published without title in *Poems, in Two Volumes* (1807), but in Dove Cottage MS 1807/15, the text Wordsworth used for making corrections for his collected edition of 1815, he added 'Daffodils', seemingly as a title.

14. DWJ I. 132.

15. Published in *Poems, in Two Volumes* (1807).

16. 16 April 1802, LEY 348.

17. 16 April 1802, ibid., 350.

18. Dove Cottage MS 41, headed 'Sarah Hutchinson's Poets' and also containing poems by Coleridge and by Sara herself.

19. DWJ i. 139–40.

20. Ibid., i. 142.

21. Published in *Poems* (1815).

22. DWJ i. 172–3.

23. First published in Wordsworth's 1807 collection with the title 'Composed upon Westminster Bridge, Sept. 3, 1803'; the year was corrected to 1802 in the edition of 1838. They had been back in London three days by then, and the weather was not so fair, so it is most likely that the sonnet was not 'composed' on this date, but may have been written down or polished then. There can be no doubt that the *experience*, as recorded in Dorothy's journal, was that of the early morning of 29 July.

24. DWJ i. 175. The de Selincourt edition misses a line due to editorial eyeskip, so the quotation is corrected here from Pamela Woof's edition of Dorothy Wordsworth, *The Grasmere Journals* (Oxford, 1991), p. 125.

25. 'In the cottage of Town-End, one afternoon, in 1801, my Sister read to me the Sonnets of Milton. I had long been well acquainted with them, but I was particularly struck on that occasion with the dignified simplicity and majestic harmony that runs through most of them – in character so totally different from the Italian, and still more so from Shakespeare's fine Sonnets. I took fire, if I may be allowed to say so': FN 73.

26. Published in the 1807 collection.

27. 'Composed in the Valley, Near Dover, On the Day of landing', published in the 1807 collection.

28. 'Nuns fret not', published in the 1807 collection.

29. 'Lying in Abraham's bosom' was a conventional expression for being dead, used most famously in Mistress Quickly's account of Falstaff's death in Shakespeare's *Henry V*, a work that in

33. 'Ode', in *Poems, in Two Volumes* (1807).

34. Published in *Poems, in Two Volumes* (1807).

35. Beaumont to Wordsworth, 24 Oct 1803 (Dove Cottage MS WLL/Beaumont, George/1).

36. LMY 1. 64 (1 Aug 1806).

37. Coleridge to Wordsworth, 10 Sept 1799, STCL 1. 527.

38. STCL 2. 975.

39. FN 87.

40. *Monthly Literary Recreations*, July 1807, CH 169–70.

41. *Critical Review*, Aug 1807, CH 171–76.

42. *Le Beau Monde*, Oct 1807, CH 177–85.

43. *The Satirist*, Nov 1807, CH 201–4.

44. *The Simpliciad* (1808), CH 262–84.

45. LLY 2. 324 (Sept 1830).

46. LMY 1. 146 (May 1807). It should, however, be noted that Wordsworth did care about his immediate reception. When Southey told him that C. V. le Grice, the lead reviewer of the *Critical Review* (who had panned Southey's latest epic, *Madoc*), was hostile to Coleridge and all his circle, Wordsworth wrote to an influential London friend asking him to persuade the editor not to give the volumes to le Grice. 'But alas!' he would later write, on seeing the unsigned hatchet job that appeared in August, 'it has been out of the frying-pan into the fire!' (LMY, 1. 173.)

CHAPTER 16: FROM NEW SCHOOL TO LAKE SCHOOL

1. Jean-Jacques Rousseau, *The Confessions*, trans. J. M Cohen (Penguin, 1953), p. 16.

2. 1 May 1805, LEY 586.

3. Lady Morgan, *Italy* (1821), 2. 140.

14. Robert Southey, *Specimens of Later English Poets* (1807) 2. 420.

15. 27 Feb 1799, LEY 256.

16. *Poems, chiefly in the Scottish Dialect* (Kilmarnock, 1786), p. 159.

17. Wordsworth knew the novel; the parallel is noted in David Chandler's excellent essay, 'In the end despondency & madness: Werther in Wordsworth', *The Wordsworth Circle*, 30 (1999), 55–9.

18. FN 38.

19. Published in *Lyrical Ballads* (1800).

20. 'To H. C., six years old', published in *Poems, in two Volumes* (1807), almost certainly first drafted around this time: in a letter of October 1803 to Tom Poole, Coleridge quoted Wordsworth's phrase: 'Hartley is what he always was . . . a strange strange Boy – *"exquisitely wild"*!' (STCL 2. 1014).

21. 1799 *Prelude*, 1. 17–26.

22. [Henry Fuseli], *Remarks on the Writings and Conduct of J. J. Rousseau* (1767), p. 20.

23. Ibid., p. 25.

24. See Roger Shattuck, *The Forbidden Experiment: The Story of the Wild Boy of Aveyron* (1980).

25. Published posthumously in *Memoirs of the late Mrs Robinson* (1801), prepared for the press by her daughter Maria.

26. Summer 1809, STCN 3538.

27. John Home, *Douglas: A Tragedy of Five Acts* (1789), p. 15.

28. LEY 518–19.

29. Ibid., 520.

30. A. A. Milne, author of *Winnie-the-Pooh*, absorbed the pun when he entitled his famous book of children's poems *Now We are Six* (1927).

31. Final stanza of 'The Idiot Boy', in *Lyrical Ballads* (1798).

32. FN 159.

NOTES   **539**

Wordsworth's time, as in the two world wars of the twentieth
century, was never far from the minds of English patriots in
times of war.

30. DWJ 1. 176.
31. Ibid., 1. 182.

CHAPTER 15: THE CHILD IS FATHER OF THE MAN

1. Published in *Poems, in Two Volumes* (1807), untitled, as
   the fourth of a sequence entitled 'Moods of my own Mind'.
2. DWJ 1. 125.
3. Published in *Poems, in Two Volumes* (1807).
4. Verse letter to Sara Hutchinson, headed 'A Letter to − −
   April 4, 1802. − ', STCL 2. 790–8.
5. 21 Apr 1802, DWJ 1. 135–6.
6. 3 Oct 1800, Ibid., 1. 63.
7. Sara Hutchinson's fair copy of the first draft of the poem that
   was eventually published as 'Resolution and Independence', in
   the volume headed 'Sara Hutchinson's Poets' (Dove Cottage,
   MS 41), transcribed in *Poems, in Two Volumes, and other Poems,
   1800–1807*, ed. Jared Curtis (Ithaca, 1983), pp. 317–19.
8. Sara's spelling is 'despondencey'.
9. Remaining quotations from published version of the poem,
   since (maddeningly) the next leaf of Sara Hutchinson's
   manuscript has been torn out.
10. To Sara Hutchinson, 14 June 1802, LEY 366–7.
11. July 1802, STCL 2. 808–13.
12. *The Mirror of Literature, Amusement, and Instruction*, 8 (1826), p.
    239.
13. See Nick Groom, 'The Death of Chatterton', in *From Gothic to
    Romantic: Thomas Chatterton's Bristol*, ed. Alistair Heys (Bristol,
    2005).

4. Novalis, Fragment 105, *Schriften*, ed. R. Samuel (Stuttgart, 1960), 2. 545.

5. *New Monthly Magazine*, 9 (1823), 175.

6. Hunt deliberately omits Southey out of disgust at the turn in his politics and his acceptance of the post of Poet Laureate. I have written at length about the importance of Shakespeare for the 'Romantic revolution', in *Shakespeare and the English Romantic Imagination* (Oxford, 1986), *Shakespearean Constitutions: Politics, Theatre, Criticism 1730–1830* (Oxford, 1989), *The Romantics on Shakespeare* (1992) and *The Genius of Shakespeare* (1997).

7. Hippolyte Taine, *History of English Literature*, trans. H. van Laun, vol. 2 (1872), p. 227.

8. Edmund Gosse, *English Literature: An Illustrated Record*, vol. 3, *From the Age of Johnson to the Age of Tennyson* (1903), pp. 199–200.

9. Isaiah Berlin, *The Roots of Romanticism*, ed. Henry Hardy (2000), pp. 1–2.

10. A tendency that began with A. O. Lovejoy's classic essay 'On the Discrimination of Romanticisms', *PMLA*, 39 (1924), 229–53. See also, Peter Cochran, *'Romanticism' – and Byron* (Newcastle upon Tyne, 2009), pp. ix–li.

11. Published anonymously in 1744, then widely disseminated via an anthology called *A Collection of Poems by Several Hands*, published by Robert Dodsley in 1748.

12. See, for example, Joseph Farington's diary, 17 June 1806: 'Wordsworth dined with Taylor [a Tory journalist] while He was in London. – Taylor found Him strongly disposed towards Republicanism' (CH 130).

13. Sydney Smith to James Mackintosh, 13 Jan 1802. See Alan Bell, 'An Unpublished Letter on the *Edinburgh Review*', *Times Literary Supplement*, 9 April 1970, p. 388.

14. *Edinburgh Review*, 1 (Oct 1802–Jan 1803), article VIII, 'Southey's Thalaba: a metrical romance', 63–82.

15. Albeit in a translation by Elizabeth Inchbald that watered down its sexual transgressions.

16. *Edinburgh Review*, Oct 1807, CH 185–201.

17. *Literary Gazette*, April 1817. See Peter A. Cook, 'Chronology of the "Lake School" argument: some revisions', *Review of English Studies*, n.s. 28 (1977), 175–81. Cook notes that Coleridge's nephew mentioned in a review in April 1814 that the group had become colloquially known as 'the Lake Poets'. He misses the usage of that nomenclature in Hunt's *The Feast of the Poets*, discussed in chap. 18.

18. '*To the Lady E. B. and the Hon. Miss P*, COMPOSED IN THE GROUNDS OF PLASS NEWIDD, NEAR LLANGOLLIN, 1824'.

19. Chateaubriand, *Génie du christianisme* (Paris, 1802), translated as *The Genius of Christianity* (Philadelphia, 1871), p. 271, translation adapted.

20. Goethe, *The Sorrows of Werther* (English trans., Boston, Mass., 1884), p. 73.

21. 'The Songs of Selma', in *The Poems of Ossian* (1801), 2. 15.

22. Goethe, *The Sorrows of Werther*, p. 101.

23. See especially Fiona Stafford, *The Sublime Savage: A Study of James Macpherson and the Poems of Ossian* (Edinburgh, 1989).

24. 'Glen Almain; or, The Narrow Glen' (composed on Scottish tour, 1803; published, 1807). As noted earlier, the same phrase was used (in plural form) in 'The Brothers'.

25. 'Essay, supplementary to the Preface' (1815), PrW, 3. 77.

26. Defoe, *A Tour thro' the Whole Island of Great Britain* (1724), 3. 223–4.

27. Lecture (in Italian) by Joyce on Defoe at Università Popolare, Trieste, March 1912.

28. Lakedistrict.gov.uk.

29. Marjorie Hope Nicolson, *Mountain Gloom and Mountain Glory: The Development of the Aesthetics of the Infinite* (Ithaca, 1959) remains a wonderful introduction to this theme.

30. Published in the *London Chronicle*, 24–26 April 1766, then as a pamphlet (Newcastle, 1767) that was reprinted several times.

31. Gilpin, *Observations on the River Wye* (1782), p. 1; *Essay on Prints* (1768), p. xii.

32. Letter to Richard West, 16 Nov 1739.

33. *The Poems and Letters of Thomas Gray* (1820), pp. 362–3.

34. 1780 edn, pp. 79–80.

35. Opening of 'The Brothers' in *Lyrical Ballads* (1800).

36. W. H. Auden, 'Bucolics III Mountains', in *The Shield of Achilles* (1955).

37. *The Journal of Elizabeth, Lady Holland (1791–1811)*, ed. The Earl of Ilchester (1908), 2. 231.

38. De Selincourt edition, p. 39. Subsequent quotations from this edition, which divides the text into three sections: 'View of the Country as formed by Nature', 'Aspect of the Country, as affected by its Inhabitants', and 'Changes, and Rules of Taste for preventing their Bad Effects'. This division was introduced in the work's first publication as a self-contained guidebook, *A Description of the Scenery of the Lakes in the North of England* (1822).

39. *Guide to the Lakes*, pp. 61–8.

40. Ibid., p. 72.

41. Ibid., p. 92.

CHAPTER 17: SURPRISED BY GRIEF

1. John Wordsworth, *Letters*, ed. Carl H. Ketcham (Ithaca, 1969), p. 155, quoted in Alethea Hayter, *The Wreck of the Abergavenny:*

The Wordsworths and Catastrophe (2002, repr. 2003), p. 5, a highly readable account of this episode. See also Richard Matlak, *Deep Distresses: William Wordsworth, John Wordsworth, Sir George Beaumont, 1800–1808* (Delaware, 2003).

2. Letter from Thomas Gilpin to Wordsworth, 25 Apr 1805 (Dove Cottage, WLMS 3/11), quoted, Hayter, *Wreck of the Abergavenny*, p. 92.

3. Thomas De Quincey, *Recollections of the Lakes and the Lake Poets*, ed. David Wright (Harmondsworth, 1970), p. 157, denying the 'calumny'.

4. 11 Feb 1805, LEY 541.

5. Ibid. 586.

6. '*Elegiac Verses* IN MEMORY OF MY BROTHER, JOHN WORDSWORTH, COMMANDER OF THE E. I. COMPANY'S SHIP THE EARL OF ABERGAVENNY, IN WHICH HE PERISHED BY CALAMITOUS SHIPWRECK, FEB. 6TH, 1805. Composed near the Mountain track, that leads from Grasmere through Grisdale Hawes, where it descends towards Patterdale. 1805', published 1815.

7. 7 Feb 1805, LEY 534.

8. De Quincey, *Recollections*, p. 269.

9. To Catherine Clarkson, 9 Dec 1810, LMY 1. 454.

10. Scott's *The Lay of the Last Minstrel* went through nine editions within three years of its publication in 1805.

11. PrW 1. 341

12. *The Friend*, 28 Dec 1809, in *The Collected Works of Samuel Taylor Coleridge: The Friend*, 2. 258–9.

13. *The Friend*, 22 Feb 1810, ed. Rooke, 2. 334–46. Wordsworth also wrote about the process of development from childhood through youth to adulthood in another essay in *The Friend*, a response to 'Mathetes' (pen name of two young Scotsmen, John Wilson and Alexander Blair), who had proposed that

Wordsworth was the great 'Teacher' of the age (*The Friend*, 14 Dec 1809).

14. 11 Aug 1810 and 4 June 1812, *The Love Letters of William and Mary Wordsworth*, ed. Beth Darlington (Ithaca, 1981), pp. 62, 229–30.

15. 1 Aug 1810, ibid., p. 46.

16. Sept 1808, STCN 3383, 3386.

17. Dorothy to Catherine Clarkson, April 1809, LMY 1. 398–9.

18. Reported by Dorothy to Catherine Clarkson, 12 May 1811, LMY 1. 447.

19. 28 April 1811, STCL 3. 319.

20. Coleridge to his friend John Morgan, 27 March 1812, STCL 3. 382.

21. Reported, Coleridge to Morgan, March 1812, STCL 3. 383.

22. Sara Coleridge to Tom Poole, *Minnow among Tritons: Mrs S. T. Coleridge's Letters to Thomas Poole, 1799–1834*, ed. Stephen Potter (1934), p. 16.

23. Remarks to Henry Crabb Robinson, in *Henry Crabb Robinson on Books and their Writers*, ed. E. J. Morley (1938), 1. 75. Hereafter HCR.

24. Lost, but drafts survive among the Dove Cottage papers (printed STCL 3. 404–6).

25. 11 May 1812, STCL 3. 407.

26. 13 May 1812, *Love Letters*, p. 146.

27. Ibid., p. 197.

28. *Suspiria de Profundis* (*Blackwood's Magazine*, 1845), repr. in Thomas De Quincey, *Confessions of an English Opium-Eater and Suspiria de Profundis* (1864), p. 175.

29. Letters printed in *De Quincey to Wordsworth: A Biography of a Relationship*, ed. John E. Jordan (Berkeley, 1962), pp. 30–7 (31 May 1803, 14 Mar 1804).

30. De Quincey, *Recollections*, pp. 130–1.

31. Dorothy's observations: LMY 1. 365, 389.

32. See Grevel Lindop, 'Did Wordsworth's Daughter have Down's Symdrome?', https://grevel.co.uk/andanotherthing/catherine-wordsworth-a-romantic-poets-downs-baby/. The argument is primarily based on Wordsworth calling her his 'little Chinese Maiden' (LMY 1. 365), but the context of his remark was her Chinese-doll-like baldness at the age of eleven months. She seems to have spoken in lively style at the age of three and a half (LMY 2. 6).

33. Dorothy's letter to De Quincey, quoted further, immediately below.

34. LMY 2. 23.

35. 11 June 1812, HCR 1. 103.

36. *De Quincey to Wordsworth*, p. 265.

37. 5 Jan 1813, LMY 2. 62.

38. 27 Dec 1812, Ibid., 2. 56.

39. 1 Dec 1812, Ibid., 2. 50–1.

40. 2 Dec 1812, Ibid., 2. 51.

41. 7 Dec 1812, STCL 2. 599.

42. 5 Jan 1813, to Catherine Clarkson, LMY 2. 61.

43. 2 May 1813, the day after they moved, to Jane Marshall, ibid., 2. 95.

44. Published 1815; he told Isabella Fenwick that it was 'suggested by my daughter Catharine long after her death' (FN 76). In his 1820 edition, Wordsworth changed 'I wished' in the second line to 'I turned' – one of the more felicitous of his many revisions of his poems.

CHAPTER 18: THIS WILL NEVER DO

1. *The Excursion* (1814), 9. 1–9. Original draft in MS D, into which Dorothy copied 'The Ruined Cottage'.

2. *The Excursion* (1814), 1. 240–64. Italics from later editions. The vision in the clouds in book two was a particular inspiration to John Ruskin, as I show in *Romantic Ecology: Wordsworth and the Environmental Tradition* (1991), pp. 69–71. It was also much admired by Sir George Beaumont, who described it as 'the fairest flower of British Poesy'. 'It perfectly fascinates me', he wrote, venturing to ask whether it was 'suggested by that marvelous effect we saw in returning thro Patterdale amongst the mountains of Ulswater [*sic*] . . . I remember you were struck dumb for an hour at least, and then you told me words might do little but not much in describing it – you have proved yourself mistaken' (Beaumont to Wordsworth, 30 Nov 1814, CH 506).

3. George Borrow, *The Romany Rye* (1858), chap. 22.

4. *The Excursion, being a portion of The Recluse, A Poem* (1814), pp. vii–ix.

5. Ibid., pp. x–xiv.

6. Annotations to *The Excursion* and Wordsworth's *Poems* of 1815, in *Blake's Poetry and Designs*, eds Mary Lynn Johnson and John E. Grant (New York, 2008), p. 467.

7. HCR 2. 436.

8. Again, according to Crabb Robinson (HCR 1. 332).

9. Benjamin Robert Haydon, *Diary*, ed. W. B. Pope (Cambridge, Mass., 1960–3), 2. 312.

10. *Edinburgh Review*, 24 (November 1814), 1 (unsigned).

11. The review is reprinted in CH 381–404.

12. *Edinburgh Review*, 25 (October 1815), 355 (unsigned).

13. 'The Prince on St Patrick's Day', editorial in *The Examiner*, 22 March 1812, p. 179.

14. *The Reflector*, Dec 1811, CH 329.

15. Letter to Tom Moore, Sept 1813, written in Surrey Gaol, in Thomas Moore, *Memoirs, Journal and Correspondence*, ed. Lord

John Russell (1853–6), 8. 157.

16. Leigh Hunt, *The Feast of the Poets* (1814), p. 13.

17. Ibid., pp. 77–8.

18. Leigh Hunt, review of Keats's *Poems* (1817), in *The Examiner*, 1 June 1817, 345.

19. Hunt, *The Feast of the Poets*, pp. 88–90 (the full note – the longest in the book – is reprinted in CH 332–9).

20. Byron to Hogg, 1814, reported by Crabb Robinson in Dec 1816 (HCR 1. 199).

21. Leigh Hunt, *Autobiography*, ed. J. E. Morpurgo (1949), p. 223.

22. Hunt, *The Feast of the Poets* (2nd edn, 1815), CH 331.

23. 'On Gusto', in *The Round Table* (1817), *Complete Works*, 4. 77.

24. Thomas De Quincey, 'William Wordsworth', *Tait's Edinburgh Magazine*, VI (1839), 251; One of Hazlitt's biographers, Duncan Wu (*William Hazlitt: The First Modern Man* [Oxford, 2010]), takes De Quincey at face value. Others are more sceptical, as am I. Knowing Hazlitt's proclivities, it is more likely that he made some kind of pass at Dorothy.

25. Southey, letter to Richard Duppa, 14 Dec 1803, online edition of *The Collected Letters of Robert Southey*, https://romantic-circles.org/editions/southey_letters; STCL 2. 958.

26. March 1804, LEY 446–7.

27. 'Character of Mr Wordsworth's New Poem', *The Examiner*, 21 Aug 1814. Subsequent quotations from this review and its continuations on 28 Aug and 2 Oct 1814, repr. in CH 368–81, and 'On the Living Poets' (1818), CH 894.

28. *The Excursion*, 4. 262.

29. *The Examiner*, 28 Aug 1814, CH 375.

30. Mary Wordsworth, *Letters*, ed. Mary E. Burton (Oxford, 1958), p. 24.

31. 'A Reply to "Z"' is quoted here from *William Wordsworth: Interviews and Recollections*, ed. Harold Orel (Basingstoke, 2005),

p. 54. Hazlitt owed his knowledge of the conversation to Wilson.

32. 'Mr Wordsworth', in *The Spirit of the Age* (1825), *Complete Works*, 11. 86–95.

CHAPTER 19: AMONG THE COCKNEYS

1. *The Champion*, 25 June 1815, CH 527.
2. Benjamin Robert Haydon, *Diary*, ed. W. B. Pope (Cambridge, Mass., 1960–3), 1. 450; entry of 12 June 1816, misdated by Haydon as 13 June.
3. Ibid., 1. 451.
4. 20 Nov 1816, *Letters of John Keats*, 1. 117. In Keats's final line, I find it hard not to hear an anticipation of Shelley's famous line in 'Ozymandias', 'Look on my works, ye Mighty, and despair'. Keats's 'Listen' becomes Shelley's 'Look'; Keats's 'mighty workings' from the previous line become Shelley's 'works'; Keats's 'ye nations' becomes Shelley's 'ye Mighty', and, decisively, Keats's 'and be dumb' becomes Shelley's 'and despair'. Keats's poem is about the 'great spirits' of the present who will one day be recognized as immortals; Shelley's is about the great rulers of the past who have proved mortal, all too mortal. The politicians die and their monuments are broken; the creative artists live and influence the future through the endurance of their work. In this sense, Keats's poem inspires not just 'Ozymandias', but Shelley's vision of poets as unacknowledged legislators of the world. The image of creative artists as spirits standing apart 'Upon the forehead of the age to come', one of whom is Keats, self-effacing yet ambitious for his own art, chimes with the climax of the 'Defence of Poetry' in which poets are described as 'the mirrors of the gigantic shadows which futurity casts upon the present'.
5. 'To Joanna'.

6. Published in 1820. 'The Lady was Miss Blackett, then residing with Mr Montague Burgoyne at Fox Ghyll. We were tempted to remain too long upon the mountain; and I imprudently, with the hope of shortening the way, led her among the crags and down a steep slope which entangled us in difficulties that were met by her with much spirit and courage' (FN 67).

7. 3 Apr 1815, STCL 4. 554.

8. *Letter to a Friend of Burns* (1816), PrW 3. 127–8.

9. *The Letters of Sir Walter Scott*, ed. H. J. C. Grierson (1932–7), 12. 324.

10. *Biographia Literaria* (1817), chap. 22.

11. Ibid., quoting *The Excursion*, 1. 219–31.

12. Ibid., chap. 14.

13. Sept 1817, LMY 2. 399.

14. Letter from Haydon to a colonel named Wild, 6 Oct 1831, transcribed by Marcia Allentuck in *The Art Bulletin*, 44 (1962), 53–4. Hazlitt's quotation was from *Peter Bell*.

15. 'My First Acquaintance', *Complete Works*, 17. 116.

16. Haydon to Edward Moxon, 29 Nov 1845, in *The Keats Circle*, ed. H. E. Rollins (Cambridge, Mass., 1948), 2. 143–4.

17. To J. H. Reynolds, 3 May 1818, *Letters of Keats*, 1. 279.

18. Ibid., 1. 281.

19. To Richard Woodhouse, 27 Oct 1818, ibid., 1. 386–7.

20. Keats, 'Lamia', in *Lamia, Isabella, The Eve of St Agnes, and other Poems* (1820), p. 41.

21. *Life of Benjamin Robert Haydon Historical Painter from His Autobiography and Journals*, ed. Tom Taylor (1853), 1. 353–7. Two fine books have been devoted to the evening: Penelope Hughes-Hallett, *The Immortal Dinner, A Famous Evening of Genius and Laughter in Literary London, 1817* (2000), and Stanley Plumly, *The Immortal Evening: A Legendary Dinner with Keats, Wordsworth and Lamb* (2014).

22. Exchange of letters, 10–11 Jan 1818, *Letters of Keats*, 1. 202–3.

23. *Blackwood's Edinburgh Magazine*, 1 (June 1817), CH 611.

24. Ibid., 2 (Oct 1817), CH 612.

25. *Blackwood's*, 2 (Oct 1817), p. 38.

26. In addition, according to Francis Grose's *Dictionary of the Vulgar Tongue* (1811), s. v. COCKNEY, 'the interpretation of the word Cockney, is, a young person coaxed or conquered, made wanton; or a nestle cock, delicately bred and brought up, so as, when arrived at man's estate, to be unable to bear the least hardship': these implications of both sexual profligacy and effeminacy served Z's damaging purposes very well indeed.

27. *Blackwood's Edinburgh Magazine*, 2 (Oct 1817), 40.

28. Ibid., 3 (Aug 1818), 520.

29. *London Magazine*, 1 (May 1820), 495.

30. Ibid., 2 (Nov 1820), 515.

31. Ibid., 2 (Dec 1820), 676.

32. These and subsequent quotations relating to the affair are from *Statement, &c. The Editor of the London Magazine Thinks it Necessary to Publish a Statement of what Has Recently Taken Place Between Himself and Mr. John Gibson Lockhart, of Edinburgh, an Understood, though Unavowed, Conductor of Blackwood's Magazine* (1821).

33. Dialogue from Lockhart's and Christie's accounts, in *The Life and Letters of John Ginson Lockhart*, ed. Andrew Lang (1897), 1. 292–6. My account of the affair is also indebted to Leonidas M. Jones, 'The Scott-Christie Duel', *Texas Studies in Literature and Language*, 12 (1971), 605–29.

34. Reported by his friend Joseph Severn to his publisher John Taylor, 6 Mar 1821, *Letters of Keats*, 2. 378.

35. To Thomas and Jane Monkhouse, 9 April 1821, *The Letters of Mary Wordsworth 1800–1855*, ed. Mary E. Burton (Oxford, 1958), p. 79.

36. To Henry Crabb Robinson, March 1821, LLY 1. 43–4.

37. Shelley, *Adonais* (1821), stanzas 36, 37, 42.

38. Haydon, *Diary*, 5. 554.

39. Frances Blanshard offers a full account of the many likenesses in *Portraits of Wordsworth* (1959).

40. 'On a Portrait of Wordsworth by R. B. Haydon', in *The Poems of Elizabeth Barrett Browning* (1844), 2. 125.

CHAPTER 20: THE LOST LEADER

1. 'Michael', 33–9.

2. Preface, in Shelley, *Alastor; or, The Spirit of Solitude* (1816), pp. iii–vi, slightly misquoting *The Excursion*, 1. 500–2.

3. 15 Sept 1814, *Mary Shelley's Journal*, ed. F. L. Jones (1947), p. 15.

4. J. H. Reynolds, *Peter Bell. A Lyrical Ballad* (1819), p. 17.

5. Ibid., Preface, pp. iii–v.

6. *The Examiner*, 25 April 1819, 270.

7. Preface, p. iv. Sara Hutchinson recorded that Wordsworth thought that the parody was by Hazlitt, because the latter had heard the original *Peter Bell* many years before (Sara Hutchinson, *Letters*, ed. Kathleen Coburn [1954], p. 154).

8. 1798–9 manuscript text of *Peter Bell*, 1312.

9. Wordsworth, *Peter Bell, A Tale in Verse* (1819), p. 81.

10. *The Examiner*, 2 May 1819, CH 651.

11. Shelley, Prologue to 'Peter Bell the Third' (published after his death by Mary Shelley in her 1839 edition of his *Poetical Works*); Robinson reported by Mary Lamb to Sara Hutchinson (Mary joked that she longed to join them and make a fourth) – *Letters of Charles and Mary Lamb*, 3. 233.

12. Lines 703–7 of 'Peter Bell the Third', in *Shelley's Poetry and Prose*, eds Donald H. Reiman and Sharon B. Powers (New York, 1977), pp. 323–47.

13. *Childe Harold's Pilgrimage*, canto 3 (1816), stanzas 71, 72, 75.

14. Quoted, and the claim dismissed, by Wordsworth – LLY 3. 1306 (March 1847).

15. To Henry Taylor, Dec 1823, LMY 4. 237.

16. Thomas Medwin, *Journal of the Conversations of Lord Byron, noted during a residence with his Lordship at Pisa in the years 1821 and 1822* (1824), p. 135.

17. *English Bards and Scotch Reviewers* (1809), 175–82.

18. *Don Juan* (1819), Dedication, stanza 1.

19. Ibid, stanza 6.

20. *Byron's Letters and Journals*, ed. Leslie A. Marchand (1975–82), 8. 66.

21. Medwin, *Journal of the Conversations of Lord Byron*, p. 135.

22. 'Sweet birthplace' is Coleridge's phrase in 'Frost at Midnight', quoted by Wordsworth at the beginning of *The Prelude*.

23. FN 65.

24. *The River Duddon*, sonnet XVI, 'American Tradition'.

25. Ibid., sonnet XXI.

26. John Beer, *Providence and Love: Studies in Wordsworth, Channing, Myers, George Eliot, and Ruskin* (Oxford, 1998), chap. 2.

27. *The River Duddon*, sonnet XXXIII, 'Conclusion', later retitled 'After-thought'.

28. PrW 2. 84–5.

29. LLY 1. 519.

30. Hemans, 'Remembrance of Grasmere' (1834).

31. Wordsworth's phrasing at the time of her death: LLY 3. 75 (to Henry Southey, July 1835).

32. LLY 3. 74, 27 June 1835, to Edward Quillinan, a Peninsular War army officer, Wordsworth's future son-in-law: his first wife had died from burns, leaving him with two daughters. Twenty years later, in 1841, he married Dora Wordsworth.

33. First published in the *Newcastle Journal*, 30 Nov 1835.

34. *Kilvert's Diary*, ed. William Plomer (1938–40), 1. 318. Wordsworth's letter to the editor of the *Newcastle Journal* added a note, a version of which was published as a footnote to the poem: '*note*. In the above is an expression borrowed from a Sonnet by Mr G. Bell, the author of a small vol: of Poems lately printed in Penrith. Speaking of Skiddaw, he says – "yon dark cloud *rakes* and shrouds its noble brow." These Poems, tho' incorrect often in expression and metre, do honour to their unpretending Author; and may be added to the number of proofs, daily occurring, that a finer perception of the appearances of Nature is spreading thro' the humbler Classes of Society.' (LLY 3. 128.)

35. Published in Wordsworth's collected edition of 1843.

36. Quotations from Emerson's *English Traits* (1856), chap. 1.

37. 23 April 1831, LLY 1. 378.

38. 'The Lost Leader', in Robert Browning, *Dramatic Romances and Lyrics* (1845).

39. Crabb Robinson to Mary Wordsworth, 7 Mar 1848: 'I recollect once hearing Mr W. say, half in joke, half in earnest – "I have no respect whatever for Whigs, but I have a great deal of the Chartist in me". To be sure he has. His earlier poems are full of that intense love of the people, as such, which becomes Chartism when the attempt is formally made to make their interests the especial object of legislation as of deeper importance than the positive rights hitherto accorded to the privileged orders', in *The Correspondence of Henry Crabb Robinson with the Wordsworth circle, 1808–1866*, ed. Edith J. Morley (1927), 2. 665.

CHAPTER 21: A MEDICINE FOR MY STATE OF MIND

1. Southey to John Rickman, 15 June 1814, electronic edition of *The Collected Letters of Robert Southey*, no. 2442.

2. To Edith, *Letters of Southey*, no. 2997 (17 May 1817).

3. 7 Oct 1820, LMY 2. 642. The date 1792 for his 'last visit' might tell against Carlyle's report of Wordsworth returning the following year and witnessing the execution of Gorsas, but on the other hand he did sometimes misremember important dates.

4. To Dorothy, from Paris, 25 Mar 1837, LLY 3. 385.

5. To Isabella Fenwick, from Paris, 24 Mar 1837, LLY 3. 380–1.

6. Thomas De Quincey, *Recollections of the Lakes and the Lake Poets*, ed. David Wright (Harmondsworth, 1970), p. 121. Subsequent quotations also from this edition, which reproduces the original *Tait's Edinburgh Magazine* texts, as opposed to the revised versions gathered in book form in 1854.

7. Ibid., pp. 131–2, 205.

8. Dorothy to Rogers, 3 Jan 1823, LLY 1. 181. The plan to publish was abandoned after she expressed further 'scruples and apprehensions' the following month (to Rogers, 17 Feb 1823, LLY, 1. 189).

9. Ibid 3. 83.

10. Crabb Robinson, *Correspondence with the Wordsworth Circle*, 1. 283.

11. Ibid., 1. 421, 12 Jan 1841.

12. Dove Cottage MS 120. 22ff.

13. Quoted from text published in *Poems, chiefly of Early and Late Years* (1842), pp. 230–1.

14. 'Thoughts on my sick-bed', Dove Cottage MS 120. 27.

15. LLY 3. 528. The line from Spenser is slightly misquoted. One further brief letter survives, written to Mary on 22 Oct 1853 (LLY 4. 918).

16. John Stuart Mill, *Autobiography* (1873), chap. 5, 'A Crisis in my mental history', pp. 133–4. Subsequent quotations from the same chapter (pp. 135–49).

17. *The Autobiography of Mark Rutherford* (1881), pp. 34–5.

18. Ibid., pp. 35–6.

19. Emerson, *English Traits*, chap. 14.

20. Quotations from Mrs Humphry Ward, *A Writer's Recollections* (1918), pp. 78–80. Mrs Ward was born Mary Augusta Arnold, Matthew's niece; her million-selling novel of religious faith and doubt, *Robert Elsmere* (1888), was set in the Lake District and contains many allusions to Wordsworth. Its sympathy for the clergyman protagonist's crisis of belief was partly a reaction against a pious sermon by Wordsworth's great-nephew John.

21. *Harriet Martineau's Letters to Fanny Wedgwood*, ed. E. S. Arbuckle (1983), p. 105.

RETROSPECT EPIGRAPH

1. Gerald Haylett, *New Chronicle*, 27 Jan 1937, praising Sir James Frazer, author of *The Golden Bough* – but the phrasing captures exactly my sense of Wordsworth's influence. I owe the reference to Mary Beard's fine article, 'Frazer, Leach, and Virgil: The Popularity (and Unpopularity) of the Golden Bough', *Comparative Studies in Society and History*, 34 (1992), 203–24.

CHAPTER 22: A SORT OF NATIONAL PROPERTY

1. Preface, *Poems of Wordsworth*, chosen and ed. Matthew Arnold (1879), pp. xvi–xxiv.

2. Ibid., p. xii.

3. Ibid., p. vi.

4. PrW 2. 155.

5. To Sidgwick, Mar 1842, LLY 4. 309–10.

6. 1853 edn, p. 219. Other quotations are from *Wordsworth's Guide*

to the Lakes. The Fifth Edition (1835), ed. Ernest de Selincourt (Oxford, 1906, repr. 1977).

7. Dated 12 Oct 1844.

8. PrW 3. 350.

9. George Heald, 'Reply to Wordsworth's Sonnet on the Kendal & Windermere Railway', *Kendal Mercury*, 17 April 1847.

10. As in *Through the Wordsworth Country* (1891), the title of an illustrated guide by William Knight, founder of the Wordsworth Society. 'Wordsworthshire' seems to have been a coinage of the American poet James Russell Lowell in his *Among My Books 2nd series* (1876), p. 240.

11. Quoted, Saeko Yoshikawa, 'Railways, Tourism, and Preservation in the Victorian Lake District: from Wordsworth to Rawnsley', in *Victorian Ecocriticism: The Politics of Place and Early Environmental Justice*, ed. Dewey W. Hall (New York, 2017), p. 22. Yoshikawa offers a wonderful account of the changing face of nineteenth-century Lake District guidebooks and related developments in *William Wordsworth and the Invention of Tourism 1820–1900* (Aldershot, 2014).

12. John Muir, *Journals*, 'June–July 1890, Trip to Alaska; June-August 1893, Trip to Norway', 6 Aug 1893, MuirReel27Journal08RearP04–05.tif, Holt-Atherton Special Collections, University of the Pacific Library. After a brief period as an Oxford don, which ended because of his alcoholism, Hartley Coleridge had returned to Grasmere, where he died in 1849.

13. Articles of Incorporation of the Sierra Club, written by Muir, 4 June 1892.

14. *The Century*, 40, no. 4 (Aug 1890).

15. Ibid., no. 5 (Sept 1890).

16. Stopford Brooke, *Dove Cottage: Wordsworth's Home from 1800–1808* (1890), pp. 5–6.

17. *Dove Cottage Minute Book* (Wordsworth Trust Archive), quoted, Polly Atkin, 'Ghosting Grasmere: The Musealisation of Dove Cottage', in *Literary Tourism and Nineteenth-Century Culture*, ed. Nicola Watson (New York, 2009), p. 93. Letter from the trustees on the occasion of the donation of the editor William Knight's vast cache of books and manuscripts, the original core of the now incomparable collection of the Wordsworth Library.

18. Lake District Defence Society,- Carlisle Records Office. DSO 24/15/1, quoted, https://www.hdrawnsley.com/index.php/conservation/lake-district-defence-society.

19. Hill, 'The Kyrle Society', *Charity Organisation Review* 5 (1905), 314, quoted, Robert Whelan, '"The poor, as well as the rich, need something more than meat and drink": the vision and work of the Kyrle Society', chap. 5 of *Octavia Hill, Social Activism and the Remaking of British Society*, eds Elizabeth Baigent and Ben Cowell (2016).

20. Quoted, John Sheail, 'The Concept of National Parks in Great Britain 1900–1950', *Transactions of the Institute of British Geographers*, 66 (Nov 1975), 41–56.

21. Report developed and published as J. Dower, *National Parks in England and Wales*, Command Papers 6628 (1945).

22. Stegner's essay 'The Best Idea we ever had: an overview' was published in *Wilderness* magazine in 1983. He attributed the phrase to Lord Bryce, the British ambassador to the USA before the First World War, though Bryce's 1912 lecture 'National Parks: the need of the future' did not use the exact phrase. See further, Alan Maceachern, 'Canada's Best Idea? The Canadian and American National Park Services in the 1910s', in *National Parks beyond the Nation: Global Perspectives on 'America's Best Idea'*, eds Adrian Howkins, Jared Orsi and Mark Fiege (Norman, Oklahoma, 2016), chap. 2. Like most

comparative accounts of the history of National Parks around the world, this very informative collection of essays never mentions Wordsworth.

CHAPTER 23: LOVE OF NATURE LEADING TO LOVE OF MANKIND

1. W. H. Auden, 'In memory of W. B. Yeats', in *Another Time* (New York, 1940).

2. Keats to the George Keatses, 21 April 1819; to J. H. Reynolds, 3 May 1818 and 21 Sept 1819, *Letters of John Keats*, ed. H. E. Rollins (Cambridge, Mass., 1958), 2. 102, 1. 282, 2. 167.

3. Ralph Waldo Emerson, *Representative Men* (1850), 'Napoleon; or The Man of the World'; 'Goethe; or, The Writer'.

4. Matthew Arnold, 'The Study of Poetry' (1880), reprinted as the lead essay in his *Essays in Criticism: Second Series* (1888; repr. 1925), pp. 1–54.

5. 'The Study of Poetry', p. 3.

6. F. W. H. Myers, *Wordsworth* (1881), in the 'English Men of Letters' series, pp. 130–1. Though 1881 is on the title page, the volume actually appeared in December 1880.

7. Myers to George Eliot, drafted 7 Dec 1872, Trinity College Library, Cambridge, MS Myers 11, quoted in John Beer's fine 'Myers's Secret Message', in his *Providence and Love: Studies in Wordsworth, Channing, Myers, George Eliot, and Ruskin*, chap. 4.

8. Myers, 'George Eliot', *Century Magazine*, 23 (Nov 1881), 62–3.

9. Myers, *Wordsworth*, especially pp. 137ff.

10. *Proceedings of the Society for Psychical Research*, 1 (1882), 2. 147.

11. 1850 *Prelude*, 6. 600–2, 14. 108.

12. Myers, *Human Personality and its Survival of Bodily Death* (1903), 2. 110–11.

13. *Proceedings of the Society for Psychical Research*, 17 (1901), 1–23; 18 (1903), 33.

14. For these connections, see David E. Leary's excellent essay '"Authentic Tidings": What Wordsworth Gave to William James', *William James Studies* 13, no. 1 (2017), 1–26.

15. William James, *The Varieties of Religious Experience* (1902; repr. Cambridge, Mass., 1985), pp. 34, 312. His italics.

16. Ibid., p. 402.

17. 'Océanique': Rolland to Freud, 5 Dec 1927, in *Selected Letters of Romain Rolland*, eds F. Doré and M. Prévost (Delhi, 1990), pp. 86–7. The immediate influence on the idea was Rolland's reading of the Hindu mystic Ramakrishna.

18. Sigmund Freud, *Civilization and its Discontents*, trans. James Strachey (New York, 1961), pp. 13–14.

19. *Prelude*, 2. 238–9, 242, 247–50, 275–9.

20. W. H Auden, 'In memory of Sigmund Freud', also published in *Another Time*.

21. *Prelude*, 8. 1–79.

22. Ibid., 8. 80–118. 1805 text only, perhaps because the secularization of the image of the Good Shepherd did not sit well with the later Wordsworth's Anglican orthodoxy.

23. William Blake, 'London', in *Songs of Experience* (1794).

24. Miscellaneous Sonnets, 18, in *Poems in Two Volumes* (1807).

25. For Wordsworth's influence on Ruskin, see further, chap. 3 of my *Romantic Ecology: Wordsworth and the Environmental Tradition*.

26. *The Excursion*, 4. 760–2.

27. *The Library Edition of the Works of John Ruskin*, eds E. T. Cook and Alexander Wedderburn (1907), 27. 90–3.

28. Shelley, 'The Defence of Poetry'.

29. *Prelude*, 13. 442–52.

30. *The Excursion*, 2. 380–2.

INDEX